1980

The Collected Plays
of
Jack B. Yeats

Also by Jack B. Yeats

The Bosun and the Bob-tailed Comet (1904)
A Little Fleet (1909)
Life in the West of Ireland (1912)
Modern Aspects of Irish Art (1922)
Sligo (1930)
Sailing, Sailing Swiftly (1933)
The Amaranthers (1936)
The Charmed Life (1938)
Ah Well (1942)
And To You Also (1944)
The Careless Flower (1947)

THE COLLECTED PLAYS
OF
JACK B. YEATS

Edited with an Introduction

by

ROBIN SKELTON

SECKER & WARBURG
LONDON

This collection first published in England 1971 by
Martin Secker & Warburg Limited
14 Carlisle Street, London W1V 6NN

SBN: 436 46820 4

Printed in Great Britain by Morrison & Gibb Limited
London and Edinburgh

CONTENTS

Introduction   1

Note on the Text and Acknowledgements   12

Part One: Plays for the Miniature Theatre
    My Miniature Theatre   17
    Timothy Coombewest   21
    James Flaunty   37
    Onct More's First Circus   49
    Onct More's Great Circus   55
    The Treasure of the Garden   57
    The Scourge of the Gulph   73
    The Wonderful Travellers   81

Part Two: Plays for the Larger Theatre
    The Deathly Terrace   93
    Apparitions   121
    The Old Sea Road   141
    Rattle   163
    The Silencer   207
    Harlequin's Positions   251
    La La Noo   297
    The Green Wave   329
    In Sand   333

Appendix A:
    First Productions   377

Appendix B:
    Sources of the Texts   379

Appendix C:
    How Jack B. Yeats Produced his Plays for the Miniature Theatre:
    by the Master himself   380

INTRODUCTION

Jack Butler Yeats was the fifth child of John Butler Yeats; he was born in London on 29 August 1871 at a time when his father, aged 32, having given up his career in the law, was beginning a new career as a painter and, after two years at Heatherleigh's Art School, was working at the Academy School under Poynter. When asked, in a radio interview of 1948, to give his reasons for becoming a painter, Jack Yeats said emphatically that it was because he was a painter's son. He did not, however, spend more than a small part of his childhood in his father's house, but lived in the main with his maternal grandparents William and Elizabeth Pollexfen in Sligo, and Sligo remained important to him throughout his life. Sligo was at this period much more of a seaport than it is today, and talk of the sea, of sailors, smugglers, and pirates was certainly very much a part of Jack Yeats' early education. One great-grandfather, William Middleton, had been a trader and smuggler in the eighteenth century, and another, Anthony Pollexfen, had been an owner of sailing ships. William Pollexfen himself was born in Devon, where his grandson Jack was later to live, and ran away to sea as a lad, later becoming a ship-owner and flour-miller in Sligo. Jack's paternal grandfather, William Butler Yeats, was a red-headed clergyman, the rector of Tullyish in County Down, and as famous for his prowess on horseback, and his hunting and fishing, as for his idiosyncratic preaching. Jack Yeats' fascination with tales of the sea and his love of horse-racing, pugilism, and the active life must have had its beginnings in his Sligo childhood. Art, however, was by no means absent from his grandparents' home. His grandmother painted watercolours, and his older brothers and sisters were all given to drawing and painting. The Yeats children and their mother spent a great deal of time in Sligo at this period, for John Butler Yeats was both generous and impecunious, and could not always afford to support his family in London. Jack's earliest drawings, according to his father,

> were never of one object, one person or one animal, but of groups engaged in some kind of drama. For instance, one day I picked up one of his drawings and made out that there was a cab and two men and a telescope; one looking through the small end and the other man looking through the large end. The telescope itself, which was of monstrous size, lying on the ground—and I asked what it meant and was told that the man at the larger end was the cab man and that he was trying to find out what the other was looking at. At this time Jack's education had not got beyond learning his letters.

Jack's formal education was not to progress very far. When Mrs Yeats and the rest of the family returned to London he stayed behind in Sligo and attended a private school run by three spinster ladies, the Misses Blythe, where he was consistently at the bottom of the class. He was more interested in roaming Sligo and the surrounding countryside, making drawings, and going to every fair, circus, and race-meeting he could find. He early showed a taste for dramatic events, not only in his drawings, but also in his games. He made a dolls' house which he called 'The Farm' and carried it with him wherever he went; it was his first attempt at creating his own theatre.

John Butler Yeats returned to Dublin in 1880, but in 1887 decided once more to try to make a living in London as an illustrator. The family settled at 58 Eardley Crescent in Earls Court, and Jack spent almost every day of that summer at the American Exhibition, being particularly impressed by Buffalo Bill's Wild West show, with its 'Deadwood Coach' and fierce Indians. In the autumn of 1887 he began studying at the South Kensington School of Art, and in later years he also studied at the Chiswick Art School and the Westminster School. In the summer of 1887 Mrs Yeats had a stroke and was an invalid for the remainder of her life. (She died in 1900.) At the end of 1887 the family moved to 3 Blenheim Road, Bedford Park, and the house became a centre for the artists' colony of the area. Among the frequent visitors were John Todhunter, the poet and playwright, the painter J. T. Nettleship, Oliver Elton, G. K. Chesterton, Florence Farr, Harry Paget, Joseph Nash, and York Powell. Paget and Powell were both devotees of boxing and the latter became one of Jack's closest friends. On 7 April 1888 he appeared in print as an illustrator for the first time with some drawings in the Children's Corner of *The Vegetarian*. From this time onwards he worked hard on his drawings, and contributed regularly to *The Vegetarian* until the end of 1893. He began drawing for *Paddock Life* in 1891 and continued to do so until 1893 when the paper stopped carrying so many drawings. He illustrated Ernest Rhys' *The Great Cockney Tragedy* (1891) and W. B. Yeats' *Irish Fairy Tales* (1892). His drawings were published in *Judy* (1892–1897), *Chums* (1892–1896), *Sporting Sketches* (1894–1895), and other papers. He only published two prose pieces during this period, one in *The Success* and one in *The Boys' Own Paper*, both in 1895. He had three exhibitions before the turn of the century, one in November 1897 at the Clifford Gallery in London, one in February 1899 at the Walker Art Gallery, London, and a third in May 1899 in Dublin.

On 23 August 1895 Jack Yeats married Mary Cottenham White, whom everyone called 'Cottie', and they went to live in Surrey. In the spring of 1897 they moved house to Devon and a two-storied cottage a mile and a half from Strete just off the Totness Road. It was here that Jack Yeats set up his miniature theatre and began to learn to be a writer as well as a painter. He had for some time been collecting nineteenth-century prints and ballad sheets, and had also developed a great interest in the theatrical prints of Redington, Pollock, and Webb, and their cut-out scenes and characters for such plays as *The Corsican Brothers*, *Paul Clifford the Highwayman*, *The Smuggler*, and *Three-Fingered Jack*. In the spring of 1900 he showed a play of his own writing, *Esmeralda Grande*, to the children of Strete, and thereafter, for several years, he showed plays, pantomimes, or circuses, each one written and designed by himself. His method of work and the nature of his theatre he later described in an essay in *The Mask*. This is printed elsewhere in this book so there is no need to discuss the subject here. What does, however, demand comment is the drama itself, for it was in these early plays, directed at an audience of children, that Jack Yeats began his career as a playwright and laid the basis for such later and important plays as *La La Noo* and *In Sand*.

The first of the series, *Esmeralda Grande*, is the least interesting. The story lacks that ironic power which is characteristic of the later plays. Nevertheless, there are hints, in the description of the burial of the green emerald, and in the repeating of the Adventurer's Oath, of that poetic intensity and verbal exuberance which makes others so strangely disturbing. The second play, *James Flaunty*, John Butler Yeats called, in a letter to Lady Gregory, 'a most *poetical* play—it assures for ever Jack's fame—and people will study that play as presenting the right model for all plays big and little.' If we take John Butler Yeats seriously and consider the poetry of the play we do discover a number of powerful speeches and memorable phrases. Florry refers to 'Men who have hung by Scraw Wallaw—the shaking Scraw that hangs o'er the mouth of Hell.' Gillen tells Flaunty that the Navy 'have money and a king behind them, but we have nothing but the living we can claw off these coasts'. The plot of the play is simple, but the speeches are intense, and at the end Pine's last words before he is killed are heroic and cast a dark shadow over the whole drama. The dark shadow which colours the conclusion of *James Flaunty* broods over the whole of *The Treasure of the Garden*, which opens and closes with imagery of death. Less of a pure fantasy than *James Flaunty*, it deals with the way in which unscrupulous ship-owners made profits from the emigration trade by sending Irish families off to America in unseaworthy boats. It refers, indeed, to the specific disaster of the *Maid of Galway* which sank with everyone on board her. The hero, Willie McGowan, presents us with the theme of man in search of his dream; his dream is to find enough gold to marry his sweetheart. As soon as he has done so, however, he hears of her death. The same theme of frustration is used to much more telling effect in *The Scourge of the Gulph*, where Miles revenges himself upon Captain Carricknagat and thinks to possess himself of the captain's treasure, only to discover that the box contains the skull of the captain's murdered wife. His last speech ends with a question that recurs in many forms throughout Jack Yeats' writings: 'An empty skull, a black box, a dead skipper! Have I done anything or nothing?'

It is obvious that in *The Scourge of the Gulph* and the *Treasure of the Garden* Jack Yeats had gone far beyond the requirements of his juvenile audience. That he was aware of this seems certain. He knew his audience's taste well enough to write the pantomime, *The Wonderful Travellers*, in

C.P.Y.—I*

which ancient practical jokes combine with ingenious stage-devices to give his customers an entertaining half hour. He was particularly pleased with the staging of this play and wrote to T. A. Harvey 'I think it amused the children more than any other of the entertainments I have given them. It really wasn't half bad. I had some working figures of which I was very proud. A town crier who rang a bell, and a figure of the clown which smoked a pipe (real smoke which I blew through a tube from behind the scenes).' Although he was delighted by the children's reaction to these effects, he seems to have lost his enthusiasm for writing new plays for them after 1906. He continued to take pleasure in tales of piracy, however, and, with his friend John Masefield, made many ships with which various adventures were acted out; he told the story of these ships in his book *A Little Fleet* (1909). He did not, however, turn to literature again for some years, contenting himself with illustrating Masefield's work, and with imitating the nineteenth-century prints he loved in his *A Broadsheet* which he edited and published with Pamela Coleman Smith during the years 1908–1915. He also made many prints for the Cuala Press. In 1910 he moved from Devon to Dublin, where in 1916 he fell seriously ill. After his recovery he did little work for five years. His father died in 1921. His painting was now becoming freer and more expressive of personal convictions, less concerned with recording the life around him than with exploring the life within. He became opposed to the photographing of his pictures, and in 1925 turned against the Cuala prints he had made and wrote to W. B. Yeats, 'The last two or three prints I have given them against my will. These reproductions are a drag, and a loss to me in my reputation. I refused to two different people several years ago the right to reproduce my "Old Ass". And last year I would not make a design for Bristol publishers who wanted one similar to the Cuala Prints. If I had the ready money I would try and buy up the copyrights of all the prints of mine which Cuala publishes.' On 6 February 1926 he wrote to Lolly Yeats, 'I have coloured the proofs and send them now. When you send me the "Hurley Player" I will colour it also. These reprints from the Broadside are the last I can give leave for.'

It was in the middle twenties that Jack Yeats' paintings began to develop the energy and originality which made him Ireland's greatest painter.★ At the time his father died in 1921 he was 50 years old. At almost the same age in 1914 his brother W. B. Yeats had published *Responsibilities* which, together with the first edition of *The Green Helmet* (1910) had signalled a change in his poetry. John Butler Yeats had, in 1887, at the age of 48, abandoned Dublin for London's Bedford Park and thought to change the direction of his work. It seems that in middle age the males of the Yeats family were destined to attempt a change of direction.

It was in the late twenties, when he was approaching 60, that Jack

★ For accounts of Yeats as an artist, see James White, *Jack B. Yeats, Drawings and Paintings*, Secker & Warburg 1971, and T. G. Rosenthal, *Jack Yeats, 1871–1957*, no 40 in The Masters series.

Yeats turned again to literature, and began to produce the series of plays and prose works which mark him out as one of the most original writers of his time. The first of his plays, *The Deathly Terrace*, is clearly a further development of the melodramatic tradition he utilized in his earlier plays of piracy and romance. Its characters are all involved in a world of imaginery events, in the world of the cinema. Just as in his children's plays he created a highly mannered mode of speech appropriate to the never-never land of pirates, treasure-hunters, and romance, so in *The Deathly Terrace* he created a mannered diction which, while including many of the clichés and stock phrases of the popular romantic cinema of the period, also has a wayward vitality of its own. The plot of the play is as fantastic as are the plots of the earlier ones. It does, however, introduce a theme that remained central to Jack Yeats' writings from this period onward. Nardock, the man whose supposed death opens the play, and who also pretends death at the close of it, is one whose vision and way of life contrive to irradiate and give meaning and perspective to the lives of others. He tells Andy

> . . . for a moment of every day or every age I bit into the crust of the rainbow, and that is only a figure of speech for what I bit into. . . . I whistled to the wind and it whistled back, an endless whistle, that had a colour and a form, a rope of whistling making and unmaking itself into knots nautical, and starry knots, a cable twisted of three, four, seven, strands, and again it became a single strand like a whigging snake of blue light on a marble sea. . . .

Nardock has wandered everywhere, and has spent much time as an inventor. He invented, he tells Andy, both the circle and fire, which is to say that he saw the wonder and originality in all things; he became himself involved in that vital principle which caused the creation of the world. Andy, the other man in the play, has lived by chance and not by choice, and thus has also steeped himself in the feeling for life as miraculous. When these two men, at the end of the play, give the actress the impression that they have 'died' for love of her, their sacrifice transforms her into something approaching a goddess, even though she may, as Cinema Star, open bazaars or kick off (*sic*) cricket matches, she, 'with her lovely soul shining through her gorgeous eyes will look benignly on all the world as it . . .' The sentence is left incomplete with the words 'as it'. The world goes on turning. It has all been a fantasy, but it has suggested that our beliefs about ourselves, our attitudes towards the universe, can transfigure not only our own lives but those of others, and that spiritual goodness can spring from an acceptance of the life of the intuition and the imagination. The truly valuable individual is the man who, like Nardock, can be so assured of his individual uniqueness, and yet so willingly involved in the life of the world around him, that he can truthfully describe himself as 'an Egotist steeped in generosity and seethed in affection'.

Nardock is, in some respects, a practical joker; like the Clown and Pantaloon in *The Wonderful Travellers*, his life's work appears to be to astonish and awake the sensibilities of those around him. The practical joke is also a motif in the three plays collected together under the general title *Apparitions* in 1933. The title play is a small enough comedy, in which the townspeople are gulled. *The Old Sea Road* is less conventional in structure and more bitter. The last practical joke of Ambrose is murder and suicide; it is hinted that this is as much a deception as his two previous practical jokes in which he sent the villagers looking for the results of a non-existent earthquake and caused them to believe that the Grand National had been cancelled. The inconsequence of the play is marked. It is so organized as to suggest the wayward fluctuant progress of life, and the finally desperate attempt of man to give it shape, even by mocking and denying it. *The Rattle*, the last of the three plays, is just as formless; the characters spend the majority of their time discussing the possible future of the family business. It ends, however, with the death of a central character in South America in a conflict which is clearly meaningless; and yet the death is given dignity by the vitality of the imagination of the dying man, who finds that just as 'To know all is to forgive all', so 'To forgive all is to know all.' To forgive life its inconsequence, its brutality, its meaninglessness, is to find it consequential, innocent, meaningful. The viewpoint is almost oriental, and it is perhaps no accident that in Jack Yeats' next play *The Silencer*, the Chinese are seen as 'neither watching, nor waiting, nor regretting'.

In *The Silencer*, the central character, Hartigan, impinges upon the lives of a group of businessmen engaged in discussing house prices and finance and begins, with his talk of wonders and foreign lands, to alter their lives. Employed by one of them, his love of talk causes a business investment to be lost; on another occasion, eager to help a stranger with a long and detailed discussion of his problems, he is robbed. After this his ability to capture and hold an audience is utilized by robbers; he is set to talk to a plain-clothes policeman and distract his attention from a robbery. This scheme does not work; the majority of the thieves are arrested, and one of those who have escaped kills Hartigan in revenge as he is talking to a man on the street. In this last speech before he dies Hartigan identifies his role for us; it is Socratic, but also something more. He tells his listener:

> All deaths are game deaths; death sees to that. It's the penultimate moment that shakes the brave. Chinamen in all the parts of the world where I have seen them, appear to me to be neither waiting, nor watching, nor regretting. And you are doing the whole three this moment I know; I know it in my bones. And you can't deny it; and you don't want to deny it.

Hartigan, as the man who is aware, as the man who knows himself, as the man who rejoices in life, is an embodiment of the spirit of life itself which the majority deny. His murderer, visiting a seance in order to ask forgiveness of his victim's ghost, is told by that ghost:

> In comfort of body I recall dreadful days of old, fighting odds too heavy, far too heavy. But then I was held in a body that could ache and fear. But this body now is

the fun of a body which has neither fear nor ache, unless the misty vapour of the lake can ache. Do the clouds ache in their hearts because the lake distorts their reflections? Not they! They say if there were no clouds there'd be no lakes. And what are lakes but little puddles grown up. And what are little puddles but little drops of water, and little grains of sand too; they make the mighty ocean and the pleasant land too. A song of innocence; little drops of water and little grains of sand are innocent because they are little. But why not big lakes and roomy mountains innocent too! Is a little innocence better than a big innocence? No, a thousand times, no! Ten thousand times ten thousand innocences are just that and nothing more, and what a lot that is.

He is told of death

So that's where we leave down one gangway, we come aboard skipping up the next. Ever ashore, ever a-floating; before the wind and in the wind's eyes, in the trough and on the crest, forgetting where the foaming stars come down and the twinkling waters rush up.

He is arrested, but by fake policemen, party-goers in fancy dress. The punishment of crime, the thoughts of Truth and Justice, are as insubstantial as is all else. They are all aspects of the delusive Maya, the figment which is mortal events and existence. There is, finally, nothing but the current of life itself, and that finds death meaningless, a delusion. The state of the heart, of the soul, is all that matters and that survives to other places, dimensions, and, maybe, other lives.

The Silencer is a fantasy, but also a philosophy. Filled with marvellous speeches, its sense of the marvellous is integral to its philosophical theme; its ironies and absurdities are at one with its message. It is a play filled with both gaiety and profundity, and in its emphasis upon life as flux, as change, as delight, explains and anticipates the structures and attitudes of Jack Yeats' later prose works, *Sligo* (1930) in particular, and justifies the almost casual treatment of death in the earlier plays for the miniature theatre. Those who take death seriously, those who cry out 'An eye for an eye' and speak of Truth, Justice, and Vengeance in the same breath, are those whose eyes have not been opened to the glory, innocence and splendour of the life process.

In *Harlequin's Positions*, the first of his plays to be performed, Jack Yeats denied himself his usual verbal exuberance, and presented what appears at first blush to be an entirely naturalistic story of the relationship between a small group of people in an Irish country town and a visitor from abroad. The visitor, however, early in the first act makes it clear that the drama is intended as something more than a 'Slice-of-life' episode. He tells the relatives he is visiting of a harlequin he once met and adds:

I discovered that those positions the harlequin takes with the wand in his hands all have names. I don't know if his were peculiar to himself. He turned always from one to the other to complete the series, five in number:
Admiration.
Pas de Basque.

> Thought.
> Defiance.
> Determination.
> I committed them to memory—Harlequin positions—and have made them my order of—order of existence, if I may put it in that way.

He endeavours to show how these five positions can be applied to every human act, and thereafter the play appears to bear him out in its sequence of events. The first act is dominated by his relatives' admiration of him and their wonder at his experiences. The second act presents the first steps of the relationship. In the third act a great deal of time is given to philosophizing, and in the fourth Annie, who has just sold the Cinema, shows her defiance of the limits set upon her life by circumstance by planning to set off with her friends on a sea voyage. The voyage is postponed because of rumours of war, and in the fifth act the Guard exhibits the mood of determination as he goes down to the little town talking of heroic matters. The scheme is not carried through with any rigidity, but the whole clearly follows a plan. Jack Yeats was, in his later drama, much concerned with the depiction of life's changing tones and moods; in a notebook for *The Deathly Terrace* he showed the progress of the drama in terms of colour-progressions and rhythms in a series of pastel designs. He was not, in *Harlequin's Positions*, concerned to present a philosophical viewpoint so much as something for philosophical contemplation. In this the play resembles the apparently inconsequential short late plays of Samuel Becket where little that is dramatic occurs, but where an episode from life is held up to us for our scrutiny, and for us to make of it what we will. In *Harlequin's Positions*, Alfred, the visitor, tells his relations:

> There is something in everything. There was a group of young men in Buenos Ayres when I was there who tried to found a religion on that—something in everything. One of them, the Secretary of the Society, picked up a horseshoe nail, walking with me one day near the Market and he began, on that nail, expounding, expounding. At first I was dizzied, but after a little I was completely bored, and so was he. If I could have reconstructed the ambling pad, the horse, Aunt Claire, from the horseshoe nail, I would have mounted it and ridden away from the Secretary, leaving him nothing but my dust.

He also tells Johnnie 'Everything's symbolical if you look at it in the right way.' It was Jack Yeats' intention not to interpret the symbolism he presented, but to offer it upon the stage in such a way that perfectly ordinary events appeared to be of more than usual significance. He dealt in hints, in nods, in sly suggestions.

La La Noo, which was first performed in 1942 when its author was seventy years old, is more compact than *Harlequin's Positions* and more obviously symbolic. The story is simple. Seven women, caught in a rainstorm, are forced to shelter in a lonely pub. The publican shows them to an inner room and they strip off their clothes and hand them out for him to dry them at the nearby smithy. The stranger, a much travelled man, later agrees to drive them in a lorry to catch the bus, but he runs into a tree and is killed. The drama exists in the talk and its intimations of death. The Fourth Woman says of men:

> I never seen them die. I seen them wither and when my back was turned they died on me. Wouldn't they put the life across you. They'd like to with their tricky ways. They're in hands with death the whole time, the dirty twisters.

It is she who leaves before the accident, almost as if the act of turning her back were a curse upon the stranger. The Fifth Woman follows her speech by saying 'I don't care what you say, I'll see a man die and then I'll die myself and it won't be long either', and the first half of her prophesy is quickly fulfilled. The Fourth Woman tells the company 'You're all talking about death because you think 'tis so far away' and refers to deaths on the roads. There is in the whole of the conversation a building-up of pressure towards the climactic event, the stranger's death. If we attempt, however, to give the women labels, to regard them as fatal sisters, to allegorize, we face the impossible. They cannot be schematized, any more than their nudity in the heart of the play can be fitted into any thematic pattern. It is merely, yet potently, a hint at the nature of unaccommodated man, a pointer to the nakedness we share beneath all our pretensions and our talk. The story has an eeriness to it, and it tells of a strange turn of events, but it is resolutely not a myth. It is what we might these days call a happening, the record of an unplanned occasion, an apparently spontaneous act of the life-and-death process. Jack Yeats discovered in *La La Noo*, as Beckett and others discovered later, that the presentation of any event as if it were theatre creates theatre; the frame of the stage is almost all that is needed to give symbolic power to the inconsequent, the casual, the insignificant. It is all in the way we look at it, for 'everything is symbolical if you look at it in the right way.' It is the business of the stage and also of the cinema screen to make us look in a certain fashion, to manipulate the quality of our attention. Thus, the heirs to *La La Noo* are not only the smaller late plays of Beckett, the happenings of modish New York in the sixties, some of the films of Andy Warhol and much work stemming from the *cinéma vérité* tradition, but also, even, the 'found' poem, and the 'found' novel.

Something of this is indicated by *The Green Wave*, a one-act conversation piece intended as prologue to *In Sand*. In this short piece two elderly men are looking at and discussing a painting of a green wave which one of them has bought. The second man asks the first:

> What is it?
> 1ST MAN It is a wave.
> 2ND MAN I know that, but what sort of a wave?
> 1ST MAN A green wave—well—a rather green wave.
> 2ND MAN What does it mean?

1ST MAN I think it means just to be a wave.

2ND MAN I like things to mean something, and I like to know what they mean, and I like to know at once. After all, time is important, the most important thing we know of, and why waste it in trying to find out what something means, when if it stated its meaning clearly itself we would know at once.

1ST MAN If that wave could speak it might say, 'I'm an Irish wave and the Irish are generally supposed to answer questions by asking questions,' and the wave might ask you what was the meaning of yourself!

This is a key to the Socratic stance of Jack Yeats' drama. He is presenting us, in all his mature works, with green waves that disturb us with questions, first as to their nature and then as to ours. There are fewer answers than questions. 'Truth,' said W. B. Yeats once, 'is an attitude of mind.' Jack Yeats would, I think, have agreed with him, feeling that 'to forgive all is to know all', which is to say that our knowledge of life's meaning and of the meaning of ourselves can only be achieved by the humourful and affectionate acceptance and admiration of the whole of the business of living and dying. It cannot be achieved by taking thought, by great plans, or by the will. Those who plan gain, who hunt the treasure, end with a skull in a box; those who pursue are trapped; those who trick are tricked. The ultimate prank of the practical joker who aims to impose his will upon others can only be death, and death is itself the funniest joke of all, that which makes Hartigan caper with glee at the fake policemen and the 'arrest' of his murderer.

Death is a recurrent theme in Jack Yeats' plays, or perhaps it would be better to say, a recurrent event whose significance and insignificance is dwelt upon by the dramatis personae. *In Sand* opens with the death of Anthony Larcson whose last wish is that a young girl should write upon the sand at low tide the words 'Tony, we have the good thought for you still.' The message is written by the young girl, Alice, who by means of the inheritance Larcson leaves her, gets a husband. On her travels she writes upon every strand she comes across, the words 'Tony, we have the good thought for you still.' At the close of the play, after her death, when the plans for making the island an autonomous republic have to be delayed by the early commencement of the tourist season, two young people are found writing the words once more on the sand, not understanding them, but knowing that they bring good luck. Thus the simple, even meaningless phrase, carries more weight than all the pretentious slogans that the Governor contemplates putting on his list of slogans permitted to be written. The reality of this message of simple affection, of reverence, can withstand the ravages of time and the accidents of circumstance more successfully than can the Governor's and Visitor's plans for political advancement and for roads, swimming pools, and personal aggrandizement.

The plans of the Visitor and the Governor to create their own republic are ludicrous, but carry a serious message. What matters is not, perhaps, the provision of actual things, of real roads and swimming-pools, but the idea of them. The picture gallery can be made to exist as a notion if not as a fact; the swimming-pool can be created by a notice board stating its existence. We are, it seems, not what we are but what we think we are; we are all fantasists and the best of us, the wisest of us, are so assured that our life is illusion, that our wealth and power are insubstantial, that we can create from the insubstantial a world in which we may find our roles, our selves, our identities. The viewpoint is, as I have said before, strangely non-occidental, somewhat oriental. Life is a flux of illusions; death is a subterfuge of life; the dream is as powerful as the fact and the fact can be transformed by the smallest word. This wonderful creature, man, once released from his bondage to rents and revenues, once able to let chance, providence, and fantasy, move him along its natural path, may find sorrow and solitude but will also find strength, and a kind of security, free from dogmas about art, politics, or meaning.

Jack Yeats' drama is, one might suggest, anarchic in the proper sense. It mocks and teases notions of government and politics. It opposes materialist values. After its beginnings, it frees itself from the conventions of the drama of its time, breaks all the laws of unity, and challenges all contemporary preconceptions of what is dramatic. It utilizes inconsequence and chance, with a little nod as if to suggest that chance is itself a guiding principle to which we have forgotten to pay homage. It is ironic, it deals always in irony, but the final irony is that the event which traps us, death, is not the trap we have supposed it to be and that the glory we desire is not the glory we suppose; the desire itself is the glory. Thus Jack Yeats' drama points away from the schematized philosophy of the symbolist drama of his brother as well as away from the social naturalism of such successful contemporaries as Galsworthy, and the rationalist approaches of George Bernard Shaw. Poetic in that it is the imagination which is the hero of every play and the power of the imagination and fancy which is the real protagonist in every drama, it nevertheless eschews poetic posturing, and, in the last work of all, refuses to pontificate. Belonging to no school of thought, not even being easily allied to the Irish writers' drama of its day (though one suspects an influence of George Fitzmaurice's fantasy plays on occasion), it has been largely forgotten by all save a few. Nevertheless, the drama of Jack B. Yeats, especially in his major plays, *The Silencer*, *La La Noo*, and *In Sand*, is both inimitable and likely to become, once it is given the attention it deserves, seminal. It challenges orthodoxies and promotes questions, but does so with an affectionate humour and a dazzle of wit that few playwrights have equalled in our time, and to the question 'What does it mean?' it gives the calm answer 'I think it means just to be.'

The University of Victoria,   ROBIN SKELTON
Victoria, British Columbia.

NOTE ON THE TEXT
AND ACKNOWLEDGEMENTS

As this book is intended to present the plays of Jack B. Yeats to a wider audience than they have previously enjoyed, rather than to provide the specialist scholar with a fully documented and minutely meticulous record of the exact texts of frequently chaotic manuscripts, I have chosen to take a number of editorial liberties with those plays which the author himself did not see through the press. The manuscripts of the previously unpublished plays for the miniature theatre are very casually punctuated, contain many mis-spellings, and frequently omit necessary stage directions. The author was, after all, the producer as well as the whole cast, and did not need to tell himself that for a character to re-enter the stage it was necessary for him first to have left it; nor did he need elaborate punctuation, but could be adequately informed by occasional dashes and a sprinkling of commas. To present the text of these plays as they are written down would be to set up unnecessary obstacles for the reader. I have therefore chosen to amend the punctuation wherever its absence or oddity could lead to confusion or cause the reader to stumble; I have replaced a number of dashes by full stops; I have capitalized the beginnings of sentences; I have made the names of the characters consistent throughout each play; and I have added entrances and exits where obviously necessary. The extent of my meddling should perhaps be illustrated here. In *The Wonderful Travellers* the policeman is given the following speech:

> Heres a nice howdododo Heres countrytomtom—a couple of villians have escaped from a dark Donjohn, and are expected to arrive in this town at any moment I have just received a warrant to arrest them immediately on sight if I dont see them sooner, or before that—the warrant which I have here in my hand gives a description of the rascals—
>> The first villian is described thus nicely
>> middle height
>> Hair Black
>> Eyes one blue the other pink
>> dress—large blue ruffle round neck
>> sleeves striped red and blue
>> Red spotted trousers
>> and white shores with pink rosettes
>>> oh the miscreant

I have edited this fairly typical passage to read:

> Here's a nice howdododo. Here's countrytomtom—a couple of villains have escaped from a dark Donjohn, and are expected to arrive in this town at any moment. I have

just received a warrant to arrest them immediately on sight if I don't see them sooner, or before that—the warrant which I have here in my hand gives a description of the rascals—

       The first villain is described thus nicely:
       Middle height
       Hair Black
       Eyes One blue, the other pink
       Dress Large blue ruffle round neck,
       sleeves striped red and blue, red spotted
       trousers and white shoes with pink rosettes. Oh the miscreant!

In this passage I have corrected 'villians' to read 'villains'; in other places, wherever there was any possibility that the spelling was intended to indicate a particular pronunciation or to be humorous, I have left the text alone. Jack Yeats' orthography was frequently unorthodox, and I have chosen to keep his spellings whenever they are more likely to amuse than obstruct the reader in order to retain some indications of the rich idiosyncracy of his style.

With the published plays there has been less to do, though in *La La Noo*, after the Fourth Woman has been sent off stage, we are given the stage direction:

Women file out into the kitchen. Their clothes are wrinkled and pathetic looking. First and Second Woman side by side. Fourth alone. The Seventh alone. Then Fourth and Sixth side by side.

Obviously one of this batch of Fourth Women is the Third Woman and the other the Fifth; I have altered the text accordingly. One play has been omitted: the only text of *James Dance or The Fortunate Sailor Boy* that has so far been discovered is too fragmentary to deserve publication.

The illustrations are taken from both printed and manuscript sources, from the printed texts, from notebooks in the possession of Miss Anne Yeats, and from materials in the Special Collections Room of the Macpherson Library of the University of Victoria. These last have appeared previously in *The Malahat Review*. The map of Pirate Island on p 20 is taken from *Ernest Marriott: Jack B. Yeats* (Elkin Matthews, 1911). All the photographs were taken by The Green Studio, Dublin, with the exception of those illustrating *La La Noo* which were provided by The Morriss Printing Company, Victoria, British Columbia.

'Of making many books there is no end,' says *Ecclesiastes*, and, similarly, there is no end to the editing of them. I am sensible that this particular volume does little more than furnish an adequate text of Jack Yeats' plays, whereas it might well have included much ancillary material relating to his life and work and some more thorough documentation concerning the productions of the plays themselves. Jack Yeats has, however, waited a long time for an editor, and having been fortunate enough to have been given the task, I have thought it better to avoid 'letting "I dare not" wait upon "I would" ', and to risk the obloquy of the pedant rather than delay the pleasure of the ordinary reader.

In working on Jack B. Yeats I have been greatly helped by a number of people and organizations. I am indebted to the University of Victoria and to the Canada Council for grants which enabled me to visit Dublin, and study the relevant manuscripts and typescripts. Liam Miller has on this, as on so many other occasions when I have been concerned in studying Irish writings, been a tower of strength, and the firm of Bertram Rota, Ltd, has once again earned my gratitude for helping me discover necessary texts of the published works while Miss Elizabeth Havelock has been of great assistance in a number of matters during the final stages of the editorial process. Above all, however, I am indebted to Senator Michael Yeats, and to Miss Anne Yeats who made the papers available to me and allowed me to study them in her house.

The University of Victoria,   ROBIN SKELTON
Victoria, British Columbia

Part One

PLAYS
for the
MINIATURE THEATRE

MY MINIATURE THEATRE

Every Christmas for a number of years it has been my habit to entertain the children of the valley in which I live, and for their amusement I first set up my miniature stage. The size of the proscenium of my theatre is three foot nine inches wide and one foot ten inches high. This shape lending itself better to my mind to the artistic and realistic compositions of the scenes, than the lofty style of the real prosceniums which is responsible for the incongruity, which we sometimes see, of the heroine and her little boy, starving in garret, with so much top room that they could have floors put in and let the place out in flats. The scenes in my plays are pasted on cardboard and painted in water colours. I find great brilliancy is got in a large mass of colour by using coloured papers—indeed long before I start the mounting of a new play I begin collecting in my property box every bit of good coloured paper and tinsel I can lay my hands on.

The characters are also drawn on cardboard and cut out. They are about nine or ten inches high, so that an audience of two or three dozen people can sit comfortably and yet not be too far away to see them well.

The whole idea of my theatre was suggested to me of course by those fine old penny plain and twopence coloured plays of our grandfathers; indeed every successful play that appeared on the London boards and was sufficiently exciting was immediately issued in sheets for the Miniature Stage, at a penny plain and twopence coloured. And delightful the sheets of characters are, magnificent pirates and robbers, and graceful lovely Nancies with the smallest of hands and feet, and combats too. All done from copper plates, and full of the real dignity and romance of the traditions of theatricals. The scenes too are beautiful things, there is one of a cottage interior in Skelts Floating Beacon that seems to vibrate with the electricity of dramatic excitement. But has not Robert Louis Stevenson told people what fine things these plays were? But as these plays were abridged editions of the full grown ones for living actors some of the actions of the characters were very difficult to carry out with paste-board players. Take stage directions such as these:

Enter Mainyard L H Plate 2—I have ye now foul pirate swab. *Draw off* Mainyard *and* Theodore—*put on* Mainyard *and* Theodore *with swords fighting* R H Plate 5. *They fight. To give noise of weapons clash two dinner knives together behind scenes.* Mainyard *strikes* Theodore *who falls draw off* Theodore *and* Mainyard *put on* Theodore *wounded* R H Plate 2 *and* Mainyard *wiping sword* R H Plate 3. *Red fire.*

Now that is good to read but difficult to carry out so as to be convincing.

Seeing that to make a play go without a hitch the *business* must be very simple, I write all my plays with as little movement for the figures as possible, they slide into their place; I fix them upon slides of thin lath coloured to match the flooring of the stage, and unfold the plot by the dialogue—though most of my characters do little but talk, and walk, majestically, I have had some characters of whose *business* I am very proud. In the Harlequinade of *The Playful Pilgrims* or *The Gamesome Princes and the Pursuing Policeman*, there was a town crier who moved his arm, and rang his bell, and a clown in the same play who smoked a pipe with real smoke. The town crier's arm which rang the bell was worked with a string which ran down his back and along the side of his slide, and the clown's smoke was blown from behind the scenes through an india rubber tube.

My footlights are candles with small reflectors, and sometimes at the back of the scene, when it is intended to shine through a transparent part of the backcloths as in the shipwreck scene in *Esmeralda Grande*, when the lightening was illuminated from behind, or in the moonlight scene in the *Treasure of the Garden*. For great effects red, and green fire's the thing, the smoking and spluttering of it adding more and more to the horror of the scene.

The best scenes are I think the deep ones with many side wings, and the back cloth far back as is the last scene in *Esmeralda Grande*, when the Hero returns from sea and is married to Miss Marjorie Morning. Solid built-up scenes are effective too like Scene IV in *James Dance* or *The Fortunate Ship Boy;* it had a *practical* road down which on ponies James Dance and the mysterious dwarf passed on their way to that treasure cave among the mountains which opened only to a certain strange spell which had been imparted to James Dance by the unearthly dwarf.

It is curious to notice what my audiences like best especially if they are children. A mounted Arab received an ovation every time he came on, why I could not understand; there were other Arabs also mounted but they left my audience unmoved—I was finally satisfied that it was the metal top off a champagne cork which did duty as a shield on the Arab's breast which was responsible for his joyful reception. The piece of bright tin certainly did catch the light from the footlights. In *The Playful Pilgrims* a clown disguised as a parrot in company of the pantaloon as a sailor man was also always received with honour.

The emerald in *Esmeralda Grande* which was borne aloft in the processions by four Nubians upon an oaken tray and was of the shape and bigness of a pineapple, was a pretty fine thing and much admired.

The parts in these plays are of course spoken behind the scenes and it is at times hard to make the voices of the characters sufficiently different, and after talking for some time in the husky voice of Captain Teach, you find that for a scene or two, all the characters are speaking their lines in the same deep notes—for the time you have acquired the throat of piracy and you must be very careful—shuler Pine must not speak with the same voice as Eldorado Gillen or James Flaunty.

As to the plays, I write them all myself. So what shall I say of them, but that I admire them all but I like the piratical ones best—and always feel very proud of myself when reciting in two voices the Adventurer's Oath in *Esmeralda Grande:* it requires two voices a deep roar for the captain and a fearstruck wail for the crew which gradually grows feebler as the thing goes on.

CAPTAIN Will you swear by the Adventurer's Oath.
CREW (*shuddering*) The Adventurer's Oath! the Adventurer's Oath!
CAP Then say after me slow and distinct.
By the Wind from Carrick-na-Gat.
CREW By the Wind from Carrick-na-Gat.
CAP By the light on the Blennick.
CREW By the light on the Blennick.
CAP By Shule-na-meala.
CREW By Shule-na-meala.
CAP By Poolhoya.
CREW By Poolddhoya.
CAP By Benbulben and Knock-na-rea.
CREW By Benbulben and Knock-na-rea.
CAP By the Spanish Main.
CREW By the Spanish Main.
CAP By the old trade and the merchants of the old trade.
CREW By the old trade and the merchants of the old trade.
CAP We swear to stand by Captain Blackbeard the second.
CREW We swear to stand by Captain Blackbeard the second.
CAP In fair or in foul.
CREW In fair or in foul.
CAP In smooth or in breakers.
CREW In smooth or in breakers.
CAP Until our Bones are White.
CREW Until our Bones are White.

JACK B. YEATS

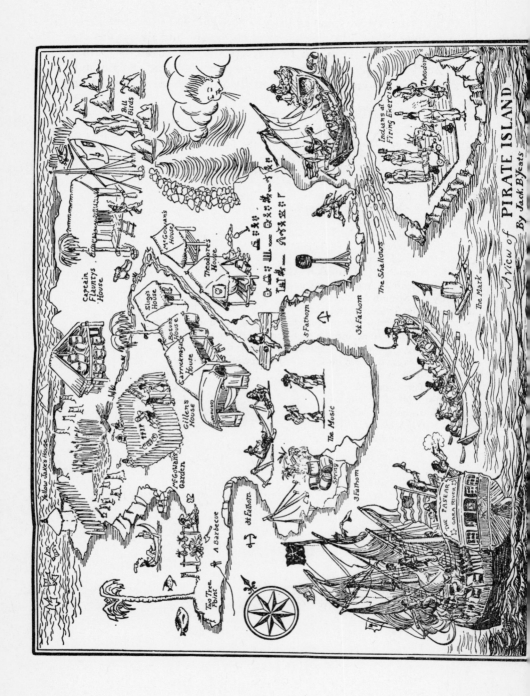

A View of PIRATE ISLAND
By Jack B. Yeats

Timothy Coombewest

or

Esmeralda Grande

Playwritten and Played
1900

JACK·B·YEATS
ESMERALDA GRANDE
PLAY WRITTEN AND PLAYED
1900

Jack B Yeats

CHARACTERS

Men

TIMOTHY COOMBEWEST *first a farmer's boy.*
CAPTAIN SHEAF (*ashore but afloat known as*) *Captain Blackbeard the Second.*

HARRY THE DANDY (*Bosun*) ⎫
BILLY THE CAPSTANBAR ⎪   *Crew of The Green*
MARK ANTONY ⎬   *Linnet Brig*
MCGOWAN THE PRIVATEERSMAN ⎪
COLORADO MADURO ⎭

DAVY JONES *the owner of the well known* LOCKER.
TOWN CRIER *of the old Seaport Town.*
SAILORS *fishermen &c &c &c.*

Women

MISS MARJORIE MORNING *afterwards Mrs Timothy Coombewest.*

SCENES

ACT ONE

Scene 1: Ankersknowle Valley.
Scene 2: The Old Sea Port.
Scene 3: Deck of the Linnet.

ACT TWO

Scene 1: Linnet at Sea.
Scene 2: Below decks on the Linnet.
Scene 3: The Wreck.
Scene 4: Davy Jones's Locker.

ACT THREE

Scene the last: Fore Street of Old Seaport Town.

ACT ONE

Scene 1: *Ankersknowle Valley.*

Enter TIMOTHY COOMBEWEST *and* MISTRESS MARJORIE MORNING.

MARJORIE   Where are you going, Master Timothy Coombewest?

TIM   Away!

MARJORIE   Where tew?

TIM   To seek my fortune on the Sea. Since Father died, Aunt and Uncle
have treated me so mortious bad that I must away; but before I go I
want you to promise me something Marjorie dear.

MARJORIE   Yes Timothy.

TIM   When I come back will you marry me?

MARJORIE   Yes Tim, if I am alive when you come back I will marry you—
and how long will it take you to make your fortune?

TIM   Perhaps five years, perhaps ten—but not more than ten.

MARJORIE   Goodbye Tim!

TIM   Goodbye Marjorie, think of me every day.

(*Exit* MARJORIE M.)

TIM (*running after her*) Give me the flower you wear dear—(*returns with flower*) Goodbye old valley, Goodbye!

Curtain.

Scene 2: *The Sea Port.*

Enter TIMOTHY.

TIM Blackberries for breakfast aren't very satisfying but—if I was at home now I'd be having a lump of barley bread and a drink of milk in my brown mug—But here's a ship—and here—comes the Captain too.

(*Enter* CAPTAIN SHEAF.)

CAPTAIN What do you want my lad, eh?
TIM I want a job aboard your ship sir.
CAPTAIN What can you do my lad, hé?
TIM I can plough and I can sow, I can reap and I can hoe and I can top turnips.
CAPTAIN Can you box the compass, hé?
TIM I don't know 'un, but I dare say I could wrastle 'un. . . .
CAPTAIN What do you say eh? if I took you aboard and make a cabin boy of you, hé?

TIM   Thankee Sir, and I'd be obliged if you'd let me have some breakfast. I can smell it a-cooking.

CAPTAIN   Alright, go aboard and tell the cook that Captain Sheaf said he was to inside line yer.

TIM   Thankee Sir.

(*Exit* TIM. *Enter* TOWN CRIER, *passing along.*)

CRIER   Lost or strayed from a gentleman whilst playing dominoes with some other gentleman, a pair of knee buckles—a pair of fine gold shoe buckles—a ruby ring—and an Indian silk sash—Anybody finding the same and returning to the watch house, will be rewarded!—Five shillings reward!!——Lost, stolen or strayed, a Farmer's Boy, black hair—eyes of blue—brown leggings—and carries a walking stick. Anybody finding the same and returning all sound to his sorrowing uncle, Benjamin Coombewest, Flint Farm, Ankersknowle Valley— will receive the above Fine reward—

(*Exit* CRIER.)

CAPTAIN   Ha! Ha!

(*Exit* CAPTAIN)

Curtain.

Scene 3: *Deck of 'Linnet'.*

CAPTAIN   Tim! Tim! hurry up you young schemer or I'll have to rope's end you again, like I did yesterday.

TIM Coming Sir.
CAPTAIN Send Bosun Harry here, Harry the Dandy.

(*Exit* TIM.)
(*Enter* HARRY.)

CAPTAIN Harry, pipe all hands on deck, I've got news for them.

(HARRY *pipes. Enter* CREW.)

CAPTAIN Are you all there? Billy the capstan bar!
BILLY Here——
CAPTAIN Mark Antony!
MARK A. Here——
CAPTAIN McGowan, the privateersman.
MCGOWAN Here——
CAPTAIN And you, you cursed Spaniard Colorado Maduro.
COLORADO Here, Captain Sheaf.
CAPTAIN Don't call me Sheaf—afloat I'm Captain Blackbeard the Second—
the Dauntless Desperado of the Southern Seas. . . . Well—the whole
happy family of you are there—and I have news for you my cheerful
companions. It isn't piracy this time or ebony goods—but Treasure—
ready for the finding——

My Christian friends, listen to the words written on this parch-
ment which two years agone I took from the captain of the 'Scottish
Warrior' schooner before she gurgled down to Davy Jones with all
aboard. (*Reads*) I, Jamesee Henderson, write down these few lines for
the good of my family for fear at anytime I should pass away sudden.
In the South Pacific about Lat ——Long ——on a sandy island not
marked in the charts, I have buried an emerald stone of the size of
which I dare not speak—and shaped wondrously in the form of a
pineapple—under 10 foot of sand it lies, a foot of sand will wash away
in a twelvemonth so that I must dig him up ere ten years, else the
dazzling green-ness of him will so shine forth that every passing vessel
shall see it.

Now those who gave me this jewel of the world and who shall
never be named by me, told me, whereas to those to whom it was given
it brought all prosperity, but those that stole it, enjoyed it for but one
year, then perished fearfully—Now what I propose to do is to search
all islands in those latitudes for the jewel which must be of great
value—to search until we find—if need be until the sand shall wash
away, and guide us to it by the green light on the sky. Now will you
swear to stand by me and to the end?
CREW (*slowly*) Ye-e-es Captain.
CAPTAIN Will you swear it by the Adventurer's Oath!

C.P.Y.—2

CREW (*with bated breath*)   The Adventurer's Oath! The Adventurer's Oath!

CAPTAIN   Then say after me, slow and distinct: By the wind from Carrick-na-Gat.

CREW   By the wind from Carrick-na-Gat.

CAPTAIN   By the light on the Blennick.

CREW   By the light on the Blennick.

CAPTAIN   By Shule-na-meala.

CREW   By Shule-na-meala.

CAPTAIN   By Pooldhoya.

CREW   By Pooldhoya.

CAPTAIN   By Benbulben and Knock-na-rea.

CREW   By Benbulben and Knock-na-rea.

CAPTAIN   By the Spanish Main.

CREW   By the Spanish Main.

CAPTAIN   By the old trade and the merchants of the old trade.

CREW   By the old trade and the merchants of the old trade.

CAPTAIN   We swear to stand by Captain Blackbeard the Second.

CREW   We swear to stand by Captain Blackbeard the Second.

CAPTAIN   In fair or in foul.

CREW   In fair or in foul.

CAPTAIN   In smooth or in breakers.

CREW   In smooth or in breakers.

CAPTAIN   Until our Bones are White!!

CREW   Until our Bones are White. Oh-h-h-h-h-h (*shudderingly*).

(*The voices of the crew get weaker and weaker
as they repeat each part of the Oath.*)

Curtain.

End of Act One.

ACT TWO

Scene 1: *The 'Linnet' at Sea.*

(*Eight years are supposed to have passed. Distant voice of the*
CAPTAIN *across the sea.*)

CAPTAIN Eight years have worn away and no sign of the green jewel.
(*starting*) Is it!—ah!—the green light on the sky. (*exultingly*) Yonder
island holds the Wonder of the World! (*to men*) Lower the longboat.

Same Scene: *On the Island.*

(*They search.*)

CREW Not here, not here. Where is it then?
CAPTAIN I cannot see the light. Some ship must have seen it before we did,
and got here before us. No matter! The 'Linnet' is the fastest vessel in
the Southern Seas, nothing can live in front of her—and—nothing
29

shall! We will lay her on the chase of every ship we see, board her, and search so we must at last find this wondrous jewel.

(Exit all.)

Curtain.

Scene 2: *Below decks on 'Linnet'.*

(Sailors heard shouting.)

Give us a stave Harry, or give us the piece old Fergusson gave us before he went down aboard the 'Scottish Warrior'—the piece he said he read in a book—Though *I* believe he made it up.

HARRY THE DANDY   All right, only hold on a minute 'til I crouches meself up like the old rattle bones (*singing*)

            Three days we sailed to norrard
            Three days without a night—

VOICE ABOVE   All hands on deck to shorten sail.

(Exit CREW. Enter COLORADO MADURO and TIM.)

COLORADO   Tim, you have acted fair by me when the Captain put me in irons and would have let me starve—you brought me food. Now, I will act fair by you.

    Take my sea chest—in that chest I hold a wondrous sight——The Emerald.

TIM   The Emerald!

COLORADO   I got to it first on Sandy Island and hiding it in my coat carried it aboard—You remember, he who steals it can only hold it for a year, though to whom it is given it brings blessing. I give it to you. I stole it. 'Tis a year tonight. Tonight I perish. Look!

(*Opens chest and then slowly closes lid. Exit* TIM *and* COLORADO.)
(*Enter* CAPTAIN.)

CAPTAIN   I am weary of these endless chasings and killings. Yesternight we came upsides with a Scandinavian barque and put all to the sword— But the emerald was not there. Tomorrow—I will end it all, set the 'Linnet's' course for home. Once ashore I will never sail again. I'll be a farmer and grow flag-poles.

A VOICE   Captain!!

(*The* CAPTAIN *stands stlll.*)

VOICE   There are breakers around us—Captain!—There are *rocks* around us—Captain!!——

(*Crash.*)

Curtain.

Scene 3: *The Wreck.*

CAPTAIN   Nothing can save her.
MATE   Shall we burn a flare Captain?

CAPTAIN   It is of no use, these rocks are the Desolate Deadman's Teeth!——
There is not a human face for a hundred miles.

(*Burns flare. Ship sinks.*)

Curtain.

Scene 4: *Davy Jones's Cavern under the sea.* DAVY *discovered seated by Locker.*

(*Enter* TIM.)

DAVY   What's your name, young man?
TIM   Timothy Coombewest, Sir.
DAVY   Then Tim, I've got a whacking great lump of old green rock for you.
TIM   The Emerald?
DAVY   That's it, go and pick it out.
TIM   But how will I carry it?
DAVY   Haven't you got a nosekerchief?
TIM   Of course!
DAVY   Then tie it up in that, and good luck to you!

(TIM *passes across and off stage and returns with* 'emerald'
shining through 'nosekerchief'.)

Curtain.

End of Act Two

ACT THREE

Scene the Last: *Street of Seaport. Half-light. Fishwives and a Charlie discovered.*

Enter HORSEMAN *on grey horse.*

HORSEMAN (*gasping*) Captain Coombewest is near, I saw his ship, the 'Happy Return' passing Frighted Point (*pause*) And this good grey has galloped the whole 14 miles as hard as he could clink—Shove his muzzle in a trough of wine—and let who will make a song of it!!

(*Dawn lights—people arrive—*TOWN CRIER *on barrel.*)

CRIER Hail! Hail! Hail! Burghers of this Borough. By order of the Mayor and Burgesses of this ancient town, let ye all keep holiday! For today our fellow-countryman, Captain Timothy Coombewest, sails up the bay with Esmeralda, the Emerald of the World, at the prow—and we are glad to do him honour.—Today he weds Miss Marjorie Morning,

33

the fairest maiden in these lands. Today there will be a procession in this ancient town—the horses are even now champing their bits— (*order of procession*) First, the Sailormen of the 'Happy Return' supporting, on a carven sea, an image of their ship. Second, a high mettled racer. Thirdly, the oldest and youngest burghers of this ancient town. Fourthly, a troop of Merry Andrew clowns to make old and young laugh. Fifthly, the town band of this ancient town, marching in solid phalanx. Sixthly, a fish-chariot from Startle Point. Seventhly, the King of the Gypseys on his celebrated mare 'Moonless Light'. Eighthly, Borne aloft by four Nubians on an oaken tray the Wonder, The Wonder of the World—The Emerald! Ninthly Mistress Marjorie Morning, now the fair young wife of he who stands beside her, Captain Timothy Coombewest. Hail—Hail—Hail. (*dismounting from barrel*) Here they come! Mind yourselves you little children, and don't get trod on to. Hail—Hail—Hail.

(*Procession.*)

CURTAIN

THE END

Timothy Coombewest
of Ankersknowle Valley. Devon

Miss Marjorie Morning

THE *TOWN CRIER* OF THE OLD SEAPORT TOWN

Captain
Sheaf
Blackbeard
The Second
The Dauntless
Desparado of
The Southern
SEAS

. Billy The Capstan Bar.
of the LINNET CREW.

James Flaunty

or

The Terror of the Western Seas

Published 1901

JACK B. YEATS'S

~~PAGE~~ PLAYS:

In the Old ~~(Skeltian)~~ Manner.

JAMES FLAUNTY

OR

THE TERROR
OF THE
WESTERN SEAS

NANCE   FLAUNTY

JACK B. YEATS

ELKIN MATHEWS,

NEAR THE ALBANY;

And by most Booksellers in Town and Country.

CHARACTERS

JAMES FLAUNTY *The Terror.*
NANCY MCGOWAN *the Daughter of McGowan, the Landlord of the 'Happy Return.'*
CAPTAIN GIG *of His Majesty's Ship 'Cormorant'.*
LIEUTENANT FLORRY *of the same.*
ELDORADO GILLEN *A Pirate.*
WILLIAM PINE *A Shuler.*
BEACHCOMBERS AND MAN-O'-WAR SAILORS.

Scene: The Western Ocean.

Scene 1: *Coast of Western Africa. Inn on Right. Beachcombers discovered attacking Pine, who retires R., breathing hard.*

PINE   I haven't got any money—not a tosser. I swear to you. Stop a-throwing stones at me, and the first bit o' brass I picks up I swear by the vartue of me oath I'll—

BEACHCOMBERS *(yelling)* Hev him in the creek and make a cockshy of him till he sinks.

(Enter JAMES FLAUNTY. *With sword drawn he advances and pushes crowd slowly back before him.)*

FLAUNTY Will ye back or will ye not?—Back, I say, creek rats! or let each man wait and see me spit his fellow on this sweet sword.

(Exit COMBERS.*)*

IPNE   Thanks for my life to thee, cap.

(*Enter* LIEUTENANT FLORRY.)

FLORRY   A word with you, Mr Flaunty, in private. (*Exit* PINE.) His Majesty's
   brig 'Cormorant' lies on the farther shore, and I am instructed by Captain
   Gig to secure your services. (*Whispers*). To-night we propose to make an
   attack on the pirate Blackbeard's ship, the 'Spitting Devil'. In one of the
   creeks to the norrard she lies, but in which we do not know. Captain
   Gig has been informed that you have been many years upon these coasts,
   and that you will likely know where the 'Spitting Devil' lies to-night,
   and be able to lead us through the difficult channels to her. He has bid
   me ask your services as a pilot. As one white man to another white man
   I ask you, and fifty guineas he will pay you for these services. Can we
   depend on you?
FLAUNTY   Then you are in certain earnest. This is to be a crushing blow—
FLORRY   Aye, a crusher; every gun double shotted, every man full of fight.
   We have a crew, Mr Flaunty—ah, such a crew! The cream of fighting
   men picked from four frigates on these coasts. Not boys, you understand me, Mr Flaunty, but toughened men. Men who have hung by
   Scraw Wallaw—the shaking Scraw that hangs o'er the mouth of hell—
   and come back again.
FLAUNTY   You have said enough, sir, my knowledge of these treacherous
   creeks is at your disposal, and my arm. Step with me along the beach
   and we will arange the hour and mode of our attack.

Scene 2: *The Parlour of the 'Happy Return.'* NANCE *and* FLAUNTY *discovered.*

NANCE   So you will be for leading the man o' war sailors agin the—the
Quicktraders? I listened at my window and heard you, O cruel Jim.
Every one of them Quicktraders has a sash full of swords. How many
have tried to wipe them off the coast? Scores. They came the quick,
they went back the dead.

FLAUNTY   What of that, Nance, 'tis but the chance of war. If I come back
alive, fifty guineas; if I die, a roundshot and a canvas bag. But, sweet
Nance, with fifty guineas I can pay my tally to your father, marry his
daughter, and receive his blessing.

(*Voice heard without.* Nance, Nance, Nance!)

NANCE   'Tis my father's voice. Good-bye, Jim, and, mind you, keep out of
danger; let the horrid old hoss-eaters do the dirty work.

(*Exit.*)
(*Trap door opens slowly. Dripping pirate shows.*)

GILLEN   Lock the door, Captain Flaunty. (FLAUNTY *goes behind wing. Sound of falling bolt heard. He then re-enters.*) Good, then hear me, Captain. You receive fifty guineas to sell us to the English—to double on us. We offer you one hundred guineas to sell them to us. Fifty guineas for the double, one hundred guineas for the double double. I have the money about my waist, and, O Star of the Sea! it was a heavy cargo to swim the creek with to-night.

FLAUNTY   Back to those that sent you, and say that Captain Flaunty said no, not for a hundred thousand guineas!

GILLEN   But, Captain Flaunty, though you have never been altogether with us, you have many a time taken part in many a good adventure from the valorous devil that burns under your ribs. You have passed your word of honour to lead the British brig to us. Then do so; but take her by the White Bones sandbank. We will be there. You are promised to both us and them, Captain. They have money and a king behind them, but we have nothing but the living we can claw off these coasts. Ours is the finer cause, Captain. You are with us, Captain, I see; by the red on your cheek you are with us, Captain Flaunty.

FLAUNTY   Yes, by the old trade and the merchants of the old trade I am with you. Now, begone.

(GILLEN *sinks through stage. Trap closes.*)
(*A knocking at door.* FLAUNTY *goes and unbars. Enter* PINE.)

PINE   Ah, Captain, I have heard all.

FLAUNTY   What do I care. Ere to-morrow's sun is in half his strength I will
  be leagues away on the main.

PINE   I know that, and that is why I come. I come to serve you like a dog, if
  you will but take me with you. Tell the captain of the brig that I am
  your body servant, and then, when to-night they are delivered into the
  hands of the pirates—and I wish them no better fate, though I sailed on
  a brig myself from Plymouth in years gone by—then let me follow you
  with the pirates to the main, and let me serve you hand and foot till a
  merchantman too poor to rob comes rolling home for England, then
  force them to give me a passage home. Captain, I would sell every limb
  of my body so that I go home. I have tried as a seaman, but I am too
  weakly, they will not take me. I have tried as a stowaway, but every
  time was discovered, put ashore, and had to cut my way back through
  the jungle. Ship me for home, Captain—home! I ask you to do much
  for me, but only promise me you will put me on a homeward bound
  and my body and my soul are yours till I stand on her deck.

FLAUNTY   My poor fellow, you shall go home. I have said it—'tis enough.
  Meet me in the shadow of this house at midnight—and now—away!

Scene 3: *The Cabin of the 'Cormorant'.* FLAUNTY *discovered.*

FLAUNTY   She touched the sand then ever so lightly—but now—now—
(*sound of grating without*) now, by the pirate's moon, she's fast! (*Shot
heard without*) Blackbeard soon sets about his work. I must take up on
deck a bit, and hack the air till I see a chance to slip into one of the
pirates' boats.

(*Exit.*)
(*Red fire, explosions, clashing of arms heard off.*)

Scene 4: *The same, with windows open and hanging figure.* CAPTAIN GIG *and*
MIDSHIPMAN *discovered seated at table.* FLAUNTY *between two seamen with
drawn cutlasses.*

GIG   James Flaunty, you have been judged by this court guilty of conspiring
with the pirate Blackbeard to betray us into his hands last night. Have
you anything to say why your fate should not be the same as that of
this pirate taken alive by us last night when we drove off his comrades?
Turn your eyes to the stern windows, James Flaunty. Do you see his
body swinging there?

FLAUNTY   I do, captain.

GIG   Have you anything to say, James Flaunty?

FLAUNTY   Very little, Captain Gig. During my life I have spoken by deeds in preference to words. All I would say now is—what one Brave might say to another Brave—I would ask a last request that I may be executed in a more honourable manner. I request that I may be shot by your men on the shore of the creek when the sun is just sinking behind the palms.

GIG   Your wish is granted.

Scene 5: FLAUNTY *standing R. against tree. Officer on left. Enter* NANCE.

NANCE   Oh, Jim, Jim, is this the end of it?

FLAUNTY   Ah, sweet Nance, 'tis even so. They cannot tame the eaglet, let it once feel the long sweep of its pinions, and they cannot tame James Flaunty but in death. Farewell, sweet Nance.

OFFICER FLORRY   Ready!—present!

(*The clank of muskets heard without after each word of command.*)
(*Enter* PINE).

PINE   Oh, stop officer! This must not be! The captain is not the guilty one— he would not speak. He would have shielded me, for 'tis I who warned the pirates, and 'twas I who told Captain Flaunty that there was a clear

passage when it was thick with banks. Officer, shoot! men, shoot!
(*Sailors advance left, with muskets at the present.*) What care you, officer,
so long as you shoot someone. He is not guilty, let him go.

FLORRY   Anything you like, only be quick about it. I must get my men back
aboard the brig before nightfall.

PINE   Get back, Captain. (*He shoves Flaunty away off.*) Sailors, do your duty.
To-night I'll be on Sligo Quay.

CURTAIN.

Onct More's
First Circus

Played to Strete Schoolchildren
January 3rd 1901

PART ONE

PROGRAMME

(Entry of Attendants.)

RINGMASTER *(tall)*   The first item on the programme is the celebrated DON GONZALVAS in his FIRST JOCKEY ACT.

The next item—THE COUNTESS CASTILLA in her great high school act on her highly trained arab, THE NUBIAN CLOWN— SAD ALPHONSO.

(Enter Clowns TUFFCAKE *and* CREAM.)

TUFF   I am going to ask you a riddle.

CREAM   He's going to ask me a riddle, boo boo.

TUFF   How many wells make a river?

CREAM   How many wells? I dunno.

TUFF   Then I suppose I must tell you—one if it's big enough. Now I will ask you another riddle.

CREAM   Now he'll ask me another riddle, boo boo.

TUFF   If a boy and a $\frac{1}{2}$ with a boot and a $\frac{1}{2}$ takes an hour and a $\frac{1}{2}$ to walk a mile and a $\frac{1}{2}$—How many days will it take 6 boys to walk to London?

CREAM   One if it's long enough.

(Enter TALL RINGMASTER.)

TALL RINGMASTER   Get hout hof the way you hignorant hignoramuses and make room for the SEÑORA FLORA FINA.

(Exit CLOWNS.)
(Enter SEÑORA FLORA FINA.)
(Enter Clown CREAM.)

CREAM   The man who said, 'Dough as I dough' was a baker.
The man who said 'I will if it soots me' was a sweep.
The man with the hatchet face was a woodman bold.

(Enter Clown TUFF.)

TUFF   But the man who said 'I see yer' was a sawyer.

51

(Exit clowns.)
(Enter RINGMASTER, *Blue.)*

BLUE RINGMASTER   The next item we will have the pleasure of showing you is the SIGNOR MAC DERMOT, the justly celebrated bareback rider.

(Enter Clowns TUFF *and* CREAM.*)*

TUFF   I have brought you here to recite a piece of poetry to you.
CREAM   He's brought me here to recite a piece of poetry to me. Boo. Boo.
TUFF   Ba ba black sheep don't lose your wool.
CREAM   No, not that one.
TUFF   Sing a song of sixpence and I'll promise not to cry.
CREAM   No, not that one.
TUFF   Ride a cock horse to Banbury Cross to see a green lady get on a blue horse.
CREAM   No, not that one.
TUFF   Little boy Blue, come blow me tight.
CREAM   No, not that one.
TUFF   Hickery Dickery Dock, the mouse pulled up his sock.
CREAM   No, not that one.
TUFF   Little Tommy Tucker tucked into his supper.

(Enter TALL RINGMASTER.*)*

TALL RINGMASTER   Clear the way for the great race between the celebrated Sioux chief MAN-WHO-HAS-EATEN-SNAKE (on his celebrated Mustang, SPOTTED EAGLE) and young GREEN FEATHER. They will race a measured mile, giving you a haccurate repreagentation of the sports of the pampas plains of America—are you ready for the great Race?

(Indian Howls.)

TALL RINGMASTER   The first part of the entertainment will conclude with M. ONCT MORE'S celebrated himpersonation of an Irish Ballad Singer, a repreagenation which the entire inhabitants of the two worlds have unanimously owned to be truly life-like.

(Enter mounted man with card.)
3 MINUTES INTERVAL

PART TWO

RIDE OF ALL NATIONS

RIDERS: 1. ANCIENT ROMANS
2. COWBOYS
3. EGYPTIANS
4. JAPANESE
5. HUNTSMEN
6. RED INDIANS
7. PICADORS
8. JOCKEYS

BLUE RINGMASTER   The hentertainment will conclude with a repreagentation of the ride of ALL NATIONS in which we will show you mounted on matchless horses the RIDERS OF THE WORLD from the ARTIC to the TORRID ZONE.

Firstly let me introduce to your notice the Riders of Old Rome who in Prehistoric days guided their antediluvian hosses mid the catacombs and byramids of that noble city without saddle or bridle.

Secondly let me introduce to your notice The Cowboys, the daring and intrepid horsemen who skeour the Perrairies of the Pacific slope of the United States of America in pursuit of their prey.

Thirdly let me introduce to your notice The Egyptians, stated to be without herror the most marvellous hossmen in the entire universe from the Hindian Ocean to the Carrabeean Sea.

Fourthly let me introduce to your notice the Japanese, some of the finest riders of the known world—have come from the East, the birthplace of the Hoss.

Fifthly let me introduce to your notice the green-coated hunters of old England.

Sixthly allow me to have the pleasure to introduce to your notice the untramelled Red Man or Hindian Warrior of the Bounding Perraries of the United States of America as they enter. The chief nearest you is surnamed MAN-AFRAID-OF-NOTHING. Next him sits LITTLE-HORSES, while the inmost chief is known as SAY-THAT-AGAIN-SWEENEY.

Seventhly, let me introduce to your notice the Bullfighters of Old Spain. These are the hidentical Hidalgos and these are the hidentical hosses which have kicked to the topmost tier of the Arena the sanguinary sawdust of Seville.

Eighth and lastly let me introduce to your notice the Jockeys, each of which are about one foot and a half high and weigh from 28 to 36 pounds. These little men keep themselves so small entirely by eating nothing but Mustard

That will conclude
The Entertainment
This Evening. I thank
You one and all for
Your kind attention.

ONCT MORE'S GREAT CIRCUS SECOND YEAR
1902

Cloun cream

Changes of costume.

Cloun Tuff cake

change of costume

Cream

Tuff.

change of
costume

Tuff.

change of
costume

The Treasure
of the Garden

First performed, October 1902

ONE OF JACK B. YEATS'S PLAYS
FOR THE MINIATURE STAGE

THE TREASURE
OF THE GARDEN

COLOURED BY THE AUTHOR.

PUBLISHED BY
ELKIN MATHEWS, VIGO STREET, NIGH THE ALBANY, LONDON

DIRECTIONS

The pages with the scenes and characters of this play should be cut neatly out of the book, then pasted on cardboard—thin for the figures and thicker for the scenes. The figures should then have their names and in what scenes they appear written on their backs.

After the characters have been cut out, any little white edges left by the scissors may be touched with some dark colour, which will take away any ragged appearance.

Instead of fixing the feet of the figures directly into the tin slides, it is better to gum a small strip of cardboard to the back of the figure, leave the end loose and slip that into the clip of the slide.

Before pasting the last scene on cardboard a piece should be cut out of the board to correspond to where the moonlight falls on the water, then at the moment when McGowan rises out of the pit with the crock of gold in his arms, if a candle is held behind the scene it will shine through and illuminate the track of the moon.

For the lamps colza oil must be used, paraffin would not do at all as it would smoke.

Candles may be used at the wings instead of footlights.

In this play none of the characters *cross* the stage, but are only pushed on a little way, and withdrawn from the same side as they enter.

In the last scene the mound of earth should be fixed to the stage in front of the open trapdoor with a couple of drawing pins, the foot piece of the mound having been first folded inwards; and, of course, only the head of McGowan is shown until he finds the crock of gold, and is raised up far enough to show it in his arms.

A spoonful of earth should be thrown up on the stage from the trap each time McGowan counts. It is better to have the stage raised well clear of the table on books, so that he who throws up the earth can get his hands comfortably under the stage.

The lights must be turned low during the last scene, and lower still as Bosun Hardbite enters.

Those who move on the figures and recite the parts should be hidden, of course, from the audience by curtains.

In conclusion, the words of the play should be learnt and *not* read from the book, and those who speak should be careful to speak from the side of the stage nearest to which the characters which he or she represents is standing.

And now to those who take the trouble to cut out, set up, and play this little play, I wish good success, and I hope that the resulting pleasure may be worth the labour.

JACK B. YEATS.

R.H. *means Right Hand.*
L.H. *means Left Hand.*
Pl. *means Plate of Characters or Scene.*
The Reader is supposed to be on the Stage facing the Audience.

PERSONS REPRESENTED

WILLIE MCGOWAN *The Man Hunter of the Gulf.*
OLD HENDERSON *A Ship Owner of Poolthoia.*
OLD MAN OF THE EMIGRANTS.
BOSUN HARDBITE *of the 'Gleaner.'*
BALLAD SINGER.
JESSIE HENDERSON *Daughter of Old Henderson.*
EMIGRANTS AND CREW OF THE 'GLEANER.'

SCENES

Prologue: The Deck of the 'Pearl of the Gulf.'
Scene 1: Shore opposite the village of Poolthoia.
Scene 2: The Garden by the Beach.

PROLOGUE

Scene: *The Deck of the 'Pearl of the Gulf' (Pl. 1).*

PROLOGUE.   PLATE I.

WILLIE MCGOWAN (Pl. VII.) (*the Man Hunter of the Gulf*) *discovered. Dead bodies of seamen in the shrouds and on the deck.*

WILLIE MCGOWAN   Men call me the Man Hunter of the Gulf, and that seems a fine thing to be called, and it is a fine thing; and it is a fine thing to be the foremost skipper in these waters—under the Free Flag. What a roaring life it is, too, chasing the rich ships—the big fat pigeons with crops full of gold—chasing of 'em with every stitch on her, chasing of them and nearing them every minute, chasing of them through the narrows like a flash—up, up under the guns of the walls. First quieting the guns, then taking what you've a mind to, and out again—on the highway of the sea, and as like as not the decks aren't swabbed before up there comes another—then it's racing again! Oh, that's the sort of life while the blood's hot. You get a wound or two, and lose a man or two; but no one minds, even the men you lose dies laughing. But it's the other trig that sickens—fighting two great ugly frigates in a little ditch of a creek. On the top of the sea we can outsail them, and out-seamanship them too. But bad sailing's their best holt among the Islands; they fall across you and lie on you like a dead horse; and all the time you're fighting them you know it's a one-sided game. If they ever take us we know what it'll be. I ship no sick-hearted ones aboard the 'Pearl', they're all stiff upper lip men here—they don't mind dying, but they don't want to die of the long neck. And if we take them, what is it worth? A hogshead or two of washy rum and the little gold watch that the midshipman's mother gave him. But it's generally like it was this morning, they come slopping alongside of you at the break of the day as you lie, and then it's up anchor and fight, fight, fight, and run, run, run, until, with everything aloft a wreck, you bump over the sand and leave them; and its' but a poor consolation to know that they're stuck fast behind you, when you come to take tally of the living—fifteen men left out of forty that was my darling crew. 'Tis a horrid trade! To-night, when all is quiet and clean again, I'll give the 'Pearl' as she sails and two hundred doubloons to Jack Westaway, and to-morrow the crew shall take him as their skipper; and I, I will be landed on the coast, dressed in sober clothes, and none will know me, or dare know me. So I will slowly make my way back again to that Connaught village where I was born, where I will stay until I pick up some quieter, less melancholy trade than this.

END OF PROLOGUE.

Scene I: *The Shore opposite the Village of Poolthoia (Pl. II.).* WILLIE MCGOWAN (*Pl. VII.*) *discovered seated on an iron mooring post.*

SCENE ONE.   PLATE II.

WILLIE MCGOWAN   I've been at home now three long comfortable years—
and I've liked it—up and down the Western coast for Old Henderson
in the 'Gleaner.' She's pretty near falling to pieces; but he pays well, so
what of that? But I don't care about this last job, and, what's more,
Willie McGowan's stomach doesn't care about it. It isn't a kind heart I
have, but a weak stomach. (*Enter* OLD HENDERSON (*R.H., Pl. VII.*).)
Good morning, Mr Henderson.

OLD HENDERSON   Well, what's your answer? Are you going to take the tide
for America with the emigrants?

WILLIE MCGOWAN   No, Mr Henderson, I don't care about it. The 'Gleaner'
isn't fit for sea, and if we was to experience rough weather she'd go
down in three days.

OLD HENDERSON   All the better for you and me, Willie; you have a good
yawl aboard, and the sooner she sinks the sooner you'll be back in the
village with every pocket full; for I'll pay you all as though you'd been
to America and back again. And it'll pay me all right, my boy, for she
is fully insured, and all the gamios have paid their passage money.
Come, lad, you'll soon be back again.

64

WILLIE MCGOWAN No, I don't go.

OLD HENDERSON You're afraid; afraid of a couple of days in a good new yawl. Some of them say you were a low and murdering pirate when you were on the other side, so it can't be that you're too fine in the feelings. You're afraid, my lad, that's what's troubling you!

WILLIE MCGOWAN Yes, I *am* afraid, you cross-eyed old devil! I'm afraid to do a dirty trick on them poor gamios!

(*Exit* OLD HENDERSON. *Enter* JESSIE HENDERSON (*R.H., Pl. VII.*).)

JESSIE I'm not going to say one word to you, Mr McGowan, you've been saucy to my father; and now he says you won't ever stand on the 'Gleaner's' deck again. You've made a pretty pickle of yourself young man. I did mean to marry you, and so I will still, Willie, if you'll go back to my father and make all square with him again. I don't seem, Willie, as if I could ever marry a poor man; but I don't care a tosser for dad—and that's God's truth. You make some money—with him or without him—and I'm yours, dear sweetheart. Here comes the gamios, I hear them crying. Poor creatures!

(*Wailing heard off and getting nearer.
Enter Emigrants (R.H., Pl. VI.).*)

OLD MAN OF THE EMIGRANTS Go-morrow, captain.

WILLIE MCGOWAN I'm no captain.

OLD MAN Is she a good ship, captain? and will the old gentleman put good food on the ship for us? and will she make a quick passage, captain? Oh, I see her there. She's a fine ship, she's bigger than the old 'Maid of Galway.' A lot of fine young boys and girls went away in her, and sure she was wrecked, and the creatures never saw Amerikay. Come away, neighbours, the poor captain is feeling sad in his heart. The poor man, like the rest of us, doesn't like leaving the dear milk of the kine.

(*Exit Emigrants. Singing heard off.*)

The sailors' life is bright and free,
With a ho, ro, the Yankee packet.
Fire a gun, don't cher hear the racket!
Ho! the rolling river, the rolling, rolling river.'

(*Enter Bosun and Crew (R. H., Pl. VI.).*)

BOSUN HARDBITE Come on board with us, captain. Never mind old Comushala, he's offended with you, but never take notice of him.

The 'Gleaner's' a rotten old schooner, 'tis true, but what o' that—'All the sooner back,' old Comushala says. Four months' pay for four weeks' work, cap—plenty of sprees in the village then. Well, goodbye, cap, sit there on yer old iron mushyroom till the seaweed grows on you.

(*Exit Crew. Enter Ballad Singer (R.H., Pl. VII.).*)

BALLAD SINGER   Go-morrow, captain, are you for the ocean to-day?
WILLIE MCGOWAN   I don't know.
BALLAD SINGER   Then I'll give you a stave, captain. (*Sings.*)
    Oh, rise up, Willy Reilly, and come along with me,
    I mean for to go with you and leave this coun-te-rie,
    To leave my father's dwelling, his houses and fine land;
    And away goes Willy Reilly and his dear Colleen Bawn.
How do you like that, captain? You don't care about it, eh, captain? Then here's:
    We drink the memory of the brave, the faithful, and the few!
    Some lie far off beyond the wave, some sleep in Ireland, too;
    All, all are gone, but still lives on the fame of those who died.
    All true men, like you, men, remember them with pride!
Here comes poor old Henderson.

(*Exit* BALLAD SINGER. *Enter* OLD HENDERSON (*R.H., Pl. VII.*).)

OLD HENDERSON   Have you made up your mind, Willie?
WILLIE MCGOWAN   Yes. My answer is No, you old leg of the devil!
OLD HENDERSON   All right, my bold fellow, look what you're missing; in a few days you earn the wages of months. I can't say fairer. For the last time, Will you drop out with the tide? No answer? All right, you're a foolish young man. I'll take her out myself. I'll take her round to Shunabeg myself, and I'll find a better man than you there that'll take the job you refuse; and I'll take my daughter with me, I'm not going to leave her to be falling in love with a broken-down skipper like you. This venture is bound to turn out lucky I know, for why?—I dreamt last night I found myself digging in the old garden down by the Point, and I dug up a crock full of gold. Just by where the stream runs down on to the strand, on the seaward side of the stream, I was digging. That sounds lucky, doesn't it, my bucko!

(*Exit* OLD HENDERSON.)

Scene 2: *The garden by the beach. (Pl. III.).* WILLIE MCGOWAN (*Pl. VI.*) *discovered in a pit digging, he throws up earth with his spade.*

SCENE TWO.   PLATE III

WILLIE MCGOWAN   It's a hot night and very still, and it's hot work digging.
I will throw up seven more spadesful and then I'll jack it up. (*Throws up
earth and counts the spadesful.*) One, two, three, four, five, six, seven—
What is that that rings so hard? It is (*he stoops, and his voice comes up from
the pit*), it is the crock! the cover comes away in my hands, (*He rises up
with the crock of gold shining in his arms, the moonlight full across him.*) Oh,
sweetheart, it *is* the crock of gold!

(*A noise without. Enter Bosun Hardbite* (*R.H., Pl. IV.*).)

HARDBITE   Oh, Captain, listen! We're back again, you'll never sail the
'Gleaner' again no more. We was crossing the bar at Shunabeg, the old
man was steering, and he kept her too far to norrard, and she touched.
There was a sea running on the bar, and it broke on her—she was
heavy as lead. It struck her again, and the old hen-coop couldn't stand
it—she stove—she was going down. We got the yawl clear. At first
some of us was for saving ourselves, but the women cried so, we had to
take 'em, and the rest of the gamios hung to the gunwales. We was all
saved—all except—oh, I must tell you. Old Henderson was the first

man out of the yawl when she touched the shore, and he slipped on the seaweed and cracked his little old brain on the rocks.

WILLIE MCGOWAN   Is Miss Jessie safe?

HARDBITE   Oh, when we struck she was on the deck beside me. One screech she let out of her, and leapt inter the sea. We never seed her again.

CURTAIN.

PROLOGUE. WING L. PLATE IV.

PROLOGUE. WING R.

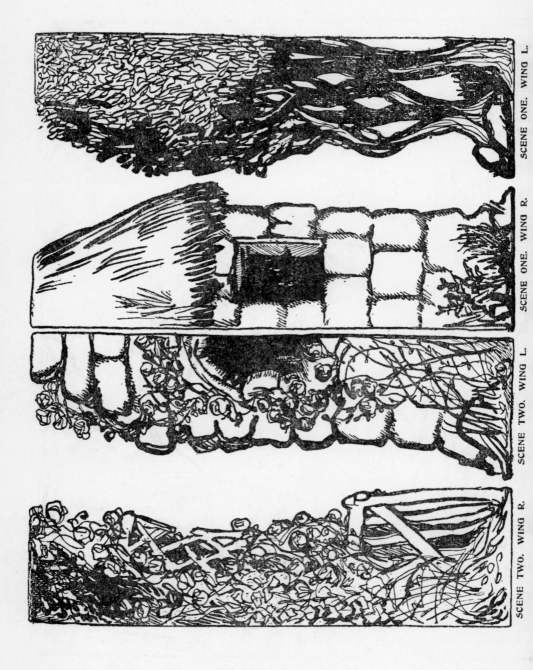

SCENE ONE. WING L.

SCENE ONE. WING R.

SCENE TWO. WING L.

SCENE TWO. WING R.

Jack B. Yeats

mound of earth Scene II

Emigrants Scene 1

Willie McGowan Scene II

Crew Scene 2

PLATE VI.

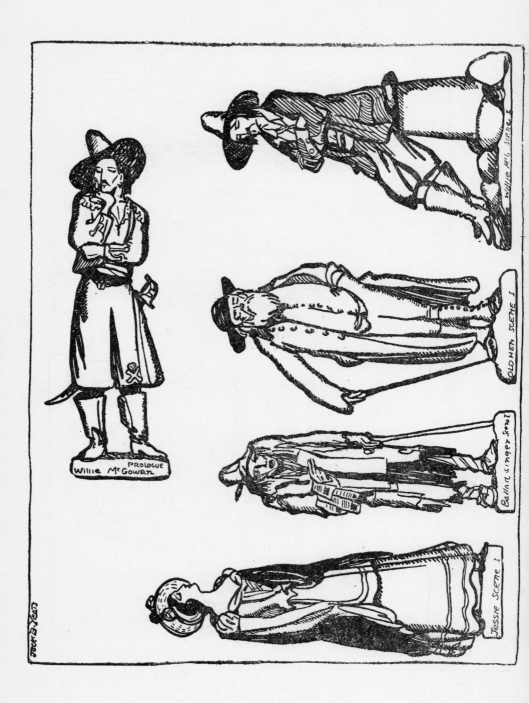

Willie McGowan PROLOGUE

Willie McG Scene I

Gold Hen Scene I

Ballad singer Scene I

Jessie Scene I

The Scourge of the Gulph

or

Fierce Revenge

Published 1903

ONE OF JACK B. YEATS'S PLAYS
FOR THE MINIATURE STAGE.

THE SCOURGE

OF THE GULPH

LONDON

Published and Sold Wholesale and Retail by ELKIN
MATHEWS in VIGO STREET (nigh the Albany);
also Sold by most Booksellers in Town and Country.

Price One Shilling net.   Copies coloured by
the Author, Five Shillings.

CHARACTERS

CAPTAIN CARRICKNAGAT *A Pirate, Captain of the schooner 'Distant Land'*.

JAMES BROAD *Bosun of the 'Distant Land'*.

JOE MILES *The Scourge of the Gulph*.

LA LOLITA *The Belle of the Pacific, Wife of Captain Carricknagat*.

CREW *of the 'Distant Land'*.

SCENES

Scene 1: The deck of the 'Distant Land'.

Scene 2: Captain's cabin aboard the 'Distant Land'.

Scene 3: The Grove of Heads on the Savage Island.

Scene 4: The woods of the Isle of Plumes.

This play is in the manner of those ancient plays which Robert Louis Stevenson delighted in, and of which he wrote under the title of 'A Penny Plain and Twopence Coloured.' A Penny Plain and Twopence Coloured was the price paid for each scene and each sheet of characters, which were afterwards to be pasted on cardboard and cut out.

All that was then wanted was a little wooden stage, some tin slides to move the characters on with, and plenty of red fire.

The illustrations to the 'Scourge of the Gulph' show the various scenes set with the characters on the stage.

Scene 1: *The Deck of the 'Distant Land'.*

SCENE ONE.

CAPTAIN L.H., LA LOLITA *in hammock* L.H., BOSUN BROAD *with cat-o-nine-tails* R.H., MILES R.H., *and* CREW *discovered.*

MILES She comes from the same street in Panama as I do.

CAPTAIN Silence! Joseph Miles, you spoke saucy to the wife of Captain Carricknagat, the Wolf of St. Domingo. You have received but fifty lashes; think yourself lucky to escape with life. Now give him his coat, and put him ashore.

MILES That's rough talk, Captain Carricknagat, but hear this: You have flogged me—me that's now nothing but a seaman, but was once known as the Scourge of the Gulph. Listen to this, Captain Carricknagat: You think life is a pleasant passear; but one of these flaming days, or black nights, I'll settle your passear—for ever!

Curtain.

76

Scene 2: *Captain's Cabin aboard the 'Distant Land'.*

SCENE TWO.

CAPTAIN *discovered at table.*

CAPTAIN We landed on Savage Island to search for water, but savage natives, to the number of fifty score, came down on us; we fell away before them. The party who were with my wife (she being in a litter), by my orders made a rush for the coast; while I with twenty of my steadiest men stood up to the natives, till seven of us were all that was left, and we ran for the sea. Not to the bay where the long boat had been left, for my wife was to be taken in that to the schooner; but to a point nearer to where the schooner lay. We reached the beach, we hailed, and three men put off in the small boat. It was the mate and the two men left on board when we started away that morning. My sweet wife had *not* returned. That was two days ago; since then we have searched the woods and shores of this island, but have seen nothing— no natives, none of my wife's guard, nor her own dear self. (*Sound without.*) Who's that? Any news?

(*Enter* BOSUN.)

BOSUN 'Tis I, Captain; and I bear a horrid tale here in a letter from the lady, written on these pieces of bark before—before——

CAPTAIN (*takes letter and reads*) 'This is good-bye Paul. In a few moments now I will have gone. I have one request: After they have killed me they will burn my poor body, but my poor head they will hang at the mouth of the cave, on the middle tree of seven. I write this letter, dear heart, because I want you to take my head from that tree, and bear it away in my box with the silver hinges—away to our Island of Plumes, and there bury it on the round hill. When you find my head 'twill be nothing but a little white skull. I send this letter by James Broad, if he live to deliver it. They have saved his life that he may teach them to cook their meat, and to tattoo their cruel faces. God be with you, heart!'

       Oh! Jim, this thing has not happened! Oh! tell me I am mad! tell me you gave me no letter! Oh! tell me—tell me—the truth!

BOSUN The lady, my Captain, is dead. She must have hardly felt it, her lips still smiled. They cut my bonds, and told me to throw more wood on the fire; but I leapt through the flames. They feared to follow—all but one, he came on. He got up to me, he took off my arm at one hack; but I ran faster still. I reached the coast; and I am here to lead you back again to that cave.

CAPTAIN Let the surgeon bind you up; then I will take the 'Distant Land' to the nearest point to the cave, and I will take all that are left of my crew, and you will lead us.

Curtain.

Scene 3: *The Grove of Heads on the Savage Island.*

Enter CAPTAIN *and* BOSUN.

CAPTAIN None of my brave crew are left; and how bravely they went through the savage men that came down on them in myriads—they went through the first pack of them like the shuttle through the loom; but we were penned in at last, and only you and I got through, Jim. My ship is sunk; though it was no one's fault but my own. I piled her on the coral, and now she lies in thirty fathoms with 50,000 pieces of eight in her. You'll get no share this run, Bosun; but the blessed head shall yet be mine. I see the middle tree of seven; I have the box she wishes it carried in. In the darkness, while they lie around the fires that burn my bully men, we will crawl to the coast; search along it till we find some canoe, then put to sea, and the burning flame within me will keep me living till I reach my own Isle of Plumes.

Curtain.

SCENE THREE.

Scene 4: *Isle of Palms.*

SCENE FOUR.

CAPTAIN *discovered.*

CAPTAIN   I am left alone to do her bidding. How gladly poor Jim would
have worked to the end; though, if all my crew were alive again and
now around me, not one would I allow to bury this sad piece of ivory
but myself, and I would not even let Jim do it. No, I must do it by
myself, making the grave with my useless sword. For what is a free-
trade captain without a ship, without money, and without a crew?
How terribly lonely it was when the last of them, my poor Jim,
turned over on his side and died of the black thirst within sight of this
island. We were twenty days on the canoe, seven without water—and
then to die in sight of all he wanted—water!

(*Enter* MILES.)

MILES   At last! there he stands before me with the money in his arms. How
long he has been a-coming; but now he's in my power! I will settle
him with the old piece! break open the box, go back and find his crew,
let them see a little of it; and then the people who thought him a
buccaneer will laugh at him when they see what I'll bring them to.
Oh, what a fierce revenge! I have waited for him, living on what I
could pick up in the woods, and many a gaudy parrot fell to my
gun—here goes for a gaudier! (*Fires,* CAPTAIN *falls.* MILES *goes over, and
presently is seen on his knees at wing, with box open, holding up skull.*)
An empty skull, a black box, a dead skipper! Have I done anything or
nothing?

CURTAIN.

A Pantomime

The Wonderful Travellers

or

The Gamesome Princes
and The Pursuing Policeman

First performed January 1903

THE MYSTERIOUS TRAVELLERS

OR

The Gamesome Princes

and

The Pursuing Policeman

A PANTOMIME.

Played

Before Valley Children Jan 1904.

CHARACTERS

POLICEMAN.
CAPTAIN OF THE 'DOLPHIN'.
CLOWN.
PANTALOON.
HARLEQUIN.
COLUMBINE.
OLD BUFFER.
DUDE.
MYSTERY.
POSTMAN.

Scene: *Dartmouth by a Boat float.*

(*Enter* POLICEMAN, *Left.*)

POLICEMAN   Here's a nice howdododo. Here's countrytomtom—a couple
of villains have escaped from a dark Donjohn, and are expected to
arrive in this town at any moment. I have just received a warrant to
arrest them immediately on sight if I don't see them sooner, or before
that—the warrant which I have here in my hand gives a description
of the rascals—
   The first villain is described thus nicely:
      Middle height
      Hair Black
      Eyes One blue, the other pink
      Dress Large blue ruffle round neck, sleeves striped red and
blue, red spotted trousers and white shoes with pink rosettes. Oh the
miscreant!
   The second villain is described more so.
      Hair Piebald
      Eyes Pale blue
      Dress Yellow and green jacket, green trousers—Oh the
miscreant villain!
   And I am imperformed these scoundrels may arrive at any
moment. I will go and look for them with my truncheon, and in the
meantime I will sew.

(*Exit.*)

(*Outcries*) O Ye! O Ye! O Ye! Lost, Stolen or Strayed! (*Heard off,
Whistle, Bell, Shouting*) Easer. Stopper. Back her. A turn a starboard.
A turn ahead. A turn astern. Stop her. (*Enter 'The Dolphin' with* CLOWN
with bandbox on head and luggage in hand. CLOWN *steps on quay.*)

CAPTAIN OF 'DOLPHIN'   Back her—

(*Exit 'Dolphin'. Whistle off.*)

CLOWN   Hello lo lo lo lo lo lo lo lo lo lo—stop—I've arrived where from,
ah Foreign Parts—I've come for my health and for sport. I'm on a
fishing excursion. But where's my antient friend. Hello lo lo lo lo
lo lo—stop— (*Enter* PANTALOON, *Right*) Ah there you are—give the

84

pony to the pony man to put it into its little bed, and then come and talk to me while I fish.

(*Exit* PANTALOON. *Exit* CLOWN.)
(*Enter* CLOWN, *Left.*)

CLOWN   Hello Hello Hello lo lo lo lo lo—Stop—you'll make the fishes nervous. (*Enter* PANTALOON) Ah Pantaloon, there you are! Don't talk. Watch me fish.

PANTALOON   Whatcher going to catch?

CLOWN   Herring salmon trouts flounders pike soles haddocks whales hake skate plaice dace and winkles. We won't catch any mackerel because there aren't any. We must get a large frying pan at the ironmongers or perhaps we ought to get the blacksmith to make a real big one—because we'll want a big one to cook all these fish on—hello lo lo—stop—I've got a bite—oh such a monster!

PANTALOON   Haul him up then.

CLOWN   Course I will. You waint, he's *so* heavy—There must be a great many fish all on the hook at once, poor little hook. Oh dear, it is heavy, but I'll have him out in a minute (*hauls up iron pot*).

PANTALOON   You're a nice sort of fisherman.

CLOWN   What do you mean, fellow?

PANTALOON   To go and hook an old iron pot and think you'd got a fish.

CLOWN   Nothing of the kind you impertinent fellow—I got this pot on purpose to cook the fish in, of course.

(*Exit Both. Enter* POLICEMAN.)

POLICEMAN   I have had information those scallywags have arrived but I haven't caught them yet—(*walks up and down*)—but when I do I'll—I'll tackle them, I'll thump em. I'll put handcuffs on their hands and feet cuffs on their feet.

(*Exit. Enter* PANTALOON *and* OLD BUFFER.)

PANTALOON   So Sir, you want to purchase a nice parrot.

OLD BUFFER   Yes. A talking parrot. Have you got one?

PANTALOON   No Sir, but a friend of mine, a sailor, Old Ben Stunsail Boon has just returned from a voyage round the world two times and he has a lovely parrot with him, that talks most beautiful.

OLD BUFFER   Let's see him, my man.

PANTALOON   I'll just run round and get him. He's rather a big bird, Sir, you won't be frightened will you?

(*Exit. Enter* CLOWN *as Parrot and* PANTALOON *as Sailor, Left.*)

PANTALOON   My old friend in the green and yaller told me you wanted a talking parrot. I'm a man of few words. This is her.

OLD BUFFER   It is indeed a fine bird. Can it talk?

PANTALOON   Yes Sir. (*To Parrot*) Speak up, Poll.

CLOWN   Pretty Poll. Whats a clock. Scratch my pole. Pretty Polly. Whats a clock.

OLD BUFFER   Can he talk any more?

PANTALOON   He can count.

OLD BUFFER   Can he? Clever bird!

PANTALOON   Count for the gentleman, Polly.

CLOWN   One Two Three (*up to about* 30 *or* 40).

OLD BUFFER   That'll do. Tell her to stop it. It certainly is a fine bird. I'll give ye a sovereign for her.

CLOWN   Hello hello.

PANTALOON   You can have her Sir and I dare say you could teach her to say a lot more things.

OLD BUFFER   I dare say I could, my good man, but I don't want it for talking. I'm very fond of parrot. I want to eat it.

CLOWN   Eat me. You lobsided old ruffian. Let me at you and I'll jolly soon eat you. (*Advances towards Old Buffer.*)

OLD BUFFER   Help help police!

(*Exit* CLOWN *and* PANTALOON.)
(*Enter* POLICEMAN, *Right.*)

POLICEMAN   What's the matter, Sir? Tell me and I will save you.

OLD BUFFER   A villain of a sailor man with a talking parrot was here and the parrot threatened me life.

POLICEMAN   That was no sailor man as that was no parrot—They were the pair of ruffians that I'm out after with me truncheon—Oh let me once secure them. I'll hide here by the Hotel porch and I'll catch them yet.

(*Exit* OLD BUFFER. POLICEMAN *stands by Hotel window.*
While he talks CLOWN *looks out of window.*)

POLICEMAN   What villains to deceive an innocent old man like that. But I'll wait here a week until I see them, then I'll give one great jump and spring on them. To give one blow to the top of each of their heads with me faithful truncheon, overpower them, put the handcuffs on them, and drag them to the deep dark cavern underneath the fountain will be the work of a moment, then I will get the reward. One hundred pounds reward is offered for their apprehension and I'm the man to apprehend them, if I stay here all the winter, rooted to the spot like a pillar box of salt. (*While he talks, towards the end he gradually moves off.*)

(*Enter* DUDE, *Right.*)

DUDE I wonder what upon earth is the hour. I will accost yonder yachtman with the writing on his chest. What Ho Yachtman. Would you kindly inform me what is the hour—no answer. He sleeps poor fellow after his hard day's work. I will again address him. What is the hour young friend? Hour H-O-U-R. No answer. Are you asleep? (MYSTERY *shakes his head.*) He shakes his head, so he must be awake, poor dear. Are you awake now, mystery? (MYSTERY *shakes his head.*) Strange—strange.

(*Enter* PANTALOON.)

PANTALOON Don't ask that man any questions. He's not himself today.
DUDE If he's not himself, who is he?
PANTALOON He's his brother.
DUDE Strange. Strange. Kind Sir, would you be so good as to tell me the hour?
PANTALOON Look at the clock.
DUDE (*steps back and looks at clock*) But it's stopped.
PANTALOON No it hasn't. Look again.

(*Clock begins to go round.*)

DUDE I think the clock is fast.
PANTALOON Of course it is. It's the fastest clock in these parts.
DUDE Strange. Strange. Strange.

(*Exit both. Enter* HARLEQUIN *and* COLUMBINE. *They dance.*)
(*Enter* POLICEMAN, *Left.*)

POLICEMAN Now then, out of this. Get away. Get away. You can't dance here in the public thorough fare. You may be a fairy but this is *not* a thorough fairy.

(*Enter* POSTMAN, *goes to pillar box* (CLOWN *inside letter box*), *opens it, snaps to, and comes back. Enter* PANTALOON, *Left.*)

PANTALOON What's troubling you, Postman?
POSTMAN There's somebody in the letter box.
PANTALOON Nonsense. Go and open the box. Perhaps there's a letter for me.

(POSTMAN *goes and opens box again.*)

CLOWN Hello. Hello. (*He withdraws.*)

(Enter CLOWN.)

CLOWN   I say, Old 'un, shall us go for a row in the boat float?
PANTALOON   Oh let's!

(Exit both.)
(Enter POLICEMAN, *Right.)*

POLICEMAN   I've got those skeroundrels now. I'll stand here and watch the
windows and the Pillar Box. I brought both my truncheons. Hello,
Mystery, have you seen two miscreants in spotted clothes?

(MYSTERY *shakes head. Enter* CLOWN *and* PANTALOON
in Boat, right, and pass slowly along.)

POLICEMAN   They cannot possibly by any manner of means escape my eagle
optics—I'll be a match for them but I wish I'd brought another
truncheon—never mind I'll thump em, I'll bump em, and every time I
hit them I'll say Would you sell parrots to nice old gentlemen would
you—Would you frighten postmen would you?

(Exit all. Enter CLOWN, *Right, with pipe.*
Enter PANTALOON.)

PANTALOON   What are you doing now you old reprobate?
CLOWN   I'm resting my thinkograph, whiffing a few whiffs. I'm tired, you
old deceiver *(smokes)*. But I've had a pleasant time. I hope you have had
a pleasant time too—But the question is, has everybody had a pleasant
time? *(smokes)*. Anyway, I hope they have *(smokes)*.

(While he talks POLICEMAN *enters at back.)*

POLICEMAN   Here they are—but now I've forgot my truncheon—They've
got it at home a stirring up the Christmas pudding with it. I will listen
to what the villains say.

(Lamp lit.)

CLOWN   They are lighting up the lamps my friend. It is getting late. We
soon must be winging it away. Meet me round at the back and then
together we will come back once to say good night before we go.
POLICEMAN   Ha Ha, this is my chance. I will run and get help and catch them
both together.

(Exit POLICEMAN.)

CLOWN   Come let us go and get our cablet.

(*Interval.*)

(*Enter Left,* OLD GENTLEMAN, BUTCHER'S BOY *with pitchfork,* POSTMAN, *and others. Enter Right,* POLICEMAN *with three truncheons,* DUDE *and others. Balloon comes down. Crowds move towards centre to catch* CLOWN *and* PANTALOON. *The words 'Good night' appear on Balloon—which slowly rises.*)

CURTAIN.

GALANTY SHOW TO
VALLEY CHILDREN
JANUARY 1905

GALANTY SHOW
SHOWN TO CHILDREN
JANUARY 1906

Part Two

PLAYS
for the
LARGER THEATRE

The Deathly Terrace

A Play in Three Acts

CHARACTERS

WILLIAM NARDOCK *Unemployed.*
ANDY CARMICHAEL *Film Producer.*
SHEILA DELGARVAY *Cinema Actress.*
ABSOLUTE VOSP *Youthful Cinema Actor.*
WILLIAM WILBERFORCE O'GRADY *Youthful Cinema Actor.*
CHARLES CHARVILLE *Elderly Cinema Actor (Stout).*
DEL MONTE GRANVILLE *Elderly Cinema Actor (Tall Spare).*
JIM *Camera Man.*
JAKE *Camera Man.*
CHOCOLATE USHER.
RENTERS.

Left and Right Directions are as seen by Audience.

ACT ONE

Scene 1: *Yellow-white stone terrace by sea. Yellow-white pillars left and right: De Venta notice on right-hand pillar. Blue sky. Green-blue sea. Purple bougainvilleas hanging on pillars. At end of balustrade to right beginning of slight cliff path. Enter* NARDOCK *from behind pillar right. He wears rather worn grey tweed clothes, soft grey felt hat, turned-down collar, bright blue tie in sailor knot, revolver in hand he advances three paces towards balustrade, looks slowly to left and slowly to right, places revolver under chin. Sail of small boat, falling as it comes, enters behind balustrade from left.*
ANDY CARMICHAEL *stands up in boat, he is wearing black trousers, wine-red sash, soft shirt striped broad blue stripes on grey ground, no coat, soft felt hat, crown pushed up. He springs from boat, throwing small anchor and rope over balustrade, and struggles with* NARDOCK. *They continue struggle about the stage: revolver goes off and falls to ground,* NARDOCK *presses hand to side and crumples under balustrade to left. During struggle* SHEILA'S *voice is heard, left, singing at time of shot.*

SHEILA (*singing*)   Row brothers row, the stream runs fast
The rapids are near, and the daylight's past!
Blow breezes blow, the stream runs fast,
The rapids are near, and the daylight's past!

ANDY *wrings hands, feels* NARDOCK'S *side, sees blood on fingers, throws away burnt shred of cloth, lifts* NARDOCK'S *hand, lets it fall limply, picks up revolver from stage, goes over and puts it behind* NARDOCK. *Enter left, heads and shoulders of people showing, also tall prow of boat.*
SHEILA DELGARVAY *still singing. She is dressed as a beautiful Spanish lady in dress of the seventies, with bustle, bright yellow dress, yellow rose behind ear, square cut opening top of bodice, pink parasol.*
ABSOLUTE VOSP *in light grey flannel suit, no hat.*
CHARVILLE *in black frock coat, striped trousers and silk hat.*
DEL MONTE, *white suit, large grey sombrero.*
JIM *and* JAKE *in seedy brown suits.*
VOSP *and* O'GRADY *are rowing, standing up facing the way they go.* JIM *and* JAKE *hand* SHEILA *over balustrade and follow with cameras.* JAKE *makes painter of boat fast to one of the uprights of balustrade.* SHEILA *takes* JAKE'S *arm and walks up and down.*

SHEILA   Gee, some jolt hitting sand banks coming here, but I sung out and
    heartened them little boys. You been long here?

ANDY   Quite a while, lovely soul.

SHEILA (*Seeing body of* NARDOCK)   Ah, so you got it then.

ANDY   Yes, I got it, full of good wine, but a business head, accepted some of
    his native paper in advance, and fell off the slumber end again. Lovely
    still I calls him. He agrees, and I agree, to lie undisturbed while we shoot
    our heavy stuff with him in the back. He says, in his native idiom of
    course, that his house, his castle, his palatzio, is ours. I doubt if it's his'n.

SHEILA   Child, a word in your ear. Yonder lad looks to me very steady.

(*Goes over to* NARDOCK *and peers into his face kneeling beside him.* ACTORS
talking, grouped around cameras and CAMERA MEN *do not see* SHEILA *nor*
ANDY. ANDY *watches,* SHEILA *comes closer to* ANDY, *both over on left, two or
three paces from* NARDOCK.)

SHEILA   Too steady. That lad is going to sleep it out tomorrow morning,
    and all the mornings. Andy, you haven't done anything careless, have
    you?

ANDY   No sweet sister, all is as you see.

SHEILA   Andy, speak freely to little sister and tell her. How much experience
    have you had of making the movies?

ANDY   None yet.

SHEILA   Boy, you are brave. Watch me and the rest goes easy. I'll talk to
    these lads, and you nod, just nod, nod, nod, nod. (*Raising her voice.*)
    Boys, this is where we shoot the scene of the unwanted dead by the sea.
    I am one of the imperious ones, irresistible but pure, The first shoots we
    shot—Saw you boys plotting down in the Chink Dive to rid me of my
    enemy my alleged Uncle, the Slicer. Who, as you know, has the
    secret of my birth hidden in a place only known to himself. Well, you
    are all met here on the old time Spanish Terrace prepared to wring the
    secret from old Slicer, who, to your horror, you discover has already
    done himself in.

ANDY (*quietly to* SHEILA)   I suppose you've had a lot of experience on this
    business.

SHEILA   Now boy, nod, nod and nothing more. Come up you cripplers and
    each and all get your little stories from Auntie Del. Now Absey, you
    come on reading letter received by you from Slicer, it says:
            At the ole Terrace by the Bay
            I will tell the secret.
    Now let's see you do it, Absey.

VOSP (*walking from back towards front of stage and in front of camera, and facing
    them partly, reading letter.*)
            At the ole Terrace by the Bay
            I will tell the secret.

(Hardly saying the words, mostly forming them just with his lips. Moves away to Right.)

SHEILA   Very nicely, Abso. *(She looks at* ANDY *and waits for him to Nod.* ANDY *nods twice.)*

SHEILA   Now, O'Grady, you come in same as Absey.

(O'GRADY *repeats* VOSP'S *business reading letter.)*

At the old Terrace by the Bay
I will tell the secret.

(Hardly speaking the words, forming them mostly with his lips only, all will do so using different expressions on the lips. SHEILA *looks at* ANDY, *he nods.* O'GRADY *moves away to Right.)*

SHEILA   Now Charville, got your screedo?

(CHARVILLE *produces letter and reads.
moving in front of cameras.)*

At the ole Terrace by the Bay
I will tell the secret.

(ANDY *Nods.)*

SHEILA   Now, Monte, let's have a little more of the decrepit with determination, but not senile.

(GRANVILLE *repeats the business, reading letter.)*

At the old Terrace by the Bay
I will tell the secret.

(ANDY *Nods.)*

SHEILA   Now we'll shoot all that before the tropic twilight falls. It's like Life here. One moment the glad sunshine another moment night, with its velvet pall, palls, falls, over all. *(Shivers.)* Ah death where is thy sting. Now Jake, Jim, jump to it. We'll shoot now. Abso, O'Grady, Charlie, Monte, stand by to do it good when I—when Andy Nods.

(ANDY *Nods as they go through the performance as before,* CAMERA MEN *turning handles of cameras. The light is going as* GRANVILLE *comes on—it is only just light enough to make a photograph possible.)*

JAKE   This'll be a bit muggy, Miss.
SHEILA   Go on, go on, they'll like it, the Rembrandt touch.

(*When* CHARVILLE *moves to Right,* VOSP, O'GRADY, CHARVILLE *go back of camera men and murmur together, lighting cigarettes, except for* VOSP, *who lights a large cigar, admired by others. They are joined by* GRANVILLE. SHEILA *comes downfront to left and beckons* JIM *and* JAKE. *They come to her.*)

SHEILA   Say, chillun, you all got any special aptitude for the life of camera men, or is it just with you a learnt art, tell me, tell me truly. Speak boys.
JAKE   Well, in an amacheur way.
JIM   In an amacheur way.
SHEILA   I feared as much. The way you turned them handles looked to me as if it was something between a gift and a give away. Well, I know you will be loyal and give of your bests.

(*In a louder voice, turning towards* ACTORS.
ANDY *is standing behind her at back.*)

Tomorrow morning, boys, in the studio, we'll go on horror on finding the Slicer has taken his own life and all that. Andy or somebody'll be doing the Slicer. To your boats, boys. Andy and I will follow in Andy's little sail boat. We've got to get a note on this super's duds for tomorrow's discovery shots.

(*The* ACTORS *and* CAMERA MEN *climb over balustrade and move off left, camera men rowing, it is now dusk.* ANDY *and* SHEILA *gaze at* NARDOCK.)

ANDY   What do I do with it, drop it in the bay? Plenty sharks.
SHEILA   Tell me, Andy, truly this is as it looks, suicide or accident.
ANDY   As God's my judge, Del, I found him with his revolver under his chin and when I struggled to get it from him, it got down by his side and blew through him. You believe me, Del, so help me God, I never saw the man before and I never want to see him again. (*As he speaks he turns towards house on right.*) Ah, what's on the table in here? (*Goes into house behind pillar on right, comes out with paper in hand.*) Listen, Del, this explains the business, and we can't get mixed up, except in the mildest way in anything. Listen (*he reads*)
   'Farewell harsh world. Cold, Bitter, Nasty, Clammy, Relentless, Fatal, I bid you a long goodbye. William Nardock.'

(*As he finishes he looks over at* NARDOCK, *then goes over and carefully places the letter on ground close to* NARDOCK.)

Saves the detectives trouble to have everything close to. Now, Del, we'll be off.

(*He climbs over balustrade and* SHEILA *follows, he raises sail and they pass off to left. Gets darker, moon rises, light of moon appears on left.*)

(*All Slowly.*)

(NARDOCK *moves a little, slowly, comes to and gets on knees, feels side, sees blood on hand, sees farewell note, picks it up, then stands up staggering a little, but getting better all the time. Places note on ground in front of balustrade, on left centre. Places stones on corners of note to keep it from blowing away, looks at blood on fingers again, goes over, and kneeling in front of balustrade writes with blood on coping the word* 'Farewell'. *Then begins* 'Sig'—*stops, not enough blood. Looks about and through into house, right. Goes into house and comes out again with inkstand with black and red ink bottles. Dips fingers in red ink and continues Sig.* 'Signed the Impresario of Despair,' *finishing last part of word* 'pair' *with own blood. Dabs some blood on top of coping of balustrade, to right of centre in each case carefully using different fingers for blood and ink. Scuffles feet on ground, then steps up on top of coping of balustrade, pressing feet well down, comes back on ground, looks about for revolver, sees it, places it carefully in an accidental-looking position against foot of balustrade. Takes off hat, throws it out into water. Sits down on ground, takes off coat, arranges handkerchief round body, to take up any blood from wound. Takes off shoes, and with them in hand walks along to right up on balustrade and up slight cliff path and off.*)

Curtain.

ACT TWO

Scene 1: *Cinema Hall. On left small portion of edge of picture shown, dark, voice of* SHEILA.

SHEILA   Well, so far so good, good, good, goodie. Chink diving doing well. But there isn't quite enough of the deep calling to deep in the bit when Granville defies Charles. Still, what's done is done and now the Great Moment. I always knew it. There, there where O'Grady bites his nails and Mister Vosp hands him the letter behind the barrel, and they swear to save me, come hog, dog or devil. Ah wait boys. Shu, shu. But look Andy, oh Andy, look at yourself, some shooting that! Oh Jim, Jake, hug yourselves. I will never forget it to you. The way you hung on to that bit. Lovely, lovely, lovely, lovely. I am there now. See me, see me. (*Her voice is rising constantly and sinking a little again.*) But wait, wait. Here comes the close-up, no one's seen it, but me and Jake and Jim, and I tell you I played it with my face as near nude as the camera could swallow, swallow, swallow me. Boys, this is the greatest picture ever thrown. Andy, fame and fortune's on your either hand, all you boys are made for ever.

ANDY   Oh, Del, shut up.

> (*All the time figures of men, some smoking cigars,*
> *are moving about, some going out.*)
> (SHEILA *gives two or three loud sobs.*)

SHEILA   I find this bit a bit low brow. If I had my absolute way there would be nothing in this picture but the pure, straight, noble, refining drama of Life seen once and seen nobly acted by a natural nobility like you and I and all of us, isn't that so Andy?

ANDY   Oh very so so. This is a Trade Show not an intellectual treat.

SHEILA   I don't care, I feel, I feel as if I was standing where two clouds meet, the golden cloud of prosperity and the pale blue cloud of Art like a polished dagger of beauty leaping, by its own volition, from the scabbard of crepe-bound dull-witted obscurity.

(*Lights go up and discover on right, second row,* ANDY, SHEILA, O'GRADY, CHARVILLE, GRANVILLE, *also in front row, in front of* SHEILA, JAKE *and* JIM, *further along front row to right.* SHEILA, *fashionably dressed in modern clothes,* ANDY *wearing quiet dark grey suit, soft felt hat, but red silk sash showing. All others dressed much as before, in quiet grey or brown suits:* VOSP *still in light grey flannels,* GRANVILLE *still with sombrero, three or four men in each of the third, fourth and fifth rows. Cinema gallery men renters, most of them smoking.* ANDY *gives* SHEILA *a cigarette and lights one himself, all actors and camera men, except* GRANVILLE, *smoke cigarettes, but* ABSO *lights large cigar.*)

SHEILA (*puffing cigarette*) Andy, this is your great day. I don't believe you have realized it, but Del does. I do boys, don't I? We all do.

O'GRADY Sure thing.

CHARVILLE True, every word of it.

GRANVILLE True, indeed.

ABSO Absolutely.

ANDY (*looking round*) Now, Chocolate Usher, this way, hi.

(*Gets up and walks off signalling, comes back, right, followed by* BOY *with Chocolates.* BOY *very smart in bright blue uniform, gold braid, crimped golden hair.* ANDY *buys largest box of chocolates, hands it to* SHEILA, *gives* BOY *note,* BOY *fumbles for change and then goes off to get it.* ANDY *turns over back of seat and, with determination, says to* STOUT RENTER *in corner seat, third row.*)

ANDY Well, sir, how's she going?

STOUT RENTER Finely, finely.

(SHEILA *throws away cigarette into aisle over her shoulder behind her,* ANDY *has to put his foot on it, getting up to do so. She begins rustling paper and eating one or two chocolates, she turns her head, sees* STOUT RENTER, *looks hard at him.*)

STOUT RENTER Congratulations, congratulations Miss Delgarvay.

JACK (*in low voice*) I'm not so certain about the next bit, I know it'll go, but it's not for me.

JIM Nor me either.

(*Lights go slowly down, as they do so* NARDOCK *enters right,* BOY USHER *asks for card by signs,* NARDOCK *signs 'got none', gives boy paper money and slips along gangway with face turned left and sits down in corner seat, second row left of gangway, keeps face well to left, he is wearing same dress as in Act One, but grey silk tie, sailor knot.*)

SHEILA This is where it drags. It's old steady stuff.

ABSO (*murmuring*) They'll like it.

SHEILA Oh, they'll simply love it. The old houses all hanging over. There you go, Charles, creeping along the moonlight wall. Do you remember the nail in the wall, spikey end out, that hurt? I was on it once or twice. That was good, Charles, that pawing you gave the window. All

of this was yours, Jake and Jim, every single thread in it, and it does you
credit, poor dears, you worked it well. If anything could lift the story
along here it's your shots that would do it. Now the long avenue with
the Cactuses and the Eucalyptuses and everybody creeping, creeping,
creeping to the sea. What's that?

(BOY USHER *with change at* ANDY'S *side.* ANDY *turns to get change from him,
notes and coins.* SHEILA *looks over* ANDY'S *shoulder to watch,* USHER *turns his
electric lantern on money, and on reaching in his pocket for more money turns
lantern on* NARDOCK. SHEILA *sees* NARDOCK *and screams.*)

SHEILA   Oh God, the stiff from the Terrace, the Dead Man come to haunt
you Andy, and me.

(*Uproar, people jump out of seats.*
NARDOCK *moves along aisle and out right.*)

STOUT RENTER   Lights.
ANOTHER RENTER   Turn 'em on.
ANOTHER RENTER   Something wrong here.
ANOTHER RENTER   Lady fainted.
ANOTHER RENTER   No, not fainted, it's Miss Delgarvay.

(*Lights go up.* SHEILA, *hanging on* ANDY,
points up aisle and off.)

SHEILA   Find him, Andy, dead or alive, ghost or human being. Follow him,
Andy.

(ANDY *throws her off, leaves by aisle right,
preceded by* BOY USHER *dashing off first.*)

Curtain.

Scene 2: *Side Exit of Cinema. Daylight.*

(*Enter* BOY USHER *down steps left of centre with a run,
looks to left and right, is followed down steps by* ANDY.)

ANDY (*Looking off to right*)   Is that his taxi?
BOY USHER   Yes, that's it, boss. But there's another on the hazard. Hi taxi.

(*Points at* ANDY *and away right and after first taxi, to right.*)

BOY USHER (*To* ANDY, *slapping him in the middle of his back and shoving him towards right*)   After him old Sleuth. (*Shoving him off to taxi, shouts to taxi man off*) Hurry up, get her jumping, follow that taxi, five pounds if you get him before he makes the docks.

ANDY (*Going off right*)   Hi. I'm coming, make her throb.

(BOY USHER *comes back slowly to stairs looking off right,
and begins to go slowly upstairs. As his legs disappear curtain falls.*)

Curtain.

ACT THREE

Same as Act One. Time towards evening. Balustrade and writing on balustrade a little aged, creepers longer, De Venta notice older, all a little mouldy and mossy.

(Enter from left ANDY *and* NARDOCK *in boat, prow of boat showing over balustrade. Head and shoulders of* ANDY *and* NARDOCK *showing, both rowing back to bow usual way.* ANDY *in bow, he is wearing the same clothes as in Act Two, but has field glasses in old black leather case with sling round shoulder.* ANDY *steps over balustrade and makes painter fast to one of pilasters. After him comes* NARDOCK *dressed as in Act One and Two, but wearing pale pink silk tie sailor knot, he is carrying a good-sized luncheon basket which he places carefully down by the side of balustrade to the left of centre, reaches over and takes two cushions from boat, bright green velvet cushions, places them on each side of basket, opens basket takes out large, old bottle of burgundy, holds in two hands then against cheeks.)*

NARDOCK   The old style.
ANDY   The old style.

*(*NARDOCK *continues unpacking basket, nice small meat pie, a country cheese, some lettuce, and oil and vinegar, mustard, pepper, salt, 2 long French loaves, some strange fruit, bright peach-like, plates, knives, forks, glasses. Closes lid of basket and arranges pie, fruit, loaves and wine on top, puts glasses, plates, knives and forks, vinegar, oil, mustard, pepper and salt on ground in front of basket.* ANDY *smoking a cigarette, he throws cigarette into sea.* NARDOCK *waves hand to cushion on right of basket, sitting down himself on left-hand cushion,* ANDY *sits down on right. They each peel and eat a fruit,* NARDOCK *doing honours, handing oil and vinegar and salt, where each makes for himself, on side plates, Romain salad.* NARDOCK *pours out wine. This supper should be eaten and the wine drunk as realistically as possible and all with quiet enjoyment.)*

ANDY *(raising his glass)*   In memory of my catching you.
NARDOCK   In memory of your catching me. I wished to be alone. But I never was so glad, after the first five minutes, that I was not alone, but had my fellow man with me, I can't say more than that can I, my fellow man? Everybody isn't my fellow man and don't you forget it. I am glad to see you here opposite me across my own table, as I may say on my own terrace.

ANDY   Are you sure you will not have a great deal of bother for yourself, reconstructing yourself and proving that you aren't dead?

NARDOCK   Ah no. For obvious reasons there was no inquest. There was no special shark taken about that time with recognizable belt buckle, or watch or sleeve links or any memorials at all. I was just missing, supposed dead, certainly a case of suicide, gone to the happy sharking grounds, and if you look you will see they are still waiting. See that sickle fin, and that. (*He turns his head, raising it a little and pointing out to sea,* ANDY *follows his looks.*)

ANDY   Busy boys.

NARDOCK   You can see (*turning his head towards house*) it is likely there has been no tenant in this house since I left it going to my watery doom, and, from what you heard them saying in the hotel last night, this house will never be occupied except by a would-be self destructor or myself or yourself. We will take our ease here, read the papers and laugh gently at the world, I will re-name the house—SHARK'S BELLY HALL—The old name was Casa Amarillo ex Now or Never ex Merry Widow ex Lord Jim ex Tara Boom de A ex El Casa Viejo, so you see it has always been changing like leaves changing.

ANDY   (*raises glass*)   Very nice burgundy. This to Shark's Belly Hall.

NARDOCK   To Shark's Belly Hall and to its guest. I will, as you have no doubt guessed, guest, he lisps in puns because the punnings come. Pun while the punnings good—I have, as I am sure you realized, made up my mind not to commit suicide. The embarrassments of a year ago have settled themselves by my estate to the ownership of which I have already established my identity, attracting the attention of some enquiring sportsman, with an itch for scratching the earth, and this individual has discovered some mineral which is extraordinary useful, and in fact absolutely justifies its existence by lending itself to all forms of adulteration. It never appears under its own name. It is a stretcher created by the great upheavals of the world for the purpose of making, perhaps, tooth powder go further, or face powder cover a larger face, without costing the manufacturers of these articles too much. The Primeval mountains of the planet cracked their joints in the ages of old, and today some Turk perhaps, mixing his explosive sherbet, may be, for all I know, quaffing the very subsoil of my Estate. But I never enquire where my incognito friend of the soil goes. I only know he pays as he goes, a very nice royalty. The Mining Company does it all, and I receive my monthly cheque. My teeth I make fast in a bowline and wash in Neptune Realm. My face I powder no more, having failed to powder it with gunpowder, and I hope you and I will not be reduced to sherbet. (*He drinks some burgundy.*)

(ANDY *drinks.*)

ANDY   My friend, I am with you. What of your promise to tell me the story of your life.

NARDOCK   Ah, that will come, a chapter at a time. I will tell you all, as today. But of course sometimes sitting on chairs (*he stirs a little on his cushion*) and with a table between us, my story may have a moral and it may not. I myself have never laid down new primrose paths, nor have I sown tares in existing ones. I have been a wandering, gambling orator, speaking when I was not listened to and picking often the subjects of my discourse at haphazard like sweep numbers from a hat.

(*Pours out more wine for both.*)

I have been among the gales of the mountain top, and among the lacey rollers of the beaches. I have journeyed over all the worlds, either in body or in spirit and sometimes in both. As a child I had as many eyes as there are points to the compass, and every eye was registering simultaneous it seemed. Time has no meaning to me, I am embedded in time, and floating in eternity. I have seen the Peruvians in pigtails and the Chinese in kilts. I have gone down into the heart of the volcano, and placed my hand where the pulse should be and called on it to shake. And I have stepped from the fragment of one star to the nucleuary fragment of another, and I have looked at myself so doing. I am an Egotist—

ANDY   Not at all.

NARDOCK   I am an Egotist steeped in generosity and seethed in affection. I first saw the light of day, and it was a good day, on an island, a sort of shooting island, or perhaps I should say a popping island, a-popping up and a-popping back into the Western Ocean. As we talk it may be there, and as we talk it may be gone, sunk beneath the blue waters. It is not Atalantis, quite another cup of tea. Older and yet friskier. It had, as far as I ever heard, no name, unless I name it with my own name, and the name I go under now is not my name. It is an assumed name. Assumed for the purposes of confusion. I left my island as it sunk beneath me and I was in—Paris. Pleasant city, but it was not what it is. And it is not what it was. It is in fact, in fact it is, perhaps it is a neverwaser, but an alwaysiser, or will be like Cork, or a don't-want-to-be-but-can't-help-being like New York, or a muffled sob like London. I shook myself and I was a silent guide to the buried cities of Tibet. I might tell you that my travelling was done in a gold coracle with silver oars foaming along on a foam of rose petals. But as a matter of fact I walked, for wheresoever I journeyed I walked, up and down, deck of ship, or gangway of train, or floor of carriage or sledge, the development of the calves of my legs—

(ANDY *looks over at legs,* NARDOCK *draws them up.*)

up to a few years ago was a marvel to behold and to pinch.

But a long time I pursued the uneven tenor of the ways as an inventor. But first I invented an extremely delicate instrument which if gently placed in close proximity to the model or plan of any imagined new invention would tell the observer at a glance if the said invention was new or old. If new a disk on the assaying instrument blushed a light pink. If the invention was old it turned a bright painful scarlet and we laid away the model specification or what not of the so-called new invention in the bottom drawer of the Tall Boy Limbo of the unwanted redundant thoughts of mankind, there to grow mossy or wilt away, or tumble into a fine dust, and await the day when it would be blown away with the short stab-like puffs of bicycle tyre inflators.

I did not invent the bicycle but I invented the circle. I did not invent smoke, I invented fire. I thought of water, not to quench fire, but to float a raft to carry fire. I did not invent the iron ship floating on the ocean, but I invented the sinking of the stone in the pond, and everything I invented caused my delicate assaying instrument, the inventor's conscience, to turn scarlet and I was glad, for I had invented continuosity and thrown away stepping stones.

ANDY   You sure were one magnificent being, and I am with you all the time.

NARDOCK   I waded in the greasy dew of the stars, and I felt depressed when the daisy closed her petals at the evening time. But for a moment of every day or every age I bit into the crust of the rainbow, and that is only a figure of speech for what I bit into.

My thoughts carried me and I carried my thoughts. Thoughts are too cold a word for what I bosomed myself upon. I whistled to the wind and it whistled back, an endless whistle, that had a colour and a form, a rope of whistling, making and unmaking itself into knots nautical, and starry knots, a cable twisted of three, four, seven, strands, and again it became a single strand like a whigging snake of blue light on a marble sea. I mean a sort of Connemara marble sea, mottled like concannon. Now concannon is a dish of mashed potatoes laced with strands of green cabbage, you should try it, excellent for the complexion.

Let us light our cigars before we get into the heavier work.

(*He takes up case and offers regalia to* ANDY *and takes out match box and lights* ANDY'S *and his own cigars. Opens small bottle of burgundy.*)

NARDOCK   Ah, the foal to foot. (*Fills glasses.*) Ah, the foal to foot, and how bred? How say you, Andy?

ANDY   By Jollity out of Good Egg.

NARDOCK   Mister Andy, you are a man of taste and intelligence and you have the gift of words. If few they are gifted. But tell me, had yourself, that marvellous lady, and the rest of that interesting group of per-

formers I first met on this Dramatic Terrace, had you and they long
lived in Hollywood?

ANDY   None of us, never. But, as the man said in the old song, we all had
'good offers,' or thought we would have. Gee, some boys and one
perfect princess.

NARDOCK   Quite so, quite so. By Jollity out of Good Egg. I continued my
inventive existence. Originally I read all books. But today I read only
jackets. By exchanging jackets and obliterating titles I have added to
the difficulties which add to the powerful digestiveness of the Human
Race. When I leave some resting place of a day I leave behind me a
book with a wrong jacket. I see the joke in that, perhaps you don't.

ANDY   I'll tell the artificial lashed eyed world I do.

NARDOCK   That's a difficult sentence for you to say, don't tax your tongue's
elasticity too far.

ANDY   I see the joke in that all right anyway. I feel when with you, friend,
that it would be impossible for me to see the joke I couldn't see.

NARDOCK   Good boy again. Now attend carefully to what I have to tell
you. Most of my youth was spent walking the roads of the world. I
was the bootmaker's friend, that is I imagined bootmakers and
befriended them. I visited every picturesque city of the world, and all
the little one horse towns which had about them any faint memory of
the horse shoes of romance. And everywhere I left I left my blessing,
and it did them a power of good. I could tell you the names of many
of these towns, right here and now, as the saying is, but I could tell
them better if I had a gazeteer handy. I am the man who holds ever a
lone hand in the descriptive game. I could, and would if nothing else
was under my tongue, describe to you an empty box so that the very
emptiness that begot it wouldn't know it. I could tell you a great many
tales of the mighty horses of the past; Dean Swift's horse, so tall that
it passed for a cathedral on the sky line. And the horse of Peter the
Great which was so unlike a horse that when it neighed the very lions
of the jungle lay down in their tracks, and sobbing, prayed for wings,
for they did not know what was come along the glade. But they soon
rose up and laughed with me at how their legs had been pulled. Leg-
pulling is a fine art. The one art which, with my great modesty, I do
not claim as my own. There is always coming nearer the day, when the
last pullable leg will be pulled. A poet has shown us the sadness of the
last man, the hangman with no one in the world left to pull his legs. But
I see another picture of the last man looking with desolated eyes
searching for the last leg but two, just to pull it, and his mind will be
brimming with splendid schemes for leg pulling—too late, and he
could not stoop to pull his own leg. Could *you* Andy?

ANDY   Never. I'd die first.

NARDOCK   Too late, that is a sad word, never say it, say too soon, perhaps.
But never say too anything, there is no such thing as redundancy to

those who are imbedded, as you and I are, in continuosity, because if there is too much of anything at any moment, we only hold it over in the heel of the fist and later link it up with the coming event, and so linked together we get continuosity, impetuosity and exuberance. We do not sit, you and I, the centre of the hub, but until our hour strikes, just off centre, moving always, but appearing to direct the spokes and rim. We will have all the fun of passing as an aristocracy ruling by position. While we enjoy all the fun of going round and round. They tell us I think, or they told us, at school that the rim moves faster than the hub or the hub moves faster than the rim. Either way it's a cowardly lie got up by Schoolmasters, and they taught me nothing. It was I who was doing the teaching, Andy. And they didn't know it.

(NARDOCK *takes up remains of French loaves in each hand.*)

NARDOCK   See if the fins are ranging around still, they'll think these are calves of legs.

(ANDY *moves round and looks over balustrade, takes out field glasses and looks through them.*)

ANDY   They are still there, but a long way off.

NARDOCK (*Throwing loaves over balustrade*)   Well, here's legs for fins. Come and help yourselves when you feel like it. But now (*leaning back and pulling at cigar*) it would be nice if you were to tell me your early life, if you are willing, and later on I will knot another thread that will become finally the bright worsted stocking of my own ravelling Life.

ANDY   I was born in Shoreditch, and I never saw either the shore nor the ditch. My father had a small newsagent's shop and the day I was born he did a thing he had never done before. He drew a racing prophecy from an automatic tipping machine which he had in the shop. The horse he drew didn't win, but father luckily hadn't backed it, and when a couple of months later it won father hadn't backed it either. In fact father had given up backing horses altogether by then. But he decided that I must be dedicated to luck, that chance should rule my life not premeditation. So when at the age of five years, my education having got beyond my mother's powers, I chanced to spell out the word 'School' without having any idea what it stood for, I was taken to board school, but on the way I lost my little shoe in the mud opposite a small house which had a notice in the window DOWTON COLLEGE. I went there. It had style, that College. There were eleven pupils. I made up the dozen and we wore mortar boards. The school caught fire and was burnt out, when I was ten years of age. So my father came to the conclusion that my school days were over. I delivered the newspapers after that, but I delivered them by chance,

as instructed by my father. I had no list of addresses. I just walked about
our neighbourhood in the early morning dropping newspapers into
letter boxes or propping them up against milk jugs, just as my fancy
took me.

NARDOCK   Forgive me interrupting you, but didn't your father find it bad
for business?

ANDY   Business improved. The people who hadn't received their papers
came to the shop and called for them and bought cigarettes and pipes
and tobacco, and the people who hadn't ordered papers in the past did
so in the future. Also I met a man who got a paper from me which was
of the opposite kind of politics from his and it contained an insulting
article about himself which he would not have seen without me. So
having a pull he got me a position as junior office boy in the Assembly
Rooms. But on the way to take up my work I stopped on the platform
of a railway station to get some chocolate out of a penny in the slot
machine, and as usual I chanced the kind of machine I was trying my
luck with. And the first time I got a box of matches and the second
time I got a bottle of scent. I tried another machine and my penny was
returned. A square-faced man saw me, he thought I looked disappointed, which of course I didn't. I was only surprised at getting my
penny back. Negative luck was new to me. But the square-faced old
lad gave me sixpence to heal my wound. But in taking out the sixpence
he dropped half-a-crown which rolled under a seat on the platform
and I went in after it, and beside it I found a second halfcrown, which
must have been dropped by somebody else. I came out from under the
seat with the two halfcrowns, and that so pleased the old lad he thought
it was a lucky omen, that he told me to keep one of the halfcrowns.

NARDOCK   Very kind of him I'm sure.

ANDY   And then he offered me a job as a cabin boy on a tug he owned, so
I went down to the docks with the old lad and I was a cabin boy a
week, going up and down the river, without seeing my home. So
when I did get home my mother was pleased to see me for myself, but
my father was more interested in my luck. It was a hot summer day,
so I thought I'd give my luck a rest, so I went to the swimming baths.
But while standing on the edge I accidentally fell in, fully dressed, so
they put me to bed while they were drying my clothes in front of the
fire in the laundry part of the baths. After that they gave me a job as
attendant in the baths, but after a while the baths caught fire and got
burnt out. So I was without a job until the Fire Brigade Captain
employed me as a sort of apprentice, but mostly as a mascot. But my
luck didn't seem transferable for they didn't have another fire for
three months, so the captain retired in disgust, and opened an Employ-
ment Agency. He took me with him. All the people who came looking
for employees employed me. I was too many things to tell you.

NARDOCK   You must write all this.

ANDY After many years the Captain lost the Agency at billiards to a sporting prophet. But next week I won it off the prophet and re-instated the Captain. I tore the cloth in doing so, but I mended it again so well that I became famous as a Billiard Table Cloth's Tailor, I'd never been that before. Of course I tried my luck at finding winners, but it only came off once. I believe the premeditation necessary to the business interfered with the luck. And the time it did come off the bookmaker was a welsher. His creditors distributed his belongings and I got his hat, but I am making a long story too long.

NARDOCK Not at all, not at all, have some more burgundy. (*Helps him to wine and himself.*)

ANDY Well, the hat was a Tom Mix affair. But I forgot to tell you that my father had died and left two wills in two sealed envelopes with directions for me to open one, and destroy the other unread. Well, the one I opened left me executor with instructions to sell the business, realise everything, and invest the proceeds in an annuity for my mother. A few years later my dear mother died leaving me her advice to trust to luck. Well, this Tom Mix hat led the lady we know as Miss Sheila Delgarvay to think I was connected with the Cinema Industry. First she got me to suggest a good professional name for her. I arrived at the result by drawing names from a hat. The surname was the result of two torn entries. She was so pleased with the name that she asked me to produce 'The Slicer' for her. We came out to this place through me taking up the wrong tickets at the Tourist Agency. I came to this house because this balustrade (*pointing to it*) was the first thing I saw to tie up to. Then you came in. I had promised Miss Delgarvay to engage some one to take the part of the corpse in the background and there you were, and here we are.

NARDOCK Splendid, splendid. You must write it all. What a life you have had. See if our friends the sharks have seen our legs yet.

ANDY (*looking through glasses, turning round where he sits to do so. Takes glasses from eyes*) Yes, they are basking about close in, chewing. (*Puts up glasses to eyes again, sweeps horizon right to left. Looks left long.*) There's a boat putting out from the shore, probably some crabber. (*Turns round again, sips wine.*)

NARDOCK You, Andy, with your marvellous faith in your luck, and myself with my enjoyment of the marvellous, will drop a crab pot over the balustrade at night and take it up in the morning full of all sorts of wonders, ancient brandy in barnacled bottles, or diamonds, or pearls by the Beard of the Prophet, or first Edition (in sealed tin cases of course). Every morning will be dedicated to the opening of the crab pot and you and I hilariously welcoming the gifts of the Gods. Or would the crab pot be too much like premeditation? Premeditation is the thief of Luck. There's a casino here. Have you ever played the tables Andy? or is that too much of a forethought for your luck to hold?

ANDY When we came here it was through taking up the wrong tickets as
I told you. Our passages should have really taken us to Nice. There I
might have given my luck a chance.

NARDOCK Well the luck was with that coast. However, the casino here is a
small affair but growing. When it is large enough to be worth your
luckship's attention we'll go in there and, after giving an exhibition of
what you can do, we will, if you are willing, hand over our winnings
to the Home for broken Wirepullers, and desist from playing the
tables again. How magnificent it will be to walk about gazing at the
nervous gamblers biting their nails and going through all the hills and
the valleys of gamblers' land, while we do nothing. Holding the magic
lamp we refuse to rub it. How magnificent to have a Giant Luck and
not to use it. But of course your luck is not absolutely dependable.
You'll forgive me saying so. But perhaps I should put it differently.
Your luck, I will say, has its own way of doing things, and I have no
doubt after a day of taking happy chances, and lunching on cream pies,
and shaking the bones you will be glad enough to come back to
Shark's Belly Hall. And an evening sacred to conversation under the
stars will not be so dusty, as the saying is.

ANDY I could listen to you for ever.

NARDOCK Ah, Andy, it's I who have the luck magnificent and it's I must
sup the cup while it brims. At no time, walking the roads of the world,
and always singing:
          'There's a land that is fairer than this'
(*Sings in a croaky way*) did I believe that I should ever find myself in a
country like this Terrace, inhabited with such as you. Once I talked all
night through to a man leaning against a tree in a plain, in a desolate
land, and I thought him a chieftain of listeners, so still, so respectful, so
understanding, and in the morning's dawn I knew why. He was a dead
man wrapped in his shroud. I talked all day to a fat man on an Arab
horse crossing a desert and I was hanging to his stirrup, and, not
knowing the language I spoke, he thought I praised his horse, and
when we reached his camp he gave me the horse. And perched on a
gold leaf saddle, I rode him over the ridge pole of the world, howling
philosophy as I rode. Ridge pole is the place for philosophy, the
essential essence of philosophy drifting upward through the hoofs of
the horse, through the horse's body along the horse's ridge pole, into
my body and mounting so to my brain. There were times then and
have been since, when I have felt that one quiver of one of my eyelashes
and I would be master of understanding knowing all things, and only
revealing them, on Saturday afternoons in the Summer time, a little
at a dose, to chosen birds who might seem to be worthy of receiving
the gift of the result of the lapidary walloping of my brain. Take a
sweep of the Bay and see if there are any more Sharks.

ANDY (*after sweeping, with the glasses, from right to left, across*) An odd fin or so more showing. But they seem to have agreed that the two lads close in now, licking the bread crumbs from their curley lips, have a special call on this edge of the bay. But I see our friend the crabber seems to be coming out steadily, well fairly steadily. A bit zigzaggy in his course, but coming nearer. He's got wind and tide against him, poor dear.

NARDOCK Poor dear, yes poor devil, rowing out to lift an ordinary crab pot with very likely nothing in it, nothing, nothing to the lucky crab pot we will be opening in the bright mornings. I will be singing, no, not singing, it's unlucky to sing before breakfast, but crooning happy songs of sun rise to celebrate the fact that we are just hitting a new rosey trail. I don't mean a trail that goes anywhere, I mean a kind of a stationary trail on which we stand and purr, while the world's best scenery, past, present, and to come, rolls by us like the back cloth of the races on the stage. How's our friend the crab pot hunter getting on?

ANDY (*looking with the glasses again, and holding the glasses down in his hand turns to* NARDOCK) It's not a hunter, it's a huntress and rowing against wind and tide is not her best line.

NARDOCK Well, I hope she finds something good in her blasted crab pot. When I say we will hit only a stationary trail I don't mean we won't be shaugharawning around the countryside refilling memories' measures against the séance of the evening when the medium (*he points at his own breast and towards the bottle*) will speak hail, rain, snow, or shine. Of course as a matter of fact they never have any hail, rain or snow here and most of the evenings the shiner will be sinking to the west in an amber glow of beatitude. All the same it looks a bit ragged tonight but stylish.

(*Sky by now has become very garish as the sun gets lower.*)

Some people are afraid of a stylish sky. Nature drawing up its embattled and highly coloured wonders to proclaim that when it comes to glory, profundity, high spots, tiger stripes, and whirlygigging refulgences the palette of the painter (alliteration I don't really like it) is but a half a half-brother to the towering jars of luminosity spilling themselves through the cracks in the firmaments and sweeping to the very feet of the observer, standing bare foot waiting for the flood to lave his ten toes. Lave is a curious word to use today, Andy, but it had its day, I suppose. Has every word, like every dog, a day, Andy? There are some words, in whose day I should not have cared to be assisting. 'Crikey' that was an awful word, like a crack on the head with spite, and yet all the bravest and the best used it, perhaps, in its day. However, what have we got to do with words of the past? The pleasant present and the gorgeous—How's the crab Huntress getting on?

(ANDY *looks through glasses.*)

ANDY   She's come on a bit. But now she's got a parasol, a pink parasol, up to keep the sun off the back of her neck perhaps, and she can't want to do that for there's no great heat in this sun now. It's nothing but showiness. Perhaps she thinks she can sail her old canoe with the parasol, especially against the wind . . . whatever idea it was she's given it up and furled her parasol.

NARDOCK   I'm sure I wish her the best of good luck. What was I talking about?

ANDY   Words.

NARDOCK   Ah words, I often do talk about them and with them too. It's a superstition, using words for speech, and I suppose the day will come when it'll be found, out, like most superstitions. That's the way with the clever ones, they think they've found how a superstition works just when it fails to work. Everyone finds out everything too late. When anything, love, or even conversation, fails to prove itself fool proof, then give it up. Never give up a riddle till you've got the answer, then give it up for good. There are clever riddles, like marriage, which themselves give the answer before the question. So they become riddles in perpetuity while grass grows and water runs. Everybody, including birds, finds out everything too late. They find out that nests wear out, too late. And so they have to begin house-building again in a hurry. If they found it out in time they'd build their nests in old boots and tin cans, and firemens' helmets, and other odd shops pitched on by the exceptional birds who prove the rule. And then there's the weather which knows itself here from day to day, except perhaps tomorrow; by the look of that sky (*he turns his face towards setting sun*) it's going to be a saucy day, with gloomy frillings on it, for the children of the sea. There was a lively volcano here spouting one time, and there was a green wave came up out of the sea and slithered up the mountain side and flopped into the crater and put out that volcano. Did you ever smell a kitchen range just when the kettle boils over onto the hot iron? Well, a thousand miles to the West-ward the people living on the Islands held flowers to their noses and sniffed very superior. When all speech dies at last the sniff superior will be the last comment, because of course you can sniff flowers silently if you like. Flowers round red brows. Bacchus. Flowers on graves 'No Flowers by request.' And the protagonist, that's a good word Andy, we must use it again—some time. Andy, would you like to sing a song to me?

ANDY   I'm only an amateur songster. But I'd be glad to.

NARDOCK   What'll you sing?

ANDY   What about 'Rolling Home.'

NARDOCK   Roll it Home.

ANDY (*singing*)   'Rolling Home':
        Call all hands to man the capstan
        See the cable run down clear
        Heave away, and with a will boys
        For Old England we will steer
        And we'll sing in joyful chorus
        In the watches of the night
        And we'll sight the shores of England
        When the grey dawn brings the light
        Rolling Home, Rolling Home,
        Rolling Home across the Sea
        Rolling Home to Dear Old England
        Rolling Home Dear Land to Thee.

        Up aloft amid the rigging
        Blows the loud exulting gale
        Like a bird's wide out-stretched pinions
        Spreads on high each swelling sail;
        And the wild waves cleft behind us
        Seem to murmur as they flow
        There are loving hearts that wait you
        In the land to which you go
        Rolling Home, etc.

        Many thousand miles behind us
        Many thousand miles before
        Ancient Ocean heaves to waft us
        To the well-remembered shore
        Cheer up Jade, bright smiles await you
        From the fairest of the fair
        And her loving eyes will greet you
        With kind welcomes every where
        Rolling Home, etc.

NARDOCK   Good song, well sung. It was written from somebody's heart.
    Do you like cats, Andy?
ANDY   I love 'em.
NARDOCK   So do I. The quiet smiling ones, who understand having the
    backs of their ears rubbed. There's nothing like a nice settled cat for
    making a home. They make complacency interchangeable and they
    don't mind what sort of clothes you wear. If Shark's Belly Hall had a
    cat with that sort of a disposition it would think as much of us in our
    tattered thinking clothes, as in our frock coats and silk hats, and striped
    trousers and white spats. If we possess such things. A cat should be
    jolly at Christmas times. Did you ever think of putting presents in a

cat's stocking? It would be rather amusing, if a cat had a stocking, to see her putting her paw down into it to pull up a white sugar mouse with pink eyes and a tail. You remember them perhaps. We never ate the tails, they were just white string. I think they should have been made eatable don't you? If I found myself one of the great sweetie manufacturers of the world I would see to it that every bit of any sweet I turned out should be eatable, so that parents might have no fear in giving their young hearty meals of our sweets to gormandize their little selves with. But perhaps, if there is a new year, this will be one of the new year leaves to turn over. For the manufacturers to turn over, to wrap their chocolates in eatable wrappings, so that there wouldn't be so much rustling in theatres and the audience could begin outside and eat straight inwards. Like the knives and forks at a dinner used to be, before the Neophytes got on to it, and the Exquisites, to make their torture more exquisite, mixed them all up again. But Mid-summer is the rational time for turning over new leaves, though it is always Mid-summer here, God bless it. Mid-summer is a handy time for turning over new leaves, because if you repent about it afterwards you've only got six months to struggle through and most everyone could keep a diary, on a vow, for six months. Even if they didn't succeed the soul would be sooner over upbraiding. Hallows Eve is the real gilt edged time for putting your fate to the touch. So few months left then till the sun sinks and the curtain falls and the candle gutters. And if you are sick, a sinking sun, a falling curtain, and a guttering candle can't be too quick about it, that is if you're really sick. Of course if you only think you're sick—look Andy, how's the yellow huntress making out her voyage?

(ANDY *looks again with glasses a long steady look, then turns round and soberly speaks.*)

ANDY   We know who she is, this huntress. She's Sheila. She got her old 'Slicer' dress on and she's coming here.
NARDOCK (*looks straight before him and says nothing for a while, then speaks*) Are you sure she's heading for here?
ANDY   Sure.
NARDOCK   How far off?
ANDY   Oh a good ways yet.

(NARDOCK *broods silently.*)

ANDY   She's a poor rower.

(NARDOCK *gets onto hands and knees and moves round to front of basket. Takes visiting card from case in pocket and fountain pen. The pen is loose in his side pocket not fastened upright with a clip, and writes on card and reads out.)*

NARDOCK   'I cannot live any more, therefore I depart.' How's that, is it like me?

ANDY   Near enough I should think.

NARDOCK   Now you (*takes glasses from* ANDY *and hands him his fountain pen*) Got a card on you?

ANDY   Yes. (*Writes*).

(NARDOCK *watches sea with glasses, being careful not to show himself over balustrade.*)

ANDY (*reading*)   'I go. I step off here.' She'll appreciate that.

NARDOCK   I'm sure she will. (*Hands glasses back to* ANDY, *and lays out cards on balustrade.*)

ANDY   She's coming on, she's advancing.

(*Both men are smoking ends of cigars all the time* NARDOCK *takes out of hip pocket revolver, lays it on basket, takes off shoes, motions* ANDY *to do the same, while he watches through glasses which he takes from* ANDY. *He hands back glasses to* ANDY, *takes shoes from* ANDY *and rubbing the soles of his own and* ANDY'S *shoes on ground, makes marks with them on balustrade top. Takes* ANDY'S *hat and his own and throws them into sea. Nudges* ANDY. *then takes up revolver and fires it off twice left, arranges revolver as if dropped on ground by basket.*)

NARDOCK   Has she heard?

ANDY   She heard all right, and turned her head, now she's put her head back again and she trying to push her old dinghy along. She's put a bone in her mouth, a very little one.

NARDOCK (*in a whisper*)   I suppose sharks don't eat hats.

ANDY (*in a whisper*)   Not unless as a very last resource I believe.

(NARDOCK *leaves his cigar stump on his plate, lifts up his shoes, signs* ANDY *to do the same with his cigar and shoes and goes off right, stooping and creeping up bank and disappearing right.*)

A WAIT

(*Sun sinks more towards the west and the edge of the sea.*)

———————

(*Enter* SHEILA *in dinghy, left, dressed as in Act One, rowing about a little. She is picking up hats. She comes up to balustrade, throws painter over on to ground, climbs over herself with a hat in each hand, shakes water out of hats. Then holds hats against breast, finds them damp, so puts them carefully down side by side, on ground by basket.)*

SHEILA   How they loved me.

(She is a little hysterical in her voice at first, but gradually her emotion becomes subdued to her words. Stoops over basket and reads each card carefully, takes up revolver, looks at it; after fussing to open it, does so, sees two cartridges have been fired, goes back to cards and reads them again.)

SHEILA   They died for love of me. Sooner than live on and see the other accepted, each did take his life. *(Looks at marks on balustrade)* And what the revolver commenced the old ocean finished. Beneath the wave they lie for me.

(She steps up on balustrade and begins to pace up and down, thinking of words to fit the occasion. She looks up at the sky above her.)

SHEILA   The darkness of night is creeping over Heaven's blue. *(She looks at the sun)* And the sun is sinking. The short tropic twilight will soon be here, and then night with its velvet pall will fall over all Sea *(looks down at water)*. Sharks! *(Comes quietly and with dignity down from balustrade and paces up and down on ground)* Sea and land. The curtain is about to fall. I, the last item. The last number. I who have often before, in Variety, played them out. Played out the last-trammers. The last bussers, the last toobers! tubers! I play them out again. Here, by Old Ocean, I make my last fond farewells to the gods, the pits, the dress circles, and the stalls. A daughter of the legitimate says good-bye to the old dear friends of other days. The days that are no more. Music, Poetry, the Arts. Thine own familiar servant says goodbye and not aurevoir. Oh Mother Eve, your daughter, for whom two brawney Adams have this evening died, bids the cold world of dirty money, grasping managers, press agents and sandwichmen, a slow and lingering farewell. As the sun sinks so sink I. But not wholly sunk, for mid the pinkey clouds of old sky I will gaze now and then on the garden parties, the picnics, the water chutes, the automobile joyful ridings in the Springtimes, that may come when daisies again star the green sward. By rock, by mountain, by lake, by tumbling water-fall, by all the inspirational and picturesque artist-belovéd beauty spots wherever the gentle daisy may find a place to root. And wherever the golden sun flowers glorious, full blown, magnificent, and not unlike myself when I was here. Wherever, I say, the golden sunflower turns to the sun there in spirit will be I, gracious but bold, forgiving my enemies, and defying the press to spancel my style. With my two ankles free.

From the cloudy heights—from the cloudy heights (*to herself*)—that's where I was, wasn't it? I will dance me in and out of the hearts of men, so that these two lads who have died tonight will be a speck on the ocean of the myriad young men who will dedicate their lives and their deaths to Sheila Delgarvay, the brightest star that ever bloomed, star is vulgar, vulgarized by lioness comiques of other days. But thou knowest kind Heaven the kind of star I mean, Delgarvay the brightest star of them all, reflected at one moment in 'Killarney' by Killarney's lakes and fells, Emerald bays and—and—and in Geneva's lake where the peace boys are. In the great lakes of the U.S.A. and in all the lakes of whose size and magnitude Thou has cognization kind Heaven as being of the first class. (*While she is speaking the rope (the painter) from her boat is slowly being drawn away, caused by her boat drifting away.*)

DELGARVAY THE IRRESISTIBLE
DELGARVAY THE GRAND
DELGARVAY——

(*here she sees the rope going, and puts her foot on it and stops it*). The Clouds the Sun, the Moon, Old Ocean, the mountians, the hills, the shepherds on the hills, the glens, the gullies, the prairies, and the deserts love me— they love Delgarvay as she trips through them, scintillating bright cheer and graceful gentility wherever she goes. They love me for myself. They love me for my art. They love me for what I have done for Art. (*While speaking she takes her foot from rope, which slides away over the balustrade and disappears*)—The Soul of Art. For kind friends Art has a soul, and when the great Delgarvay opens bazaars, and kicks off at cricket matches and opens the balls here, there and everywhere, there she will tell them of Art. The Art of life she knows so well. She will be helpful and kind to the down trodden and the temporary despairful. Her motor will be an angel's prayer for beauty, so long, so slim, so magnificent, like her mistress. She with her lovely soul shining through her gorgeous eyes will look benignly on all the world as if—

(*The sun drops below the horizon. It gets nearly dark.*)

Ah so, flop, ends the tropic day. That gets me.

(*She sinking on the ground with her back against the balustrade, takes the yellow rose out of her hair and twiddles it as the curtain goes down.*)

CURTAIN.

Apparitions

A Play in One Act

CHARACTERS

JIMMY *waiter, young, seedy.*

CHARLIE CHARLES *small, red-haired, about 50, wizened, out of work ship's steward type.*

JOHN EVERTON *big game hunter, middle aged.*

JOHN ALBERMARL, *traveller in Near East, middle aged, with fez.*

PHIL POLEAXE *ex-cowboy, about 30, with sombrero.*

BILL SCOTT *soldier of fortune, about 40.*

ERICK PARLBURY *Labour speaker and journalist, about 50. Heavy, white, fat.*

ERNEST LIVID ('Little Livid') *ex-music hall performer, about 45.*

(*All clean-shaven except* ALBERMARL, *who has heavy, old-fashioned moustache; and* PARLBURY, *who has short clipped beard.*)

HOTEL CLERK *pale, willowy-type of woman, about 25.*

(*Note to be printed on programme if the play is shown in an arena:*

WHEN WEARING WHITE GLOVES AN ACTOR IS A STAGE HAND.)

As an Overture
'JOHNNY, I HARDLY KNEW YOU'
by a distant fife and drum band

Scene: *Coffee room of Little Bridge Hotel, Pullickborough.*

(JIMMY *comes in through curtain and arranges seven chairs round table, three on one side, two on the other, one at each end of table.*
Enter CHARLES, EVERTON, ALBERMARL, POLEAXE, SCOTT, PARLBURY *and* LIVID. CHARLES *with paper in hands, points where each is to sit.* ALBERMARL *and* PARLBURY *sit on two chairs side of table.* EVERTON, POLEAXE *and* SCOTT *opposite.* LIVID *in end chair opposite entrance.* CHARLES *end chair in front of entrance. He has large leather bag with him. He puts it on the floor beside him until others are settled in their chairs. Then he opens bag, takes out tin alarum clock and puts it on the table in front of himself.*)

CHARLES   We all know, fellow brothers in arms, why we are gathered here to-night. And it is only necessary for me to remind all parties that the house is surrounded—at the present moment—and I defy any man to defy me—by the loving, watching eyes of the inhabitants of this part of the world. If this ghost, horror, or what-not appears to-night, it, he or she, will meet seven hearts as brave as any as ever beat in any part of the entire world together at the same time. It is unnecessary for us to further prove our courage. It has been proved so often in the jungle, and on the heaving deck, on the battlefield, in the arena, on the prairies and behind the footlights. The procedure this evening will be very simple. To-night is the night of all the nights of the year on which, according to accounts by the various tenants of this salubrious abode the appearance had made its appearance, and had apparently such an effect on the nerves of the beholders, that they have without further parley jumped clean out of the place, and refused to pay any more rent. These being licensed premises, the constant changing of tenants has been bad for the property, and bad for the village. But all this is ancient history to us. What we know is that we are here to scotch a ghost or goblin, or whatever it is. The new proprietor, Mr Weston, as a good citizen, I might say, as any village could have, did me the honour, over a friendly glass, to ask me to pick 'six good men as true', these were his words, to face the situation. I said to him in reply at once, I can do that without a second thought. Six you want, I says and six you shall have. Our Squire, I says, Mr Weston, leads by right of position, consanguinity and prowess in the hunting field. The hunting fields, both big game and little game has fallen to his gun, both here and beyond the marches of civilization. Also, I says, he is loved by one and all; his pocket has always been open and at the service of the village. Are you satisfied, Mr Weston, with Mister John Everton as a leader? 'I am,' he says, 'and I leave the matter in your hands and his.' Gentlemen all, are you satisfied with my choice?

ALBERMARL   Excellent! I shall be delighted to co-operate in every way with Mr Everton.

LIVID   Me, too.

PARLBURY   Squires may rise and perish, Kingdoms rise and roam—I forget the quotation. But for the time being I am very pleased to assist in what way I can with the help of John Everton. (*All slap hands on table.*)

POLEAXE   I'm with this. (*More slapping hands on table.*)

CHARLES   Agreed, agreed. All agreed. (*Turning towards* EVERTON) I am proud to salute you as leader of our band, and we will all be glad to hear what you propose to do when, and if, we find ourselves confronted with this diabolical interrupter from beyond the veil.

EVERTON (*rising with small piece of paper in his hand*)   When our little friend, Charles, asked me to take up the leadership, my first idea was to refuse and tell him to get a parcel of the young people of the village to run the ghost, or whatever it is, out of the village. My second idea was to come down here with my elephant gun and let him have it. But on further consideration I came to the conclusion that this room was not suitable. I forgot for the nonce that I would not be hurtling through my jungles where man, as Kipling says, can be:

> 'Red in tooth and claw and
> Devil take the hindmost.'

I finally came to the conclusion that if this supernatural appearance was genuine it would be wily and up to all the tricks. Therefore it behoved us to have a proper plan prepared, and after consultation with Charlie here, I decided to lay out my forces in a certain manner.

LIVID   Hear, hear.

EVERTON   My idea (*Consulting paper in his hand*) is this. The spectre, spook, or whatever you like to call it, will land, from God-knows-where, on the table—green attracts them—most likely in front of me. I will, using my left, get a hold on arm or neck, and force it towards Mr Poleaxe, who has experience in handling all sorts of cattle, he will concentrate on the other arm of the intruder. My friend, Scott, will then administer a couple of body punches, just, well—just, above the belt. There's no use in being too particular in handling these gentry. Little Livid here will then attack the legs of it. And by that time it should be in our hands. But if not I will blow whistle (*producing whistle*), and Mr Albermarl and Mr Parlbury will charge in, head downwards, taking it in about the same place as friend Scott's blows have landed. But I do not expect to have to call on Mr Albermarl or Mr Parlbury at all as I expect that the combined efforts of this side of the table, coupled with Little Livid's tripping-up action, will be quite sufficient. When the matter is settled, Mr Charles here will no doubt succeed in switching on the light as, of course, we will have been receiving our visitor in the dark; they never come in the light; they shun it—and we'll see where we are, that is, if the appearance is some sort of a human lunatic or practical joker. But I have an open mind and if the ghost or goblin should turn out to be quite another cup of tea then, of course, my plan falls to the ground and we grab empty air. In that connection my advice to everyone is, to act exactly as it seems best to themselves, but for God's sake, not to hit me by mistake. (*Sits down and looks round at* POLEAXE.)

POLEAXE   I am ready. And what I say is, get on with it.

CHARLES   Pardon me, one moment. Having selected the name of Squire as leader, I thought of me who should make up his band. My thoughts immediately turned on Mr Albermarl; he hasn't been so long in our midst, but since he has taken Prospect he has been very much with us. No doubt his travels under the torrid sun and other—other inconvenience, have made him glad, I say glad, to settle down in the quiet of a homely, honest, pure, straightforward, motherly village like Pullickborough.

LIVID   Pull leg!

CHARLES   No, Mr Livid, not Pull-leg-borough, that's another place altotogether. Forget it. So I selected Mr Albermarl as number two. For number three I had no difficulty in choosing one with whom, perhaps, all will not see eye to eye, but one who for sterling qualities, of straightforward speech, attention to details, and a grasp of many of the economic difficulties which beset us on every side, is hardly equalled, even by our deepest thinkers on the spot, therefore I chose comrade Parlbury, and right well did I choose. The next item had to be one of the lightweights, therefore my eye fell on our friend, Little Livid, as those of us who are old enough to remember the brave old days of yore, remember his songs, and I think it says something for his heart—a man who might have lived in Monte Carlo or any other fancy place—it says something for his heart that he should take Wompan farm and settle down to a rural life far from the glitter and the glare of former triumphs. (LIVID *slaps hard on table for applause. Others clap hands.*) Therefore I chose Little Livid, a brave man and one who, in his day, as an equilibrist, had no equal. The nearest house to Wompan was Telescope Cottage and there I found (*pointing towards* SCOTT) William Scott, Esquire, fighter in all the wars. It's quite unnecessary to explain why I chose. It's obvious that a man who never stood in his tracks and never let his wounds heal, if a battle was anywhere in his vicinity, was the man for Pullickborough to-night, so he is here. I now come to Poleaxe. I didn't speak to him, he didn't speak to me. I grasped his hand and I knew he was with us. That completes our little circle and as we have a little time to spare still (*looks at clock*) I will call on Mr Albermarl to give us his views on laying the ghost.

ALBERMARL (*rising*)   During my travelling in the desert I met from time to

time a number of leading men who told me strange tales, which in the
sober surroundings of the Club, one finds it hard to credit. But in the
East, any strange affair may happen with the suddenness of the arrival
of the sandstorm. Or it may vanish like the mirage, before our eyes, or
it may remain, a fixture like the pyramids, or an anachronism, like the
harem, or rather, as the harem seems to us.

LIVID   Hear, hear.

CHARLES   Order! Order!

ALBERMARL   A dear old friend of mine, I forget his name, had his camel
stopped outside the little town where I had been to see the Italian consul,
and signed to me to come towards him. So I turned my camel's head, a
large cream-coloured camel it was I was riding, cream-coloured with
spots on it.

LIVID   With nobs on it?

CHARLES (*rising*)   Order! Order! (*And pointing at* LIVID) You do not wish me
to name you from the chair.

(ALBERMARL *sits down.*)

LIVID (*burying face in hands and pretending to weep*)   Apologies all round.

ALBERMARL   When I got close to my old friend he said, 'Go not with the
sun on thy temples but on thy backside.'

LIVID (*rising*)   Order! Order! Order! Order! Order! I rise on a point of
order.

EVERTON   Well, sit down on it.

(LIVID *sits down.*)

ALBERMARL (*rising*)   That is a literal translation. Of course he was speaking
in Arabic, or rather an Arabic patios, of which there are a large number.
And, of course, he meant that I should turn North. 'Why, O friend?' I
said. 'Because,' he said, 'there is danger for thee and thy people to the
South. For my Secretary,' and he pointed to a small Portuguese
gentleman, who was riding a pure bred piebald Arab, 'tells me that
there are grave diggers at work to the South.' 'Whose graves are they
digging?' I said. 'Perhaps yours,' he said. 'Perhaps mine.' 'But,' I said,
'can you not send your fighting men down with canes to beat them
away?' 'No,' he said, 'I cannot, for the fighting men would only beat
the air. These gravediggers are not of flesh and bone like you or me.'
And when he said that, he bared his sinewy arm. 'They are—but thou
understandest.' I certainly did, and I did not journey with my temple to
the sun. I journeyed with my camel's head turned North. But that was
in the East, and here in theWest, gentlemen, I find myself prepared to
defy the supernatural, perhaps because I feel I am in perfectly discreet
company. (*Sits down.*)

CHARLES (*looks at clock*)   Now, Mr Scott, let's have a few remarks from your-self on the subject before, or about to be before, the meeting. I daresay, you've met some lively young spooks in your time. We'd be glad to hear how you handled them and how you think we should handle the present gent, or lady, should he, or she, see fit to put in an appearance.

SCOTT (*rising*)   All wars are the same to me, feller soldiers. And if this is war, then unloose it, I say, and let's have at it. Grasp the nettle, hit him in the midriff, for hearth and home, cottage and castle, let 'em have the cold steel. I used to sing a song in my youth:

'I fear no foe in shining armour,'

(*Croons the line. Takes out handerkerchief and sniffs into it.*) But that's a long time ago, I've got a bit long in the tooth now. However, we all know why we are here, and I, for one, say I would prefer to be meeting something solid. Well, no matter. That's only the natural opinion of an old soldier of fortune, who hasn't seen a winner for years. (*Takes out handkerchief and sniffs again.*) However, what does it matter now. We're in for it, singly and together. Now, here we are to see the fight out. There's a general idea in most people's noddles that if a crowd of good lads can face out any sort of a hobgoblin, well he's faced out and retired, moocho pronto, with his tail between his legs. I trust it is so and that after midnight's come and gone that the ghost will have gone for good. I trust and hope that may be the ending of the fight, and that we will be able to go down in the bar and toss off a parting glass before we go home to our beds, to receive tomorrow the ovation, which I have no doubt whatever the inhabitants of the village will present us with, after which we'll have enough to talk about for the rest of our lives. (*As he talks, he droops into himself, but now he pulls himself together, throws out his chest and looks boldly round the table.*) But I have one thing to say, and that is, that I never hope to stand shoulder to shoulder with a finer lot of men than I see around this table to-night. They look ready for anything. That's all I've got to say, I think. That's all. (*Sits down and droops again.*)

CHARLES   Now Mr Poleaxe. (*He looks at clock.*) We have plenty of time yet to hear your views—a man from the wide spaces like yourself, if I might say so, should have wide views.

POLEAXE (*without rising*)   What I want to say won't take long.

EVERTON (*who has been looking for some time at a newspaper cutting which he has taken from his pocket*)   It has never been made clear to me why the spirit should appear at this particular date, because to-morrow night, the 31st, would seem to be the natural day for the supernatural to come forward, the last day of October being All-Hallows Eve, you might expect . . .

ALBERMARL   But this is October 31st.

EVERTON   I don't think so, it says in the cutting particularly that the (*reading*) 'famous ghost of Pullickborough Village appears every year at midnight on October 30th' and here we have the reason for that particular date. I missed it before. (*Reading*) 'that being the anniversary of the day on which the local pundits aver mine host of the Little Bridge threw a tumbler of vitriol down his throat, having first thrown his wife and her paramour out of the window.

CHARLES   That newspaper feller needn't have dragged that last bit in. It don't do the village any good.

ALBERMARL   But this is October 31st, so we're a day late.

LIVID   I think this is the 30th. Who's got an almanac?

PARLBURY   I've got a newspaper. (*Takes paper out of pocket.*) Oh, it's a weekly.

EVERTON   (*looks in pocket and produces evening paper*)   Here we are. Absolutely right. This evenin's' paper. (*Reading*) Thursday, October 31st. We're a day late, there you are.

POLEAXE   (*rising with dignity*)   I'm off.

CHARLES   Well that's awkward. Don't go Mr Poleaxe, we'd better think about this.

(POLEAXE *sits down again.*)

CHARLES   If we give up this inquiry now we'll make the village a laughing stock, not to speak of ourselves.

LIVID   Hearty laughter, clean humour.

CHARLES   If we keep this among ourselves nobody'll know a thing about it. That cutting you read, Everton, is very old. I saw it myself when it came out. The best thing for us to do is to go through with the matter just as if everything was all right. I might as well begin filling in our report while we are waiting. (*Begins writing on sheet of foolscap.*) How's this; 'Hearing a number of fantastic tales of ghostly visitations at the Little Bridge Hotel, Pullickborough, the following Committee of local citizens was formed: John Everton, Esq., squire—(you don't mind me putting squire, do you, it looks well?).

EVERTON   Just as you like.

CHARLES   John Albermarl, Esq., Phil Poleaxe, Esq., William Scott, Esq., Erick Parlbury, Esq.

PARLBURY   Not Erick, Tom, and no esquire.

CHARLES   I always thought you were Erick.

PARLBURY   I was christened 'Erick' but the boys always call me Tom, plain Tom Parlbury.

CHARLES   But this is different. Erick with the Esquire, I should say, and Tom with the plain end. What do you think, Mr Everton?

EVERTON   Whatever Parlbury likes best himself. We ought to all go in the same.

CHARLES   Well, I'll let it go with the Esquire. It's the same for all. All get the

Esquire except me. Because I come last and have my own merry ending 'Honorary Secretary'.

(*All applaud.* CHARLES *bows.*)

ALBERMARL   And a very good one too.

CHARLES   Ernest Livid, Esquire and Charlie Charles, Honorary Secretary. (*Lays down pen.*) We'll wait until the witching hour is past and then we'll just make some sort of report and file out. In the meantime (*Looks at clock*) there's no hurry, we might 'stand easy' as we say, and have a smoke.

(*Takes out shining, sparkling, fancy sort of Woolworth's case and offers cigarettes to* EVERTON *who takes one,* CHARLES *gives him a light. All light cigarettes except* POLEAXE, *who does not smoke, and* PARLBURY *who produces briar and fills it, and* LIVID *who brings out enormous calabash pipe, all smoke and turn their chairs about in easier positions.*)

SCOTT   What about a song?

LIVID (*slapping table*) A song, a song, a song from old Bill Scott.

SCOTT   Oh no, not me, I was thinking of you.

CHARLES   No, no singing, they'll hear us outside. They won't understand.

PARLBURY   Come on Livid, never mind, give us a turn, you can keep it soft and low.

LIVID   I wrote one myself, they wouldn't touch it, Charlie Coburn was all the go then, they said it would interfere. It goes to a tune most of you know.

CHARLES   Be careful now.

LIVID (*singing very muffled—to the tune of 'Cheer, boys, Cheer!'*)

> Leer, girls, leer,
> No more of idle sorrow.
> Leer, girls, leer,
> There's never a to-morrow.

(*And then goes on Mum-mum to the tune.*) All together now.

ALL (*very muffled*)

> Leer, girls, leer,
> No more of idle sorrow.
> Leer, girls, leer,
> There's never a to-morrow.

(*As they sing they all band together down to* LIVID's *end of the table, except* CHARLES, *who remains at the top.*)

CHARLES (*looks at clock*)   Of course there's still the possibility that the appearance may show up to-night, just to annoy. Or perhaps that newspaper might have got it wrong. Sometimes the newspapers do make mistakes.

EVERSON   Well, it was taken from one of the London daily papers, I believe.

ALBERMARL   I've no doubt it's correct.

SCOTT   I don't know, I'm sure.

CHARLES   However, we might as well continue our meeting in a dignified manner. Mr Poleaxe, will you kindly give your views of the supernatural and how to handle it. We haven't yet had the pleasure of hearing you on the subject.

POLEAXE (*without rising*)   What I want to say won't take long. I'm a man of few words. We are the servants of the public to-night, and what the public wants is action. I say, give them action. (*Folds arms.*)

CHARLES (*after a pause*)   Very true, very true! Now, Mr Parlbury. We haven't had the pleasure of a discourse from you yet. Kindly let us have the benefit of your well-known and ripe experience in the realms of thought and action. (*Settles himself back in chair as though to listen to a long speech*).

PARLBURY (*without rising*)   What I have to say will not take long. Every man in this hall to-night knows my views on every subject—they are Duty, and Deeds, and Determination.

CHARLES (*after a pause*)   Very nice, I am sure, put in a nutshell. Now, Mr Ernest Livid, how do you feel about it? Take a cheerful view and throw us something off your chest to meet the occasion.

LIVID (*without rising*) I am a man of few words and what I say is, we're here for a purpose—let us fulfil that purpose.

ALBERMARL (*without rising*)   I should like to say that the public looks to us, and we are ready and determined to do our Duty.

CHARLES (*after a pause, rising*)   Well, everyone has given us the benefit of his advice and accordingly there's nothing further for us to do than to wait the remaining few moments which intervene between now and the midnight hour. This (*looking at alarum clock rather sadly*) is an ordinary alarum clock. It is set for 12 o'clock midnight. Just before it goes off, it's in the habit of giving a little rattle like a cough. I shouldn't, perhaps, say rattle, rather gruesome, eh! Sounds like the death rattle in a throat. As soon as I hear that little noise, I will switch off the light, and we'll wait in the dark for whatever may come, like the lot of bloody humbugs we are.

(*All fidget a little.* PARLBURY *cleans nails with nail cleaner.* LIVID *cleans out pipe.* SCOTT *blows nose.* POLEAXE *settles coloured handkerchief in its set position out of breast pocket.* EVERTON *looks at cutting again, tears it up and throws pieces on table, then picks them up and puts in side pocket.* CHARLES *keeps looking at the clock.* ALBERMARL *takes off fez and straightens strands of tassel with fingers raked through it. Clock gives preliminary noise. All straighten in chairs and fold arms, except* CHARLES, *who takes up electric switch and switches off light.* DARKNESS. *Long alarum goes off and as it does, ghost appears.*

Tall spectre, hands on top of head. Faint light from eyes cast sideways, not strong enough to illuminate room in any way. Spectre moves round table very slowly from right to left. Stays over each of the seven chairs for a while. Only noise an occasional deep breath from EVERTON. *After a time spectre disappears. After a few moments* EVERTON *gives a series of deep breaths close together.* LIVID *gives a short cough. The light is switched on, and with the exception of* CHARLES, *all are found sitting exactly as they were when the light was switched off and all have their arms folded, but the hair of all, including* ALBERMARL'S *moustache, and* PARLBURY'S *beard, has turned snowy white. A hand is on the end of the table still holding the switch and presently* CHARLES *comes slowly out from under the table, and takes his seat.* CHARLES'S *hair is not white. The six look at one another and after a time* CHARLES *hands up a little round looking-glass from his bag: it is passed round the table from left to right.* ALL *examine themselves carefully.* CHARLES *receives it back and puts it in his pocket.*)

CHARLES   Well, I must say you're a poor lot; if your hearts are brave your heads aren't. What did you see, or fancy you saw?

ALBERMARL   Oh, it was dreadful!

EVERTON   A dreadful sight!

CHARLES   I heard you all right, old Toffee, doing your breathing exercises. I didn't have a look myself. I wasn't taking any chances. But I'll take your word for it that you saw something, and you needn't give me any description. And (*rattling paper in front of him*) we needn't fill in any report now. Your old noddles speak for themselves. (*Tears up paper and throws it about in the air: it falls like leaves*) Well, boys, I shall open the door and say 'School's out!' Well, boys, I've been the barber and hairdresser of this village since I was a boy myself, and I never saw such a sight. You know, my name ain't Charles at all. I haven't got a name. I'm a merry foundling. I suppose the Council called me something, Old-Banana-Crate, or See-what-the-tide's-washed-up or something. But Old Charlie Charles, the barber and hairdresser of this village, adopted me and gave me his name, and taught me the business, and a good old tough old Bloke he was, too, and what a memory! He knew the 'Police News' off by heart and every head he ever chopped. I wish he was alive this night to see you. One time that good old man was telling a customer a bit of a yarn with a happy ending, and when the governor finished the customer—old party, the same age as the governor—says, 'I don't care for your story!' So the governor gives him a winner for the Gold Vase, and then this party turns on the old man and says, 'If you cut my hair nicely, don't put any nasty smelly stuff on it, and refrain from any conversation whatever,

I will give you a sixpence for yourself. When I visit a hairdresser, I do so for the purpose of getting my hair cut, not conversation!' I was ashamed, I tell you. It cut the old man to the quick. He never took any notice of anything again. That fat-headed old tool-chest killed an artist that day. I had my lesson, too. I've never troubled any of you old fat-heads with my talk the few times any of you have sat in my chairs, and that's not often, with your safety razors! And some of you've got safety hair-cutters, too. Though Little Ernie comes and has his hair waved sometimes. But you know me, as everyone does, for a silent barber—silent, efficient and respectful. I haven't bothered you with my old talk, but I've listened to your blasted old balderdash because I was drawing good money for the job. And what's more you'll come to me regular in future, and you know you will, unless you up-stakes altogether and shift from the village. If you do, I won't follow you. I've listened to your old stuff long enough. While I've been the silent, efficient, respectful barber, you haven't been silent, you lot of old hear-me-outs. Albermarl, with the time he bought the sack of Scaramooches in the town of Bizzoff, or was it Buzaboowussy? And the other time he played the Jews' harp outside the har-har-harem. I've heard both them tales and I don't expect to hear them again. And honest Tom Parlbury! How he self-educated himself by reading the works of Comrade Mr Shaw. Those were the days, eh, Comrade Mr Parlbury? And you told me how you learnt to love cricket playing on the village green, or was it that you imbibed it with your mother's milk? I didn't have Old Cricket or any Old Mother. I came out of the foundry. You'd say, I suppose, if you were in my place, that you came out naked, and with your bare hands were the architect of the edifice of your own fortune. Well, I didn't come out of the Home naked. I had a pair of corduroy trousers, too short or too long like the ladies dresses; a waistcoat of tweed material, a good hard shirt, a jacket made of God-knows-what, and a cap to make Comrade Shaw laugh. He's a joker, so he ought to see a joke, even if the joke is on a little boy's head. I came out like that and old Charlie did the erecting of the architectural edifice on which you bunch of lads have put the topside pinnacle to-night. What you call a cupola with a clock in it, a clock with four faces, all looking different ways and all funny. And then there was Ernie Livid with his funny stories (he had two), with happy endings. I'd heard them first in the foundry, but I laughed, oh, how I laughed!

EVERTON We've had enough of this.

CHARLES Silence! Your time hasn't come yet, Old Toffee. And poor old Billy Scott—we musn't forget him. A great reader working his way along slow, but sure. He was going to read 'Deadwood Dick' and Jesse James, when he'd read all there was to read about Charles Dickens. He was doing more than read it, he was learning it off. I don't think he was in my shop more than three times, but each time

Paul Dombey died. I'm sorry to be so rough, Billy. I don't speak for your good, I wouldn't insult myself by saying so. I'm just holding the mirror up to nature. And nature if he don't like it, nature can county court me. But it don't matter. Next time you come you can kill Paul Dombey again. But, mind you, once again only. Hello, Poleaxe, the strong, the silent, the wide open spaces; the meshes must have been pretty wide open when they let you through. I suppose you are *just* human. You're a good listener, to yourself. But that doesn't strain your ears much. A man of few words and some of those he can't spell. (POLEAXE *makes a movement to his hip pocket*) Now, don't go reaching for an imaginary six-shooter, you know it isn't there, and if it was, you know you wouldn't shoot me with it. And you know (*looking round at all*) none of you images are going to do anything to me, because you're all busy thinking of what you *could* do to me. And the sort of thinking any of you is capable of is entirely your own little affair. Even Comrade Commune Parlbury couldn't get himself to join a general riot with the object of putting me where the good niggers go. And Old Toffee wouldn't let you; he'd veto anything that had any kind of a jump to it. I'm not forgetting you old Everton toff. Toff Everton, the man who invented standing still and reading yesterday's paper to-morrow evening. Our popular squire. Well, if he's a squire, he has to be popular, hasn't he? The name's enough, it goes with the job—popularity does.

EVERTON You're a worm, a common worm!

CHARLES That's only one of my names, my lad.

ALBERMARL What you want is backshees (*reaching for pocket book and opening it*) I've seen your sort of blackmailer before and let me tell you, in the East there are men without a shoe to their foot or a camel to their name, who could beat you blindfolded. And another thing let me tell you . . .

CHARLES Now then, Old Jack Bashuus, I told you I wouldn't let you tell me anything any more, and keep your backshees for poor old Billy Scott, who never backsheesus a winner these hard times.

PARLBURY I'm absolutely done with you.

CHARLES Why, you bunch of old fools, don't you know you're Brave Men. The Spirit was willing, but the colouring matter supplied by nature was weak and disappeared when wanted. But I'll show you how Art can put right the mistakes of nature.

(*Rising with ink-stand in hand and approaching* ALBERMARL. *He has taken two shaving brushes from his pocket. He stands behind* PARLBURY *and shows him black ink.*)

I'm afraid you'll all have to be a black-haired flock of happy ravens!

(*Behind* ALBERMARL's *back; dips shaving brush in red ink and colours hair red. Making faces and winks at others not to give the joke away. Others laugh at first and victim laughs, just thinking the idea of inking hair at all is funny. But others sober up their faces.* CHARLES *leaves* ALBERMARL *and goes over to back of* PARLBURY, *half-whispering,* 'I'll keep it dark, nice and dark.' *Lets him see black-inked shaving brush, and winking towards* ALBERMARL, *who is busy looking down at his white moustache. He proceeds to red-ink* PARLBURY's *hair.*)

ALBERMARL   What about my moustache? Aren't you going to black it?
CHARLES   After I've done all the others, I want to make certain of not using up the Ravens Renovator. I'll come back and give your moustache a light touch or two, and on your beard Comrade. (*Tapping* PARLBURY *on the head with brush. He then turns to* LIVID *and half-whispers to him*) Don't laugh until I've been all round.

(LIVID *nudges him with elbow and smiles.* CHARLES *red-inks his hair also. Next* CHARLES *moves to* BILL SCOTT *and whispers something in his ear. He is sitting crumpled into himself and his head is red-inked.* CHARLES *then turns to* POLEAXE. POLEAXE *turns round to meet him, looking very nasty.*)

POLEAXE   You understand—no jokes!
CHARLES (*looking towards others*)   I take the trouble of blacking these gentlemen's hair just because I'm a hairdresser—and you say 'No jokes!'
POLEAXE (*looking solemn*)   I was thinking of something else.

(*His head is red-inked.*)

CHARLES   And last but not least, the squire, who when all is said and done, in spite of Bolshie Parlbury and his Red flag, is the squire, our mainstay and our pride; the most dignified personage in our village (*half-whispers in his ear*) and the only dignified one in the room.

(*Proceeds to red-ink* EVERTON's *head.* CHARLES *then walks over to coal-box and empties black ink into coals and throws brushes in also.*)

ALBERMARL   What about my moustache? Are you going to touch it up?
PARLBURY   And my beard?

(ALL *the others laugh, and instantly suppress their laughter.*)

CHARLES   Oh, I clean forgot you! But you'll find it doesn't really matter; you'll be as well off.

(ALL *the others suppress their laughter.*)

ALBERMARL   I think, Charles, you are damn careless. (*Suddenly sees all the others again with their red hair*) But I don't know that you are.

PARLBURY (*who is looking down ruefully at white beard, looks up, looks at* ALBERMARL *and all round at the others*) Albermarl, you're being funnier than you ever were in Buzzobuzuso, or whatever Charles calls the place.

(*The whole crowd continue for some time looking round the table at the others, and subsiding into solitary laughter.*)

CHARLES (*resuming his chair at head of table; raps table with fist*)   Silence, now, while your raven locks are drying. I won't tell you any more about yourselves. I've finished that. But I might say of myself that I consider myself a man of courage, a self-made man of courage; my courage is entirely of my own invention. Some of you might not appreciate it. It's a work of art. Talking about works of art, I'm sure there's one you're all well able to appreciate. (*Gets up his leather bag, takes out looking-glass and hands it to* ALBERMARL) Have a look at the tableau and pass on the reflector.

(*The glass is passed round the table and* ALL *know the truth.* CHARLES *takes back looking-glass and folds his arms in a defiant manner.*)

CHARLES   Well, what are you going to do about it?

EVERTON   Worm!

LIVID   You said that before.

PARLBURY   Dirty worm!

LIVID   That's better. But it's not enough.

ALBERMARL   Kismet! We'd better get the two taxis and go home.

POLEAXE   And will *you* go out and order the taxis?

EVERTON   And there's no use asking Charles.

CHARLES   Old Toffee, you called me a worm, and Comrade Parlbury called me a dirty worm!

PARLBURY   I'll take back the dirty. I can't take back worm, because I didn't originate it.

EVERTON   Well, in the interest of peace, I'll take back worm. I'll say you're not a worm.

POLEAXE   No, take back nothing. I don't agree.

LIVID   Hear, hear! I am a man of few words. Take back nothing.

ALBERMARL   Well, we must do something. Send for Jimmy. Waiters are used to all sorts of things; they're dumb by nature, and even if they weren't, nobody would believe a word they say.

SCOTT   I believe Jimmy's got a heart. I'll appeal to it.

PARLBURY   You'll do nothing of the kind. That'd spoil everything. We'll just get Everton to tell him to get the taxis and keep his mouth shut.

I'll call him. (*Goes to door and shouts*) Waiter! Waiter! Waiter! Jimmy! Jim-e-e-e-e.

(*Enter* JIMMY. *At first when he looks round he is doubled up with suppressed and delighted laughter.*)

EVERTON   Pull yourself together and take no notice of anything you see here in this room. Your position as a waiter should, if you have the true interest of your profession to heart, inure you to all strange sights. Sufficient for you be it, that your orders are to get Muldock's two taxis to deliver us to our respective homes and bring the taxis round to the door, but I implore you to bring us in our hats.

(JIMMY *goes out and returns with cricket cap with badge, small black felt Trilby hat, a hard felt black hat, a blue beret and a large-sized tweed cap.* ALBERMARL *has his fez and* POLEAXE *his sombrero. Exit* WAITER. ALL *try and cover up as much of red ink hair as possible with hats and caps, but it is no use.* EVERTON'S *cricket cap leaves all back exposed;* PARLBURY'S *black felt very small.* SCOTT'S *hard felt and* LIVID'S *beret all are quite inadequate to cover up red heads.* CHARLES *slaps his own tweed cap cheerfully on the back of his head and hands round his little looking-glass for each to try and see themselves.*)

(JIMMY *enters.*)

ALBERMARL   Well, have you got the taxis? Have they got the hoods up?
JIMMY   No, sir. They're down.
ALBERMARL   Well, speaking very distinctly, Go And Get Them Put Up. You damn fool!

(*Exit* JIMMY. EVERTON, ALBERMARL, PARLBURY, LIVID, SCOTT *and* POLEAXE *draw apart and pace up and down gloomily.* CHARLES *sits in his chair, looking at them sleepily with his arms folded.*)

(*Re-enter* JIMMY.)

JIMMY   The chauffeurs say the hoods are broken and they can't get them up.
ALBERMARL   Now, what are we going to do? (*To* JIMMY) Don't stand grinning there—and suggest something.
JIMMY (*composing face into solidity, which expression he keeps all the rest of the time he is on the scene*) Shall I go and get Harvey's cab?
EVERTON   In heaven's name, go!

(*Exit* JIMMY.)

SCOTT   But the cab'll only hold four inside.

ALBERMARL   Two will have to wrap their heads up in something and ride outside, one on the box and one on the roof. That's the only thing we can do.

PARLBURY   Yes, that's the only way.

LIVID (*striking attitude of Martin Harvey*)   It is the only way. And you two are the only ones to carry it off—Albermarl with the fizz on his head and Comrade Tom Parlbury, Honest Tom, the idol of the Toilers. I propose these two gentlemen have the honour of the box seat and the roof of the cab.

SCOTT   I second that.

LIVID   Those in favour say 'Aye'.

(ALL *except* ALBERMARL *and* PARLBURY *say* 'Aye'.)
(CHARLES *does not speak, he is dozing.*)

LIVID   The 'Ayes' have it.

(*Re-enter* JIMMY.)

JIMMY   I sent a boy down to Harvey's to turn him out and the taxi men want a bob apiece for turning out themselves.

EVERTON (*putting hand in pocket and taking out two shillings*)   Give them this money and tell them to go home and go home quietly.

JIMMY   I'll tell them, but I'm afraid they won't go. You see, gentlemen, the villagers are getting up and dressing or putting top coats and jackets over their nightwear, and hurrying out, and the first ones are sitting in the taxis. You see, sirs, when the taxis came through the village at this hour of the night the inhabitants, being used to keeping early hours themselves, thought something special was happening.

(*Motor horns outside.*)

Ah, that's to let us know that Harvey's cab's at the door. Have you, gentlemen, decided whose to go on the top?

LIVID   Parlbury and Albermarl have been elected.

ALBERMARL   That's most unfair.

(*Motor horns outside.*)

PARLBURY   I don't care. I'll take the roof, but for God's sake, Jimmy, give us a bit of something to wrap round our heads a bit.

(*Exit* JIMMY.)

(*He returns with two lace antimacassars, which he drapes carefully round heads and lower part of the faces of* PARLBURY *and* ALBERMARL, *hiding moustache and beard.*)

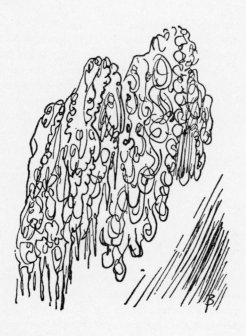

EVERTON   It is time for us to go.

(ALL *push* ALBERMARL *and* PARLBURY *to the front and then move out in the following order,* LIVID, SCOTT, POLEAXE, EVERTON.)

JIMMY (*to* EVERTON)   The last to leave the ship!

(EVERTON *turns in a temper and kicks* JIMMY *more or less viciously in the coat tails.* JIMMY *cringes to receive the kick, then suddenly turns round, throws off his coat and gives* EVERTON *a thump on the nose.* EVERTON, *off his balance, falls into the arms of* POLEAXE, *who reaches for imaginary revolver. Others crowd round.*)

LIVID (*coming to the front*)   Now, let by-gones be by-gones.

(*Takes a hand of* EVERTON *and* JIMMY *and makes them shake. Tableau with* PARLBURY *standing slightly behind* LIVID.)

PARLBURY   Brute strength and intellectuality shake hands. All's right with the world, lead on! (*He points to exit.*)

(They file out, in this order: ALBERMARL, SCOTT, POLEAXE, LIVID, EVERTON, PARLBURY. *As they go out they* ALL *tip* JIMMY. *After they have gone,* JIMMY *slowly puts on coat and wakes up* CHARLIE *with some difficulty, gives him his bag, and shows him out: picks up torn paper, puts it in coal box, straightens chairs, and then goes out himself. Re-enter* JIMMY *with ghost mask and ghost costume, open to show his waiter's clothes underneath. He is leading by the hand pale, tall, willowy type of girl, about 25, dressed in black, carrying a typewriter under her arm. She is the clerk of the hotel.* JIMMY *takes off mask and puts it on the table.* CLERK *sits down to table in chair at the head, nearest entrance; puts her typewriter in position and puts paper in and looks up at* JIMMY, *bright and ready.* JIMMY *dictates, striding up and down and round the table as he does so.)*

JIMMY Chapter eight. 'As turns the Worm at Eventide.' Quotation mark and 'anonymous'. In my last chapter I beguiled the reader, and I trust I did beguile him, for the worm-like sufferings of another, are as balm and wormwood—no, not that—not wormwood; balm and—balm and—balm and—balm and what? I've lost it. Sufferings of another are a joy untold to the observer from the safe vantage place of—no, not vantage place, it sounds like some sort of silly joke about lawn tennis—'love all' and that sort of thing—a joy untold to the observer from the Olympian heights of safety in the front—oh dear, oh dear! in the front row of the best seats, which surround the arena. That's not very good. I'll come back to it and alter it later on. Surround the arena, where the victim's heart throbs. In short, in my last I described the indignities I had put up with from bull-necked, ignorant, inaesthetic clods. But the point in my career at which I had now arrived will show the reader what . . .'

CLERK Jimmy, I love you.

(Rises, catches him by the neck and pulls him into the seat beside her.)

JIMMY *(looking at her stiffly)* Why?
CLERK Because you're so funny.
JIMMY Well, that's useful, anyway.

(CLERK ruffles up his hair, making it stand up on the top of his head.)
(When play is in an arena he takes a pair of white gloves from his pocket puts them on and from under the cloth of the table takes the card. Folds it to stand up on centre of table to be read from both sides. He takes off gloves and throws them on the table.)
(CLERK takes up mask and prepares to carry it away, but JIMMY takes it from

her after a little struggle. He offers her the typewriter; she does not take it. Exit CLERK.)

(JIMMY *puts on mask again with face toward the back looking toward the audience. Exit* JIMMY.)

CURTAIN.

The Old Sea Road

A Play in Three Acts

CHARACTERS

JOHN NOLAN ⎱ *labourers.*
JOHN DOLAN ⎰

POSTMAN.

JOSEPHINE CURRAN, *school-teacher.*

JULIA *pupil.*

AMBROSE OLDBURY.

POLICEMAN.

MOLLY GILLANE.

CHRISTOPHER CONNOR.

BALLAD–SINGER.

JOHN DWYER *student.*

MICHAEL OF THE SONG.

ANDY DOWD *publican.*

('Left or 'Right' directions are as seen by the Audience.)

SUGGESTIONS

All the characters should be dressed in fairly dull coloured clothes. Except for the dark plum-coloured velvet dress of Julia, and the rather pale blue costume of Josephine and the small dark green muffler of the ballad-singer.

The sky, sea and land are brighter than the people.

The speech is slow, and not high, until, towards the end of the second Act, when Ambrose is shouting at times; last Act, speech determined and crisp.

'BELIEVE ME, IF ALL THOSE ENDEARING YOUNG CHARMS'
from the strings only.

ACT ONE

Scene 1: *Heathery grassy slope in foreground, with some out-crop rocks. Old turf cutting on right. At top of slope is the road. Beyond the sea. Early morning yellow light from left. There is a lark singing overhead at intervals for a while. Faint sound of sea, every now and then, breaking on the rocks beyond, and below, the road. This goes on all through the play.*

SECTION OF SCENE IN THE OLD SEA ROAD

(Enter Left, by road, NOLAN and DOLAN, two country-road workers each about 60 years of age, but both hale men, black haired with very little grey, in working clothes worn and old. NOLAN has a soft felt hat, DOLAN an old cheese-cutter cap, both men are clean-shaven. NOLAN has not got a red nose but a redder face than DOLAN. They are both, at first, smoking old briar pipes. Both have long-tailed shovels with which they begin spreading a few stones on the road, which stones they take from off stage on the Right.)

NOLAN   Well, this is a Hell of an old road in the morning early. But *(he stops)* hark to the lark. That's a noted lad, he's up early getting the sun on his breast, and watching you and me breaking our backs, our poor old backs, for a blasted contractor. However, it's a long road has no turning, and some day the Nolan's will come into their own my boy. If I was in Boston now I suppose I'd be drunk, even allowing for the difference of the time.

DOLAN   You're too fond of the drink.

NOLAN   I'm wedded to it. But the wedding was celebrated in a Registry Office on a Registrary till, and now we're broke, Dolan, my old friend, and I wish I'd never left America.

DOLAN   Aye, the Land of the Free.

NOLAN   And the Home of the Brave. But (*Looking Left*) I see a burst of light in the gloom, Andy is after opening the door, and taking a look at the world he owns. He's had his morning bath. I can get his first hard shot (*sniffing the air*) he must have taken it pure. (*Carefully placing shovel alongside road on slope*) Come on we'll touch him for a morning zephyr.

DOLAN   No, not till the sun is over the main yard, and that's a while yet.

NOLAN   To hell with main yards. I'm for the bright breezes that blow o'er Erin's Isle so early in the morning oh, and the sun that shines through a half one, so early in the morning oh.

(*Trips off Left in road.* DOLAN *goes on working, humming over to himself soft and low*

> With me hi fol de diddle I do
> With me hi fol de diddle di do
> With me fol de di
> With me fol de do
> With me fol de diddle diddle
> Diddle diddle diddle di do

over and over again three or four times with silences in between, in a miserable doleful voice.)

(*Enter* NOLAN *by road, slowly. He has been to the village and back, and takes up shovel.*)

NOLAN   That Andy deserves to find himself begging his bread with his tongue hanging out. He's got a heart bent in on itself. He wouldn't give me the sight of the squeeze of a rag, he said I was too early for them follies.

(*Goes on slowly, crossing Right, getting a shovel full of stones and spreading them Left.*)

Well, it's a wonderful thing the inventions we have in the world these times. Did you see the photograph in the paper of the flying boat that's able to cross the Atlantic in the fore part of a day. They'd hardly have time to enjoy the sea air. So you see now the improvements they put on us aren't so grand at all. Did you hear about the man that won the sweep? He didn't know what to do with the money. God help him. Ignorance is a dreadful affliction. I'd sooner be dead than ignorant. Reading is a great invention. Where would you and I be if we didn't have the newspapers to be reading, and what would we know about racehorses, and the great events of the universe, if it wasn't for the newspapers spreading their education everywhere? Now my niece, Miss Julia, well, the amount of intelligence that that innocent child has absorbed from reading the newspaper would astonish you. When I was in Chicago I never had time to throw my eye over a newspaper at all, all bustle and work, and enjoy yourself. But I was laying the ground work of an education, on which I've since been able, here at home, in my native land, to build up—to build up my present position. But it's time I retired, but the times we live in won't let me. Fancy me, let alone yourself, spending the whole blessed day laying stones on the Old Sea Road. We spread them here, and in the fullness of time they roll down the hill until they reach the charming village of Cahirma- hone, where they lie night and day to trip up the feet of the ancient warriors of the place—well what about going down to our breakfast. Though in the days of old I never took breakfast on an empty stomach. Well, come on, we're for it.

(NOLAN and DOLAN shoulder their shovels and exit Left, by road.)

Curtain.

Scene 2: *The Old Sea Road as before, about an hour later. Sky brighter, sea sounding at intervals.*

(*Enter* POSTMAN—*elderly man—Left, by road. He moves slowly along road to Right, reading postcards and looking into ends of circulars, stopping from time to time and looking out to sea. He turns stones, lately laid on road, about critically with his stick. Exit Right along road. After a time enter Left on road* JOSEPHINE CURRAN, *about 22 years of age, good-looking school-teacher; no hat. She is wearing a rather pale blue costume, and is carrying an old dispatch case in right hand, first finger keeping case shut; in her left hand she holds a school-book and a bright paper-covered novel. She moves along road toward Right. Enter* JULIA, *Left on road. Girl about eleven years of age, in dark plum-coloured dress. She skips along until she is near to* JOSEPHINE, *when she walks sedately behind for a little. Then* JOSEPHINE *looks, pretending to have only just noticed* JULIA.)

JOSEPHINE (*speaking rather nicely*) Good-morning Julia, have you your lessons off?

JULIA   Perfectly, all but the Euclid. There I'm stumped.

JOSEPHINE   Well of course, in a sense that's a speciality for you. But you'll soon get the way it goes. (*In a more natural voice, while she stops and looks out over the bog left and right*) Did you hear the bees buzzing about the heather? That's a happy sound, Miss Julia. (*Turning to the sea*) There's the old sea, listen how he sounds.

JULIA   He makes a noise like a child that'd be eating stirabout.

JOSEPHINE   Stirabout yourself, pupil and teacher will be late for school.

(*Exit Right on road hand in hand and swinging them. After a while NOLAN and DOLAN enter Left by road, with shovels, and begin spreading the stones about.*)

DOLAN (*looking away Right*)   Here's the joker coming. What's the game on with him to-day I wonder?

NOLAN   The story he put out about Jacksport being blown up with an earthquake got a lot of innocent people to go to see the hole in the ground.

DOLAN   Yes, I nearly went myself.

NOLAN   Well, I thought of it, but I asked how it was we didn't get a stir here at all, and he said it was a local earthquake. Well, I thought to myself, that'd have to be a very small earthquake that'd only jolt one town in (*with an oratorical voice*) the length and breadth of Holy Ireland, the Home of Saints and Chisslers. The Grand National was a good idea; (*laughs*) a brewery bursting and flooding the course so that there was no race, but it didn't take with the people any more than the earthquake did.

DOLAN   I don't suppose more than five people, most of them childer, started for the earthquake.

NOLAN   And young Andy was the only one who went to the railway to countermand his ticket for Liverpool.

DOLAN (*looking again Right*) Come on up to him. He's standing now looking out over the ocean and plotting some mouldy old divilment. We're finished here, we'll spread the heap beyond. (*Moves off Right.*)

NOLAN (*moving with him off Right*)   And now we'll get first whiff of whatever he's up to, the common omadhawn.

DOLAN   He's what they call a practical joker, God help him.

(*Both exit Right.*)

(*After a time enter Left, by road, POLICEMAN in uniform, passes along road and exits Right. After a while, enter Right on road, POLICEMAN and AMBROSE OLDBURY. AMBROSE is wearing a tweed hat, dark blue college*) *blazer, with shield on pocket, loose flannel trousers, soft collar and dull coloured tie, all rather slovenly. He is a man about forty, rather unshaven and smokes a pipe. He offers* POLICEMAN *cigarette from a packet which he takes from his pocket, stops and gives the* POLICEMAN *a light, shading hand from sea breeze.*)

POLICEMAN   You know, Captain, you don't want to worry the people here too much, they're not able to stand it. It amuses us at the barracks, but the unfortunate people here are not able to grasp things, and what you want is to go easy.

(*They move along road, towards the Left.*)

AMBROSE   But they liked the first one.

POLICEMAN   Those that went to see the result of the quake didn't, and in a way nobody did. You see they don't take the joke like you do. It's all the point of view, and what you ought to do now is to go down and take a bit of a sleep in the back room at Andy's, don't keep staying about in the open. There's a gale coming up and it's all not too good. You want rest, and the whole place wants rest. A couple of practical jokes is enough for a small place like this for a while.

(*Exit both along road, Left.*)

(*Enter Right from bog, not by road,* CHRISTOPHER CONNOR, *elderly peasant in worn old clothes, and stick to help him along. Also enter Right from bog* MOLLY GILLANE, *elderly woman, neatly dressed in old blue serge bodice and skirt; old checked apron.*)

MOLLY   Now Christopher, if you're long away the crows will have the spuds ate on you.

CHRISTOPHER   Oh I gave them a good extra scaring the last five minutes, that'll keep them in their place, wherever that is, for a time anyway. I'll have the tobacco or I'll perish.

MOLLY   It's an awful thing the slaves men are to the pipe.

(CHRISTOPHER *hobbles up on to the road with a kind of gay swing and goes off Left.* MOLLY *gazes after him, then out to sea, gives a couple of happy sighs and exits Right, over bog. Enter Left along road,* BALLAD-SINGER, *worn clothes, small old green muffler, has coloured ballads under his arm, waves off to* MOLLY.)

BALLAD-SINGER (*shouting*)   Will you buy a ballad mam? Will you buy a ballad mam?

(Enter MOLLY, *Right, over bog. She stands on the bog* BALLAD-SINGER, *stands on the road above her. He hands her down his bundle of ballads. She goes through them, chooses three, gives the* BALLAD-SINGER *money which she takes from a little bag with a string round it, which she takes from a pocket in her petticoat.)*

BALLAD-SINGER   The blessings of God on you mam, and safe home.
MOLLY   And to you sir, also.

(Exit BALLAD-SINGER *Left, and reading one of the ballads as he goes.)*
(Exit MOLLY *over bog, Right.)*

Curtain.

ACT TWO

Scene: *Same as Act One, but later; it is getting towards evening. The sunlight is gone more to the Right. As the scene goes on the sky becomes wilder, lurid. The sun is sinking.*

(JOHN DWYER, *discovered sitting Left of centre on bank. He is a young man, he wears a large tweed cap, he is dressed in an easy dim coloured tweed suit, trousers, not plus fours, turned down collar, dark blue tie. He is reading a book, and sometimes referring to another book, a dictionary perhaps. He is smoking a cigarette, he lights another from the butt of it, he brings his knees up and makes himself comfortable for his reading. After a time enter Right along road* MICHAEL OF THE SONG, *a tall rangey man past middle age, but well built, dressed in worn clothes like the* BALLAD-SINGER, *but no muffler, old soft felt hat. He stands gazing down at* DWYER.)

MICHAEL The little student. Is it Nat Gould you're studying or astronomy?

JOHN Neither, but (*folding his arms in a Napoleonic manner*) in my time I have studied both.

MICHAEL Good boy, you haven't got a bit of meat on you, just the smallest bit would be acceptable?

JOHN No, I'm sorry I haven't. What would I be having meat on me here for, at this time of day?

MICHAEL (*sitting down beside* JOHN *on his left hand*) I just thought you might chance to be the proud possessor of a small piece, but no matter.

JOHN Have a cigarette?

(*Hands cigarette case, a little black Japanese Woolworth's case and match-box.* MICHAEL *lights cigarette, but after a little he lets it out, and making certain that it is out, places it carefully on the ground beside him.*)

MICHAEL I suppose Cahirmahone is the same as ever it was?

JOHN Pretty much. But though it's only down there (*jerking head Left*) I wasn't in it this summer. Jacksport's more exciting.

MICHAEL You're right there. Jacksport for excitement. I floated out of it this evening after only ten hours in the place. I was like to die of the throb of my heart. I didn't note you there, but to tell the truth, most of the time I was sleeping.

JOHN Well, it's livelier than Cahir, though that doesn't say much.

MICHAEL Aren't I saying it's exciting. Why the whole world's exciting.

149

If it was the least tint more exciting the unfortunate inhabitants would be exploding into fragments making star sparks of themselves.

JOHN   Well the world wags.

MICHAEL   It's you that's the wag.

JOHN   Why are you so hard on Jacksport, and why did you leave it so soon?

MICHAEL   Well, I had a song twenty-one verses and all about nothing but your old waggin' world, and a crumb or two from the starry heavens. Me old song went to a melodeon I had. My idea was to sing my song and get the people interested in me, and after that I planned to set up a small dancing school, but as soon as I hit the second verse of my song the unfortunate people thought it was personal and they never let me finish, and they'd give me neither bite nor sup, nor so much as a tanner on the old melodeon. Well I paid less for it, I got it as the price of my song—and perhaps it was the price of me too—from a kind of a travelling man with a Grand National muffler on him, I met him in the County Kerry a while ago. He said it had a broken heart anyway. Don't tell the man if you know him, but I threw the heartbroken melodeon to the tide crossing the old mill bridge. Let it mix its noble bellow and its small moan with ocean's sentimental sighs. (*Listens to sound of sea and jerks thumb over shoulder*) Well, John?

(JOHN *gives a little start and looks up with a smile.*)

MICHAEL   I see your name on your book large and fine 'John Dwyer'; are you a student of philosophy, John?

JOHN   Mathematics is supposed to be my subject.

MICHAEL   Well, gaze on this (*placing his hand spread out on his own breast*). A philosophy. The thing not the student of it. But it's souring on me, I don't know if I was to take up mathematics if it might ease my troubled spirits. But I doubt if the old skull (*slapping his hand to his brow*) would stand it. I've tried poetry: The sky is blue, the grass is green, the greenest grass I ever seen. 'I thank you mam,' says Dan, to the muse of poetry I suppose. We're not told what colour Dan was or the muse herself for that matter. Keep pointing at the blade of grass, they say, and presently you'll see two blades sprout where one sprouted before. The commercial instinct.

JOHN   Isn't that a necessity?

MICHAEL   God give you sense, and don't interrupt me, you and your commercial instinct. Isn't that an attempt to roll all the instincts into one big instinct, like the old-fashioned Transport Union? To Hell with the departmental store, all under one roof. I'm under my own roof, and I don't want yours, nor to interfere with yours. Every man under his own thatch and the ladies (*looking Right*) under their own, if you like. (*Taking off hat and putting it beside him on the ground.*)

(Enter Right along road MISS JULIA *and* JOSEPHINE.)

JOHN *(pulling off cap and putting it on again)* Hello, Miss Julia and Miss Curran.
The day's work over you return to the salubrious village of Cahirmahone. I trust, Miss Curran, you have not overtaxed the willing intellect
of Miss Julia unduly, unJulia-ly.

(Laughs, so does JOSEPHINE; JULIA *doesn't.)*

JOSEPHINE   Julia is my star pupil right enough.
JOHN *(indicating* MICHAEL)   My friend here, and I, have been discussing
philosophy and in fact all the highbrow . . . er . . . er . . .

*(*MICHAEL *lifts hat from ground and waves it in courtesy to
ladies when indicated by* JOHN.)

MICHAEL   Ingredients.
JOSEPHINE *(coming to edge of road and looking straight down at* MICHAEL *who
leaning back, looks straight up at her)* I hope you didn't tell him anything
that wasn't good for him.
MICHAEL   I never thought of that Miss.

*(*JULIA *and* JOSEPHINE *move Left along road.)*
(Enter Left, POLICEMAN *in plain clothes.)*

POLICEMAN *(taking off soft felt hat to* JOSEPHINE)   Good evening Miss Curran.
JOSEPHINE   Good evening.
POLICEMAN   I hope you're getting your health in the sea air.
JOSEPHINE   Oh fine.

(Exit JULIA *and* JOSEPHINE, *Left.* POLICEMAN *turns to
sea and looks out over it.)*

MICHAEL   Plain clothes cop.
JOHN   You recognized him.
MICHAEL   It's a miracle *(Puts on hat).*
JOHN   It's a gift.
MICHAEL   It is indeed.
POLICEMAN *(turning round and coming over to edge of road Right of centre and
looking down on* JOHN *and* MICHAEL)   Good evening, men.
JOHN   Good evening to you.

(Exit POLICEMAN, *Right.)*
(After a little while.)

MICHAEL   Authority passes on its way. (*Looking Right*) Authority returns linked with convenience.

(*After a while. Enter Right, on road,* POSTMAN *and* POLICEMAN. POSTMAN *nearest front.*)

JOHN   Did you have any letters for me?

POSTMAN   I left a couple for you beyond?

MICHAEL   Any good ones for me?

POSTMAN (*rummaging in his bag*)   There's a couple of advertisements here that nobody wants, addressed wrong. What's your name sir?

MICHAEL   Michael.

JOHN   Michael of the Song.

POSTMAN   Oh there's nothing for you me bold feller, not in Jacksport, good night to you. I'm on my way with this strange young man. I'm directing him to the lovely village of Cahirmahone, he doesn't know, the way.

(*Exit with* POLICEMAN *Left along road.*)

MICHAEL   Very chatty.

JOHN   Will you come down into Cahir with me, and have a bit of supper? I'm sure Andy'll be able to stir up his Missus enough to give us a slap of bacon and eggs.

MICHAEL   Ah no, thank you. I think I'll take a bathe.

JOHN   You can't bathe on this coast, it's all rocks and cliffs.

MICHAEL   Oh it's not in the sea I'll bathe. But here (*pointing Right*) in the old bog hole. Have you got a towel on you?

JOHN   I have not. What would I be having a towel for up here at this time of day?

MICHAEL   I didn't know. I thought you might.

(*He goes Right, taking off his hat and coat and putting them down on the ground. Then sitting down takes off his boots, worn boots, and his socks, good ones, one bright blue, the other grey. He goes down hole in bank, Right, and presently throws up trousers, and standing up, so that his body shows over edge of hole in bank, pulls off his shirt and puts that on bank sinks down and splashes about, looks up with dripping arms, takes tufts of grass to dry himself.*)

MICHAEL   What about a touch of a poem, what about my Dark Rosaleen Iween, sheen, has been?

JOHN   My dark Rosaleen.

MICHAEL   My life, my hope, my soul of souls, my hope of hopes, my Dark Rosaleen.

(JOHN *standing up gives the whole of the 'Dark Rosaleen,' with passion, while* MICHAEL *goes on drying himself and dressing, occasionally stopping to listen with a bunch of grass in his hand, another time with his shirt in his hand.* MICHAEL *comes up and lies down on bank.*)

JOHN   Have a cigarette?

(*Hands case to* MICHAEL *who takes a cigarette.* JOHN *lights it for him,* MICHAEL *smokes a little and then lays down cigarette beside him as before, having put it out with his finger.*)

JOHN   What about coming down to Cahir for a bit of supper now.
MICHAEL   No thank you, I think I'll take a bit of a rest.
JOHN   (*looking at watch*)   Better come on down and have a drink anyway. (*Looking at watch again*) It's time I was off for Jacksport. But I'll have time to go down to Cahir for a while anyway, and I'll borrow a bicycle or something.
MICHAEL   Not at all man, you're best chance is to make for Jacksport while the evening is young, and (*looking off Left*) anyway two figures approach.
JOHN   (*looking off Left*)   One's an old lad called Christopher Connor and the other's the Great Practical Joker, Ambrose Oldbury.
MICHAEL   Is that who's in it.

(*Enter Right along road,* NOLAN *and* DOLAN. *Enter Left, along road,* CHRISTOPHER *and* AMBROSE.)

JOHN   Good-evening Connor. Mister Oldbury, I hope you're not deceiving Christopher in any way.
AMBROSE   It couldn't be done.

(NOLAN *and* DOLAN *lean on their spades towards Right, waiting for some practical joke to begin.*)

JOHN   Now did you find any earthquakes down in Cahir?
AMBROSE   Not a sign of one. (*Looking down at* MICHAEL) Is our friend here ill?
MICHAEL   (*waving his hand in a half salute to* AMBROSE) Not at all.
AMBROSE   I'm glad to hear it. I thought you looked a bit pale. (*Turning to* NOLAN *and* DOLAN) Still on the stony paths my lads.
DOLAN   Stony enough.
NOLAN   Stonybroke. Well, good night all.

(*Moves off Left along road with* DOLAN.)

CHRISTOPHER (*to* AMBROSE)   God save you kindly.

(*Goes off Right front by bog.* JOHN *gets up, puts books in pocket, climbs up bank and goes along road, Right.*)

JOHN   Good evening.

(*Exit* JOHN *Right.*)

(AMBROSE *comes slowly down bank and sits beside* MICHAEL *on* MICHAEL'S *right hand. The evening is darker.*)

AMBROSE   Well, my old son of brass, how goes it? I never saw you before to my knowledge, but you look like a son of some kind.

MICHAEL   I'm a son all right.

AMBROSE   What do you think of these people here? The raw material I thought. But now my opinion, I give it for what it's worth, is that they're more raw than they are material. In fact what they are or are not—is immaterial. They don't appreciate a joke, they don't know one when they see it, or when it's shown to them.

MICHAEL   They're the limit.

AMBROSE   Limit, yes, but which end, are they bang in front with nothing to beat, or are they down aft on the fundamental ribs of it? Fundamental, is the accent on the fun, the mental, or on the dementia?

MICHAEL   Search me boss, they aren't worth it.

AMBROSE   Search you. I'll search you all right, my old son of brass.

MICHAEL   What's the big idea, these practical jokes. Do you get anything out of it?

AMBROSE   Of course I do, or I wouldn't do it.

MICHAEL   But there's plenty of people doing things they don't get anything out of, drawing the breath of Life for a starter.

AMBROSE   Well, as you say for a starter, we've got to do that for a starter. Some people aren't content with that, they have to inhale cigarette smoke. I do myself.

MICHAEL   I hate to see good smoke disappearing down into the dark caverns of the unknown. I've got a stomach, that if I filled it full of smoke would soon be asking me to send down something more solid.

AMBROSE   That's it, solid, solid's the word. Solid jokes. If I could bring off a solid joke with four dimensions I'd be satisfied. But I never saw one that had more than two, here and there. All I ask is reasonable fun and that's denied me by a benighted people.

MICHAEL   That's because you are not able to consume your own amusement as it comes, and carbonize it for further use, if you did . . .

AMBROSE   Pardon me, if I did I wouldn't be sitting out on an old bank talking to you at this time of evening. I'd be sitting in lonely study regaling myself on my own regalia and chuckling to myself.

MICHAEL   You've had your last chuckle long ago. You've lost the instinct, you common omadhaun.

AMBROSE   I've lost nothing, everything is sticking to me. I'm smothered with it. I tell you I'm the feller with the grand piano legs that carried the world on his back. I'm the feller that's full to the brim. I'm the brim myself in fact, I'm not myself, I'm the end of everything.

MICHAEL   You flatter yourself, you've just come on the wrong pitch and now you're all hit up about it. What you want is a good sleep, and a think it over.

AMBROSE   I'll think nothing over again. I'm done with thinking things over either before or after the event. I'll open my mouth and swallow the wave.

MICHAEL   You're right. Take the cream of it, and, so ends another day.

AMBROSE   Cream's a good word. It's the skim milk I've been getting up to this.

MICHAEL   I don't think you have a great deal of sense, or ever had, but you know more than most and as the saying is, you'll go far. What's the best practical joke you ever made?

AMBROSE   I never made but two, the Grand National and the Earthquake, but no matter, I have another, a good one up my sleeve, and who'll be the common omadhaun then? The two I made failed because the material I had to work on was too materialistic to be either taken in or taken out. What a genius . . .

MICHAEL   Genius, you've said it.

AMBROSE   What a genius like me wants is a large canvas, as the saying is, to spread myself on, and by God I'll get it or die in the attempt. But what's the good of me talking to you who never made a joke yourself and you're nothing but a joker queerer.

MICHAEL   That's not the truth.

AMBROSE   No it's not the truth, you're worse, you're a dead centre, you're a revolving climax.

MICHAEL   Well, that's healthy anyway.

AMBROSE   Healthy is it. I'll show you what healthy is in a minute. You wait, and don't sit grousing there, as if the end of the world had come, you keep your eyes skinned and watch clever boy do his stuff. I'll show you something you've never seen before, I warrant you. I'll show you Man upright defying the slings and arrows and getting away with it. I'll show you how the rich can dissolve in their own essence in the twinkling of an eye.

MICHAEL   I wouldn't put it past you, but let me take your word for it.

AMBROSE   No. I've got two jokes left in the pack. Two. I said I'd got another up my sleeve. I've another, and then another, and then perhaps you won't be giving me your airs, your high and mighty airs. I'll show now, watch this.

(The sky is by now a dark evening sky with some livid streaks on the Western corner. Right, AMBROSE *takes out of his breast pocket a large wallet and from one side takes a pack of notes, turning them in his hand so that the sinking sunlight shines on one side after the other. He then takes patent pipe-lighter out of his pocket, and after fumbling with it with several misfires and getting irritated and burning his fingers a little, he gets it going and holding the pack of notes by a corner, burns them and throws the ashes on the ground.)*

AMBROSE   Now that's all the money I had left in the world and I've burnt it and from now on I'm a living joker starting in on the ground floor. That's what they call a gesture, you sneering son of Hell.

MICHAEL   I never sneered.

AMBROSE   No you didn't. I'll take that back—and you're no son of Hell either, but you are very hard to amuse. That's my last word.

MICHAEL   Never say that. The last word was never said in my hearing yet.

AMBROSE   Do you know I thought at first that you were what they used to call a bit of a card, but now I'm . . .

MICHAEL   It's you that's the card.

AMBROSE   But now I'm not so certain. So help me God I think you're almost the whole pack of them, and I'm only a second hand leg-puller. I mean I'm second-hand at leg-pulling, I don't mean that the legs I pull are second-hand, if you get my meaning.

MICHAEL   Sure thing. I got it before you said it.

AMBROSE   Well, I make a clean breast. That bundle of notes I burnt were made of newspaper, except for the top one and the bottom one. But

I tell you what I'll do now (*Taking out and opening his wallet again and taking another pack, this time all genuine notes and showing them by turning the leaves of them close to Michael's face*) I'll finish the genuine lot.

MICHAEL   Why should you?

AMBROSE   I'll wipe it all out. I owe nobody. I've left enough and ample to pay all I owe Andy down here (*nodding head towards Cahirmahone*). I sent a cheque that emptied my bank balance to an old friend to settle up where I come from, and now I'm down to zero. (*Fussing again with automatic lighter*) And I'll walk the roads of the world with you.

MICHAEL   Well, thank you, but I wouldn't walk the Heavenly paths with a man so little in sense as yourself.

AMBROSE   Then I'll walk behind you. (*He is burning up the notes as he talks, as they are finished he blows as if he blew away the smoke, as one does of a cigarette*) Now I'm naked and fit to fight for my life with my two hands. Naked I came and naked I go. Now aren't I a son of old Adam like yourself?

MICHAEL   I'm sure you are, you're looking well.

AMBROSE   I feel well, I'm free.

MICHAEL   What's that?

AMBROSE   Freedom, don't you know what freedom is? I'm out of harness, I'm on my own, I'm loose-O.

> Turn key and lift bar
> Loose Oh bolt and chain!
> Open the door and let him out.
> And then lock up again, if you like.

I'm out and on my own.

MICHAEL   Good luck to you and safe home.

AMBROSE   What do you mean by home?

> I'm on the road
> Rattling the stones
> Over the bones of
> The old ones
> Dead and gone.

I tell you it's great.

MICHAEL   Didn't you know that without all that fire-burning business?

AMBROSE   You're a hard man. No, I wouldn't say hard, but you're cruel. I don't know that I'd say that either. But, by the way, I don't think you've seen even this joke. Never mind, we'll have a drink on it. I suppose you've no objection to joining me.

(AMBROSE *turns away, takes large flask from inside breast pocket. Takes off top with right hand, smells bottle and smacks lips, puts stop in left hand with flask. Then takes little bottle from waistcoat pocket, draws cork with teeth, pours contents into flask, gives flask a shake quickly, spits cork out of mouth, puts empty bottle back in waistcoat pocket, takes silver cup from bottom of flask, fills it from flask as he turns towards* MICHAEL, *and stooping down hands the cup to* MICHAEL.)

AMBROSE Here's to good going. (*He drinks himself from the flask.*)

MICHAEL That's hairy stuff.

AMBROSE It has its kick.

MICHAEL It has indeed. (*Taking another deep drink from the cup. After a moment letting his hand with the cup fall by his side. The sleepy poison is beginning to work.*) So you think you've done the trick.

AMBROSE (*sinking on the bank beside* MICHAEL, *the poison is working in him also*) I think I have. No I don't think I have. But anyway if I haven't I've had a good try. But what's the good of that.

(*He takes another drink from the flask. The drink works in him and he lets his hand with the flask in it fall to his side. As he sinks down he leans over almost on* MICHAEL'S *breast. They are both sunk down now on the bank well below the road, so that they are not in view from the road except for a person standing immediately above them. The sun is nearly gone down, and only the faint after-glow remains.* MICHAEL *and* AMBROSE *are almost lost in the shadow, but the movements of their faces can just be seen. The road crest is in silhouette.* MICHAEL *mutters a little. He is praying but unable to raise his hands. After a while,* MICHAEL *speaks with slow difficulty into* AMBROSE'S *ear.*)

MICHAEL Would it be any offence if I said a prayer for you?

(AMBROSE *moves his head a little from side to side and then downwards.* MICHAEL *moves his lips as though muttering a prayer thickly. The cup falls from* MICHAEL'S *hand as he dies quietly, he opens his eyes looking about him with difficulty at* AMBROSE *and then again about him over the distance.* AMBROSE'S *eyes are closed, he is dead.* MICHAEL *dies.*)

Curtain.

ACT THREE

Scene: *As before. Sunlight from left, a fine clear morning. Bodies of* AMBROSE *and* MICHAEL *on the bank.*

(Enter Left, NOLAN *and* DOLAN *with long-tailed shovels far side of road. They do not see the bodies of the dead men. As they move along they move into its place an odd stone which has got displaced. The lark begins to sing up aloft and continues off and on through the scene.)*

NOLAN   Ah, he has his eye on us, good morning (*waving hand upwards*), me old comrade of the skies.
DOLAN   Oh, that feller doesn't give a damn.
NOLAN   I dunno. Maybe that feller's as full of his old thoughts as I am.

(As they talk they move off on road Right. After a time enter POSTMAN *along road Left. He does not see bodies, he is looking through the ends of circulars and at the postcards which he takes out of his bag as he walks slowly along. When he reaches Right of centre he takes out one circular, makes out the address, then takes his whistle from his bag and blows long. Waits and blows again. Then holding up circular, shouts.)*

POSTMAN   Christopher, it's not much, it's only an advertisement of some sort.

(He is trying to make his voice carry out over the bog. After a time a voice, CHRISTOPHER'S, *off Right)*: 'My God what is it!'

(He has seen the bodies.)

POSTMAN   'Tis nothing but an old sewing-machine advertisement.

(Enter CHRISTOPHER *Right front over the bog, he hurries to the bodies, gazes on the faces, touches each hand. The* POSTMAN *has come forward and is looking down at the bodies now. The circular falls from his hand.)*

CHRISTOPHER   Cold. (*He crosses himself and says a prayer as does the* POSTMAN.)
CHRISTOPHER   (*climbing up the bank*) Stand your ground, touch nothing, I'll away for Priest and Doctor.

(He hobbles off along the road, Left.)

POSTMAN   And the Police.
CHRISTOPHER   Aye, the Police.

(*Exit* CHRISTOPHER *Left*.)

(POSTMAN *stands stiffly, picks up circular and puts it in his bag, stands again very stiff, a sort of sentry. After a time enter* BALLAD-SINGER *Left along road, hurrying*.)

BALLAD-SINGER   What did they do to him? Is he dead? Is the man dead? I met an old man on the road.

(*He stumbles down bank to the two poor dead. He looks at them and cup and everything. Touches nothing. Then goes over and sits on the bank on* MICHAEL's *Left, rocks himself a little, clasps and unclasps his hands, then sits quiet. After a time enter Left along road* JOSEPHINE *and* MISS JULIA. BALLAD-SINGER *takes off hat from* MICHAEL's *head and throws it down on the ground on his—*BALLAD-SINGER's—*Left.* POSTMAN *turns towards* JOSEPHINE *and* JULIA. *They have not yet seen the bodies*.)

POSTMAN   Did you meet Christopher Connor on the road?
JOSEPHINE   No, we did not. I expect he went by the short path.
POSTMAN   Well, you'd better stay where you are.

(JOSEPHINE *and* JULIA *come forward along the road tentatively*.)

POSTMAN   Stand where you are, I tell you.

(*He turns again front on his sentry duty.* JOSEPHINE *and* JULIA *come forward on to the edge of the road. They look down and see the bodies.* JOSEPHINE *puts her hand to her mouth in horror of the sight.* JULIA *pokes her head forward.* JOSEPHINE *sways a little, then sits down on the roadside, Left.* JULIA *stands beside her and cries into her side.* JOSEPHINE *cries quietly into her handkerchief.* POSTMAN *stands sentry. Enter Left along road, hurrying,* ANDY DOWD, *Publican, sturdy man about 50, hardy, stout, unshaven, old yellow hard felt hat, yellowy grey old homespun worn trousers and jacket, dark tweed waistcoat*.)

ANDY DOWD   Christopher told me to come on up here to look at what's here. 'Tis a terrible thing to happen. (*He comes down the face of the bank and looks down on the dead men*.)

(*Enter Right along road* NOLAN *and* DOLAN *without spades, they are hurrying*.)

NOLAN   What's up here? (*He comes forward to edge of road and sees the dead*.) Is

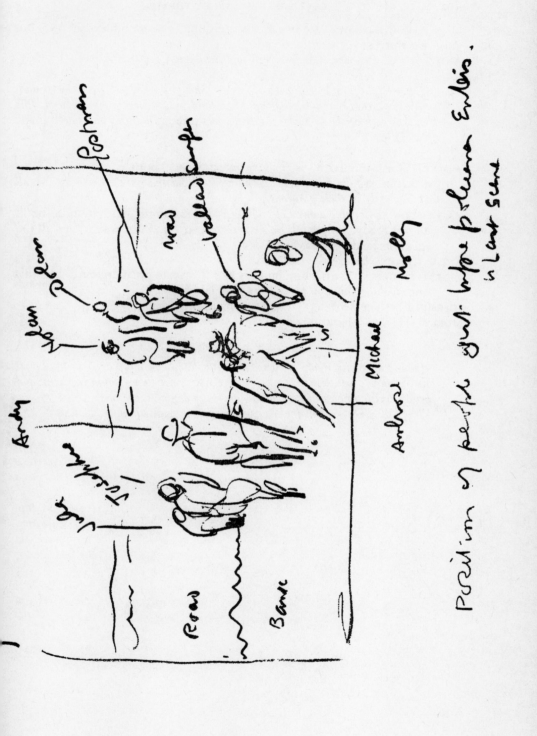

Position of people given before Evelia's
in last scene

it dead they are? We never saw anything, us coming along. Aye, but
we were the other side of the road.

ANDY   Dead they are. (*He lifts each cold hand and lets it fall.*)

(*Enter Right from bog,* MOLLY GILLANE. *She goes quietly over to the bodies,
takes* MICHAEL'S *soft felt hat up off ground puts it neatly on his head. She
touches each of the hands of the dead. She takes up the cup and smells it and
the flask.*)

MOLLY   'Tis poisoned he is (*looking at* MICHAEL), both of them. (*Looking
at* AMBROSE, *she sits down on the bank below the* BALLAD-SINGER. *So all
are listlessly in their positions.*)

BALLAD-SINGER (*looking away Left*)   The Police is coming, with his note-book
all out ready, his pencil, he's sucking it. If I had my way, that's all the
suckling he'd ever have got . . .

ANDY   Shame, before the ladies.

BALLAD-SINGER   . . . . It's him and his like that have great creatures like this
one (*looking down on* MICHAEL'S *face*) laid low.

JOSEPHINE (*raising her head*)   He was a handsome man.

MOLLY   He was a lovely man.

(*Enter Left along road,* POLICEMAN *with note-book and pencil in his hand.*
ANDY *moves a little back to Left and* POLICEMAN *comes down the bank and
begins writing notes in his book as he gazes down on the bodies.*)
(*The lark sings loud in the air.* NOLAN *and* JOSEPHINE, *only, look up.*)

CURTAIN.

Rattle

A Play in Three Acts

CHARACTERS

JAMES BECKERTON *sort of tally clerk, about 50, tall, rather stout, small grey moustache.*

OAKIN *messenger and porter, about 65, rough moustache, unshaven chin.*

JOHN GARDEYNE, *40, tall, rather cadaverous, clean-shaven, except for side-whiskers.*

ALEC GARDEYNE *cousin of John, 55, short, stocky, black-haired, florid, clean-shaven, heavy face.*

WILLIAM GARDEYNE *brother of John, 35, sour, youngish face, clean-shaven.*

CHRISTIE GOLBACK *widow, sister of John and William, 45, dark-haired, handsome, broad-shouldered.*

TED GOLBACK *son of Joe Golback (brother-in-law of Christie and dead 10 years). Ted is 32, clean-shaven, medium height, fair hair beginning to turn prematurely grey.*

JOHN BOWLEY *barge skipper, short, spare, dark full moustache.*

LOUIS BARLOCK *cinema proprietor, clean-shaven, big man, about 40.*

J. BULLWHACK *solicitor. Heavy, long, fattish, clean-shaven face. About 45.*

GINGER *lighterman, about 35, small, square, moustache and head red.*

CAPTAIN FORMORE *from Pakawana. Pale olive complexion, small black moustache.*

GENERAL GOLMOZO *from Pakawana. About 40, small, handsome, dark, black moustache.*

DOCTOR CANTY *secretary to General Golmozo; clean-shaven, heavy.*

GOSSGOGOCK *about 25, curly gold hair, brown complexion.*

THE PROPRIETOR OF THE NONILLION *clean-shaven.*

FIRST WAITER, OTHER WAITERS, SAILORS, PALANQUIN BEARERS.

(All words not in English are written phonetically. Rough translations into English given within brackets.)
'Left' and 'Right' are as characters appear to the Audience.

'LET ERIN REMEMBER'
by the whole orchestra.

ACT ONE

Scene 1: *Office of* GARDEYNE *and* GOLBACK. *Street door on Left; stairs on Left going to loft above, small table under stairs, window centre and to Right of centre. River door in two pieces, upper and lower, to Right, with stairs going down to wharf. High desk and office stool in front of window. Outside stores on opposite side of river.*

TIME: *afternoon.*

As the scene goes on the stage begins to get a little darker; towards the end it is dusk.

(BECKERTON, *sitting on high stool smoking old briar pipe (strong tobacco). He is sorting some papers in his desk; lid of desk is open, showing two large coloured lithographs of very fine-looking women, head and shoulders, taken from the top of chocolate boxes; not too décolletée, but magnificent. He turns his face upwards and shouts.*)

BECKERTON   Oakin, Oakin! Those chairs—rout 'em out. (*Looking at clock inside desk*) They'll be here in half a tick.

(OAKIN *moves about overhead and at last appears at top of stairs with a couple of old wooden chairs, brings them down into office, goes upstairs again, and comes down with two more chairs.* OAKIN *is in working clothes, with an old-fashioned sleeved waistcoat and is wearing an old greasy cap and apron made out of sack. He has a rough moustache and an unshaven chin. His boots are old, strong and lumpy but well polished.*)

OAKIN (*seeing lithographs in* BECKERTON'*s desk*) You'll have to do away with them gels now.

BECKERTON (*unpinning lithographs, going over to the river and throwing one out*) So ends Romance—the Shallow to the Deep.

OAKIN (*coming up behind* BECKERTON) Not both?

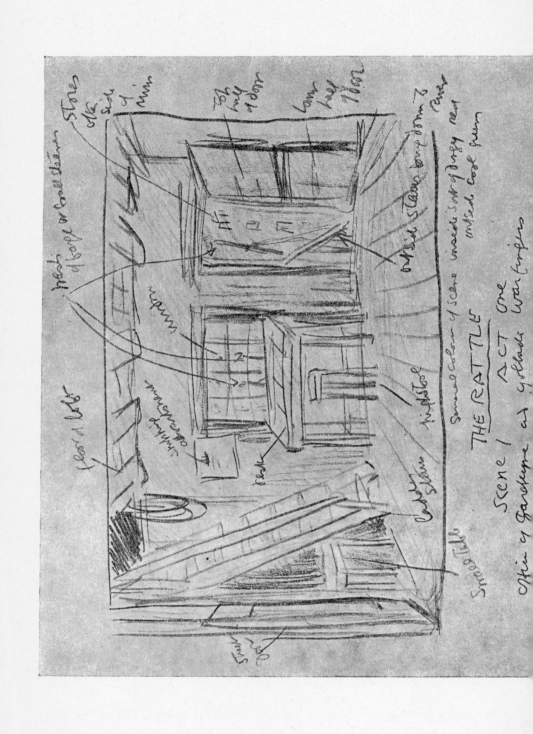

THE RATTLE

SCENE 1   ACT ONE

Office of Sanatorium at Golders-War Engine

(BECKERTON, *taking second lithograph from under his arm, hands it to* OAKIN. OAKIN *carefully folds it up, and puts it in left breast pocket of waistcoat and pats it.* BECKERTON *busies himself arranging chairs in a half circle towards Left of stage and facing audience.* OAKIN *helps him a little, but mostly stands gazing.* BECKERTON *closes both halves of river door, opens top half again and knocks out pipe into river. Puts pipe in pocket, hunts about in desk, finds rough mop head, dusts chairs with it. Rat-a-tat tatt, tatt, tatt, tatt at the street door.* BECKERTON *puts mop head back in desk.*)

BECKERTON   A lady comes.

(OAKIN *begins slowly climbing stairs.* BECKERTON *opens the street door and* JOHN GARDEYNE, *in dark grey tweed suit, dark grey soft felt hat, strides in in stately manner, followed a pace or two later by* ALEC GARDEYNE, *in brown tweed suit, light soft felt hat.* OAKIN *is nearly at the top of the stairs as they come in.*)

JOHN GARDEYNE   Mouldy place!
ALEC GARDEYNE   Picturesque; out of date.

(*Enter* WILLIAM GARDEYNE, *black jacket and waistcoat, striped trousers, hard felt hat.*)

WILLIAM   Sorrowful!
JOHN (*turning towards* BECKERTON, *who is standing holding door open*)   Well, Mr Beckerton, the weather is taking up.
BECKERTON   Yes, sir. Quite brisk. A nip was coming off the river this morning, but later the sun came out and it was like a summer day— so balmy!
TED GOLDBACK (*heard off*)   That's what I always hoped.
CHRISTIE GOLBACK (*first words heard off, rest as she comes through door*)   Ah, Ted, you were always trying to be cleverly weak. But you never took anyone in outside your own family.

(TED *and* CHRISTIE *enter,* TED *making way for* CHRISTIE. TED *wears a light tweed suit and light felt hat.* CHRISTIE *is quietly but fashionably dressed.* BECKERTON *closes the door; they all sit down in rough semi-circle, all the men with their hats on. They sit thus, reading from left:* JOHN, ALEC, CHRISTIE, WILLIAM, TED; BECKERTON *opens desk, takes some ledgers out, closes lid and puts them on it, and stands by desk.* OAKIN *can be heard walking about and pulling things about in store above.*)

JOHN   Mr Beckerton, please quiet that man.

(BECKERTON *goes upstairs and can be heard murmuring to* OAKIN. BECKERTON *returns downstairs.*)

CHRISTIE (*turning her face towards* BECKERTON) Thank you.

JOHN Well, I have myself gone into the books with Sparlings. They say 'sound'. I say 'no'. I detect the rattle in the throat. I can always tell. It's an instinct. Old Andrew Gardeyne in the eighteenth century had it. He could always tell when the end of a business was near. Then he got out of it. He had the instinct—I have inherited it. The wharfinger business in this port is not what it was. I say, sell the whole box of tricks for what it will fetch. Perhaps you would like to see over the place. None of you have ever seen it. The freehold should be worth something.

ALEC As the site of a cinema hall?

WILLIAM With the audience, or whatever is the proper term for the people who pay to see these things, coming from the river, I suppose. (*With a sneer.*)

ALEC Oh, I suppose they could get in the same way as we did, and a large illuminated sign over the door would attract the public easily. It is quite easy to get people to go to see anything if you only have a big enough sign. Lots of coloured lights, all revolving and going up and down. Some of these American Syndicates would give a large sum for a site like this, if it was only brought to their notice in a clever way— made attractive and all that. A champagne lunch and that, and big cigars. It could be got in. Some caterer would do everything. Tables could be arranged, couldn't they, Beckerton?

BECKERTON I dare say, sir. But the street is rather narrow.

ALEC But that doesn't affect the tables.

BECKERTON Narrow for lorries to bring the tables in.

ALEC Yes, that's rather a bother, yes. But I know. Listen! Get them by barge. That could be managed, Mr Beckerton? I'm sure you have the necessary ropes and pulleys.

BECKERTON It could be done.

JOHN Don't let's talk. Let us go over the premises. Mr Beckerton, show us up.

(*They mount the stairs in this order:* BECKERTON, JOHN, CHRISTIE—*taking note-book and pencil out of her bag*—ALEC *and* WILLIAM, *almost side by side.*)

WILLIAM A cinema is a ridiculous idea.

ALEC Ridiculous? I don't like that word.

WILLIAM Well, not ridiculous—impossible.

ALEC Well, impossible—possible, possible, impossible! They are matters of opinion.

TED (*taking books from desk, puts foot on bottom step of stairs*) Do you want these books up there?

JOHN Damn it, no!

(TED *follows others up. They all are heard moving about overhead. After a time they come downstairs again in this order:* CHRISTIE, TED, WILLIAM, ALEC, JOHN, *and* BECKERTON. OAKIN *stands on top looking at them going down, then returns to the loft. They sit down in the same order as before:* JOHN, ALEC, CHRISTIE, WILLIAM, TED, *reading from left to right.* BECKERTON *stands in front of desk as before.*)

JOHN   We have only ourselves to consult. The profit of the business can be divided equally between us, according to Aunt's Will. Or the whole concern can be sold as a going concern, if it will fetch anything. Or the freehold can be sold as a site, which in my idea is the best we can do—and the proceeds divided equally among us, according to the old lady's Will. There you are. I'm for a sale, Alec agrees, with a special suggestion as to a cinema. What do you think, Christie?

CHRISTIE   I shall speak my views after I have heard all of yours. William, I am sure, has something very careful to say.

ALEC   One moment, dear. Before hearing William's views, I would like to amplify my Picture House—that's the word I've been trying to think of. My Picture House idea is that, while selling the freehold to the Picture House Company, we should insist on retaining an interest in the takings, say ten per cent, which should be divided equally among us all. We could all, of course, have season tickets, and could come here whenever we liked and see that everything was suitable in—in— every way. The whole thing seems to me rather attractive, eh?

WILLIAM (*with a sweep of his hand*)   Produce your Cinema Buyer, and tell him to bring his cheque book.

ALEC   Ah well, even that I can manage I have no doubt.

WILLIAM   My plan is that Christie be appointed to go into the whole thing with Sparlings herself, personally, and then spend a week or so in Sparlings' office getting the general hang of business, so that, when she has everything at her fingers' ends, she can come down here and take charge. And, if after a year she finds that she can make nothing of it, she be empowered, at her own discretion, to wind up, as she thinks fit, dividing—equally with herself and us—the proceeds.

CHRISTIE   Thank you, William, but I am not quite so clever as you think— as you think—you are, and I have certainly no intention of bothering myself with a large unwieldy business like this. What do I know of wharfing, or whatever the thing is called? No, William, you are the one to be in charge here. Father, I believe, insisted on you taking a course of book-keeping, double entry, and didn't you have a certificate? I think I remember you bringing it home from school at the end of the term—all you brought, and father said, 'See the conquering hero comes with bays about his brow.' And though I was years older than you, I didn't know what 'bays' meant; so had father neglected our education, with his ridiculous ideas about the young learning whatever they wished, and leaving the rest unlearned. The only bays I ever heard of was a pair of bays in a carriage. And now you ask me to take charge of a wharf business.

WILLIAM   The business requires the deft hand of a fayre ladye.

CHRISTIE   Oh, do shut up!

WILLIAM   Oh, very well. And if the whole thing goes to the dogs, we'll have to share the blame around among us, for certainly—by a look I see in John's eyes—I'm not going to be entrusted with making the crooked straight. But who says it's crooked, anyway? Sparlings said it was 'sound'. How say you, Beckerton?

BECKERTON   Three years ago there was a drop in profits owing to a heavy bill for repairs on the riverside. But everything was paid out of income and, except for that one year, the profits have always been maintained. (*Pronounced as spelt.*)

JOHN   No matter, I have the instinct. I hear the rattle. The end is not far off. The thing is decrepit.

BECKERTON   Oh, don't say that, sir.

(*Boots of* OAKIN *are heard walking about overhead.*)

JOHN   Silence above there! (*Roaring very loud.* OAKIN *becomes quiet.*)

ALEC   Before we do anything else, we must have my Cinema idea tried out to the utmost—(*shouting*) to the utmost, I say.

WILLIAM   Well, if it's an idea, go and try it as soon as you like.

CHRISTIE   Not so fast. We haven't had the wonderful opinion of Ted yet. I see by a sort of radiance that is shining from his face, that he has something up his sleeve—an Idea, perchance. (*Shrugging her shoulders in a comic actress way.*)

TED   (*taking large long envelope from his inside breast pocket*) An idea, I believe, but not mine. (*He takes typewritten letter on large paper from envelope and shakes it out.*) The heading is in a sort of Spanish I can't find in any dictionary and also in English, and my thrilling correspondent (JOHN *fidgets about*) it appears is an attorney, a Commissioner of Oaths, and representative of the Republic of Pakawana. His name in English is Albert Bullwhack. His letter is as follows:

'Honourable Sir,—Your distinguished father, may the pampas grass and the bougainvilia blow lightly o'er his grave, ere he died, bequeathed property in mines, houses, lands, forests, and lakes; as to the house to the State of Pakawana; as to the mines, lands, forests, and lakes to his son, Edward Golback, absolutely, ten years after his, the most noble Joseph Golback's, demise. The rents and profits of said mines, lands, forests and lakes, to be paid to the State of Pakawana until the expiry of the said 10 years, when it should become the duty of the State of Pakawana to hand over the property to Edward Golback. I have had full inquiries made, and established the fact that you, sir, are the Edward Golback referred to, and after the signing of a number of documents, which can be accomplished at my office at an early date which suits yourself, the title deeds, etc. etc., will be handed over to you. For myself I wish to add that the property, especially the mines, is worth a very large sum indeed. Also, I understand that General Golmozo, representing the Republic of Pakawana, is now approaching Europe and, I imagine, will wish to make a formal presentation of the property to yourself, with some ceremony suitable to the occasion. This will not be a substitute for the actual handing over of the title deeds which, as stated above, can take place at my office at an early date. General Golmozo, on behalf of Pakawana, will invite you to visit the country. I have never, though the European represent-ative of the country, visited it myself since I left it, at too tender an age to have any personal memories. I understand, though, that it is a pleasant place, with a friendly and intelligent population. I have the honour to remain, Yours faithfully, Albert Bullwhack.'

(*All the time he is reading,* BECKERTON *is gazing at him, thrilled.*)

TED   I take it—that's very satisfactory?

WILLIAM   Does Bullwhack ask you to let him have fifty pounds on account of stamps, string, packing, etc?

TED   No, he doesn't.

JOHN   Not yet. That comes with the next letter. My dear Ted, have you ever heard of the Spanish Prisoner Swindle?

CHRISTIE (*interrupting*)   Don't, for goodness sake, say you have heard the death rattle in his throat! The letter and everything to do with it is, of course, ridiculous. And if Ted takes my advice, he will ignore the whole thing.

ALEC   No, no. Write a letter back asking for further particulars. If you let me, I'll dictate a letter that'll draw the Attorney further—and we'll have some fun.

WILLIAM   And then we can ask *him* for fifty pounds on account.

ALEC   Yes, if you like we could do that. But I think the whole thing could be made very amusing to while away a rainy day.

TED   I don't care what you say, any of you; I think this is genuine.

CHRISTIE   You would!

JOHN   And I believe that the explanation of the whole thing is that this State of Whackawana, or whatever it is called, is in a bad way and just trying to advertise itself by connecting itself, even indirectly, through the Golback name, with the Gardeyne family. But I can hear the rattle.

CHRISTIE   There, dear, I knew you would.

TED   Well, father did die out in that part of the world, ten years ago.

CHRISTIE   Just the sort of place Joe Golback would die in!

ALEC I don't think that is the way to talk of Ted's father before him.

CHRISTIE Well, his father was my sister's husband.

TED Sounds like one of those old riddles.

CHRISTIE When Louise died, twenty-five years ago almost to a day, I decided to watch her interests.

WILLIAM If I were you, Ted, I'd say 'you would', wouldn't I, Ted?

(TED *chuckles, waves hands about, then lightly kisses long envelope and clasps it to his chest.*)

CHRISTIE We are all being rather ridiculous.

JOHN Yes, yes.

(OAKIN *walks overhead, not so very loudly, but enough to be heard.*)

ALEC Yes, and my Picture House idea is the only one before us. Beckerton, do you happen to know if the freehold is perfectly in order?

BECKERTON (*coming to earth from his thrillings*) So far as I know sir. Of course it would want very careful going into. These riverside properties overlap a bit sometimes. And then there's the tides.

JOHN Ah, the tides.

ALEC Still, I daresay we have enough to go on, and if you are willing, I'll try and get in communication with a likely customer for the site, as a place on which to put up a good Cinema Hall. And then I could arrange a meeting with the customer and all of us, at a restaurant—a regular slap-up one. They do these things best over a glass of port and a cigar, after a good dinner. Is that all right? Can I go ahead?

CHRISTIE Yes, go ahead. I dare say there's a lot of money in Kineemas.

TED That's a new one on me, 'Kineemas'.

CHRISTIE Well, what do you say?

TED I say anything you say. What does John say?

JOHN I don't know. I think I've always said Kinama. But Alec seems to think he knows about them, and he says Cinema, don't you, Alec?

ALEC Yes, I say Picture House sometimes, and sometimes Cinema.

TED What does Beckerton say?

JOHN What do you call these entertainments, Mr Beckerton?

BECKERTON I just say 'pictures'.

(OAKIN *is heard walking about above.*)

TED What does old Oakin say? Let's call him down and ask him.

BECKERTON I wouldn't advise it. They excite him too much as it is.

CHRISTIE I dare say there's money in them, properly run. They have two in Upper Halton, and three in Lower, at least one of them is only a sort of Moving Show in a piece of waste land, with coker-nut shies and swings. I think people like it in the summer, because they are more in the open air, or they think they are. Of course, there would be a great deal of open air here, and that's a good thing always, we none of us get enough . . . Well, if Alec is to arrange this dinner with his Picture House Promoter, where are we to dine? It should be one of the very smartest restaurants.

ALEC   You choose. The lady should choose the restaurant.

CHRISTIE   She should be offered the choice, and then she should defer to the male.

WILLIAM   There is a new one just started called 'The Obvious'.

JOHN   I wonder is that a good name? Is it a success?

WILLIAM   It's only just started; it's expensive and very grand, and it's crowded so far, they say.

JOHN   I wonder will 'The Obvious' be a good name. It might seem too clever to some people—a sort of forcing you to agree with the proprietor that it's the only place. Rather like making use of the diners as advertising mediums. As you come away, people say, 'Where were you?' and you say, 'That's Obvious'. But then you might look dyspeptic, and that mightn't do the restaurant any good.

WILLIAM   Well, they say it's a good place.

ALEC   I expect the best sort of a name for a restaurant is one that grows gradually. I don't mean that the name grows gradually longer as the restaurant gets more established. I mean that—well, I mean there never was a good horse of a bad colour, and there never was a good restaurant with a bad name.

JOHN   But it might have been better with a better name.

CHRISTIE   I think Rose is a nice name for a restaurant.

TED   That's mental suggestion. The Rosey God. That's funny, too, because people always think of champagne when they think of restaurants, and champagne isn't very rosey, only very faintly rosey ever.

CHRISTIE   But there are yellow roses, just almost the colour of champagne.

JOHN   I am sorry, but I'm certain that rosey referred not to the wine the god drank, but to the colour of his cheeks, and perhaps—nose!

(*The evening is drawing on, and the time of dusk getting nearer.*)

CHRISTIE   It doesn't matter, anyway.

JOHN   Have you any idea yourself, Alec, of where the dinner should be given? You said something about a lunch here. You wouldn't think of having the dinner here?

ALEC   Oh, no. The lunch is for the Opening Ceremony in connection with the first showing of the Pictures.

JOHN   I got that, of course.

ALEC   And, of course, we haven't sold the site yet. So the idea is to meet the buyer in town in as impressive a place as we can think of. Impressive, but not overpowering. There are rather a lot of us, and we don't want to appear to be taking any advantage of the man. We don't want to appear to be trying to influence him by the lure of food and drink in their gilded forms. No, I will look in at a number of places which seem suitable, then arrange a couple of nights, either of which may suit the great man, whoever he is. Then I will communicate with you all, and we'll meet, have a pleasant dinner, with perhaps some entertainment after it, or during it. A troupe of musicians, or a couple of acrobatic dancers, or jugglers or balancers.

TED   I wouldn't. I'd just concentrate on the food.

JOHN   No, no. No entertainment.

CHRISTIE   We might just have a musician, behind a curtain, touching a lute—just touching it occasionally. Or twanging a guitar. Suggest Eastern magnificence.

ALEC   These Cinema Owners are simply filled with Eastern magnificence, I'm afraid.

JOHN   No, no. Best to just have the best of everything. Just light conversation on general subjects during the meal. And then lay our cards on the table. Say to him, 'So much. Take it or leave it.'

ALEC   Yes, that's it. But how much shall we say?

JOHN   Oh, ask Sparlings how much we ought to get.

ALEC   Oh, Sparlings don't know anything about Picture Houses. They'd say too little. No. We'll ask him how much he'll offer; he'll say so much; then we'll say so much. Then we'll hit on something between us, and whatever we decide we'll have our ten per cent coming in from the attendance.

(*Tug-boat whistle heard on the river.* OAKIN *stumps downstairs and out at river door. He is carrying a coil of light rope.*)

CHRISTIE   Where's he off to now?

BECKERTON   That's the tug. A barge is just going to tie up here.

ALEC   One of our barges?

WILLIAM   Our barge, fancy! There is a barge then?

BECKERTON   The barge doesn't belong to us. But it'll unload here on our wharf.

(ALL *get up from their seats,* CHRISTIE *and* ALEC *look out of river door.* JOHN *and* WILLIAM *out of window.* TED *stands behind* CHRISTIE *and* ALEC. BECKERTON *is at desk. He takes out bunch of papers and closes desk; in doing so he obscures the view of* JOHN *and* WILLIAM.)

BECKERTON   I beg pardon! A moment.

(*He closes desk again quickly, and moves towards river door, looking through bunch of dockets and papers in his hand.*)

ALEC ⎱ (*together*) ⎰What's the cargo?
CHRISTIE ⎰ ⎱What's in it?
BECKERTON   Barley.

(BECKERTON *goes out of river door and down steps.*)

VOICE (*out on river*)   Let go!
WILLIAM (*looking at* JOHN)   Old John Barleycorn!

(*He slaps* JOHN *on the back, with a sudden burst of gaiety. Then solemnly continues to look out of the window. Sound below of a coil of rope being thrown through the air. Then the dragging of a mooring rope. Short indistinct murmur of deep voice from barge.*)

BECKERTON'S VOICE   Pretty good. Yes, that's right. (*Short deep voice from barge, indistinct.*) Good passage, skipper?
DEEP VOICE (*from barge*)   Well, we made it. But there were a lot of lads about. (*Sound of walking about below*) Yes, fine. That's all right. Seven o'clock.
CHRISTIE   Our wharf!
JOHN   Yes, our wharf. (*A little sadly.*)
ALEC   Yes. But we'll keep the wharf and even if William thinks, and I'm sure he does, that it is impracticable to bring an audience by water, we'll be able to have a balcony, private for us, overhanging the river, just outside the window. And we'll be able to come here in a motor boat.

(BECKERTON *and barge skipper come up steps from river and in at river door.*)

BECKERTON (*with hand towards the people*)   Owners come to see the wharf. John Bowley, master of the 'Now's Your Time'.

(BOWLEY, *short man, spare, dark, with small dark moustache, not nose-ender moustache, but reaching all across upper lip. He is wearing a rather worn suit of brown, and a dark blue cap, new. He removes cap, and bows towards* CHRISTIE. JOHN, ALEC, WILLIAM, *and* TED, *who have been wearing their hats till now, remove them.* CHRISTIE *shakes* BOWLEY'S *hand. He goes round all and shakes hands.* BECKERTON *stands by his side and after a moment* BOWLEY *and* BECKERTON *go to desk, where* BOWLEY *lays down his cap and begins carefully to sign some forms.* ALL *very silent. It is now fairly dusky in the room except by the window.* JOHN *takes out large gold repeater watch; it strikes six.*)

JOHN   Grandpapa says it's time for us to go.
CHRISTIE   Good evening. Mr Beckerton.

(*Bows to* BOWLEY. *Goes towards street door.*)

(JOHN *bows, and waves hat in his hand, moves towards street door.* ALEC *bows, and with his hat pressed against his breast follows towards street door.* WILLIAM *puts hat on, waves hand, and follows others to street door.* TED *waves hand with hat, turns and moves towards river, looks out, then follows to street door, putting on his hat.* JOHN *and* ALEC *put on their hats at door and* ALL *go out.* BECKERTON *and* BOWLEY, *who had turned to receive bows, now turn back to desk, and* BOWLEY *goes on writing.*)

Curtain.

ACT TWO

Scene 1: *'The Cathedral' private dining room at the Nonillion Restaurant. Stained glass windows high up on wall; wall imitation yellow stone; dark purple velvet curtains over doorway back, Left. Heap of wood shavings and mortar on right of door with brush. Towards right of stage oval table on large oval crimson carpet. The floor is yellow stone tiles. Champagne magnum in ice bucket, also bottles on table. Large cigar box, flowers. At table, on Left at end, LOUIS BARLOCK, cinema owner—he and the rest of the guests are in full evening dress. Then CHRISTIE at back of table, fashionably dressed. Then TED and ALEC. JOHN at end of table opposite BARLOCK. WILLIAM in front by champagne bucket. At intervals sound of lute being touched behind door curtain. As scene opens WILLIAM is helping himself to champagne. Enter, Left, WAITER in light pink (much paler than hunting coat), velvet dress coat, black trousers and waistcoat, black tie. He has black soft felt hat on as he comes in, but plucks it off and throws it off stage, Left. He is carrying a pink enamelled tray (Japanese wooden with a small tray on it); both large and small trays are oval and pink, the same tint as waiter's coat. On the large tray is a very much cut glass bottle with special Nonillion liqueur in it and glasses. Coffee pot (gilt) are on the small tray inside the larger one. The small tray is put in front of CHRISTIE, and the larger tray with the liqueur brought round to ALEC, who fills out the glasses.*

ALEC   Now you must test this Nonillion liqueur. It is their very own, or made for them on an Island Fortress, somewhere in some extraordinary place. And they intend to never have any other liqueur here. It's a bold scheme and as we are the first diners who have ever dined here, as you know (*holding up menu and waving it about*); as you know, we are really opening the restaurant. In fact, this is the Opening Ceremony, and we cannot do it better than to drink the health of the Restaurant in their own liqueur.

(*He fills out glasses and they are passed by the WAITER to the others. ALEC rises. They ALL rise but CHRISTIE. Then she rises. Enter Left the PROPRIETOR of the Nonillion, a small dark man in a dinner jacket. He is wearing white kid gloves which he takes off and puts in his breast pocket. He stands in an attitude showing pleased dignity, just a few steps within the stage. ALL the diners turn towards him.*)

WAITER   Himself it is.

ALEC   Prosperity, health and happiness to the Nonillion, and all who dine, all who cook, all who open wine, all who wait (*looking towards the* WAITER), and to the genius who thinks of it all. (*He bows to the* PRO- PRIETOR.)

(*They sit down and sip their liqueur.*)

BARLOCK Magnificent!
WILLIAM Heavenly!
CHRISTIE Very attractive!
JOHN Strangely disillusioning!
TED Grand!

(ALEC *just looks round on them all and smiles. While they are talking the* PROPRIETOR *has withdrawn. Lute is heard behind curtain.*)

CHRISTIE (*listening with finger up*) Hark to the lute! (*She pronounces it 'leut'.*)
BARLOCK There used to be a song in the days of old (*singing*)

> Reut a teu teut
> She played on the fleut
> In a very charming manner.

TED Bootiful!
CHRISTIE Now you're mocking me. I pronounce as I have always under- stood I should.
BARLOCK Not at all. Anything I hear from you is music in mine ear. This has been far too memorable an evening to me for me to question any way of saying anything. And (*bowing towards* CHRISTIE) any lady so charming can say anything she pleases and she pleases me.

(CHRISTIE *smiles benignly on* BARLOCK. BARLOCK, *whose cigar stump is out, puts it on plate.* JOHN *motions him to cigar box.* BARLOCK *takes a fresh cigar and lights it.* WILLIAM *passes box to* JOHN, *who takes out cigar and lights. These cigars are long fine ones.* BARLOCK *takes the band off his cigar and puts it on his left little finger, holds it up and admires it.*)

This evening has been a delight to me and not the least of its parts has been the, ah—the music, soft, unseen. I wish I could bring it to a happy close for us all, by making you an offer for your site. But as I have explained to you, it is impossible. I would have to buy all that side of the river and build a whole suburb myself to get me a public for my Picture House. And I am afraid I cannot hold out any hopes that anyone, or any group of people, however much money they could command, could make your site a paying proposition. At the same time, if you like to go on entertaining goats like myself to such

delightful dinners, I am sure you will find plenty who will entertain
the idea of being entertained. And there it is. Now, what can I do for
you?

JOHN   Nothing more than you have done. You have entertained us yourself
most regally. In fact, though my experience of regal personages is
tiny, I believe none could equal your narration of your experiences on
the front of the —er—Silver Screen. I have only twice visited a Cinema,
but I shall go there now many times, and I will always think of you.
Alec, this man is a miracle!

ALEC   Trust me to find the roses in the bouquet.

WILLIAM   Break him and shatter him
And-whatever-it-is him still
The scent of the whatever-it-is
Will whatever-it-is to him still.

TED   Clear as a bell.

JOHN   Now, what do you advise us to do with our site?

(*The lute sounds several times.* ALL *listen very quietly.*)

BARLOCK   What can I say? For all my talk, my experience of the general
world is very little. People say 'a garage'. I don't know how madame
would say it.

CHRISTIE   You're mocking me. But I would say it as the Italians do. (*She
smiles kindly.*)

BARLOCK   A 'Garrajio' I suppose? But Italians, or Spanish, or North of
England, or whatever language they like, they're uncertain and make a
nasty tinny noise all night, and get you disliked in the neighbourhood.
No, what you really want is something that will pay you a nice income,
at least equal to what the wharf has been producing in the past, and will
be amusing to all in some way. So that your romantic complexes, if
there are such things, go on all right. I'm thinking (*He sits pensive with
his chin in his hand and his cigar in his mouth.*) No, nothing comes to me.
Nothing very striking. Tea Gardens, perhaps. Riverside Maypole
Dancing, bells on their fingers and bells on their shins, smocks all
a-blowing:

> Here we go round the mulberry bush,
> The mulberry bush
> The mulberry bush,
> Here we go round the mulberry bush
> On a cold and frosty morning. . . .

No, that goes with rum and milk. No. Now, I must really know of
something you could think about. (*Sits again pensive.*) If I knew anything about factories I could advise you. You see, a riverside position is

very good and worth a lot, if you had someone on your site making something that was best carried by water. I can't think of anything. There's money in folding boats, I believe, if they can be made to fold up small enough. The Life Boat in the waistcoat pocket. No; you want something in general use.

ALEC   Would you think of anything of marine engine making?

BARLOCK   Well, I don't know anything about it. I wish I did.

WILLIAM   Marine engines are not what they were.

BARLOCK   No, I expect you're right.

CHRISTIE   What do you think, Ted?

TED   The word 'Marine' seems to be good. It seems as if whatever is done, the position of the site by a flowing river should be taken into account.

JOHN   Marine glue?

BARLOCK   Yes, Marine Glue. But Glue Factories are not popular with the neighbours any more. No. I know if I could get away to a library I could hit on something for you. I could look up in a dictionary under 'Manufacturers'. I wonder have they got a dictionary here?

ALEC   Oh, I don't suppose so yet. They are only just started we know.

WILLIAM   A telephone directory would be a long business. But any time any of you are waiting in a telephone box any time, it will be an occupation to be turning over the leaves and noting, I mean just in the mind, any manufacturers, especially having to do with marine situations.

BARLOCK   That's the idea. Have an open mind. And now, my friends, I'm desperately sorry to break up this most delightful festival, but I have to catch a very early boat train, and before then I have to try and do something about getting an estimate from a contractor, for standing up the roof in the Cinema I'm interested in in Smarthkin. It's threatening to fall.

WILLIAM   Where's Smarthkin?

BARLOCK   Oh, it's a Garden City in the North East.

JOHN   And you'll forgive me—isn't this a late or strange hour to interview a building contractor?

BARLOCK   It is, indeed. But he's an enthusiastic creature, who has taken to dancing late in the day in every sense. Begins late and ends early—or never ends at all. I'll run him down, when I catch him, to Smarthkin. Think of us both, perhaps just before the peep of day, Madam (*he looks towards* CHRISTIE), hopping about a girder in the sky.

TED   But won't you have to get home and change before you catch the . . .?

BARLOCK   Ah no, that won't matter. I'll have to turn in so soon when I get aboard. I'll breakfast, I expect, at the Cape of Good Hope.

JOHN   Oh, you need never suffer from sea-sickness if you fix your eye on some fixed object. I cured my sister that way. Now she's never sick at sea.

BARLOCK   That's fine; I'll try that.

WILLIAM   The trouble is to get a fixed object in a rolling sea. I think they should arrange some mechanism which would introduce some object rolling in the opposite direction to the ship. Something to counteract the ship's roll on the mind.

TED   The whole concern is mental. When you are falling out of a window, think of being blown up in an explosion, and you get a soft bump.

BARLOCK   Mentally, I suppose, sir?

TED   Oh, mentally, of course!

BARLOCK   On a soft bump I leave. (*He rises from his chair.*) This has been the most delightful evening I have ever had, and it has been a privilege to meet you all.

(*He bows over* CHRISTIES' *hand.* TED *gets up and comes round table behind* CHRISTIE. BARLOCK *takes* TED'S *hand and rolls him about on his heels affectionately.* JOHN, ALEC *and* WILLIAM *stand up,* BARLOCK *walks around front of table, takes* JOHN'S *hand in his right and puts his left on the top of it. Then back of* JOHN *he takes one each of* ALEC'S *hands and shakes them. He then comes to* WILLIAM *and gives him a firm, strong, long-armed, manly shake of the hand.* JOHN *looks about on the wall and on the table for bell.* WILLIAM *points to rose among the others in the long bowl.* JOHN *takes out a rose with flex attached. He presses rose. Sound of a silver bell tinkling off.* JOHN *puts down rose. Six waiters in pink tails come in carrying silk wrap of* CHRISTIE'S *and dark coats and opera hats for the rest, except for* WILLIAM, *who has a grey-brown top coat and grey soft felt hat. They are all helped into their coats and, shepherded by the waiters, move off, Left.*)
(*The Lute sounds.*)

Curtain.

Scene 2: *Office of Gardeyne and Golback. Same as Act One, Scene 1, only broad daylight. Both upper and lower half of river door open.*

(*Seated in rough semi-circle as before,* JOHN, ALEC, CHRISTIE, WILLIAM, *and* TED, *reading from left. The men's hats are on table under stairs.* BECKERTON *standing by desk, as before, with ledgers.*)

JOHN   Back again where we were before. What to do with Gardeyne and Golback's ancient wharf? You haven't any new suggestions to make? No manufacturer seems to want to manufacture anything here. And if we dwell any longer on a settling-up of some kind, we will find ourselves manufacturing cobwebs in our brains.

WILLIAM   Never while reason holds her sway!

CHRISTIE   Good for you, William.

ALEC (*shaking head*)   Every avenue seems hopeless.

JOHN   If an avenue can be hopeless. Surely a hopeless avenue would be like the old joke of the rope without an end, because somebody had cut the end off.

CHRISTIE   That's an idea. A rope factory making endless ropes.

JOHN   The means being the end, I suppose?

CHRISTIE   That's the sort of remark that Ted will be able to afford to make if these millions of his come true. How are things going with Mr Bullwhack?

TED   I have a letter from him here. (*Holding up letter in his hand.*) He says that General Golmozo and his Staff may arrive any day, and that he understands the General's first move will be to invest me, Ted, with the highest honour of Pakawana, the Order of Badge of the Golden Wave. (*Opening letter and glancing through it.*) Oh! Bullwhack says the Insignia, of which he has seen a photograph, is very magnificent—a circlet of gold waves with pearl crests, and emeralds studded on the lower edge to represent bubbles. It is worn round the neck.

CHRISTIE   You will be magnificent.

TED   I'll have to live up to it.

JOHN   And you will.

ALEC   If—and when!

JOHN   Ah well, of course, we must always hope that there will be no dashing of hopes for Ted.

WILLIAM   Yes, and remember this, Ted; even if the whole thing turns out a false hope, old Ted will stand up to his fortune good or bad. I believe in Ted.

JOHN   Well, there's still Gardeyne and Golback unsettled. What about all of us putting our shoulder, or our shoulders, to the wheel and running a variety of businesses; anything that occurs to us.

CHRISTIE   We could have the loft (*pointing upwards*) divided into compartments and each of us have an office. The ramshackle old place is big enough.

JOHN   Oh yes. That would come.

ALEC   Our clients, or whatever we would call them, would all have to come up the same staircase. (*Pointing at ladder, turning round in his seat and gazing at it. Calling up.*) Oakin! Oakin!

(OAKIN *appears at head of stairs.*)

I suppose, Oakin, you would be able to be on hand any time you were wanted to help people up these stairs? I mean, old and infirm people who didn't know their way about.

OAKIN   Aye, aye, sir.

(*For the rest of the scene* OAKIN *remains standing at head of stairs unless otherwise mentioned in directions.*)

ALEC But that wouldn't bother us because whatever businesses we were engaged in they wouldn't be the kind to clash with each other. For instance, if I were a Company Promoter, my clients would be quite different from Christie's. Christie would very likely run a Cottage Industry, or John might.

JOHN I won't run a Cottage Industry.

WILLIAM Why not a Palace Industry?

TED That's an idea.

CHRISTIE You won't be here, Ted, if your ship comes home.

TED That's true.

JOHN I don't want to run industries. As I grow older, as I do day by day—I don't mean that to be funny—I mean as I grow weightier—I mean I grow faster in avoirdupois than I do in time. As I grow older I have less desire to run industries and more desire to have industries to run me. (*Turning to* BECKERTON.) We don't bore you, do we?

BECKERTON Mr John, it's a delight to hear you. But I don't know where you're heading.

JOHN Wherever it is, you can bet your bottom dollar it isn't dangerous.

CHRISTIE Is that on account of your gift of hearing death rattles?

JOHN Don't talk of it. I never hear it now. It's not a nice gift, anyway.

CHRISTIE Well, I'm really glad. People with second sight should only see roses.

WILLIAM The thorns come quick enough.

BECKERTON They make themselves felt, sir.

WILLIAM Indeed they do. Scratch no more fair heart, scratch no more!

ALEC You're thinking of a thorn in the side.

WILLIAM I don't think I was thinking of anything, if you ask me.

JOHN Well, let us get on to business. What is to be done with Gardeyne and Golback?

(OAKIN *sits down on top step of stairs.*)

ALEC My disappointment about the Picture House has depleted me for the time being. But no doubt, if I had a long rest somewhere, I could lay out a plan of some sort. But of course I see that something must be done almost at once.

WILLIAM That's it. It's this 'almost at once' business that bothers me. There's something in this 'almost at once' which grits against. . . . No, grits is not the word. But there's something that stems the flow and ebb. Can you be said to stem an ebb? There is something which is the exact opposite of the steady ebb and flow, flow and ebb, of the tide up and down this river, just at our doorstep, as we might say. Why yesterday, (*he gets up and walks to river door and looks out*) ah, and there it is still! Why yesterday there was a piece of broken wood, off a packing case with some letters on it. P.E.A.C., I think—and then it was broken off.

It may have been for peach or peaches, perhaps tinned peaches. But there's the bit of wood again. Yesterday I watched it go up with the tide, and again come down with the tide. And then I saw it get caught in an eddy just beside our wharf where there were some other things floating. There it stayed caught up. It seemed to me as if it was symbolical of something. It was specially odd that I should see it because, if I hadn't got the day for our meeting wrong, I wouldn't have been here at all yesterday, and so I would not have seen the peach on the deep (*he laughs*) going up and down. But there is some symbol there. Perhaps this vagrant wood is to show that the rhythm that cannot be mastered can be enjoyed until it laps you gently into a state of static bliss with a number of other pieces of drift.

CHRISTIE   And how would you apply the symbol to us, dear?

WILLIAM   Well, I don't know. But perhaps . . . (*Double knock at the street door.*)

(BECKERTON *goes to door. Express* MESSENGER *comes in with letter.* BECKERTON *signs receipt and goes over and gives letter to* TED.)

CHRISTIE   Something thrilling?

TED (*opening letter, cautiously excited*)   Well, yes. It's from Bullwhack. He says that (ALL *lean forward, but* WILLIAM *first looks out on river and then comes a step forward into the room.*) He says that the Shroneshraw—that's what it looks like!—has arrived sooner than expected and—and that General Golmozo and Doctor Canty will arrive here any time now. They are coming in the Shroneshraw's own boats. He says that the tide is against them, and that will give him time to change and be with us, he hopes, before they arrive.

(OAKIN *stands up and stretches himself spreading out his old arms to do so.*)

CHRISTIE   Well now, this is really getting exciting. It's almost more than I can bear.

ALEC   Oh, bear up. There's more to follow, I'm sure. Let us hope that Bullwhack gets here ahead of the General and the Doctor.

JOHN   And the boats' crews. (*To* BECKERTON.) Have you any idea of what we can do now? There are not enough chairs. We cannot ask them to sit on the floor (*looking down at it*) though I do think you keep it wonderfully clean considering there's a good deal of traffic, I suppose, with one thing and another. If we have a lot of cushions we could throw them about, and pretend that we're a sort of artistic people. By Jove, that's an idea! We might let this place as an Artist's Studio. We could let it (*chuckling*) to Alec: you used to make sketches one time (*Looking at* ALEC). But I'm being silly or giddy, which is worse. What can we do, Beckerton? Is there anything?

BECKERTON   Best wait until Mr Bullwhack comes in. And if the gentlemen
   come before he arrives, we can stave them off a bit with talk until Bullwhack blows in. Then he'll take charge and everything'll be all Isle of
   Wight.

WILLIAM   That's right. We wait on Bullwhack. It's a race—the Doctor and
   the General against Bullwhack. I'm backing Bullwhack at six to eight.
   Six-and-eightpence a time. That's rather good! Did you ever notice
   that six-and-eightpence is a third of a pound? The tertium quid. I say,
   I'm getting rather funny. It must be nerves.

CHRISTIE   Nerve, I should think, to try and foist a joke like that on us.

ALEC (*ponderously*)   Christie Golback, you'd say that at any joke. Even if it
   was so new you could smell the starch on it. You recognize all jokes as
   your hereditary enemy. You are the Eternal Woman.

TED   My God! I hope not.

CHRISTIE   Oh, you mean that you hope I'm not Eternal, or that Woman is
   not Eternal, or that I do not recognize jokes as my enemy?

TED (*jumping up and striking attitude*)   The answer I will carry with me to the
   grave.

(*A thump on the street door, which flies in, and in comes* BULLWHACK. *A large
heavy man, but quick on his feet. He is wearing a black overcoat and carrying a
silk hat. He takes off overcoat with* BECKERTON'S *help and puts it with hat on
desk. He is seen to be in full evening dress—tails—white waistcoat, white
flower in buttonhole. He has a gold watch chain with locket. He is wearing
brown kid gloves which he takes off and tosses into his hat. On his left little
finger is a diamond ring, single stone, very fine. He has a long, fattish, clean-
shaven face, and is about 45 years of age. His hair is prematurely grey but
waved.*)

BULLWHACK   On time. A bus, a steamboat, a taxi. You'll say gentlemen, and
   (*bowing to* CHRISTIE) Mrs Golback 'and why not one of these only?' And
   I'll say, the answer is geography, which thwarts our hopes, unless we
   have a flying machine, which cuts corners. (*As he is talking he strides
   round into the middle of the semi-circle of chairs.*) Now, let us know exactly,
   or more or less, what is before us. I have myself the vaguest idea of the
   ritual which will be followed on this auspicious occasion. But I understand that it's absolutely essential that Mr Ted here should be draped in
   the Insignia of the Order, which henceforth he is to adorn in his particular
   person. When the General, the Staff, the Doctor and the boat's crew, or
   the crews of the boats, arrive, as many as possible will come in here, and
   the General, after being introduced by (*waving to* JOHN) Mr John here,
   to the rest of the assembled company with special reference to Mr Ted
   as the chosen vehicle of the honour of Pakawana, so that there is no
   mistake and the wrong person is not invested with the investiture.
   Then the General will bow and probably make a speech in his native

tongue. But of course, I am forgetting the Doctor, who will be here the whole time, and quite able to translate everything, even a gesture, I have no doubt, into Pakawanan. I wish now that years ago I had revisited the country. I had a chance. There was a cargo of road rails going out, and, if I could have left my business, I might have gone out with them, and got some knowledge of the country I presume to represent in this part of the world.

WILLIAM Perhaps you are as well off. A little knowledge in this case, perhaps in this case only, might have been dangerous.

BULLWHACK I believe you're right.

(OAKIN *sits down heavily on top step.*)

WILLIAM Yes, the twilight of knowledge is the mist of understanding.

ALEC I hate Chinese proverbs. They are so trite and so useful.

TED But still they are ornamental, too.

ALEC Yes, in Chinese. But ornamentality is not translatable and . . .

TED I know what you are going to say. But it works the other way, too. And quite an obvious remark in the original may be deliciously wistful . . .

CHRISTIE I never heard of delicious wistfulness before.

TED Well now you do. You are getting in on the ground floor. What I say, and what I think, is that a thing deliciously wistful when translated into a fresh language, may be the feeblest sort of old shoe leather in the original. If we had an interpreter of Pakawanan here we could turn things like 'A stitch in time saves nine' and 'Honesty is the best policy' and 'When is a door not a door?' and things like that to Pakawanan and try them on the General, and he would think them perfectly beautiful and have them taught in the Secondary School System of his blessed country.

CHRISTIE Which soon, Ted, will be your blessed country.

TED (*soberly*) True. Pakawana for ever! Pakawana I love thee!

BULLWHACK Something tells me that it would be as well not to try any—if you'll excuse me saying so, any funny jokes on the General. I mean, it will be our cue—I mean, it will be our cue to keep our eyes on the Doctor and be guided by him.

JOHN I'm very sorry to be a nuisance. But as it is possible that Mr Golback will be a very long time in Pakawana, and we know that after the investiture, or whatever we are to call it, has taken place, he will be taken straight on board the Pakawanan vessel, and as likely as not sail straight away. Taking these things into account, and as the General and the Doctor and the rest, may arrive at any moment, let me beseech you all to arrange something about the firm of Gardeyne and Holback. Mr Bullwhack, you will excuse us going into session, as it were, in front of you, without consulting you professionally. We cannot do that owing to Sparlings being the firm's solicitors, and we in this case, acting entirely as our own masters we cannot—well, you understand. The matter is serious and the time short. Once again, I call on you all to come to some decision.

WILLIAM and ALEC (*speaking together*) What about Beckerton? Hasn't he thought out something?

WILLIAM Yes . . .

ALEC Yes, while we have been so busy burrowing among our Chinese proverbs he has been looking very pensive. Speak, Beckerton! have you anything new to suggest for us to do with this romantic business of ours? And remember, no Chinese Proverbs. No!

CHRISTIE Please, Mr Beckerton!

BECKERTON Well, the only thing I can think of is that, owing to general upset and all that and owing to Mr Edward going away from us for the time being, and nothing coming in the Cinema Trade, as far as we are concerned, might I suggest, if you are willing, that myself and Oakin should continue running the wharf in the future, as in the past. And think I can promise you that profits will be maintained.

JOHN No, no, not quite the same, for the salary of yourself and Oakin must be doubled, I feel, and then the profits can be divided equally among us according to the late lamented lady's Will. I don't mean that she is only lamented in the past. I'm sure those of us who ever saw her lament her still; she had a great brain—I take it all of you agree to this as only fair. I mean, I trust that we all agree that Mr Beckerton and Oakin are worth this at least, if they save us from a quandary.

(OAKIN *gets up, walks about overhead,
and comes back to sit down again.*)

CHRISTIE Oh, certainly.

ALEC Quite! Quite true.

WILLIAM Hail to thee, Beckerton. Thou hast saved the situation!

TED Agreed, agreed. Couldn't be better. John you, have inherited some of the same brain as the old lady.

CHRISTIE I'm very glad it is all settled.

BULLWHACK If you'll excuse me saying so, it has been a pleasure to have heard you. You've saved yourselves a lot of expense, I'm certain.

BECKERTON (*coming slightly forward*) Myself and Oakin are overwhelmed. We'll do our very best.

(*Whistle heard from river.* OAKIN *walks about aloft and
comes down with light rope and so out river door.*)

CHRISTIE Is that the General coming?

BECKERTON It's the tug. And there's a lighter for us—fire bricks.

CHRISTIE   One of our lighters?

> (BECKERTON *opens desk, searches bunch of papers*
> *for docket; finds it.*)

WILLIAM (*looking out of river door*)   And here's a couple of stylish-looking boats coming full of men rowing. (*He clasps his hands above his head.*) Pakawana approaches!

VOICE (*from the river*)   Hi, Oakin! Are you asleep?

OAKIN'S VOICE   All right, Ginger. Captain Ginger.

BECKERTON (*after fussing at it, opens window and shouts*)   Oakin, leave room for the boats approaching.

OAKIN'S VOICE (*below*)   Aye.

> (*Sound of ropes slapping about lighter; thumping against wharf.*
> *Cry in voice of command below on river.*)

VOICE   Odoesh! (Easy all!)

(BULLWHACK *bustles about arranging people. Upstairs from river comes* OAKIN, *looks in, disappears again; presently comes up again, followed by* GINGER, *lighterman, about 35, small square man in rough working clothes with old brown cap, red moustache and red head.* GINGER *goes over to desk to* BECKERTON. OAKIN *stations himself at bottom of stairs to left. Immediately upstairs from river marches* CAPTAIN FORMORE, *naval officer, about 20, pale olive complexion, slight black moustache, pale yellow uniform, dress coat cut, gold belt with sword, gold epaulets, high white waistcoat with gold buttons, low white turned-down collar on shirt and black tie in sailor knot, ends of tie outside waistcoat. Rather voluminous pale yellow trousers, patent leather shoes. His hat, a sort of panama with a high crown but black; there is a narrow gold band round it with a gold button in front. After him come 12 sailors, pale brown complexions. They are wearing short pale yellow jackets, white soft shirts, white trousers, black belts and black sheathed daggers. Hats the same as the officer's but with pale blue bands and buttons. The men take up positions, three on each side of the steps going down to the wharf and three fanned out into the room on each side of the river door.* CAPTAIN FORMORE *takes his stand on Left of river door, in front of sailors. Almost at the same time as* FORMORE, *comes up the stairs from the wharf,* DR CANTY, *a heavily built medium-sized man, clean shaven, pale. He is in a black morning coat, with rather low cut waistcoat, but not as low as a dress waistcoat, black trousers, patent boots, turned-down collar, no tie but an emerald and diamond front collar stud, 2 front studs, small plain gold. He is wearing a black felt roll-up evening hat, which he rolls up and puts in breast pocket. He takes his stand on the Right near* BULLWHACK.)

OAKIN Fever colour, yaller, quarantine, fever boys.

DR CANTY (*in a clear, loud, and sweet voice. His voice should always be sweet and clear, sometimes loud, but generally low*) Yes, fever. The fever that flows for ever in the blood of the people of Pakawana.

(*He bows towards* JOHN *and the assembled people generally.*)

BULLWHACK (*stepping forward*) Dr Canty, I presume? Allow me to make the introductions. Mr John Gardeyne, Dr Canty. Dr Canty, Mr John Gardeyne. Mrs Golback, Dr Canty; Dr Canty, Mrs Golback. Mr Alec and Mr William Gardeyne, Dr Canty; and Mr Edward Golback, the gentleman you have—you have—come particularly to see, Dr Canty. Dr Canty, Mr Edward Golback.

(ALL *bow*.)

DR CANTY My mission here is well known to you all, who are I suppose, friends or perhaps relations of Mr Edward Golback?

BULLWHACK Mrs Golback here (*coming towards her*) is Mr Edward's Aunt; Mr John and Mr William are brothers of Mrs Golback and so uncles-in-law of Mr Edward; Mr Alec is a cousin.

DR CANTY It is a pleasure. My mission here as you know is to act as interpreter between the country of Pakawana, which will be represented in a moment to you in the person of Golmozo. (*He looks out through river door and downwards as if to the wharf, and holds up right hand, a staying hand*) As soon as the General steps within the office he will hand me the document, which I will translate to Mr Edward and all assembed here. But first I will introduce those present. (*He whispers to* BULLWHACK *who writes names on a piece of paper torn from his notebook and hands it to* CANTY, *who keeps it in his hand.*) I will introduce those present to the General and Captain Formore, after which the General will proceed to invest Mr Edward Golback with the Order of the Wave, Cloak and Collar. On the completion of which Captain Formore will give the opening of the National Song for a Friend of Pakawana, the Guard of Honour singing. After that Mr Edward will accept the right hand of the General, and the left hand of myself, and so we will pass down to the boat, and join the ship which will carry us back to Pakawana.

(*He looks through river door and down to wharf as before and with a very quiet gesture of his right hand, palm upward, moving it from the right upwards and towards the left, signals for the* GENERAL *to come up. Enter* GENERAL GOLMOZO *up steps and through river door. The* GENERAL *is a small, black-haired, handsome man about 40, with a black moustache, long, and fairly sweeping. His complexion is a dark olive. He is wearing a white high-crowned sort of panama hat, the same as the naval captain's, but it has an emerald green cord and an emerald stone as button. He has also a fine emerald ring on the little finger of his left hand. He has a military frock coat in yellow, pale blue trousers and patent shoes. He has a gold sword and gold belt. He is wearing a turned-down collar with a black tie, worn outside, similar to the naval officer's. On his left breast he wears a straight perpendicular line of seven emeralds. On his left arm he carries a claret-red cloak, a sort of poncho with a hole in the centre for the head, and in his left hand he is carrying the gold Wave Collar—a round gold collar but about 4 inches deep at the deepest. Pearls at the top to represent foam, and emeralds at the bottom to represent bubbles. And in his breast, where one button of his coat is undone, he carries a bright yellow paper, with claret-coloured ribbons from it. As soon as* GENERAL GOLMOZO *is in the room,* GINGER *and* OAKIN, *gazing at him with admiration, take off their caps.*)

DR CANTY (*consulting paper*) General Golmozo representing the country of Pakawana (*waving his hand towards the assembly, and consulting small paper given him by* BULLWHACK) Mr John Gardeyne, Mrs Golback, Mr Alec Gardeyne, Mr William Gardeyne, Mr Bullwhack, Pakawana Fore-onoad (Pakawana welcomes), and Mr Edward Golback. Oh Pakawana oh monodore doeh grodogo (Pakawana's chosen son is welcomed).

(GENERAL *bows to all, but to* TED *he bows with his hands held in front of him like a cup.* DR CANTY *whispers to* BULLWHACK *and looks towards* OAKIN *and* GINGER. BULLWHACK *whispers back but shakes his head when it comes to* GINGER.)

DR CANTY (*waving hand towards them*) Mr. Oakin, Mr Beckerton, Mr—Mr—
GINGER Wilton.
DR CANTY Mr Wilton.
GINGER Ginger Wilton.
DR CANTY Mr Ginger Wilton.

> (NOTE—*The audience can laugh as much as they like,*
> *no one on the stage laughs.*)

GENERAL GOLMOZO I am aprouded, ahappied. (*He bows towards the three.*)
DR CANTY (*congratulating him on his English*) Looloonrock! Looloonrock!
(Splendid! Splendid!)

(GOLMOZO *looks towards* CANTY *and smiles.* DR CANTY *lightly touches scroll in* GOLMOZO'S *breast.* GOLMOZO *takes out scroll with left hand and gives it to* DR CANTY.)

DR CANTY (*unrolls scroll and begins*) Pakawana stoeore loge zoeown. Pakawana is filled with pride and joyousness to honour the Nation and its
rock, sand, rivers, mountains, lakes, buildings and ideals. Its civilization
and its thought, its—its—its—(*hesitating*) hope, (*looking closely*) its
hopes, its aspirations, and its daily achievements, by offering a part
within this to Edward Golback, the son of the distant, but near,
Joseph Golback, Friend of Pakawana, when friend was wanted. A
friend in the small compact carrying thought—thought that can be
carried away—and the large Lantern Thought, where Moon and Sun
were crossed and made a Star, to Joseph Golback's son I, Pakawana,
look asking nothing to cream the measure already filled by his great
father. I ask only the courtesy—the politeness, smoenomone, there is
no word, perhaps, in English for it. (*He turns to* FORMORE) smoenomone
Gon dorezon loze.
FORMORE Zoeoanee zoack doe moan. (Pulsing tides to and from us).
CANTY Good wishes like tides always between us—and we do now with
the hand of General Golmozo, assisted by the hand of Dr Canty, make
you, Edward Golback, a brother of the Golden Wave, and do wrap
you in the cloak of the waves. And to sweeten the cloak literally
bundled in the cloak, General Golmozo is given the pleasure of
handing over to you, yourself, the title deeds of your property in
Pakawana. (*Turning to* GOLMOZO) Zopporone oh ozzo! (The title deeds
now!)

(GOLMOZO *takes small packet of three papers from breast pocket, hands them
to* DR CANTY, *who, making his left knee a desk, not kneeling on the ground
with his right, just stooping; and, taking a fountain pen from his pocket,
signals to* TED *to come forward and sign.*)

CANTY (*to* BULLWHACK, *who has been looking about in a bothered way*)   Will you witness, Mr Bullwhack? Also Mr John Gardeyne?

(THEY *witness. And then* CANTY *signals* GOLMOZO *who comes over and signs papers:* FORMORE *and* CANTY *witness his signature. In each case each of the three papers are signed. One of the papers* DR CANTY *puts in his own breast pocket. Two* TED *puts in his.* CANTY *and* GENERAL GOLMOZO *whisper.* GOLMOZO *takes emerald ring from his finger and presents it to* BULLWHACK, *who puts it on and admires it. During the signing of the deeds the* DOCTOR *has had the scroll which he has been reading, tucked under his left arm; he now takes a white silk handkerchief from his right breast pocket and lightly pats his forehead, unrolls the scroll and continues reading.*)

CANTY   And to General Golmozo also is given the pleasant amusement of taking you on a visit to Pakawana. Immediately on the completion of the investiture you, Edward, will float, be carried, with the good wish arms of Pakawana, which await you. Zoeroe Pakawana, zoroash (Friend of Pakawana, come).

(*He signals to* GOLMOZO, *and rolling up the scroll, hands it to* TED, GOLMOZO *comes forward and puts cloak over the head of* TED, *who comes in front of river door.* GOLMOZO *then places collar round* TED'S *neck, fastening it at back.* GOLMOZO *then steps back and stands sideways so that his right hand is to* TED'S *right.* DR CANTY *steps out and stands with his left side to* TED'S *left.* CAPTAIN FORMORE *takes flute from breast pocket and plays while the* SAILORS *sing.*)

SAILORS (*singing*)

> Allogo lahgo, allogo lahgo,
>   Allogo ho
> Allogo lahgo, allogo lahgo,
>   Allogo ho!
> (Our country calls you, our country calls you
>   Calls you
> Our country calls you, our country calls you
>   Calls you!)

(*Slowly while they sing* GOLMOZO, TED *and the* DOCTOR *pass downstairs walking sideways. As they pass the last of the sailors followed by the others, fall in behind them, in pairs. Last comes* CAPTAIN FORMORE *who steps on the step of the river door, takes off his hat and from the inside takes a handful of about eight golden-yellow rose-like flowers which he strews in a half-circle*

on the floor about the river door. A voice of command below cries 'Onozoe'
(Oars). There is the sound of oars in rowlocks going away. ALL *in the room*
stand quietly, except BECKERTON *and* OAKIN, *who walk over to the river*
door and stand looking out, but not crossing the flower half-circle.)

Curtain.

ACT THREE

Scene 1: *A glade in a wood in Pakawana; gnarled old tree trunk, with heavy roots above ground, on Right. Also towards Right an opening in wood making a window through which can be seen the capital of Pakawana rising over the forest. The trees around the glade are mostly flowering trees, bright yellow flowers, like giant evening primroses. Toward the Left, at the back, there is a path going into the woods. There are leaves and some twigs on the ground. The sun is fairly low and shining golden behind the capital in the distance. Later the sun gets redder and finally sinks until the stage is in a dusk. Discovered are* DR CANTY *and* TED. DR CANTY *is wearing light yellow duck trousers tucked into untanned leather half-Wellington boots. He has a white shirt with a stud as before and a short yellow duck jacket. He has a high-crowned panama hat, yellowy-white.* TED *is standing by tree to right. He is wearing a yellow-white high-crowned panama hat, with a gold band and emerald stone in front. He is dressed as the doctor is dressed except that his shirt is pale blue silk with a narrow black tie, sailor knot, long ends. He is carrying on his arm the ceremonial cloak and a black patent-leather case with the Wave Collar in it.* DR CANTY *has a bundle of yellow thin reeds with which he is brushing the leaves and twigs away from the stage on the Right and making a little heap of them toward the Left and back. He is not a very good brusher, but he is being as methodical as he can about it.*

194

TED (*putting down Wave Case with the Cloak on top of it by the tree*) Let me bear a hand with that.

CANTY (*going on brushing*) Oh no, you mustn't. Until sunset of the first day you are just a guest, a very grand guest, but still a guest, of Pakawana. After sunset you are as free of Pakawana as its birds, and they are capable of taking the bread out of your mouth willy nilly, the saucy little jokers.

TED (*looking about, and listening*) There are no birds here.

CANTY And why would there be birds here, in thick wood only a few miles from a city, where the inhabitants are in the act, at this very hour, I'm sure (*looks out at the sun*) of tossing the crumbs from their napkins out of the windows and into the air, they just having taken the napkins from under their double chins?

TED I have only seen the people of the Port and, of course, Captain Formore and the General, and they haven't got double chins.

CANTY Oh, there are people in Pakawana who haven't got double chins, indeed there are. But they are not the birds' best friends.

(CANTY *goes on sweeping.* TED *sits down on Wave Case and Cloak.* DR CANTY *comes over to* TED *after a little more sweeping.* TED *gets up now and* CANTY *arranges Cloak over tree roots to make a seat for* TED, *having first brushed down roots. He then goes off Left and returns carrying a native grass rope of several colours in his left hand, and in his right a native basket. He*

throws the rope up and over the branch of the tree on Right, and makes end of rope fast to handle of basket, so that the basket hangs comfortably in front of TED *as he sits on the tree root. He opens lids of basket and fits struts into rings on side of basket, so making a little table on each side of basket. He takes out of basket a bunch of golden yellow flowers and fixes them through loop of rope above handle of basket. He then takes out of basket a bottle—old-fashioned short-necked wine bottle—and puts it carefully on the ground, then two gold cups like teacups with handles. He places one on each basket lid and beside each he places a couple of thick brown bread sandwiches. He pours the wine into the cups and hands one to* TED, *takes one himself and a sandwich.* TED *also takes a sandwich.)*

CANTY   This is the cocktail hour. But this wine is not a cocktail. It is something far more permanent, more penetrating, more holding, for it is the wine that flows while grass grows and water runs. It's the wine of gladness, it's the wine of a sort of sub-madness, as though a walker on a tight rope over a torrent walked with ease, because he had concealed invisible wings, which bore him along so that he only touched the rope with his toe-points. Ease and elegancy, with safety, painted to look like Danger. But drink up, my hearty.

(*He tosses off his cup as does* TED. CANTY *fills the cups again.*)

TED   I'm wondering where the General is.

CANTY   Oh, in Vino Veritas at first, later, Golden Slithers on a new moon with appropriate music. In Vino Veritas the wondering questioning alcoves of the brain get filled with activity and the victim wants to know, O Jehovah, why? To know all is to forgive all. To forgive all is not to want to know all. But the General is a son of the woodland, so he has left us a while, to hunt—for mushrooms, perhaps, or to commune with a mushroom, a constant mushroom, standing on guard before the mushroom palaces of the wood. But that needn't fret you. Here you wait until the palanquin from the Capital . . .

TED   What is the name of the Capital? You just call it 'the Capital'.

CANTY   More Veritas! The name is Pannikin.

TED   A pannikin is just a tin basin for food.

CANTY   I know. But some visitor, long ago, before your father's time, I believe, said 'it looks like a pannikin to me'. 'It is a pannikin to me.' He was full of Veritas, I suppose. The people were amused and so they called it Pannikin. That is, if anyone who is not a Pakawanian asks, they say 'Pannikin'. The people themselves, we ourselves, are too fond and proud to give the city a name that is a fixed name. Some call it sometimes 'that foolish place'; 'that fond place'; 'the friendly place'; 'that oblique place'; 'that everything of a place'. You will notice, as you become more deeply involved in the ideas of the place, that adjectives are substituted for proper names very often. Not proper adjectives, but changing and various ones. They will soon be calling you 'the one', and then 'the handsome one'. Perhaps 'the travelled one'. I myself as I come home have an inclination to drop into the old ways and call you 'the related one', thinking of your relations.

TED   Very good! But I wasn't thinking of them just at the moment.

CANTY   I found them fascinating. I mean, they looked fascinating.

TED   Yes, I daresay they are, and I'm sure they would be fascinated if they could picture me sitting here waiting for a palanquin. I never rode in a palanquin in my life. I'm looking forward to it, and I believe it will come up to my expectations. Have you ever noticed how whenever you imagine a future joy, just in the middle of picturing it some sort of a dirty little devil gives your arm a jog and you get frightened that the bottom is going to fall out of the whole concern? I'm not meaning any reflection on the palanquins of Pakawana. But, what I'm trying to say is that I have no feeling of fear about this palanquin not being up to my imagination's specifications. But don't tell me anything about it.

CANTY   All right. They'll send, I'm sure, the best they have and all are good ones. They are kept for ceremonials only. The bearers, you know, will be young men chosen by lot from the most popular members of the Wave Society. First, every member votes for what they consider the twelve most popular members and then all their names are rattled in a hat and from them are picked twelve to carry you to the Capital. Four take you from here, a third of the way. Then the next lot, and then the last lot. They have a short stage and they are supposed to take you in through the Gate at a trot. But what will most likely happen is that your bearers will walk along stately enough and the other eight, who have nothing to carry, will keep galloping round you and about you and singing laughing songs with melancholy choruses. That's these lads' idea of the height of politeness.

TED   And what will I be expected to do?

CANTY   They won't expect you to do anything in particular. You'll be propped up on your cushions, and you'll just nod. Nobody ever sweeps a long bow here—they are always short bows.

(CANTY *pours out the last of the wine into the cups and leaves the bottle down on the ground under the basket as before. The sun has nearly gone down and the scene is in a dusk. A distant shot is heard on the Left.*)

TED   Is that the sunset gun?

CANTY   Oh, they don't have things like sunset guns here. That's just some lad firing at a mark for practice. They are fine marksmen here.

(*Another shot is heard on the Left somewhat nearer.
The bottle is struck and broken.*)

TED   They are indeed. But that marksman was late, I'm glad to say.

CANTY   Yes, I'm glad, too, for both our sakes.

TED   It must have been a long shot.

CANTY   Oh, very long. He most likely saw the light shining on the bottle through a telescope. Didn't see us and thought some straying picnickers had failed to clear up after them, and so he had a slap at the empty shell that once was life. Have you noticed how marksmen love, all over the world, shooting at empty bottles? But they never shoot at full ones.

The idea is too repulsive. Ah yes, but then I forgot, there is a country, nameless, where with crowbars and hammers—(*He hangs his head*) your Lord Tennyson said (*He recites in a deep sonorous voice*)

> And all talk died, as in a grove all song
> Beneath the shadow of some bird of prey.

(*He stands silent, and* TED *hangs his head also. Then drinks again.*) But never in Pakawana.

TED   And yet you are Utopians.

CANTY   Don't let any native of the country hear you say that. From time to time in the past, visiting Utopians have come here, bringing with them some sort of a fit-up Utopian with about as much significance about it as the schoolboys' ancient joke of 'Have you anything to sit on?' 'Yes, but I have nowhere to put it.' These Utopians in the old days used to be given a certain amount of rope, until the time came when they asked to be deported, so we sent them to an island, a lovely island, lying off the coast. There they stay. It was given a name.

TED   Ah, that's interesting. So the people had to give a name to something?

CANTY   Well, no—(*A couple of shots somewhat nearer on the Left. He hesitates for a moment when hearing the shots, but goes on*)—They didn't name it. They asked me. So I called it Renaygia.

TED   Renaygia! Renaygia!

CANTY   Yes. The inhabitants are not allowed to leave. Indeed they never ask to. I've seen some of them occasionally when the boat comes to the port for supplies—matches and cameras are the only things they lack. The people I saw all had about them a sort of beauty, a sort of sterile beauty, like a cul-de-sac-on-a-starry-night and here-comes-the-thunderbolt. But I'm talking too much.

TED   Never, never, never!

CANTY   You are made to be a true son of Pakawana. But nevertheless—

(*Enter* GOLMOZO, *Left, from wood, dressed as in Act Two, Scene 2, except that he has a revolver holster on a belt.*)

GOLMOZO   Zawselode, zawzoonone zo zoete (These madmen are too close).

CANTY   Someohzam, ozack (You'll push them back).

(*Exit* GOLMOZO.)

CANTY   You haven't asked much about your property which is scattered all over the country. I suppose after you have settled down you will like to view it. It'll take you quite a while.

TED   Yes, I haven't thought about it. But I'm sure it will be a delight to see my possessions, especially as they seem to produce such a nice income.

But—(*Getting up and looking through hole in leaves at the city, which is now in silhouette against the sinking sun*)—I'm looking forward to your Capital, with yourself as interpreter. I expect to get on like a house on fire with my hosts. Though I have sometimes thought, when you have been interpreting me to Captain Formore and the General, that you have been improving on Ted! I'm judging by their expressions which are generally the expressions of men listening to something more than the ordinary remarks of a simple horny-handed quill driver like myself. But I don't care; perhaps if I get a reputation I'll be able to live up to it—when I learn to speak the language myself.

CANTY Do quill drivers get horny hands?

TED (*coming back from hole in leaves and towards* CANTY, *holding out the palms of his hands*) Not very: look!

CANTY Not very horny.

(*Sound of two or three shots on Right, not very near, then one nearer. Enter* CAPTAIN FORMORE *dressed as in Act Two, Scene 2, except that he has revolver holster on his belt.*)

FORMORE No soldore obee oree zois (They are right on top of us).

CANTY Srosim Omoss (Dreadful luck).

(*Exit* FORMORE. TED *sits down on tree trunk.* CANTY *walks up and down, then stops by* TED.)

CANTY They are pressing in on us.

TED I think so. But who are they?

CANTY I hoped they'd pass away or that the guard would be able to get close to them and disarm them. But they are so dunderheaded. They seem to be coming round us, and in on us. Oh dear, dear, it would provoke a Saint!

TED What's it all about? Is there a revolution?

CANTY Oh, not at all. It's not a bit like that here. It's just the General's younger brother. And then it's just a chance, and a mistake. You see the old 'Shroneshraw' outdid herself, or the chief got her to walk faster than she'd ever walked before. Or perhaps it was the fair weather and favouring winds. Anyway, she made a record passage and we got in two days ahead of calculations. You remember I told you the old dear was showing off. I didn't think anything of it because the triumphal arches and all that down at the port were ready. But you see they picked us off coming a long way off. Look at the coal we were burning; a pillar of smoke by day, and night, too, with sparks on it. Anyway, whatever they knew at the port they didn't tell the Capital, or if they did it was too late. But what's happened is that this young brother of the General's got a lot of people who just play him up to pass the time.

And he got an idea in his little curly head that there was a nice easy government post that a friend of his should have. And he tried to take the easy job by force of arms. But somebody else thought somebody else should have it, and both parties went out with guns to—well, just to demonstrate. But, unfortunately, as you have noticed, they are good shots! (*As he is talking he is untying the basket and taking down the rope, and putting it and the basket on the ground by the tree side.*) Now they're all about in the woods here. The General and Formore both feel certain it's only Gossgogock, that's the young brother, and his party. The others have gone down towards the sea, they think. The trouble is that we can't stand anything like a flag of truce here. Nothing clear white is carried into a fight here. We'd respect a flag of truce but we hate it. It makes it ticklish work for your guard. They'll try and get round trees and grab these men of the brother's and disarm them. One minute I understand their point of view completely and the next minute it escapes me.

TED   But oughtn't I to do something to . . . well, to do my share?

(*He holds out his empty hands.*)

CANTY   Oh no, you and I are non-combatants. You're a guest and they think of me as a philosopher, God help them! But you mustn't let anything bother you. If Gossgogock knew for an instant you were here the whole business would stop on the instant. The whole thing is absolutely unlike them. It's just at intervals these demonstrations are got up. A kind of giving of a hostage to whatever might be expected of a people like themselves. But the intervals between these marchings out are always getting longer. It's three years since the boys came out like this, and there was far more of them in the turn-out then.

TED   Is it some feeling for moving about in woodlands? Does it come from reading boys' books?

CANTY   Good God, Ted, these men of Pakawana don't read boys' books. The children of Pakawana wouldn't be caught reading children's books.

TED   Don't they miss something, the children, I mean? It seems . . .

CANTY   What does it seem?

TED   It seems, I was going to say, such a pity for children not to be children.

CANTY   When you meet the children of Pakawana you'll know that there is no doubt about them being children.

TED   Well, I know I'm in good hands.

CANTY   The hands will always be as good to you as they can be.

TED   I'll have a great deal to see in the Capital. The Fond Place.

CANTY   Ah yes, the Fond Place.

TED   My father's tomb is in the Capital itself, isn't it?

CANTY   Oh yes.

TED   I must see that. I don't want you to think I am expecting anything grand, or even a monument in great repair. Far from it. I am not a great admirer of the heavier exhibitions of architectural memory. Just a mound or a small stone.

CANTY   Your father's tomb is all these.

(*Two shots on the Left. Three shots on the Right a little nearer than the last. A twig or two fall from the trees. They have been hit.* CANTY *walks across to the Left and then to the Right; as he walks to the Right he pulls a revolver from his right hand hip pocket. He then comes and sits by* TED *on the tree trunk, with the revolver hanging in his hand.*)

CANTY   I wonder what your idea of the Capital is like. I mean, I wonder what you are expecting to see when you get there? Or perhaps, you are one of these happy-go-lucky travellers who form no previous ideas, like the lady who when she was taken to see Niagara said, 'How lovely, it's water!' She was in luck now, wasn't she?

TED   She was, and so will I be for I have no previously formed ideas about the Capital, except that, if it is anything like the General or yourself, then I am sure it is a place where intellectuality and good fellowship are blended in a two-handled cup. That's rather nicely put for me, isn't it?

CANTY   Very nicely, indeed.

TED   And I suppose you have some fine schools, perhaps where only the best of everything is taught under the freest possible conditions?

CANTY   Oh yes.

TED   And Picture Galleries where the best native work is shown side by side with examples of the oldest and the most modern from the rest of the world. At least that is what I think you have. But on the other hand . . .

CANTY   Oh yes. On the other hand . . .?

TED   Perhaps not. You may not need such aids to civilization. You may have only what you yourselves like.

CANTY   And do you know what that is?

TED   I think I do, and yet I'm not certain.

CANTY   Let you remain uncertain. It's your best hold.

TED   Well, I have always liked uncertainty. Even when a little boy I used to like not to be told where I was going, or going to be taken on a holiday, if it was to be pantomime, or a circus, or whatever it was I was going to see. And I delighted in having an old uncle holding a small present in each of his hands and making me choose which I'd have.

CANTY   And weren't you sometimes disappointed?

TED   Yes, of course—sometimes. But never enough to want to cry off with my chance.

CANTY   You had the spirit! Heroes are like that. Did you never want to be a hero? Of course, in your childhood like every other child—(*a couple of shots on the Right*)—like every other child you thought of yourself sword in hand leading a forlorn hope that just came off and so wasn't so forlorn at all. Or perhaps you died in the last ditch; too stately, no tinkley, no sweetly tearful music—that's the nearest things childhood gets to funeral music. But the adult pictures himself as a different kind of hero, doesn't he? How did you, as a grown man, ever picture yourself as a grown hero. Facing odds with you bare hands?

TED   I don't know that I did. But I suppose fleeting thoughts of oneself playing a leading part. Yes, the part, I believe, yes, the part of a showy hero has attracted me, I suppose—indeed I'm sure it has. Yes to die game. Oh yes, or perhaps to jump a buster off a liner and save the life of the belle of the ship. B-E- double L-E.

CANTY   I understood that. The other bell would take altogether too much saving.

TED   Yes, I had certainly in manhood these fancies—perhaps more than most men. I always had a good deal of time on my hands. I have never excelled very much at games. I think people who succeed a lot at golf, and tennis, and cards, they advance on stepping stones of small victories. That's rather good, isn't it?

CANTY   Yes.

TED   There's something in it, don't you think? And a poor performer in ordinary competition, like myself, has to catch up with an imaginary victory of some sort on a large scale, every now and then. Otherwise he'd be snowed under by the games club champions.

CANTY   Yes, and your happiness is your own. You would like Pakawana.

TED   I'm sure I will.

CANTY   Sure thing.

(*Enter* GENERAL GOLMOZO *and a sailor, dressed as in Act Two, Scene 2. He has a rifle in his hand and appears on Left rather silently. They look at* TED, *who does not see them, and at* CANTY, *then exit, Left.*)

CANTY   Yes, and it's better to imagine being a hero than to be one perhaps . . . It must be a desperate dull business being a whole time hero. A whole time hero knows nothing of the feel of it. And the recording angel must be worn out entering noble deeds after his name. I hear him say, 'Here's the mangy old continuous hero still registering the old stuff.'

(*Another shot on the Right. Another twig falls on the ground.* TED *stoops forward and picks it up: as he does so there is a rattle of shots on the Right and* TED *falls forward on his face.* CANTY, *shoving his revolver into his left jacket side pocket, picks* TED *up and props him up on root of tree, opens his shirt and feels for wound, then quietly pulls off his own jacket letting it fall on the ground, and then hauls his shirt off over his head; his body is now bare.*)

He goes to the Right; there are two more shots fairly close. CANTY *throws his shirt up on a branch of tree on right. Then he comes back to* TED *and, taking a tin case from his right hand outside jacket pocket, works at* TED'S *wound examining it carefully; finally puts a pad on it and binds it up with lint and bandage from the case. He makes* TED *comfortable on the tree root. He puts his jacket under* TED'S *arm and back to make him lie easy having first taken the revolver from the left pocket and put it in his hip pocket. He bundles the Ceremonial Cloak under* TED.)

TED (*motions towards the Wave Case*)   I'd like to wear it.

(CANTY *opens case, takes out Wave and arranges it carefully round neck so that it cannot hurt* TED *in any way and stands by him.*)

TED (*speaking quietly and slowly*)   Am I for it?
CANTY   You're all right.
TED   How long have I? Hours? Minutes?
CANTY   Ah yes.
TED   If I give any trouble, I know you've got some sort of jolter in that case—you know, give me a jolt. I don't want to die squealing.
CANTY   Oh, you won't want to be squealing. And if you did, what of it? You wouldn't mind me?
TED   Indeed I wouldn't. But for the sake of Humanity in general.
CANTY   Oh, what's 'Humanity in general?' But nevertheless, boy, have an easy mind now. I'll watch like a cat its kitten.
TED   To know all is to forgive all, and doesn't that cut both ways?
CANTY   Yes, yes. To forgive all is to know all.
TED   I forgive all. But I have nothing to forgive.

(TED'S *voice is now low, and* CANTY *sits beside him on the tree trunk and leans close to hear.* TED *whispers in his ear. As far as the audience is concerned his lips only move.* CANTY'S *lips also move after* TED. CANTY *strokes* TED'S *right hand with his right. After a time.*)

CANTY   Have you any directions to be attended to? Have you a Will made?
TED   No, I'd like to make one. (CANTY *takes a note, an old letter, from his pocket and tears off the back sheet, takes out his fountain pen and kneels down by* TED) Should I hurry?
CANTY   Take your time.
TED   I . . .
CANTY   I, Edward Golback, son of Joseph Golback, (*writing as he speaks*) late of Pakawana . . .
TED   Leave one-half of all I possess to the country of Pakawana. (CANTY *writes*) And the other half (*speaking very slowly and quietly but getting it done*) to John Gardeyne, William Gardeyne, my late father's brothers;

Christina Golback, his sister, and Alexander Gardeyne, my cousin, to be divided between them . . .

CANTY   Equally?

TED   No. Between them—in whatever proportion they themselves shall decide.

(CANTY *reads out what he has written, then gets up, goes Right and holds up hand. Enter Right,* CAPTAIN FORMORE *and* GOSSGOGOCK—*young man with curly gold hair, brown complexion, with more colour on the lips and in the cheeks than* FORMORE *or the* GENERAL. *He is wearing a uniform similar to* GOLMOZO'S (*except that there are jewels on the coat*), *and he has a bright blue band and blue button on his hat, and on his feet rough untanned leather boots with trousers stuffed into them. His uniform is worn, out at elbows, and patched. He is on the left of* FORMORE.)

GOSSGOGOCK   So fim (Can he give forgiveness)?

CANTY (*to* TED, *going over to him*)   You forgive this young man?

TED   Why, I have forgiven him a long while ago.

CANTY   So fimary. Ozat. Zawsonshe (His forgiveness flows from him in a straight stream to you).

(*He holds the Will on top of his tin case and, putting the pen in* TED'S *hand, sees him weakly sign his name, then beckons over* GOSSGOGOCK *to write his name, which he does, holding the case in his left hand, then handing the case and the Will back to* CANTY, *who signs his name.* CANTY *offers the Will to* TED *who signals, moving his hands a very little, and* CANTY *folds the Will, takes the revolver out of his hip pocket, puts the Will in and then replaces the revolver.* TED *is sinking.* CANTY *now goes to the Left and holds up hand. Enter* GENERAL GOLMOZO.)

CANTY   Zawrah (Dying).

(GENERAL GOLMOZO *goes over to* TED *and lightly holds the fingers of the dying man's right hand in his two hands.*)

TED   Friend! (*He turns his head, Right, towards* FORMORE) Friend (FORMORE *comes forward holding out his hands*) Canty, I'm away, away!

(CANTY *goes towards* TED; *as he does, with his hands to right and left, he signals to the others to withdraw into the wood,* GOLMOZO, FORMORE *and* GOSSGOGOCK *move off backwards.* CANTY *sits by* TED. TED *lifts left hand towards Gold Collar.* CANTY *takes Collar from* TED'S *neck very gently; and drops it on the ground.*)

CANTY   Yes, take the old harness off you. (*He stoops forward so as to hide the dying face of* TED *from the audience. After a time.* TED *is dead.* CANTY, *standing up.*) Zaappah (Gone forward).

(*After a moment* GENERAL GOLMOZO *enters, Left, and* CAPTAIN FORMORE *and* GOSSGOGOCK, *Right,* GOLMOZO *goes back, Left, and standing by wood, raises left arm. Enter, Left, five sailors with rifles. They stand along border of wood at ease.* CANTY *stands looking down on* TED. *He puts back the Gold Collar round the dead one's neck, and then steps back and swings out his hands as though he said, 'All ready.'* GOLMOZO *turns towards opening of path through woods. He signals by holding up his right hand. After a little enter, down path from wood, four young men carrying a palanquin. The young men are from* 18 *to* 20 *years of age, slight, moustaches, rather unshaven chins. Their faces are healthy, fairly plump, like that of* GOSSGOGOCK. *They are dressed in yellow short jackets, yellow trousers, pale blue shirts. Their hats are similar to* TED'S. *They each wear the Wave Collar and the wine-coloured poncho-like Cloak, and slippers made of plaited straw. Their clothes, cloaks and all are ragged, worn and patched: their sleeves out at elbows. The palanquin, which is slung on a pole, is of tarnished gilt and has pale stained blue curtains and wine-coloured cushions inside. The palanquin bearers advance slowly down the stage, Left. The two leading bearers draw aside the curtains and then the second bearers straighten the cushions, all to a quiet swing, as to a known ceremonial. The four bearers stand side by side, then advance very slowly in time towards the dead body, swinging, their arms hung down.*)

THE CURTAIN FALLS

The Silencer

or

Farewell Speech

A Play in Three Acts

CHARACTERS

HILDERBRAND.
MALONEY.
CURTIS.
JOHNSON.
MARSHALL.
HARTIGAN.
TYLER.
RANSOME.
TORNBY.
SAM.
HARDY.
FRED.
HILL.
SNOWEY.
FIRST CONSTABLE.
SECOND CONSTABLE.
BARMAID, OLD WORKING MEN, POLICEMAN, NEWSPAPER
    BUYER, THIN WOMAN, LANDLORD.

ACT ONE

Scene 1: *Small city bar, neat wine bar type, upside-down champagne bottle arrangement on right. Corner of larger bar with* BARMAID, *which shows to left and back. City street seen beyond that, wire screen on lower part of glass door. Nondescript men, rather City type come in to larger bar and go out.* BARMAID *of small bar, woman of about 35, old-fashioned statuesque type, neatly dressed in black, with spray of lily of the valley pinned on front of dress.* HILDERBRAND—*dark, saturnine, handsome, tall with Vandyke black beard.* MALONEY *large Father Flynn type of London Irish.* CURTIS *small busy type of man, fair with glasses.* JOHNSON, *heavy, reddish-fair type. All in city clothes.* HILDERBRAND *and* MALONEY *with tall hats. Other two grey soft felt.* CURTIS *is drinking champagne.* HILDERBRAND *and* JOHNSON *port,* MALONEY *whiskey.*

Right and left means as they appear to audience.

HILDERBRAND   The first day of Summer.

MALONEY   Very nice, too. Coming up in the train from Brighton the hedges were blazing with colour; it warmed the old cockles of my heart. Talking about cockles and hearts (*he drinks up his drink*): we'll have the same again.

HILDERBRAND   I must get back to the Office.

MALONEY   Never mind; this is a very good office for a moment or two. Miss—(*he attracts* BARMAID'S *attention*).

CURTIS   You should say Mavourneen.

MALONEY   I said Mavourneen once too often. (*All laugh.*)

(ALL *take their drinks, lifting their glasses as if giving a toast.*)

HILDERBRAND   Port.

JOHNSON   Port.

CURTIS   Champagne.

MALONEY   Mine's whiskey.

CURTIS   I see by the weather forecast this morning that we're promised another depression from the North Sea.

JOHNSON   Yes, I saw that.

HILDERBRAND   Yes, I believe we are in for a long spell of these depressions.

MALONEY   Well, you can't have hills without valleys.

CURTIS   Quite so, and in business we all find that. However, I can't complain.

ACT 1
SCENE 1
A CITY BAR

Mukted glass

Mukted glass

JOHNSON   That's the advantage of having a good article to sell.

MALONEY   Well, I sell advice and that's always a good article.

CURTIS   I see by the paper this morning that they are selling eight-room freehold villas out at Bolsey for five fifty, company's water, gas, electric, roads. I tcan't be done. There must be a screw loose somewhere. In fact, several screws loose.

MALONEY   Out at Bolshie, you must mean. (*All laugh.*)

JOHNSON   Well, I don't know. I hope we have a good summer this year. I like a bit of gardening.

CURTIS   I like good weather it's handy for getting about.

JOHNSON   I like a bit of garden and a lawn to mow; round about London Bridge. I got a fellow that sharpens up a lawn mower really first class. I belong to country stock; the country's in my blood.

MALONEY   Blood will tell.

HILDERBRAND   Undoubtedly. The point of it is that you instinctively turn to your first environment.

CURTIS   I saw in the paper this morning in a judicial separation action a feller said it was all on account of environment.

MALONEY   Well, I don't know about that.

(JOHNSON *laughs. All laugh.*)

JOHNSON   I'm very partial to primroses. They were a picture this year.

CURTIS   Yes, along the railway embankments.

JOHNSON   One spring down in Devonshire—I took my holiday early that year—the primroses and the wild violets were a perfect picture. They really were. I shall never forget them.

CURTIS   Down in Bucks, on Saturday, in the car, I noticed some of the cottage gardens were very tasty indeed. I like to saunter along sometimes. If you can spare a half hour or so, it's pleasant to dawdle along at about 12 or 15 and see how the people enjoy themselves. It does you good and you can catch up on it afterwards by pushing her along on an extra good stretch. I like speed, and it's the contrast that makes it taste good.

JOHNSON (*to* HILDERBRAND)   How many cars have you now, Mr Hilderbrand?

HILDERBRAND   Only three just now.

MALONEY   Well, they certainly are a great convenience.

(*All the time they are talking,* BARMAID *is polishing bottles with a duster settling flowers in her dress and busying herself generally about the back of her bar, not taking any notice of her customers. Enter left, through glass door at back,* CHARLES MARSHALL, *tall, heavy man about 65, grey moustache, dull grey clothes, hard felt hat.* HARTIGAN, *rather short, dark swarthy man about 45, with open expression, clean shaven, old grey suit.*)

MARSHALL   Ah, Hilderbrand! Ah, Moloney! I have a compatriot of yours here. Mr Hartigan—Mr Maloney, Mr Hilderbrand.

(*They shake hands.*)

MALONEY (*introduces others*)   Curtis. Mr Marshall. Mr Hartigan. Mr Marshall, Johnson, Mr Hartigan.

(*All shake hands.*)

MARSHALL   Mr Hartigan is a connection of my daughter's husband's. He's just blown in from all round the World in every direction. He's just been telling me all about it. It's most interesting.

JOHNSON   Travelling is wonderful. I long to see the great wide open spaces; the palms, the nuts, the blue sea.

HARTIGAN   Yes, you get a lot of sights travelling. Sometimes they are a sight too much for you. But it fills the memory.

MALONEY   What will you have, Mr Hartigan and Mr Marshall?

HILDERBRAND   No, no; this is on me. What is yours, Mr Hartigan?

HARTIGAN   Old square face, I suppose, with a dash of Angostura.

HILDERBRAND   And yours, Marshall?

MARSHALL   Port for me.

HILDERBRAND (*to* BARMAID)   As before and Mr Marshall will take port and Mr Hartigan an 'old square face' whatever that is, and a dash of Angostura.

(BARMAID *fills out drinks; all drink, looking towards* HILDERBRAND.)

HARTIGAN   I haven't been in London for years and it's changed. Every place changes as soon as your back is turned. I wouldn't know Cork, I suppose, if I saw it now.

MALONEY   As the saying is, I never saw Cork, but I often saw drawings of it. . . . (*imitates the popping of a cork and slaps his cheek to represent the liquor running out of a bottle. All laugh.*)

HARTIGAN   Wonderful drawings the Chinese used to do of ships. You couldn't always recognize the ship, but the curley sea was always magnificent. Curious thing how fond old sailors were of having a picture painted of their ships. They were very particular, too. Everything had to be just so. I suppose where every moment of a man's life at sea depends on exactness, it affects him in every way for ever. But all the old sailors I ever knew gave as good as they got. Exact they were and exacting. In the face of the overwhelming and embittering forces of rock, air and sea those old boys stood up to all their troubles. They lived and died game. I saw an old sailor man one time a good way down in the Antarctic. He stripped himself, put an iron billaying pin in his mouth and he said 'Iron to iron', and he stood up on the deck facing sleet and snow and bare to the buff, and he shouted out loud 'I'll split the wind or my breast bone', and he was slapping his old chest all the time and then stretching out his eight old fingers and his thumbs, as if he could scratch the venom out of a hurricane. It took three of us to pull him down and throw him into his bunk and sluice him well with rum. The old man sent his steward down with it—a whole bottle full. Ah, those were the days. The days of old, the days that are no more.

JOHNSON   Well, I never saw anything like that in all my life.

CURTIS   I saw the other day in one of the illustrated papers a photo of one of the last of the windjammers. It looked very old.

HILDERBRAND   Extraordinary.

HARTIGAN   I knew a cowboy once, one of the old school! He had absolutely golden hair, long straight golden hair hanging down to his shoulders. He was six foot two and rawboned. He had blue eyes. He was a very nice man except when he was full of old rye and then he was nice too—to his friend. But he didn't always know his friend when the old rye was well up between his eyes. And the worst of it was that one time in the gay old days of old some travelling quack oculist told him his sight was in danger if he didn't get a pair of glasses at once. So old Charlie Weston got a pair of gold mounted nose nips and wore them on a string from his neck. But he never used them until the Old Rye was in command. Then he would fix the glasses on his nose, take a six shooter in each hand, and go look for his friends so as to locate them before shooting up his enemies. It was serious work having him squint in your face seeing if he could recognize you while he pushed your stomach in with his six shooters.

JOHNSON   What a life these men lead.

MARSHALL   That's nothing to the individuals he'll tell you about. How he existed with them, I don't know. It's beyond me. But I suppose it takes all sorts to make a world.

HILDERBRAND   It does indeed.

JOHNSON   All sorts and conditions of men.

MALONEY   Sorting themselves out as they go.

(*All laugh a little.*)

CURTIS   I suppose, Mr Hartigan, you notice how serious the traffic problem is becoming in the city.

HARTIGAN   Seemed a lot of vehicles about.

CURTIS   I believe that if careful note was taken it would be found that the traffic through this street alone was advancing at the rate of twenty-five per cent per three months. A hundred yards east of here there was a traffic block which extended for an alarming distance. I was hurrying out to lunch, but I felt impelled to note carefully the extent of the trouble, and my considered opinion is that something must be done about it—and soon.

MALONEY   And it's no use whatever to the licensed trade, for though the chauffeurs have plenty of time usually to get down and throw a few drinks into their carburettors, still the block may break away at any moment.

CURTIS   Still these things have to go on—Progress.

JOHNSON   Progress. Yes, I suppose there's no doubt we have greater conveniences than our grandfathers.

HILDERBRAND   Oh, things are magnificent now compared . . .

CURTIS   Compared to the old-fashioned days, we live extraordinary interesting lives.

HARTIGAN   I saw a man once upwards of eighty years of age, driving six horses in a coach across the plains. They said he came from the Rio Grande.

CURTIS   Yes, I'm afraid some of our modern speed merchants would treat him as a joke, but still, eighty years of age.

MARSHALL   We're all getting older.

CURTIS   You're just as old as you feel, eh Johnson?

JOHNSON   I don't feel anything like my age except when I've got a touch of lumbago.

MARSHALL   That's a nasty thing.

CURTIS   Very nasty.

JOHNSON   Sudden changes of the weather in the spring and you've got to be very careful. Not a nice thing, is it, Mr Hartigan?

HARTIGAN   No, very nasty indeed.

MALONEY   Lumbago! Don't say a word about it.

MARSHALL   Well, the local practitioner out where I live gave me some stuff to rub on last year and by Jove it certainly was strong, it quite took my breath away.

HILDERBRAND   And that takes a lot of doing, you dirty-faced dog, you! If you'd lost your breath this morning you wouldn't have told the Westerly People that I couldn't deliver the stuff up to my sample.

(*Advances with hands down but rather threateningly
towards* MARSHALL.)

MALONEY   Gentlemen, gentlemen! Before the lady!

(BARMAID *takes languid interest, just a look over her shoulder.*)

MARSHALL (*backing towards left*)   What I said was only as a business man to a business man, and if you think you can brow-beat me, you are very much mistaken.

(HILDERBRAND *continues to advance.*)

MARSHALL (*as he retires round partition to left*)   If ever I come across you again I'll break every bone in your body.

(*Turns round and leaves through outer bar and glass door.*)

(*A short wait.*)

JOHNSON (*finishing drink*)   Well, I must be going I suppose.

(*Exit.*)

CURTIS   Well, well, well. Business is business I always say. I've got a customer in the West End; I've got to see him in his Club. I don't like these Club meetings. Goodbye, Mr Hartigan. Goodbye, Hilderbrand. Coming my way, Maloney?

MALONEY   Yes, part of it.

(*Exit* CURTIS *and* MALONEY.)

HILDERBRAND (*as* HARTIGAN *begins to go away*)   I'm sorry this occurred but it's been coming for some time. But I'm sorry it occurred now and that this Marshall is a friend of yours. I'm doubly sorry because you interest me, Hartigan. The Marshall business began two years ago. I took some of his trade away from him, without knowing it was his, and then someone poisoned his mind and he's knifed everything of mine he can since.

HARTIGAN   Why don't you sue?

HILDERBRAND   Oh no, he's always inside the law.

HARTIGAN   Well, he's only an in-law of mine, and I don't care if I never see him again.

HILDERBRAND   Still, I'm sorry it happened. However—are you settling in London for a time?

HARTIGAN   For a time. I'm at a loose end. I'm not on the rocks. I'll wait around and then look for a shore job, as the sailors say; something easy and amusing.

HILDERBRAND   Well, in a little while I'll have an easy job I could offer you. I am afraid the office wouldn't stand anything very grand in the way of salary, but I'd raise it later on. It's the desk just outside my private room, just to keep tag of my engagement book and watch out for my telephone bell, and the main thing—the main thing is to keep callers, who have to be kept waiting, in a good humour. You see, sometimes I'm talking to A. while B. is waiting, and B. has to be kept calm and amused, and kept off thinking until A. has gone off by the outer door in my room. Sometimes I want them to meet, sometimes I don't, and that's the way it goes. I'd like to have you. Well, come and see me before the end of the week and we'll fix it up somehow. Of course I'd always put you on to any good thing I had coming along.

(*As they talk they go out left through outer bar.* HILDERBRAND *holding door and letting* HARTIGAN *out first.*)

Curtain.

Scene 2: HILDERBRAND's *outer office two weeks later. On left outer door with muffed glass. Small knee-hole desk with telephone left. Private office door on right of centre, muffed glass; chair against wall. Office wardrobe extreme right. Engraving of factory on wall.* HARTIGAN *behind desk:* HILDERBRAND *sitting on edge of desk.*)

HILDERBRAND   Go on. Tell me about the parrots in the trees.

HARTIGAN   Ah, they all flew away, and I followed after in a canoe, and where they settled I became Counsellor to the King of the Palm Tree Palaces, Palatzio el Palm Oil. Ah, nothing doing! They couldn't palm anything on me. This man wanted little here below but a singlet, a pair of ducks and a belt to hold 'em up. So after Royalty had told me all he could remember of the Arabian Nights learnt out of a copy he got from a flying Mish (he told them to me as the legends of his Nation), then I started in and told him Gulliver's Travels with additions. He was tickled to death almost. He liked anything I could tell him, and tales of adventure by sea he loved best of all. He had an old State Canoe of his own, but he never was in it since he was a child. The State Canoe had a two foot beam and the old Bold Boy himself was very nearly four in a cross section. Once in the shallow end of home lagoon he made an effort, and with a couple of stately chiefs up to their waists on the port and starboard hand, he got a little way. But, well, he looked to me like a man trying to ride a Tishy full blown. I don't mean the fleshy Tishy of the days that are gone, but the indiarubber one the boys used to take in bathing with them.

HILDERBRAND (*stops and listens, looking towards door on left*)   Someone coming. This'll be Tyler. I'll see him in five minutes. But don't forget you've got to tell me more about that fat old King.

(*Goes quickly in through door right and shuts it quietly after him. Shadow appears on glass of door left; handle turned and enter* TYLER, *nondescript, pert business man.*)

TYLER   I have an appointment with Hilderbrand this morning.

HARTIGAN Yes sir, Mr Hilderbrand is expecting you. He's held up for a moment. Won't you sit down.

TYLER No, thank you. I prefer to stand. I'm rather pressed for time. Mr Hilderbrand has to settle a matter with me, then I'm off.

HARTIGAN You're rushed for time! I've seen a man rushed for time; I knew him, a racing cyclist of pedalling days. His name was Spare and they called him Spare-neck for short. He was very short when I saw him—short of cash. He'd got to get to a coast track to win a race. He couldn't steal a ride because he'd done it too often. He tried to tie his machine to the end car but they cast him adrift. However, he darted in behind her, got the suction and held his own for two hundred and fifty miles.

(TYLER *sits down, drawing chair nearer to desk.*)

Hopping over the ties. The sleepers' sleepers! He didn't sleep himself for a month. Bumpity, bumpity, bumpity, bump! He made the coast all right and won his race and offered to compensate the Railway Company for loss of Dignity, so they gave him a free pass for life. So he got fatty legs and never raced again. So it comes, so it goes. And have you ever noticed the way the luck always plays from the sleeve! I believe, and I believe you, sir, believe the same, that Pandora's Box——

(*Bell rings on desk.*)

HARTIGAN (*takes up telephone*) Yes, sir. Mr Tyler is here, sir. Will you go in, Mr Tyler?

TYLER What about Pandora's Box?

HARTIGAN It's got a false bottom.

(*Exit* TYLER *through door on right. As he goes through door he says very cheerily—*'Hello, Hilderbrand!')

(*Murmur of pleasant voices from inner room or a laugh or two.* HARTIGAN *tidies up desk, gets up, moves about, straightens engraving on wall, puts chair back in place. Opens drawers of desk, looks in, closes them, generally busies himself. Enter* RANSOME. *Tall, liverish-looking man, heavy black moustache, in long black top coat, dark grey trousers, black soft felt hat, bright blue neck tie.*)

RANSOME Is Mr Hilderbrand to be seen this morning?

HARTIGAN I'm sure he'll see you, Mr Ransome, but he's engaged at the moment. I'll tell him you're here. (*Takes up telephone*) Mr Ransome, sir, would be glad if you could see—yes. . . . five? . . . ten? fifteen? Three, very good sir. (*to* RANSOME) Just a moment and Mr Hilderbrand will see you. Won't you sit down? (*Gets up and gets chair for* RANSOME *who sits down restlessly*) Ah, Mr Ransome, how are the Chilterns looking? Very blue and beautiful I have no doubt these mornings. I hope you have a view from your breakfast room; a breakfast with a view is worth seven breakfasts with a dead wall out-look. Of course in a sense everything is a view, a point of view. Take a breakfast room with a dead wall view with a view to suicide. (RANSOME *glares at him gloomily: telephone bell rings*) Yes, sir; at once. With a view to a more circumscribed horizon, but a more cheerful one for old friends; take a cheerful view yourself and put off suicide, for Hilderbrand will see you now. (*Rises, opens inner door for* RANSOME *who sighs deeply and goes in, passing* MR TYLER *who is going out.*)

TYLER   Goodbye, my boy!

HILDERBRAND   Goodbye, Wat.

(*Murmur of low voices if possible.* HARTIGAN *continues tidying up desk, changes position of note books, ink stand, etc. Tears a letter or two from pocket and puts them in waste paper basket. Takes novel with staring jacket from drawer. No particular novel jacket, just bright dabs and streaks of colour. Tries to read from beginning then skips a lot of pages, looks at end, back to beginning, closes sadly and puts novel back in drawer, folds arms tightly on breast and looks straight before him for some time. Door bursts open. Enter* CHARLES TORNBY, *short, blooming golden-haired young man, clean shaven, very smart, light clothes, bright tweed overcoat, flower in button hole, gloves, white spats, brown boots very shiny, smoking long cigar.*)

TORNBY   I've got an appointment for 12.45 with Mr Hilderbrand. (*Looks at wrist watch*) It's just a few minutes short of that.

HARTIGAN   I'll tell Mr Hilderbrand you're here. (*Fiddles about a little and takes up telephone*) Mr Tornby to see you. Yes. Yes. Yes. Yes. Yes, sir, (*looks attentive*) Yes. (*puts back receiver*) Mr Hilderbrand will be a minute or two, but he won't keep you. He has an old family friend in with him now, very difficult to get rid of, but he'll move him on in a moment. These family friends can be a tiresomeness sir.

TORNBY   I am an orphan.

HARTIGAN   Sad, sad. But wasn't there some story about orphans braving storms, though I suppose it cuts both ways, as the sailor said when the wind backed, and the snows of yesterday came again. And I tell you that a topsil yard is a poor perch for snow gambolling and a snow-ball fight in the ship boy's eyes is a poor substitute for eiderdown quilts, footwarmers and hot grog. And there's no use telling me that if you fall overboard the temperature of the sea will seem warm and comfortable in comparison with a frozen deck. Contrast isn't everything.

TORNBY   I don't quite follow you, but you interest me exceedingly.

HARTIGAN   Don't try to follow; it's of no consequence. Sailors on frozen decks have to walk very Agagishly. I saw miners, genuine miners—all of them had red shirts—playing with a frozen deck of cards. When they prised them apart with their jack knives, they put each card on the knife point and simmered it in front of the fire a while to thaw it; but it was interesting, too, because those miners had useful memories for faces and back views and each knew the cards he himself had toasted. After a dozen hands had been played, the game became too physiological, and they turned it into Snatch, snatch, run and shoot; or shoot, snatch and run; or shoot, shoot, shoot. I was having a bird's eye view from a bird's nest of this battle. I was comfortable enough but I was nervous, for I got afraid that the owner of the nest might come home at any moment to his eyrie. I don't know what bird he was, but I feared him. By the size of his nest he must have been about as big as a calf.

TORNBY   Splendid!

HARTIGAN   Big and splendid I could handle, but you see he might have been big and punctilious and petty and it was getting toward two o'clock in the morning, when, you remember Napoleon said, the best sort of courage manifests itself. But suppose that old bird had it and I hadn't; what then? But there was a lull down around the fire, so I slid down my tree and approached the boys very carefully, and as I went I said: 'What about a game of forfeits?' They were a terrible tough crew. They'd had none of the benefits of a Home Life, and when I explained the game of forfeits to them they were delighted. They began at once sharpening up their knives on stones. (*Door in distance inside inner room, is heard to bang*) That's Mr Hilderbrand's old family friend gone, I expect. (*Bell rings*) Yes. Now. Quite so. Now, Mr Tornby, Mr Hilderbrand is quite ready for you. (*Jumps up and goes toward door to open it.* TORNBY *rises but stops and comes towards* HARTIGAN).

TORNBY   You can't leave it like that. Your miner friends were sharpening their knives—

HARTIGAN   Sharp knives are sometimes better than sharp tongues. That's a moral remark. But just then my late host—if a host can be a host in Absentia—came home with a sharp tongue and a jag on. I never actually saw him because I was busy watching my step at the time. But he darkened the sky and my miners must have taken it as an omen, and they began looking regretfully at the knives and putting them back in the sheaths. But man is but a changing arrow of the sky; a turnspit on a tower, ever wavering, ever trying to catch the wind by running before it, ever spinning on a high heel. Mister-face-all-round with a knife, one moment nestling in a pigskin sheath and next in between some human ribs. So I sailed out of camp. I got five seconds start, and my boys in the red shirts had high miners' boots on while I wore dancing pumps. So I went away doing three yards to their one. They fired a few shots, but wide. Then one of them accidentally hit his friend's hip pocket, with its pocket pistol made of glass, and all the old Rye was spilt on the earth again; produced by the earth, it went back to the earth again. The miners stopped hunting me instantly. They felt the occasion was romantic. Like all men dressed in fancy dress, they were fanciful. (*During the talk* HARTIGAN *goes to open tdoor, bu* TORNBY *holds up his hand to stop him and sits down.*)

TORNBY   I have noticed these things myself, but I find it hard to express my thought. I will begin travelling more soon; since this money came my way I have done a little touring with a tutor; very dry. But—

(*Door opens and* HILDERBRAND *looks out.*)

HILDERBRAND   Ah, Tornby; glad to see you.

TORNBY   Ah, Hilderbrand; glad to see you. I have been chatting with your—your—your—secretary; we've had an interesting chat. I haven't noticed the time going (*looks at watch*)—My word I haven't noticed indeed. I've got ten minutes to get to Paddington. I'm going down to the country for the week-end. I must be off. Not a moment. I'll see you Monday 12 o'clock, say 11.45. Goodbye, Hilderbrand, goodbye. Goodbye, sir. (*To* HARTIGAN. *He goes out of door on left with top coat tails flying.* HILDERBRAND *sits down heavily in chair which* TORNBY *has just left.*)

HILDERBRAND   Fifty thousand of the best gone west from Paddington. Hartigan, you are too expensive a luxury for me.

HARTIGAN   Oh, won't it be all right on Monday?

HILDERBRAND   On Monday, Tornby will perhaps come here, most likely he will just call me up. But there will be no fifty thousand for us; we won't be able to go to allotment. Lord Garravogue is spending the week-end at the same place, and he has something much more attractive to offer for the money. Hartigan, I am sorry. We must part. You must do what you can for yourself and I hope you'll be all right. I'll write you a cheque for a month's salary (*goes towards his own office door*). No, for two months. (*Goes into inner office.*)

(HARTIGAN *sits down in chair just left by* HILDERBRAND *and looks straight before him and round the room in a bewildered way, then looks down on the floor.* JOHNSON *comes in at door left. He has a new green watering-can, partly wrapped up, and some seed lists in his hands. He is gazing at* HARTIGAN *as* HILDERBRAND *comes into office with cheque in his hand.*)

JOHNSON   Hello, Hilderbrand! Is Hartigan ill?

HILDERBRAND   We are both not well.

JOHNSON   You haven't both eaten something queer or anything? You're not poisoned or anything?

HILDERBRAND   Yes, in a sense we are poisoned, but it wasn't with anything queer. No, our friendship is poisoned; poisoned by fifty thousand dirty quid. Hartigan has cost me that to-day, and we know I could not have him sitting here always to remind us both how much he cost. (*He gives* HARTIGAN *the cheque.* HARTIGAN *folds it nervously and puts it into his trouser pocket; goes to office wardrobe, takes out coat and hat, looks about him, and stands still.* HILDERBRAND *comes to him and shakes his hand.*)

JOHNSON   I'm dreadfully sorry about this. Look here, we mustn't lose sight of him. I don't know what has happened but I feel—

HILDERBRAND   What has happened is that Hartigan with the best will in the world held a fifty thousand pound customer too long. So long that he finally became no customer at all.

JOHNSON   That's serious; very, very serious. But still when I am working in my quiet garden this evening, I will not be able to think of Hartigan friendless, and there are no fifty thousand customers coming into our office to be lost. So if Hartigan finds himself without a job, I know I could get him the job of confidential messenger. Not very grand pay, but enough to keep him going. All we want is willingness and honesty. (*Shakes hands with* HARTIGAN) Next week, any day, call in and see me.

(*Exit* HARTIGAN.)

JOHNSON   I'm sorry.
HILDERBRAND   I'm sorry, and in a way it's my fault.

Curtain.

Scene 3: JOHNSON's *office. Desk on right. Door on left back. Behind desk new garden rake with new gardening gloves and other parcel tied on it.* JOHNSON *sitting at desk.* HARTIGAN *standing, holding dispatch case in which* JOHNSON *is putting long envelopes.*

JOHNSON   250 in Bonds and notes to 150. (HARTIGAN *locks case and puts key in pocket*) Run down to the safe deposit with these for the week-end, then come back here at once and we'll have a chat together over a cup of coffee in the Oceanwide Café. My train doesn't go till 2 o'clock.

(*Exit* HARTIGAN, JOHNSON *studies seed list, then begins putting things away from desk into drawers. Unpacks parcel with rose nippers and garden name pegs. Reads more from seed list. Fusses about. Gets out pipe from bag, fills it carefully and puts away in bag again. Door opens slowly. Enter* HARTIGAN— *hat dusty and bashed in.* HARTIGAN *and* JOHNSON *gaze at each other.*)

HARTIGAN   It's gone. The money. Two men hustled me—butted at me while I was talking to a man who wanted to know the way to get to

Commercial Road East. Said he was a sailor and asked me what chances there were for a hardworking old shell-back in Copra Trade these days. I know it was set for me and I fell into it. I tried to chase after the two that got the case but there were too many people, too much crowd. So I came back to you, Johnson.

JOHNSON   Hartigan, this is dreadful, dreadful. However, I feared something would happen to you somehow. But it's a good thing there wasn't a larger lot in the bag. (*He opens drawer in desk, takes out Insurance Policy and looks at it*) Hartigan, I was afraid for you so I insured against this. I'll be able to give you the money for you to reimburse the firm. You will, of course, have to keep it absolutely to yourself that it isn't your own money. Tell them it's your own savings from some of your old tradings in the South Sea Islands. And after that, of course, you'll have to go, and I can only promise if ever I hear of anything that might be a safe job for you, I'll let you know. From time to time let me have your address. Everything was going on so nicely, Hartigan, it is a blow to you. I know it must be; but your life has been a series of blows, blow high, blow low. I remember that wonderful account you gave me of the hurricane in the Islands—the curley one with the forked tail. An extraordinary night you must have spent huddled under the ruins of the store, with the villagers singing choruses and the leading native dancer pinned under the debris doing intricate step dancing with his feet on the section of the roof which was lying just above his head. That must have been a night with a white stone for extraordinaryness. One of the strangest you ever spent.

HARTIGAN   Well, it ranked high but I spent a better one when the Circus Ship went ashore so suddenly that her figure-head busted in the saloon wall. She was the 'Golden West', an old paddle boat, fifty years in commission. She'd started out on Sacramento River:

(*Recites.*)

In the days of old,
The days of gold,
The days of forty-nine

and when her figure-head came through the match boarding, the animals—horse, monkey, lion and bear, came in over the nose of her and the whole human troupe, with her Captain and Old Hole-in-the-Day, the Circus Owner, fighting for the honour of the rear guard. But Captain Garvey was the last to leave the ship. It was a big saloon but it played to capacity that night. Charlie the shirt and Albermarl, the bartenders, worked hard that night. But the monkeys, of course, lent a hand . . . It would make you cry tears down to see the pleased expression of a simple planter when he received his gin and tansy from a monkey's tail, neatly curled round the tumbler, the monkey's paws being engaged in tossing up some fancy drink for the one tourist who ever hit those Islands, and he was jaded when he came. That was a night! . . . Thirty-nine hours long! It came to an end when she went dry at 2 o'clock in the afternoon of the second day—but your train is at 2 o'clock.

JOHNSON   Ah, I've missed it. But it's no matter. I'll go by the slow one. (*Looks at watch*) That goes in about twenty minutes, but I don't know . . . (*hesitates*).

HARTIGAN   You mustn't miss it. I'll walk across the bridge with you and put you on your way.

(JOHNSON *slowly locks up desk, takes parcel, lets* HARTIGAN
out and follows.)

Curtain.

ACT TWO

Scene 1: *Bar of 'The Ship in Port'. Six months later. Door opening on street left, bar on right with other bar further back on right with window in end.* TILDA, *chubby small barmaid about 20, wearing glasses, reading bright paper-covered detective story by window.* SAM, *fattish, seedy, middle-aged sailor in well-worn shore clothes, a battered sailor's peaked cap, grey muffler.* HARTIGAN, *same dress as before but seedier, standing in doorway, left.*

SAM   I spotted you the minute. I got a memory for faces. You remember me?

HARTIGAN   No, I don't.

SAM   No. You lost your job and I'm sorry you did. But come and have a snifter.

HARTIGAN   I don't recall you.

SAM   Not the old sea dog—the old shell-back?

HARTIGAN   Some old ship-mate, eh?

SAM   Ship-mate, all right-o! Come in and have one. (*They come in to bar*) I'm going to tell you something for your good.

HARTIGAN   You are the lad we took off the berg down in the Antarctic?

SAM   No. No bergs. Miss! (*Taps on bar, having taken money out of a bag with string round it*) What'll you have, old son of the sea?

HARTIGAN   I'll have a glass of port.

SAM   Port, miss, and I'll have a pint. (TILDA *brings drinks, waits behind bar a moment, then takes up her book*) That's it. . . . Detective story. Nothing does these young ladies but tales of crime. (TILDA *gives a little perfunctory dusting to bottles behind bar, and goes off to her seat by the window with her book*) Here's another kind love for the Sailor Boy!

HARTIGAN   Good health!

SAM   Don't you remember in Fenchurch Court six months ago the Bold Sailor Boy who asked you about the prospects for a life for a toiler in the Islands?

HARTIGAN   You!

SAM   Yes, me. And I'm God-damn sorry you got in bad about it. I knew they'd bounced you for I see'd a new lad on your job. I tell you I didn't touch much of the stuff. Now, you're a gifted man; you have speech and you're getting nothing out of it. It's a gift, I tell you. Used properly it leads its owner to what they call Fame and Fortune. Why some of that you told me about the Copra days was a poem. Like a Hymn. But with more to it! You come along of me this afternoon and use your gift. The boys have a job on. Lock-up shop, very handy.

HARTIGAN Robbery like you did on me?

SAM No, not like that—that was a dirty little job, anyhow. No, no; there's some style to this one. (*Looks at clock behind bar*) The boys are going in now. I'm watching the street end and a nasty-faced feller called Hill the Spiller is in the arch, and on account of it's Saturday they'll be no one about but the plain clothes man that comes down regular; we've got his time, and what the boys want you to do is chat him and keep him away.

HARTIGAN I'm not going to have anything to do with it. I've seen too much of it.

SAM Well, come along my way anyhow. I wish I was back on the rolling deep myself, or a river—a rolling river. You seen some of that big river stuff, I suppose; monkeys and parrots and crocodiles and jays, and maidens all in brown?

HARTIGAN Yes; I been on the big rivers rafting it. I saw a raft one time on old Mississip, old Papa of the Waters; I seen a raft it was so big from stem to stem that they earthed a surface on it and had a trotting race track on it. The raft gang had an old three-cornered red mare of their own on board. Artful old Minnie she was. She used to sigh so loud you'd think it was a steam boat coughing against the stream. If she once got in front nothing could pass her; she had a way of swinging the turns so that the buggy went out at right angles. One time the tackle (*pronounced taakle*) gave way and the buggy and the drivers went out into the river. Those rafters won a lot of money with that old mare. She never looked herself; she always had something up her sleeve. I don't believe I ever saw her fully extended. She sighed before a race and laughed after. (*As they are talking,* SAM *is moving him towards the door*) Some people think horses don't laugh. Why, I tell you there is more sense of humour in a horse than in many a ——

(*They go out of door left*)

Curtain.

Scene 2: *Maygrove Street, Street, grey stone, corner of side street on extreme left: side street consists of locked-up goods stores. Narrow dark arch with alleyway behind it. On right of centre, locked and shuttered shop, bar and padlock across door. Name over shop* 'D. MOLES, JEWELLER'. *On right of shop, yard gate closed.* SAM *and* HARTIGAN *come along side street.* HILL, *small red-faced, hard-featured, clean-shaven, about 30, worn blue reever suit, tweed cap, dark muffler, flattened close against wall of archway, almost hidden in dark.* HARDY, *heavy, tall, plain-clothes policeman, with heavy brown moustache, soft brown felt hat, grey overcoat, comes quietly along from right.*

HARTIGAN   That was the way it always was with those boys; they were all for a life on the mountain tops.

SAM   Now go to him and keep him away. (*Pushes* HARTIGAN *round corner into front street and slides along wall of side street himself.*)

(HARTIGAN *walks towards* HARDY. *They meet right of centre.*)

HARDY   Got a light, mate? (*Produces cigarette.*)

HARTIGAN (*searches pocket*) No; last one gone. I remember I finished the box last smoke I had.

HARDY   You're a stranger about here, I suppose? Going to the Match?

HARTIGAN   No; is it a good one?

HARDY   Oh, very important. The Causeway Park Rovers and the Old-worth's Second Team. Seen any people looking as if they were gathering for going to the game? I'm expecting some relations from my old country home for the Match, and they might have lost their way. Did you notice anyone?

HARTIGAN   No, I didn't see anyone.

HARDY (*takes match box from pocket and lights his cigarette*)   You're following the sea, perhaps? It's a rough life they say.

HARTIGAN   Rough enough at times. But there are rougher lives. (*As* HARTIGAN *talks,* HARDY *turns toward right and they move slowly a foot or two in that direction*) Painting a suspension bridge over a canyon, surging in the air in a bosun's chair, in a gale of wind, and the safety man down below holding the end of your rope shooting craps with the other painter's mate, and both your chairs a-swinging to the gale, expecting every moment to meet and clash in the air and spill the red lead and the red blood down the dizzy depths below. I've never done it myself, but I've seen it done a score of times.

HARDY   What sort of men would these painters be? Desperate men?

HARTIGAN   Not at all. The last man I saw on the job was an artist painter. Used to paint miniatures of babies, but the mothers of the infants bothered him so much that he lost his nerve and took the job on the bridge for a rest.

HARDY   Rest, eh? Do these men live long? Don't the life take it out of them?

HARTIGAN   Live long! That's according to what you'd call long. I knew a man up in the mountains of Mexico. They said he was a hundred and twenty-five. He was an exhibit at a sort of a health resort they had out there. Used to show him to the tourists to show what the mountain air would do for you. The old bard himself used to have them send him down into the valley to sleep. He couldn't stand the noise the tourist invalids kicked up all night, singing and dancing and talking about how much better they were feeling. They always sent him down in a covered car. Of course, if the drift of invalids had seen old hundred and twenty-five skipping down to the valley they would have been off after him to get his secret from him. The secret of long life is the secret that people spend the most of their long lives hunting. I never met a long-lived man but he'd have a lot of 'mum mum mum' talk about it as if he'd done something clever himself. The Proprietor of that Sanatorium was about thirty-five himself, fat, and booked for his last passage pretty soon and he guessed it. But he told me if I found myself alive in another hundred years and came to see him and reminded him about me, he'd give me the job of Old-Man Live-for-ever-in-the-Mountain-Air. That is if the present old bird had pegged out, and if I wasn't too hideous looking. He said I'd make Old Bones perhaps, but if I did he didn't believe they'd be very nice old bones. That's not a very polite way to speak of an old friend's old bones. Now I ask you!

HARDY That's right. Not very polite; but still, taking everything into account, these mountain top places are, I suppose, as healthy as any situation in the world.

HARTIGAN Healthy! Healthy enough; but you've got to take the thick with the thin, and the high air made the natives very highly strung and impatient, and not a night went by but some Cabalerro got a bullet in him somewhere. The doctor in the valley used to prod the bullets out of them and when they were all tucked in asleep in the Cottage Hospital, he'd call up Old-Man-Live-for-ever-in-the-Mountain-Air to come round and look at the patient. It used to make the old man laugh. He had his own idea of fun. But the old man didn't like it at all. One time, he got a feverish cold and the proprietors of the Sanatorium got together a jury of matrons from the visitors and bribed the foreman or forewoman of the jury to bring in a verdict that the old man was teething. The old man didn't like that; he didn't mind getting younger every day, but there's a limit. Man must preserve his dignity, and I would always help a man to preserve his dignity.

(HARDY *is standing still, listening to* HARTIGAN *now most of the time. The door of the shop opens slightly (the bar having been cut through so that it looks as if the padlock and bar were still in working order), and two faces look out, and then the door is pulled to again.*)

HARTIGAN There is the dignity of the waves that sinks the ship, and there is the dignity of the wreck that sinks. There's a living dignity and there is the dignity of the dead. There is the dignity of the child's rattle and the last rattle in a throat. I have heard them all, and with a new body and a new heart, I'd hear them all again, under different circumstances. You can only cash a duffin cheque once.

HARDY Talking about duffin cheques, what's going to win the big race? You're the sort of man ought to know.

HARTIGAN That's where you make a natural mistake. I have made the same myself several times. Every horse is a winner until I find it—not that I'm what they used to call a perisher but I am too much of (*the door of the shop while he is speaking opened a little again. This time* HARDY *hears the noise made by the door and turns his head just a very little. He now watches off right behind* HARTIGAN's *head*) the ever flowing, ever bounding, ever bubbling stream of life to be allowed to roll into a winner because a winner is a static thing. But what's the good of a winner to a man without a large enough roll to make it worth while! Only a vexation of spirit, always ever after he dreams of what it'd be like if he'd had a couple of a thousand on it. What's the good of fifty to one in carroway seeds, though carroway seeds have comforted my sore heart before now. However, a sore heart is soon tied up in an old rag; if you aren't (*while he is speaking* HARDY *has been edging him away back towards wall so that they cannot be seen by any chance from crack in shop door, still always looking away right. He also takes a piece of paper out of pocket and writes on it, holding piece of paper against his left side and writing with pencil unseen to* HARTIGAN) there to do it for yourself some kind passer-by will do it for you—any old rag will do; never waste a good rag on an old heart. If you can hit the trail every day with a new heart, you are not doing so bad, and if you've got a new shiny heart, don't wear it on your sleeve but on your forehead and cheer the wayfarer that you meet in the early morning faring on his way. It's the early morning that tries them, it takes a bit of facing. But don't face it because you ought to, but because you've got a face. A face is built to meet the waves as they come. The nose is like the bow of the ship; the eyes the hawse holes; the ears the cat heads—cats' ears where the anchors hang a-dangling; and the mouth is the cream of it all, the waves that break with smiles. If you look over a ship's bow before dawn you see the white curve breaking bright—the brightest in all the world. (HARDY *is still looking right but turns carefully his head to the left now for a moment. As he does so* SAM *and* HILL *slide back out of sight and stay hid. On the right enters a policeman. He slowly passes behind* HARDY *who puts paper into his hand.* POLICEMAN *closes his hand over paper and passes steadily along stage and out left.* HARTIGAN *is talking all the time*). But a smile, only, don't laugh, before breakfast; only the gods laugh before breakfast. But they're laughing all the time and they don't need breakfast anyway. They say whom the gods love die young. It's truth. It's because the gods know that if they left them to grow old they'd grow out of their loveableness. But the ones the gods love best of all are the ones that they are able to love old. But the most difficult ones, the ones that put the gods to the pins of their collars to love, are the ones they love in the prime of life. They are like the salmon with the sea lice on him, shouldering through the seas. They ask no questions and they tell no lies. They go over nothing but through everything. They cut no corners. They give no hostages and they accept no prizes.

HARDY   True, true, very true!

HARTIGAN   No caps, no belts, no banners; they are their own banners. (*As they talk,* HARDY *gently moves* HARTIGAN *and himself forward so that they can be seen by anyone looking through crack in shop door*) They do nothing, they take; winnings suggest a winning post but they know no post; every post is with them, as the boys used to say, a winning post. Winning suggests a pulling up and a returning to the paddock; a wiping off of sweats, a receiving of congratulations, a shaking of hands, a weighing in, a taking up of winnings. And the prime boys couldn't stop for things like that; ever on and on they go, over hill and valley, river and stream, sea and strand, dry land and marsh land, road and bog, by horse and by foot, by wing and by fin, by paw and by hoof. Nothing stops them, for nothing can. They roll with the cloud and they zig-zag with the lightning. If ever anything stops them, it stops all. (*Motor horns heard left and right.* HARDY *steps away from* HARTIGAN) But that must never be for as they go they—

(*Crowd of policemen and plain clothes men arrive left and right.* HILL *backs away and disappears in alley. One elderly woman, quiet, charwoman type; one girl, quiet factory girl type; two old men, destitute, old working-men type; two little girls, one about 10, the other about 5, come in on heels of police.* SAM *mingles with these. Quietly and determinedly police, with truncheons drawn, and plain clothes men with revolvers, pull open the shop door and enter. Three more old destitute working men drift in. One* OLD WORKING MAN *to* HARTIGAN, *who is standing in a bewildered way where he was left:* 'What's it all about mate?' HARTIGAN *does not reply; just stands bewildered.*)

SAM (*coming up*)   Bolshies, I reckon!

2ND OLD WORKING MAN   Rooting 'em out, eh?

SAM   That's it, I reckon.

3RD OLD WORKING MAN   Not girls! Thought it was girls!

(*Noise of tramping about inside shop. Two policemen left outside, shove people back, though they are not really near the shop door. After a time, shop door opens and six men, handcuffed, rather seedily dressed in worn tweed clothes, with caps or felt hats. One of them, a large fat man, 'fat, a sort of Jolly Jumbo', but he must not be called Jolly Jumbo because there was a real man, Eccleston, and I am sure he never had anything to do with crooks. One small creature,* FRED, *led out between police and plain clothes men, taken away toward motor lorry on left, back of which has been backed into sight. People stand about a little, but* HARTIGAN, *after standing in the same place for a moment or two, moves off right.* SAM *moves after him.*)

POLICEMAN   Now then, move off to your 'omes, if you've got any!

Curtain.

Scene 3: *The same as Scene 2. A few weeks later, late evening.*

(*Enter* SAM *and* HILL *along street left.*)

SAM   What do you want with Hartigan?

HILL   I know what I want with Hartigan. I'm to settle up with him. There's no one to do it but me, and I'll do it if I swing.

SAM   No, don't you be silly, Spill. Hartigan got the lads took, but it wasn't that the bloody old fool meant it.

HILL   He meant it all right. Anyway, I attend to him.

SAM   Now, now; the boys don't think he did anything willingly on them.

HILL   How do you know that?

SAM   I'm sure of it. Why they always used to call him old Chatagain, and they knew it was his life, the talking.

HILL   Well, it's going to be his death now. The smallest dose them boys'll get'll be three years, and I'm not going to stand about to see that Hartigan walking in the open free, and selling his newspapers for three years while men that's tried to do work is in the hard places. I'm 'Truth and Justice'. I stand or fall by them two.

SAM   What's it to do with you if the boys don't ask for it?

HILL   I know, a life for a life, and if them hard-working chaps' times is added together, they'll come to as much as this Hartigan, if he was let live out his life, would live. A life for a life, I always said, and I say it now; and this is justice too. (*Takes parabellum pistol out of right hand pocket of jacket for a moment and drops it back again*).

SAM   You give me that thing. You'll be sorry afterwards if you don't.

HILL   Do you mean you'd put me out for Hartigan?

SAM   No, I couldn't go that far. But you aren't going to kill Hartigan.

HILL   No, I'm not going to kill him; I'm going to wipe the slate of 'im! I'm Truth and I'm Justice, and I'm dealing 'im them. I'm not a man, I'm an Avenge.

SAM   If anyone is done in, it ought in a way to be me, for it was me what introduced old Chatagain to the gang; it was my mistake. And in a sense it's not him that's responsible, it's me. (*They pace up and down while talking keeping to left of centre of stage*) It's me you ought to be shooting really, if it's justice you're so set on.

HILL   That's logic. I don't know nothing about logic. I'm truth and justice, and an infant child knows what they are. A life for a life. If they gets me, which they won't, and I goes on the drop, I'll know a life for a life.

SAM   If you're so set on it, why aren't you ready to give yourself up after you've done it?

(HILL *moves into alley and* SAM *with him on his right.*)

HILL   I'm truth and justice. They will prevail they says, and if they prevail on me I'm ready to do my bit for them. A life for a life; that's wot you can't get over. This Hartigan, Chatagain; I'll stop his chat for ever. I'll silence him. 'Silence in Court', that's what the crier says, and I'm the crier of truth and justice and when I say it, it will be silence. Silence what might be felt—Hush, hush! here comes your gifted friend!

(HARTIGAN *enters right. A little seedier in dress with evening papers and placard: 'SURPRISING DISASTERS'.*)

A VOICE RIGHT   Hi! That the last edition?

(*Enter newspaper buyer: dignified middle-aged man, short clipped beard, well dressed, thick overcoat, top hat, bank manager sort of man.*)

HARTIGAN   Yes, this is the last till to-morrow. If the world is gone in the night it will be gone without the help of the newspapers.

BUYER (*hands over money and takes paper; looks at it a moment*) What are these surprising disasters?

HARTIGAN   There's plenty of them. I've just got the papers from the van and I haven't had time to look at the news yet.

BUYER   Well, there are plenty of them but not too near this part of the world. China's a long way off, and 'pon my word they seem to like disasters there. Floods and storms, and fires and earthquakes. They seem to thrive on these things. The more Chinese are destroyed the more seems to be to take their place. I hope it doesn't mean the survival of the unfittest. Yes, but what won the race to-day? I didn't hear and I can't find the place. (*Searching paper.*)

HARTIGAN   I don't know myself and that's a fact, and the Chinamen don't know. . . . The Chinamen that were swept by the Sceptered elemental forces of their fates. Anyway, they died game. All deaths are game deaths; death sees to that. It's the penultimate moment that shakes the brave. Chinamen in all the parts of the world where I have seen them, appear to me to be neither waiting, nor watching, nor regretting. And you are doing the whole three this moment I know; I know it in my bones. And you can't deny it; and you don't want to deny it. (*Buyer moves to go away but stays*) You are afraid and ashamed of what you cannot help. You are saying to yourself that I'm one of these dud inspirational philosophers given away with a penny paper and you think I am holding you against your will, and you have no will. You are listening to me because you have nothing to say yourself. You are not going away because you have nowhere to go. You have forgotten you have a home. You have forgotten you have a tongue. The bell has forgotten it has a clapper. Anyway, you have no one to pull the bell rope for you and the bell can't get outside itself and pull its own bell rope, now can it? Speak me fair! You cannot speak me fair or unfair! You're held with a basilisktic stare. A basilisk of your own creation. You love the sound of me and you hate the sense. You love time and hate the clock. You wade in stars and hate the ocean seas that lap over you like a sinking tent.

(SAM *and* HILL, *hidden inside the entrance of the alley.* HILL *puts his hand in right pocket to pull out revolver.* SAM *signals to him with toss back of head to come away, and holds out packet of cigarettes to* HILL *who takes one with right hand.* SAM *strikes match on wall on his right and holds it to* HILL'S *cigarette. Lights one himself, then presses against* HILL'S *side where the parabellum is in the pocket.* HILL'S *right hand is engaged with his cigarette.*)

HARTIGAN   Look at your boots; they're all smeared with stars.

(BUYER *looks down at boots for a second.*)

HARTIGAN   And you don't know it, you could not say what street, what city you are in. You left a desk and you could not say where you left it. You are speechless because I talk for you. You think you speak yourself. You think I echo your thoughts. You have no thoughts; you never had thoughts. Those things that straggled across your brain were not thoughts, they were wheel tracks in the dust, and you have no idea what wheel made them. When your dust is gathered to its dust, it will make no difference to you. You have never existed in your own right. You exist now in mine. As the waves of the wind ripples the flag flying from its flag-pole, so you move and exist. As one ripple disappears on the flag's flying tail, another is beginning at the rope making its journey from the hoist to the fly. By my lips you live; by their stillness you pass away or back again into your solidity

of a poised dust mote. You could wish yourself alive but you will
never do it.

> (*While the talk goes on,* HILL *is reaching his left hand round
> behind his back.*)

HARTIGAN   The song says:
> Even the dear little fish,
> Though they can't think they can wish.

> (HILL *with his left hand has grabbed his parabellum from his right
> pocket. Hiding still along inside alley, he roars.*)

HILL   Stand clear you in the topper,
> Stand clear of that newsvendor.
> Here comes Truth and Justice.

> (SAM *tries to get at* HILL'S *left arm but* HILL *stretches it and fires, leaning
> muzzle close to corner of alley on left.* HARTIGAN *is hit in head; he has been
> standing over the* BUYER *on curb.* BUYER *in gutter.* HARTIGAN *clasps head
> which is now covered with blood and falls, carrying the* BUYER *with him in
> a heap on the roadway.* HILL *turns and disappears up alley.* SAM *goes a
> little way up alley.* BUYER *struggles to his feet covered with dust of road,
> stoops beside* HARTIGAN *who is dead. A handful of people come on; middle-
> aged women—poor, working-class, sleeves rolled up; a couple of elderly
> out-of-work men and then a young policeman.* SAM *comes running down
> alley.* POLICEMAN *inspects dead man, lifts hand and lets fall again.*)

BUYER   Someone shouted something—I do not know what—and then a
pistol shot rang out.
SAM   I heard it; it come from over there; (*pointing right.*)
BUYER   I thought it came from more this way; (*points*) but I was so confused
with the shout.
POLICEMAN   This man here has got a tattooing on his wrist. Sailor, I expect!
SAM   Looks like a sailor from foreign parts to me, and come to think of it,
when I passed a while ago, he was talking about Chinamen to this
gentleman.
BUYER   That's perfectly correct; he was talking about Chinamen. (*to* SAM) I
didn't notice anyone passing.
SAM   You was listening to what he was saying about Chinamen.
BUYER   That's perfectly correct; he was very interesting.
SAM   That's it you'll find, Constable. Chink. Revenge business! I've seen
pieces about it on the pictures.
BUYER   He certainly was talking wildly about Chinamen. But he talked
very wildly about a number of things.

POLICEMAN (*takes out notebook*)   Now, let's get some of this down.

BUYER   First of all, I have noticed the man before and indeed—

POLICEMAN   Now, just let's have your name and address, please.

BUYER   Name in full, I suppose!

POLICEMAN   Yes.

BUYER   Charles Allan Brownlow, 18 Wilholm Terrace, Wilholm Row.

POLICEMAN   Profession or business?

BUYER   Retired business man.

POLICEMAN   Now go ahead.

BUYER   —— and indeed not till this evening did I speak to him. I think it began by. . . . (SAM, *while the Buyer is talking, is quietly moving away right and off*) by making a remark about the disasters in the evening paper.

Curtain.

End of Act Two.

ACT THREE

Scene 1: *Outside the Seekers Bridge. Time; Six weeks later. Drab bare window, sickly yellow dun coloured wallpaper, door on right of centre. Card on door* THE SEEKERS BRIDGE. (*Voices heard singing. Thin voices of elderly women, gruff voices of old men.*)

> Lead Kindly Light amid the encircling gloom,
>   Lead Thou me on;
> The night is dark, and I am far from Home,
>   Lead Thou me on.
> Keep Thou my feet; I do not ask to see
> The distant scene; one step enough for me.

(SAM *and* HILL *enter, left, while the singing is going on.*)

SAM   What sort of a crib is this? Religious service! You don't get me at no religious service!

HILL   No, it's not a religious service. They're just singing a bit of a hymn to get up the atmosphere. Snowey says the spirits like it.

(*Singing goes on.*)

> So long Thy power hath blest me, sure it still
>   Will lead me on
> O'er moor and fen, o'er crag and torrent, till
>   The night is gone
> And with the morn those angel faces smile
> Which I have loved long since, and lost a while.

SAM   They didn't sing 'Amen'!

HILL   That shows it isn't a religious service. They're just working themselves up.

SAM   Give the door a whack and let's go in, so.

HILL   Oh no, you can't do that. There's a séance on, and it's only when one of the séances comes to an end that Snowey opens the door himself, draws the curtains and admits the Seeker. He wouldn't let you in if I wasn't with you. The first time I came, the landlord of the house brought me and told Snowey I was all correct.

(*Voice heard from other side of door; imitation Scots.*)

235

VOICE   Ah, weel, my friends, I'm recht glad to see ye gathered round—

(*Murmur of other voices.*)

Ah recht!

SAM   I wished we'd gone on down to Mother Taft's. The boys'll be gathering now. Anyway, I suppose you'll go down after this show is over.

HILL   It depends if his spirit answers and forgives. Then I'll have peace of mind.

SAM   The boys'll have peace of mind all right to-night, and Fat'll be the pet of the Farm. I wished I'd been in the Court when he stood up and told 'em the tale. That Fat's a genius. They come on him like a stroke from heaven. 'My Lord and Gentlemen,' he says, 'I am representing these pore innocent men,' he says. 'You says prisoners at the bar, I says sportsmen down on their luck. I am defending,' he says—

HILL   What I don't understand how he got rid of the tools.

SAM   'I am defending these pore, broken, innocent sportsmen and myself. The Police,' he says, and he looks very particular at the Inspector, 'has made a dastardly charge of housebreaking with intent to rob on the premises of a Jeweller. My Lord and Gentlemen, no such. What did the Inspector find when he and his lackeys bursted into the shop? He found a number of sportsmen a-playing a harmless (in the eyes of man, harmless; in the eye of the Law, perhaps not so): but I repeat the sportsmen were engaged in playing the harmless game of cards called "House".' The Inspector gave a nasty laugh at that. 'That was Fat's idea. He set all the gang round a box quick, handed the cards out of his pocket, and passed 'em round quick. The boys didn't get his plan not at once.

HILL   Yes, I heard all about it, but what gets me is how he got the tools hidden so's the rossers never got 'em.

SAM   Oh, Fat had a place marked down all right, before the job ever started, I dare say. He knew the lay of that shop well. Fat'll have to do his speech again tonight. 'My Lord and Gentlemen. My Lord and Gentlemen, say I, no tools, no nothing, was found on us or in our vicinity. A simple set of old English sportsmen, a-sporting themselves in a little game. The bar on the door was sawn through before we came along, in fact, it was that attracted our attention, and being wishful of a quiet spot in which to amuse ourselves in a civil and sporting manner, on a Saturday afternoon, we entered, and,' he says, 'on behalf of self and friends we are willing to plead guilty to gaming on licensed premises.' 'A Jeweller's a licensed premises, isn't it?' he says, and the police had to admit it. The Inspector—he laughed, but he saw how it was. Fat and the boys knew he couldn't find anything on them, and they were willing to do a month a-piece but no more.

And to-night's the night, Spill, I tell you. Better sort of spirits down at Mother Taft's than up in this miserable crib. Come away.

(*Murmur of voices in room and a little louder—an imitation nasal American voice.*)

VOICE Wall, I guess pards, this is changed from the days of old Kentuck. Gee, but old Hoss is glad to be with you to-night.

HILL Not yet. If he takes it off me and forgives, I'll go down with you. But you go on, I'm all right here.

SAM No, I'll stay for a bit of it anyway. Give the door a tap and hurry them up.

HILL No, you mustn't do that. Snowey comes when the time's right. (*All the time they are talking, murmurs come from the room*) I wouldn't feel so bad about it if they got a term each, but only a month! Clever Fat! I hates him. And old Chat done in. I've been here two, three times, and I've called him and he don't come. I want him to come and say he forgives me. It would not be much trouble to him, he says so much; just a little thing like that. 'Spill, I freely forgive you for what you done on me, and I'm happier now than I was selling newspapers down the Grove.' That's all I ask. If he said that I believe I'd feel all right.

SAM Yes, you'd be all right then, wouldn't you? But even if he just came and smiled at you and nodded his head, you'd be all right then and you could come down to Mother Taft's and hear the boys singing their songs and telling who they saw in the Stone House. You see, they ain't been long enough in to get their tempers spoilt; it's only been a picnic. 'Tea', she says, 'an' spirits,' she says, 'and creeses,' she says, 'a real picnic, that's what it's been.' None of 'em was in before except little Fred, so it's been quite a novelty for them. They'll be just like a lot of kids let out of school on a May Day down in Berkshire or some other of them inland places where they picks the flowers off the trees in the Spring time, and ornaments themselves with them.

(*A voice from within, muffled, but with rather a gramophone sound—it is coming from a dictaphone.*)

VOICE Dear friends, what the spirits of the dear lost ones have said to you to-night has helped you, I ween. I look down upon you and trust that you all are blessed in all your goings in and going outs, and that no sordid thought has sullied your hopes and prayers to-night.

HILL That's Snowey's unknown. That means the séance is nearly over.

(*A moment's wait. The door is opened from inside by a white fat hand and a heavy black curtain is drawn back and* SNOWEY *appears in doorway. Distant voices heard behind him.*)

HILL   Very successful! Wonderful! Exquisite!

(SNOWEY, *large, heavy, tall man in black clothes with white beard,*
pink cheeks, longish white hair.)

HILL (*to* SNOWEY)   This is a friend of mine—Mr Hornsey.

SNOWEY   An enquirer into the spirit world? You seek a word from some
dear one?

SAM   That's it, sir!

SNOWEY   The entrance fee is half a dollar.

HILL   I pay for us both. (*Hands two halfcrowns to* SNOWEY.)

SNOWEY   Thank you, thank you!

(*Holds back curtain, standing on right of door.* SAM *and* HILL *stand on left.*
Out of door come three elderly nondescript men of the lower middle class,
four women—3 middle-aged, nondescript, with bags and with umbrellas;
one younger, thin, willowy, miserable, tight small felt hat, pale face, no
gloves, no bag, no umbrella. All seven file out and stand in groups to right.)

SNOWEY   Now, ladies and gentlemen, that has been, I think, one of the most
successful of the soul-inspiring séances we have held with our little
group. The spirits seem very kind to us poor mortals to-night. All
have had some answer to their prayers for a message from the dim
beyond except sister here. (*Pointing towards slim girl*) Shall we, dear
friends, shall we open another séance ere the incommunicable night of
silence fall on us. I will just for a moment leave your friend while I
open the window within and air the room, and drive away any sordid
thought of the world which may have entered into our quiet party.

(*He goes into room, closes door. People murmur:* 'Wonderful, helpful,
exquisite.' *Thin woman says nothing. One of other women says to her:*
'Better luck next time sister.' SNOWEY *comes out again.*)

SNOWEY   Now, friends, the room is sweet again. Half-a-crown a head as
before.

(*He pulls curtain back again and opens door. The people open bags, take*
out purses and produce money. Thin girl looks at money in hand which
she takes from pocket in jacket—evidently not enough.)

SAM (*with courtly gesture, removing hat*)   May I have the honour of paying
for sister! My friend is treating me.

SNOWEY Ah, a kind thought, Mr Hornsey. It was Hornsey, wasn't it? We're all friends here.

> (*All file in with* SAM *and* HILL *followed by* SNOWEY *who pulls door to after him.*)

Curtain.

Scene 2: *Long room, dim light, bare dingy wallpaper, black curtains on door on left, dark purple curtain towards right. Heavy gilt inside window frame, ornament at top of curtain. Long table across stage from left to right. Various kinds of chairs round table. Stool without back at top of table, right. People filing in,* SNOWEY *showing them to their places. Three middle-aged women at back of table and thin woman at left corner; on the near side of table the three elderly men, then* HILL.

SNOWEY You sit here, Mr Hornsey, on my left hand. (SAM *sits down between* SNOWEY *and* HILL) As you are a new disciple of our little corner of the occult, you will like to have me near you to give my helping hand should your spirit stumble in the meshes of the darksome toils of the unknown. Now we will seek the quietness of the serene blackness that imitates the voids where no human harsh thought may enter in.

> (*He talks softly getting softer at each word, and as he talks he moves across to the wall and back right and switches off the one light, a small bulb, covered in a green silk bat shade hanging from centre, left. As he is doing this, all the group are taking hands. Darkness.*)

SNOWEY Take my left hand, Mr Hornsey, and you, mother, my right. All keep the chain complete. A little hymn, friends, another little hymn, the same again.

> Lead Kindly Light amid the encircling gloom,
>> Lead Thou me on;
> The night is dark and I am far from Home,
>> Lead Thou me on.
> Keep Thou my feet, I do not ask to see
> The distant scene, one step enough for me.

> (*All sing except* SAM.)

SNOWEY   Again, dear ones!

(They sing the verse again. This time the voice of SAM *can be heard singing low, strong and good.)*

SNOWEY   Who will be the first to call for a message from beyond the veil?

WOMAN ON HIS RIGHT   I call on old Kentuck to tell me if he has any word from my Jim, lost in the coal mine ten years ago—lost in the explosion.

SNOWEY   Come, Old Kentuck, manifest thyself and give, if ye can, some message from Jim to this poor sorrowing sister. What of Jim?

VOICE OF KENTUCK *(imitation nasal American voice)*   Gee, but I'm right glad you asked, friend, and I'm glad to see you and all kind friends here to-night. Ole Kentuck is most tickled to death with a crowd; the bigger the crowd, the more he kain talk and tell out the messages from the great Beyond. Mother, I seen your Jim right now, and say but he's happy and says you ain't ter worry about him no how and kaind love to dad.

SNOWEY   Any other message, Old Kentuck?

VOICE OF KENTUCK   I guess no more at the present. Jim's away on another star right now.

SNOWEY   Well, any other brother or sister like to try and receive some message from the deeps beyond deeps?

ELDERLY MAN   I would like to call the spirit of John Watson; used to live in Old Cottages, Dark Ferry Lane, Lambeth. He was a mate of mine.

SNOWEY   A friend of John Watson would hear him speak. Is John Watson happy? Speak, John; your friend is here.

SQUEAKY OLD VOICE   Heard. Happy and let you be happy too, old mate.

ELDERLY MAN *(in hushed voice)*   I didn't think they grew aged beyond! I thought they were for ever the same as when they was called away!

THIN WOMAN   I want to hear your voice, Patrick James Donnelly, who departed this life this day two year afore now.

SNOWEY   Patrick James Donnelly, a friend calls you. Can you give her no answer?

(There's no answer.)

WOMAN ON RIGHT *(to* SNOWEY*)*   Ask Sandy if he has heard of my sister's husband, Mackinnon, of Glasgow, who died in an explosion in the Docks.

IMITATION SCOTCH VOICE   I heered tell of Mackinnon all recht, and yesterday I met the chiel in the heather clouds and we had a braw crack together, and he sent wee greeting to ye aw and said he was braw and happy.

THIN WOMAN   I want to hear your voice, Patrick James Donnelly, who departed this life two years from this day.

SAM *(speaking very deeply)*   I am happy, girl. Be you happy too!

THIN WOMAN   That is not the voice of Patrick James Donnelly. I want to hear your voice.

SAM   Child, it's not in this place you'll hear his voice.

SNOWEY   Quietly, my friends; some disturbing element's with us. Listen to what the unknown will tell us.

VOICE FROM THE DICTAPHONE   Dear friends, the Unknown speaks to you. He tells you to dwell in quietness of souls, thinking only of ——

HILL (*speaking at same time as* UNKNOWN)   I don't want to hear the Unknown. I call out now for the spirit of Hartigan who was killed, to come and forgive me. I want the spirit of Hartigan.

UNKNOWN (*talking at same time as* HILL)   —— higher and better things, for by this means alone can our souls be attuned to the souls of the dear dead who ——

SNOWEY (*he has stopped the dictaphone*)   Mr Hill, conduct yourself! Ladies and Gentlemen, you know very well that while I am conducting these researches in a mediumistic capacity any interrupting in the flow may be a danger to my life, and at the very least may render me unable to conduct these séances. So decide for yourselves. Do you want Mr Hill or old Snowey to conduct the gathering?

VOICES OF THE FOUR WOMEN AND THREE MEN   Mister Snowey! Mister Snowey!

SNOWEY (*he has started dictaphone again*)   Now, Mr Hill; are you satisfied?

UNKNOWN   —— whose presence we crave here and now in the quiet room, sacred to the highest and the best that in us lies. With sacred humbleness let us all seek with reverence and calm minds what may come through the veil to these poor, erring, longing, hoping, human corruptibilities. If all are very still and silent to-night, I may be able to make a materialization. But bear in mind, my dear children of earth, that the slightest discordant action or thought may imperil the life of Mr Snowey, the true-hearted medium through whose kind soul I am able to reach down to your souls. I am now about to try and make my materialization.

(*For a moment nothing happens; then appear two hands, both lefts, cardboard treated with phosphorus; two eyes at about the correct position if hands were raised on each side of head.*)

HILL   I don't care! Hartigan, come and forgive me, forgive me, forgive me!

SAM (*shouting*)   You're putting my friend off his nut, I tell you; and the whole thing's a proper fraud.

HILL   Hartigan, come to me!

(SAM *jumps up with electric torch in left hand—his right is held by* SNOWEY— *turns light up on ceiling which reflects light down and so lighting up room faintly. Shows dictaphone partly exposed behind window curtain, and in*

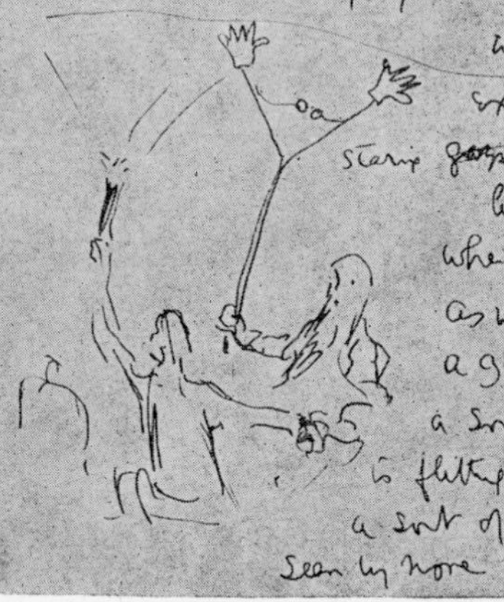

SNOWEY's *right hand an affair as in illustration. Everyone jumps up, except woman on* SNOWEY's *right, who grabs hold of* SNOWEY *and appears to almost collapse, and* HILL—*thin woman is gazing at him*—*who continues sitting staring across to left of centre of room, where ghost of* HARTIGAN, *dressed as when killed but blood on head. His figure is outlined with a golden powdering to give a sort of aura.* HARTIGAN *is flitting from side to side in a sort of weaving dance. He is seen by none but* HILL; *to all others he is invisible.* SAM *darts across room.* HARTIGAN *must weave from side to side as* SAM *passes and turns on electric light bulb, pulling off shade so that the room is in full light. He pulls blackjack from pocket and comes back down the stage in a menacing stride.)*

SAM   Now, Spill; get up and let's make this a rough house.

(SNOWEY, *with right hand, grabs at something beside him*—*the cash box.* SAM *knocks it from his hand with the blackjack and smashes the false hands, which* SNOWEY *is still holding in his left hand as a kind of shield.)*

SAM   And two left hands they were!

(*Three men and three women make for door left.* SAM *drives* SNOWEY *before him and as he passes end of table where thin woman is still standing gazing at* HILL, *he shoves her along too.)*

SAM   Now, sister; chase them home!

(*As the people are being hustled to the door, some pass on either side of* HARTIGAN's *ghost as he weaves about in his dance. Of course dance is silent.* SAM *shuts door and gently turns key. Exit all but* SAM *and* HILL.)

HILL   I thank you old Chatagain! Do you forgive me? Say you forgive me!

(SAM *takes up cash box, gives it a rap with black jack, forces open lid and slides money into his side pocket; pulls window curtain altogether aside and shows dictaphone completely.)*

SAM   The voice of the Unknown! Unknown, all right! Come on, Spill. Pull yourself together. We've got enough here to spread the dripping onto the party down at Mother Taft's. Come on. Is this a good getaway? (*Goes to door, right; opens it and looks out*) Not it; goes down to the main street. Ah, what about a window! Easy down, hard up. (*Shoves up window, looks down*) Easy as Eton. (*Throws one leg over window*) Nice ledge and a length of pipe; the slide for life. Seven foot of a drop and all is O.K. (HILL *gets up.* SAM *turns and sees he's up*) Come on, swift now, and I'll meet you at Taft's in three-quarter's of an hour. You go left and take the tram. I'll go ahead and round along by the Canal. (*His voice from below as he drops*) Very nice! Quick now!

HILL (*to ghost, which is weaving about the room in wider swings from side to side.* HILL *also weaves about following him*) Just forgive me, Hartigan! Chatagain, forgive me! It was an error of judgment. I wish I'd done myself in now.

(HARTIGAN'S GHOST *comes on dictaphone in his dancing and restarts it; as before it goes on.*)

UNKNOWN   Dear friends, the Unknown speaks to you; he tells you to dwell in quietness of soul, thinking only of higher and better things, for by this means alone can—

(HARTIGAN'S GHOST *stops dictaphone. Takes out and puts in new virgin record which he takes from little table where Dictaphone is standing.*)

HILL (*standing nearer* HARTIGAN)   Forgive me for what I done to you!

GHOST   Forgive! I can't forgive, but I've forgotten.

HILL   Look at your poor old head; I done that on you. I shot you with this bloody peter. (*Taking parabellum from right hand pocket with right hand*) I had to hit. I was made not to miss you, and now you say you can't forgive me, only forget me!

GHOST (*speaking into dictaphone*)   Forget you! Forget even to forget! Stars pass in the sky, forgetting the sky they plough, and forgotten seed stars are sown in forgotten furrows, and a harrow comes a-harrowing, a harrow that is nothing but the breath of the memory of the breaths of all the birds; like the oranges, all thoughts here are fruit and flowers on the same stem. As the basket is woven on the uprights, which are the good thoughts, and the weaving osiers the bitter thoughts, so I know that one day by forgetting here and there we will arrive at but one thought—one thought to satisfy all needs, if needs there will be for the thinker. But not yet is that one thought set for me. I cannot in the twinkling of a star be forgetting the grey beards of the seas. In comfort of body I recall dreadful days of old, fighting odds too heavy, far too heavy. But then I was held in a body that could ache and fear. But this body now is the fun of a body which has neither fear nor ache, unless the misty vapour of the lake can ache. Do the clouds ache in their hearts because the lake distorts their reflections? Not they! They say if there were no clouds they're'd be no lakes. And what are lakes but little puddles grown up. And what are little puddles but little drops of water, and little grains of sand too; they make the mighty ocean and the pleasant land too. A song of innocence; little drops of water and little grains of sand are innocent because they are little. But why not big lakes and roomy mountains innocent too! Is a little

innocence better than a big innocence? No, a thousand times, no! Ten
thousand times ten thousand innocences are just that and nothing more,
and what a lot that is. Oh, dear heart, be glad; dear heart that had to
be constantly screamed at. Screamed at into your ear to keep you up
to your best, if it did keep you so up, which I forget. But now, dear
heart, be glad. Is a taking-notice-of a heart necessary to make it glad!
But is there a point where the glad heart is so glad it doesn't know it's
glad? But glad eyes, I think, always knew when they were glad. But
that's a-going back; no, not a going back exactly but a going out sideways into the realms of the days that are no more. Not so much, no
more, as forgotten. . . . (HILL, *restless, lights cigarette, throws match on
floor. After a time lets cigarette out and throws away*) . . . or forgotten from
their order. So that where we leave down one gangway, we come
aboard skipping up the next. Ever ashore, ever a-floating; before the
wind and in the wind's eyes, in the trough and on the crest, forgetting
where the foaming stars come down and the twinkling waters rush up.

HILL   Aw, shut up! You won't forgive me, you only forget me, and then
make a lot of talk about it.

(*He goes up close to dictaphone and fires into it.* GHOST *puts mouthpiece
of dictaphone down carefully and goes dancing again, weaving from side to
side of the stage towards the back.*)

HILL   You're a nasty, selfish, sentimental, self-opinionated, insincere old chat,
that's what you are. You've got no sense of proportion. You think
you're somebody, and you think you're everybody. There's nothing
behind you but gas and you look like gas now, and that's all you are—
gas, gas, gas! You don't know nothing about Truth and Justice, but I
do. And I wish now I'd shot you twice instead of once. It'd be a pleasure.
Can't you keep still and listen; it might do you a bit of good. But you're
past doing good; you're too taken up with yourself; you're all over the
shop; you aren't straight-forward. I hate the sight of you.

(*While he is speaking he is pointing parabellum at* GHOST, *following it
as it dances. Pulls trigger. Pistol does not go off. Looks at pistol. Pulls trigger
again—another miss-fire. He walks away crossly to door on the right; as he
goes, turns and fires again at dictaphone. Pistol goes off all right. Exit door
on right. Slamming door.* GHOST *still flitting about in his dance. Door must
be constructed so strongly that it really slams, and without shaking all the
walls of the room. Noise of struggle outside door on right and bottom of stairs.
Door on left is rattled.*)

VOICE   Open this door before I smash it in. Oh, it's open!

(*Enter good-looking tall* IST POLICE CONSTABLE *in tunic, patent shoes;
in his hand he has the notice* 'Seekers Bridge'. *With him landlord—red*

faced, conventional landlord type; retired butler kind, with claret red knitted waistcoat, gold watch-chain, gold horse shoe pin.)

1ST CONSTABLE   That was the second shot just as we came up the stairs. No one here; windows open. Ah! that's where he's gone. (*More noise from stairs, right*) Ho, my fellow constable has got a prisoner, I believe. (*Moves across stage*) That was your idea, landlord, to surround the place, and that entrance was the one for my partner. They sent him out from the yard with the truncheon. He's the armed division; I'm practically a civil division at the moment.

(*Door, right, bursts in and enter* 2ND CONSTABLE, *good-looking, uniform as* 1ST CONSTABLE, *with patent shoes; he is pushing before him limp and struggling* HILL *with small streak of blood on head.* HILL *sees* GHOST, *the others, of course, do not see it.*)

HILL   Ah, there you go! Can't you forget like you said! (*Follows* GHOST *about with his head in a dazed way.*)
2ND CONSTABLE   You'll get over that in a minute. I'm sorry I gave you such a shrewd crack on the top, but you wouldn't recognize authority in a proper manner, and the truncheon (*looking at it*) is heavier than I thought.
1ST CONSTABLE   Put the beastly thing away or you'll be hurting yourself or somebody else.

(2ND CONSTABLE *puts truncheon away.*)

1ST CONSTABLE (*to* LANDLORD, *talking in a barking way*)   Now, sir; you heard the first shot at what time?
LANDLORD   About 8.47. I know, because I was looking at the clock at the time.
1ST CONSTABLE   Why?
LANDLORD   Why what, Constable?
1ST CONSTABLE   Why—were—you—looking—at—the—clock? (*said very punctiliously.*)
LANDLORD   Because it was getting time the meeting up here usually broke up.
1ST CONSTABLE   Did you hear any suspicious noise up here before you heard the first shot? Shot A!
LANDLORD   No, I couldn't hear any ordinary movement up here; the floor's thick and I'm a bit hard of hearing on my left ear.
1ST CONSTABLE   But any sound of movement up here wouldn't have come to your left ear or your right, but through the top of your head. Go on!
LANDLORD   Some time before—

1ST CONSTABLE   Some time before! Now we're getting something. (*To* 2ND CONSTABLE) Let the prisoner sit down.

(HILL *sits on chair, but all the time watches dancing* GHOST. *He is turned half-way toward back.*)

1ST CONSTABLE   Some time before—say on, and remember anything you say may be taken in evidence against you. (*To* 2ND CONSTABLE) Did you warn the prisoner?

2ND CONSTABLE   No, I forgot to, but he hasn't said anything.

1ST CONSTABLE   Well, warn him now.

2ND CONSTABLE (*in* HILL's *ear*)   Remember anything you say may be taken in evidence against.

1ST CONSTABLE   Right! Now, landlord. You heard something before—

LANDLORD   Some time before the shot.

1ST CONSTABLE   The first shot—Shot A.

LANDLORD   1st shot—shot A. I heard a number of people going down the front stairs in a hurry, and then a little later a single step went down. But I didn't think the meeting was over because old Snowey—

1ST CONSTABLE   Who's old Snowey?

LANDLORD   The old person who runs the séance.

1ST CONSTABLE   What séance?

LANDLORD   The Seekers Bridge they called it!

(1ST CONSTABLE *raises card and points to it and attracts* 2ND CONSTABLE'S *attention to it.*)

1ST CONSTABLE   What was this little game?

LANDLORD   Spiritualism; sitting in the dark; raising the spirits of the dead!

1ST CONSTABLE   That's illegal, landlord. You want to be very careful. But tell it in your own way.

LANDLORD   They used to meet here two nights a week and I hadn't anything to do with them, just let them the room. I hadn't heard it was illegal.

1ST CONSTABLE   Illegal, all right. On, on, Chester!

LANDLORD   Well, I never heard any commotion or disturbance with them in any manner whatsoever until I heard shot A. I came out of the bar door below and looked up the stairs and saw their card still on the door, and Snowey always took the card away with him when he went, so I said, he's up there, anyway. So I opened the street door and began running along the street looking for a rosser, then I seen you two constables in the taxi, and here we all are!

1ST CONSTABLE   Thank you, landlord. I congratulate you on the straight-forward way in which you have given your evidence. I will now proceed to make a thorough examination of this room, but before I do so, I will tell you that there will be no body found, for as soon as I entered I saw at once where shot A and shot B went. (*Goes over to dictaphone and shows bullet holes*) So we see, friends, the affair is as plain as a pikestaff. (*While he is talking he is walking about the three sides of room. He finds cigarette and match on floor, takes them in his hand. The* GHOST *weaving in and out of him in his dance. Looks out of window*) Snowey probably left here in a hurry; (*sees cash box*) and here is the cash box rifled; and here we have the dictaphone with which your friend, old Snowey—

LANDLORD   He was no friend of mine, only a tenant in the ordinary way of business.

1ST CONSTABLE (*to* 2ND CONSTABLE)   Have you searched the prisoner?

2ND CONSTABLE   No sir.

1ST CONSTABLE   Well, do so now.

(*Prisoner is searched.* 2ND CONSTABLE *taking money from pockets of prisoner counts it out.*)

2ND CONSTABLE   Four shillings and sixpence; part of packet of cigarettes; one handkerchief; one pistol (*opens magazine and examines*) two cartridges discharged.

1ST CONSTABLE   Anything else, comrade?

2ND CONSTABLE   No, nothing else except—a piece of pencil.

1ST CONSTABLE   Lead or slate?

2ND CONSTABLE   Lead.

1ST CONSTABLE   Nothing else?

2ND CONSTABLE   Nothing else.

1ST CONSTABLE (*coming forward and placing match and cigarette stump on table by other things*)   Very well. (*Sits down on seat back of table, left of centre; an attitude of thought for a moment*) Now, I will tell you exactly what happened. I will reconstruct the events absolutely.

Our friend here (*pointing to* HILL) an earnest seeker after the mysteries of spirits, attended the meeting to-night with the intention of taking notes of any messages received, if genuine, which he fully expected the said messages to be; in a moment of inadvertness he lights a cigarette, which reveals to him dictaphone at work and incidentally shows up whole bag tricks. Snowey, realizing the game is up, rushes toward front door, but crowd is in his way; he rushes to window and jumps out. Our headstrong young friend here, (*pointing to prisoner*) being determined to stop further fraud on the public, fires pistol, Shot A, into works of dictaphone; then finds cash box and also, being determined to reimburse himself for loss of time and temper, after a few moments with difficulty prises open the cash box, and finding in it the totally inadequate sum of four shillings and sixpence, he gives the dictaphone one parting shot, pistol shot B., and leaves by back stairs only to fall into the arms of my faithful lieutenant. That is how the matter stands. Do you agree?

2ND CONSTABLE Agreed, agreed.

1ST CONSTABLE In that case, there's nothing further to do but all to get into the taxi and buzz to Scotland Yard.

LANDLORD (*standing up*) Look here, sir; as no lives have been lost and as the only pecuniary loss is to old Snowey who has lost the contents of his cash box, which the police are satisfied was a small amount—

1ST CONSTABLE And Snowey isn't likely to put in a claim for it. In fact, landlord, you may rest assured, you will never see that fraudulent person again, and I'm heartily glad here and now to say that our friend here (*pointing to prisoner*) has done a public service in ridding the world of a pestilent humbug who has battened on the credulity of the credulous. Proceed!

LANDLORD —— under the circumstances, would the police not consider the possibility of forgetting the whole matter, and in fact not making any report whatsoever? If any little (*reaches to hip pocket and takes out note case begins fingering some notes*) little Honororium that I might ——

1ST CONSTABLE (*rising and with a gesture of the hand*) No, never! Not money. (*Landlord looks crestfallen*) But I'll tell you what; myself and colleague will agree to forget the entire events of the evening, and you on your part will put a couple of bottles of champagne in the taxi, and we'll call bygones bygones!

LANDLORD I'd like nothing better. (*Bustles out.*)

1ST CONSTABLE (*going over towards* HILL) Let us examine the wounds of our late prisoner. (*Examines* HILL's *head carefully*) Nothing but a superficial scratch, coupled with hallucinations. A good night's sleep will soon cure all that.

LANDLORD (*enters with basket with four bottles of champagne and a box of cigars*) I've four bottles of champagne here for you and a nice box of cigars.

2ND CONSTABLE Very nice.

1ST CONSTABLE Very satisfactory. Now, landlord! I have no further direction to give except that you take care of these articles; (*pointing to table*) and return same to our late prisoner to-morrow morning. In the meantime, I shall expect you to give him a shake down for the night, having first made his head comfortable for him—a little warm water and a cool rag. By the way, I might remark at this stage of the proceedings, that self and partner are not real constables. (*Takes something from his pocket and signals to his friend who does the same. They are all moving towards the door, left; first* 2ND CONSTABLE, *then* LANDLORD *with basket, then* 1ST CONSTABLE *who is followed by* HILL, *who keeps looking back at* GHOST *dancing.* 1ST CONSTABLE *helps* HILL *along sometimes*) We are fancy Constables (*puts on false nose and moustache and his friend does the same*). We are, in fact, Fancy Dress Constables and we were on the way to a fancy dress dance when your S.O.S. caught us, and I say for myself and I think I may say the same for my partner, that we are very glad to have been able to come to your assistance with our help and advice. (LANDLORD *is bewildered but happy.*)

The last words I have to say is, to tell you to see that our ex-prisoner here sleeps well and so forgets all this spiritual nonsense, and in the morning you give him a slice of rum and milk for breakfast, and return his goods and chattels plus one pound from your own personal petty cash, and minus his pistol which, if you take my advice, you will throw into the Canal where it will be unable to do any more harm.

LANDLORD   I'll be only too glad to.

(*Exit all through door on left;* IST CONSTABLE *has arm round shoulder of* HILL *as they go out of door, but* HILL *is still watching the dancing* GHOST.)

CURTAIN.

THE END.

Harlequin's Positions

A Play in Five Acts

CHARACTERS

MADAME ROSE BOSANQUET (*about 62*). *Widow of Jonathan Bosanquet who had sold a Printing Press to the 'Clarion Cry' of Portnadroleen and stayed on to work it.*

CLAIRE GILLANE *Her sister, (about 60). Widow of Captain Gillane, lost at sea.*

JOHNNIE GILLANE *Their Nephew, (about 22). Son of Robert Gillane at present serving imprisonment for a fraudulent bankruptcy 5 years—4 of which he has just completed.*

ANNIE JENNINGS (*About 26*). *An orphan who owns the spot of ground on which the post office stands, and has just sold the old store behind it to a Cinema Company, who are putting up a super Cinema which will be absolutely the finest in the South West.*

ALFRED CLONBOISE (*About 27*). *A distant cousin of Madame Bosanquet and Mrs Gillane, whose maiden name was Clonboise.*

PILOTS, RAILWAY PORTERS, GUARD, APPLEWOMAN, BOY, KATE.

Left and Right are as seen by audience.

ACT ONE

Scene: *The sitting room of Madame Bosanquet's and Mrs Gillane's house— crowded walls covered with a heavy flowered paper. Pictures in heavy frames, a large looking glass, deep claret-coloured portière over doors, one on left and one on back towards right. Window on right. Table on right with gilt bound books and a large glass ball with snow storm in it.*

MRS GILLANE *sitting on chair on left.* MADAME BOSANQUET *on settee with* JOHNNIE GILLANE *on her left.* ANNE JENNINGS *in outdoor clothes on chair in front of table to the right.*

MRS GILLANE   Annie, my child, you won't mind letting him in when he comes. I had to send Kate out down to Dolan's to get the cake. I asked them to send it as soon as they came in from the bake house. But there it is—I ordered it for eleven to be certain, and now it's just on twelve. (*She turns round and looks at small clock on a bracket behind her.*)

ANNIE   I saw her. She was looking at the site of my cinema, my super cinema! It'll be mine anyway, in a way, because Mr Aston says he'll give me a gold ticket to admit me any time. But Kate wasn't wasting her time, don't think that of her for a minute. She was looking very pursed up.

MRS GILLANE   That meant she was thinking.

MADAME BOSANQUET   Concentration.

JOHNNY GILLANE   I wish I could. When I try to concentrate I only dither.

ANNIE   She was concentrating on the bake house itself, and the back door of it. She was going for the baker himself that was delaying her cake.

MRS GILLANE   Will the new super cinema interfere with the Dolan's bake house? Or perhaps it'll be absorbing it!

MADAME BOSANQUET   I shouldn't wonder. They are to have a super restaurant with dinners and wines and teaching the old inhabitants of Droleen to dine late to music. My dear father dined at 4 o'clock, with his hat on, to the music of dear mama's grumblings.

MRS GILLANE   I'm sure Mama had cause enough for grumbling.

MADAME BOSANQUET   They both had.

JOHNNY   The last time I saw Grandpapa it was the last time he was out in the town before his final illness, and he didn't have his hat on, it was blown off his head and floating down the river. I got a boat and saved it.

MRS GILLANE   Yes, and father was in the middle of a string of such dreadful language that he didn't know his own grandson when he saw him, and just went on taking away people's characters.

MADAME BOSANQUET You see, Annie, father blamed those that built the town for the draughty winds that blow across the bridge when there is a north-easterly gale.

MRS GILLANE I am sure he'll be here before Kate gets back. These foreigners or foreign-living people are always so prompt, he's sure to be here to the tick. So, if you don't mind Annie, you'll please let him in, and then you'll get the first look at him.

JOHNNIE And he'll know we have beautiful women in Portnadroleen.

ANNIE Oh, Johnnie!

MRS GILLANE You're quite right, Johnnie, and Kate isn't too bad looking— in a rombustious way. She works a little, for her living: but she couldn't have the devastating effect of Annie, and she isn't an Heiress to a Cinema ground.

MADAME BOSANQUET He'll know all about that. He'll have made enquiries about all the two thousand people of this town, you may be sure. If he was clever enough to go to the graveyards of the whole country, to find where e'er a Clonboise lay buried, he'd be clever enough for that.

JOHNNIE Perhaps he's a man of great wealth, looking for some one to leave it to before he shuffles off this mortal coil.

MADAME BOSANQUET He's not old enough for that; he says he's twenty-seven (*takes letter from her heavy beaded black silk handbag and reads*) 'I am just twenty-seven. For the last seventeen years—we begin young in South America—I have been engaged in Mercantile pursuits, taking a holiday between enterprises. Until last month I was engaged with my firm in harnessing, part at any rate, of the passionate Orinoco.' Now why the devil does he say the Orinoco is passionate?

MRS GILLANE I expect he lost money on it.

MADAME BOSANQUET (*reading*) 'And before taking a contract to slice the tops from the mountains to fill the valley with suitable grounds for growing early strawberries, I am visiting the homes of my ancestors but how to find them that was the trouble, until I hit on the idea of searching graveyards. This very afternoon I am rewarded. I see the grave of your lamented father in the old churchyard here. I make enquiries. I find that yourself Madame Bosanquet, and your refined sister—'

MRS GILLANE How the Dib does he know I'm refined.

MADAME BOSANQUET (*reading*) 'Your refined sister, are still in the land of the living.'

MRS GILLANE And why not?

MADAME BOSANQUET '—living. I am therefore sending this note by messenger from the Imperial Hotel. I beg that I may have the pleasure of calling on you, at say, twelve, midday, to-morrow' and there you are—

(*A knock at the door is heard.*)

ANNIE   And here he is. (*She goes out through portière at back right.*)

MRS GILLANE (*looking round at clock*)   Very prompt, it's only three minutes after twelve, and I put it by the Saw Mill whistle this morning.

(ANNIE *ushers in* ALFRED CLONBOISE *through portière at back.*
MADAME BOSANQUET, JOHNNIE *and* MRS GILLANE *stand up.*)

MADAME BOSANQUET   I am Madame Bosanquet. (*Shakes* ALFRED'*s hand*) You are welcome Mr Alfred Clonboise. Let me introduce Miss Annie Jennings, no relation, just a dear friend.

(ANNIE *and* ALFRED *shake hands.*)

ALFRED   You renew our acquaintance. I met your very dear friend ten seconds ago in your hall.

MADAME BOSANQUET   My Sister, Mrs Gillane, (ALFRED *and* MRS GILLANE *shake hands*) and our nephew, Mr John Gillane.

(ALFRED *and* JOHNNIE *shake hands.*)
(ALL *sit down—*ALFRED *in the middle.*)

MADAME BOSANQUET   Well now, I must say you have been very clever to find us out with so little to go on. Let me look at you (*goes over to* ALFRED *and peers in his face*). A resemblance to the Colonboises but not so much to the Clonboises as the Meldrums. Do you recall, Claire, Aunt Janie Meldrum? They called her Janie because it was the time the Scotch boat first started running to Droleen and they thought Janie was Scotch.

CLAIRE   I can see some resemblance about the eyes. Not so much a look as a kind of toss in them.

JOHNNIE   I don't think 'toss' is a nice word to use about a man's eyes in his presence.

ALFRED   I'm delighted to have the same sort of eyes as Aunt Janie. Was she very beautiful?

MADAME BOSANQUET   One time I could have shown you her photograph. But it got speckled with spots of chemicals, like snow, until finally it was all spots and no photograph, so we tore it up.

CLAIRE   Still to the last there was something about it.

ALFRED   Perhaps the photographer who took the photograph may have the negative.

CLAIRE   Not he—he cut his throat just on the edge of the quarry, years ago, so that he could fall in and make no fuss. But they fished him out. He looked very ghastly. I went down and stood outside the crowd that were round him. I pretended to look when people made room for me, but I closed my eyes tight and said 'how sad'.

ALFRED   Was it because he was crossed in love with Aunt?

MADAME BOSANQUET   Not at all—quite another story.

CLAIRE   I only closed my eyes because I thought the sight would be unpleasant.

ALFRED   You were quite right.

JOHNNIE   Aunt Claire is always right. Aunt Rose sometimes tried to wind up the clock backwards, but Aunt Claire never. Does she Annie? Miss Jennings isn't supposed to be so partial as I am, so she has to decide this sort of thing.

ANNIE   Aunt Claire is undefeatable.

CLAIRE   What do you mean by that, I wonder? I don't think anyone would try, not because I'm so formidable, but because I'm so—what's the opposite of formidable Mr Clonboise—Alfred?

ALFRED   What's the opposite of formidable?

JOHNNIE   Yes, what is it now?

MADAME BOSANQUET   I'm sure I don't know.

ANNIE   (*opens book on table and turns over leaves*)   The Quotation book opens at 'Domestic happiness joy smooth current of'. That's anyway what Aunt Claire sets up.

ALFRED   Do you always open the quotation book to find an answer?

ANNIE   Oh, no, I never did it before. I just thought I'd do it now.

ALFRED   (*getting up and walking over to glass globe with snow turns it over and starts snow storm falling*)   Did you ever try to read an answer in the snowflakes. An old Spanish lady I knew once in South America had one of these things, and at crucial moments she used to shake it up and watch the falling flakes. She said she could read the future by the way they fell but she did not reveal her secret to me.

JOHNNIE   I suppose not.

CLAIRE   And yet there should be something in it.

ALFRED   There is something in everything. There was a group of young men in Buenos Ayres when I was there who tried to found a religion on that—something in everything. One of them, the Secretary of the Society, picked up a horseshoe nail, walking with me one day near the Market and he began, on that nail, expounding, expounding. At first I was dizzied, but after a little I was completely bored, and so was he. If I could have reconstructed the ambling pad, the horse, Aunt Claire, from the horseshoe nail, I would have mounted it and ridden away from the Secretary, leaving him nothing but my dust. I would have taken a taxi, and pushed him away as I pushed in, but at the moment, I was embarrassed to the point of not having a taxi fare. It was just before my fortunes took a sudden upward turn. You know, 'the darkest hour' and that kind of thing.

JOHNNIE   Don't you think, Annie, Aunt Rose would like us to discuss a glass of wine now?

MADAME BOSANQUET.   You'll find it in the passage. If Kate is back she won't consider herself properly cleaned up. She's, very properly, I expect, going to content herself with a squint through the crack of the door, so when you come back, just leave it open a little.

(ANNIE *goes out through door at back and returns, leaving portière and door a little open—with tray, sherry in decanter and glasses and a Madeira cake.*)

MADAME BOSANQUET   You don't find a draught I hope, Alfred my boy.
ALFRED   Not in the least.

> (JOHNNIE *takes tray from* ANNIE, *who pours out the sherry and
> cuts cake.*)
> (JOHNNIE *goes round to everyone—* ALL *take sherry and a
> piece of cake.*)

MADAME BOSANQUET (*to* ALFRED)   Do you think of settling in the old country?
ALFRED   I might, but I fear I am too much of a bird of passage, a rolling stone, here to-day and gone to-morrow but still there comes a time when something makes one say 'Kismet'.
CLAIRE   That's a dangerous thing to say.
ALFRED   I agree, very dangerous. But we cannot read our future. At least I cannot read my own, whatever I might do about other people's future. I choose a pattern and stay within it, I saw a harlequinade in Pernambuco, or Lima, or somewhere. It was given by a visiting company, and very old-fashioned—everything in tradition. Harlequin was very graceful. I was introduced to him; and I discovered that those positions the harlequin takes with the wand in his hands all have names. I don't know if his were peculiar to himself. He turned always from one to the other to complete the series, five in number:

> Admiration.
> Pas de Basque.
> Thought.
> Defiance.
> Determination.

I committed them to memory—Harlequin Positions—and have made them my order of—order of existence, if I may put it in that way. I often start a journey in a state of 'Admiration' and end it with 'Determination'.
MADAME BOSANQUET   That's interesting. But 'Admiration' for what. 'Determination' about what?
ALFRED   That would depend on the journey.
CLAIRE   That's extraordinary! But when would you execute the 'Pas de Basque'? The 'Thought' and the—what was the next one?

ANNIE 'Defiance.'

CLAIRE 'Defiance.' When on the journey would that come in?

ALFRED Just before the 'Determination'.

JOHNNIE If you got as far as 'Determination'.

ALFRED Of course my journey might come to an end prematurely.

MADAME BOSANQUET If you started wrongly.

ALFRED Yes. If I got off with the wrong foot.

JOHNNIE There is no wrong foot, they only look wrong.

ALFRED If you'll say so I won't contradict you.

JOHNNIE I can't make it so by saying it, it's just one of these facts.

ALFRED I'm sure you're right of course.

(ANNIE *gets up and pours out more wine into each glass and* JOHNNIE *follows her around with the cake. None takes cake except* CLAIRE.)

JOHNNIE But Mr Clonboise how would you work out your big five in an ordinary life? If I look out of the window here I'll probably see little Johnny Murphy (a namesake of mine, another Johnny aged four) pushing along the pavement in front of himself a little wheel fixed to the end of a stick. He thinks its a scooter, he can say 'scooter'. It isn't a scooter. Now how would you imagine your five positions 'Admiration', 'Thought' and the rest, fitting into that child's life? I'd like to know.

ALFRED They have already fitted into his life. He has 'Admired' his mother, as the most interesting being in the world to him. He has exhibited his first steps, his 'Pas de Basque'. I have wondered and considered how he managed to give his walking performance—that is 'Thought'. His mother said to him 'you stay here' and he started off with his scooter 'Defiance'. Now he knows, Johnny knows, Johnny Murphy you said his name was, wasn't it?

JOHNNIE Yes, Yes.

ALFRED Johnny knows he hasn't got a scooter but he's 'Determined' to call his wheel and stick a scooter and make it so. That's his 'Determination'.

ANNIE Yes, it fits in.

CLAIRE In a sense, but I think Alfred has enough uncommon sense to have made his positions fit into anyone's life. I've taken too much cake. I'm greedy.

(*She gets up and puts the crumbling lump of cake on the tray, and retires to her chair and sips her sherry.*)

MADAME BOSANQUET (*in a stately tone*) For what 'Admiration', 'Defiance', 'Thought' did you execute your 'Pas de Basque'?

CLAIRE I'll swear I did not trip across the room, I walked—

MADAME BOSANQUET For —?

ALFRED (*jumping up and bowing*) For our admiration, which is justly yours Aunt.

JOHNNIE Aunt Claire, if anyone could walk across a room gracefully, without fuss, it is yourself. They say that when Mary Queen of Scots walked across the scaffold to the block, she wasn't satisfied, she said 'not so good', went back and walked a second time, perfectly. Aunt Claire may, I hope to God, never find herself walking such a plank, but if she does, she will walk perfectly the first time, and so the less the harrow will go through the hearts of the people standing round. The less then, but the more in memory, when they know they've seen a queen with a crown shone on her out of the sky making her natural departure.

CLAIRE I don't want to die, Johnnie, with my head chopped off.

ANNIE And no one wants you to, dear thing.

MADAME BOSANQUET Don't you like to smoke Alfred, we have some cigarettes here. Where are they, Annie?

JOHNNIE I have some. (*Takes out case.*)

(ANNIE *goes to bracket left—takes down wooden box of cigarettes.*
Offers them to MADAME BOSANQUET, *who takes one.*)

ANNIE Aunt Claire doesn't smoke. (*Offers cigarettes to* ALFRED *and* JOHNNIE, *who take one.* ALFRED *holds the box while she takes one herself.* JOHNNIE *moves round with matches to* MADAME BOSANQUET, *and* ANNIE. *Uses a second match for* ALFRED *and then lights his own cigarette.* ALL *smoke a short space in silence while* CLAIRE *takes another mouthful of her wine.*)

JOHNNIE This business of harlequins and positions is curious in many ways. Has the harlequin's peculiar diamonds of colour costume any special meaning in your scheme of things?

ALFRED I hadn't thought of that, and my harlequin friend didn't enlarge on it. To tell you the truth, towards the end of our interview he was getting rather tired of me. He thought at first that I was a newspaper man, whereas the man who introduced me to him was a somewhat important newspaper man, and could be of considerable use to a dashing harlequin: when he discovered his mistake he was inclined to get rather snuffy and busy, and I came away. I said 'I've promised to go on a fishing excursion', which was the fact, though harlequin thought I was being just cool and off-hand with him, so he mollified himself with me and we shook hands most affably. It's perfectly true I did go fishing up the river. A party had been made up, power boats and harpoons and torches. The quarry was some unfortunate large fish that was supposed to be had about fifty miles above the city. About forty or fifty feet long with tusks and a tail—Oh, such a tail! Someone wanted to be photographed standing beside such a monster, and have the photograph in the newspapers all over. I think he was a man who was going to run for some office and he had never distinguished himself in any way. This time he chose a poor way. Mister fish never showed up. A good thing he didn't. If he had he would have got a headache laughing. As it was, on a couple of false alarms 'Here he lies,' 'That dark spot,' 'Now's your chance,' someone pitched the harpoon and each time, the rope got round someone's leg or someone's waist. One time a sportsman went over the side. Well, his leg was going, and he couldn't afford to let it go without him, so he followed over the side, splosh, dreadful, and the odd thing was I never could make up my mind which of the fools on board was the one who was paying for the whole set out, and running for the office. A lot of us had never set eyes on each other before. Some of them may have thought I was the Angel of the Outfit.

MADAME BOSANQUET   Won't you stay for lunch Alfred? Just cold lunch you know. We can have it quite soon now.

ALFRED   I wish I could but I must get back to the hotel, for I have to be there to attend to a couple of cables, and maybe a long-distance telephone call. I've never talked more than five hundred miles myself and I'm nervous about the running up of expenses. I feel as if I was sitting in a taxi in a blizzard. (*Gets up.*)

MADAME BOSANQUET   You must come and have supper. When can you come?

ALFRED   I have to go to Dublin for a few days to-morrow.

MADAME BOSANQUET   Well, will you say this day next week?

ALFRED (*takes small book from his pocket and looks in it*)   Yes, fine, that's the 17th.

MADAME BOSANQUET   Well we'll expect you at 7 o'clock, you can come Annie?

ANNIE   Oh, yes, delighted.

MADAME BOSANQUET   And Johnnie?

JOHNNIE   Yes, I'll love to come and bring my music.

ANNIE (*to* ALFRED)   You know Johnnie has no ear.

(ALFRED *shakes hands with* ALL. JOHNNIE *and* ANNIE *seeing him out to the door.*)

Curtain.

ACT TWO

Scene: *The same—After supper a week later. Electric lights, 2 lamps on table and top of glass case in centre. Stage not very brightly lit.*
MADAME BOSANQUET, followed by CLAIRE GILLANE and ANNIE JENNINGS, comes in door on left, with CLONBOISE and JOHNNIE bringing up the rear and all but CLAIRE smoking cigarettes which they are finishing.
MADAME BOSANQUET sits by round table on left. CLAIRE between her and the door at back. ANNIE on right of table. CLONBOISE between ANNIE and CLAIRE. JOHNNIE stands up and walks about getting some little vases for ash trays.

JOHNNIE Kate, I am sure, was disappointed in Alfred's conversation. While she was in the room it always happened he was talking of the most humdrum things that might have happened in the town at any time—no wild tales of the Lone Sierras.

ANNIE Couldn't Alfred stage some dramatic scene just at the moment she comes in with tea. Can you do knife throwing? Not at the furniture or the walls but perhaps on the floor. I know, we will be playing cards when she comes in, and one of us, Johnnie perhaps, or I, might—I will, yes, I'll let fall the Ace all on the floor and you'll throw your knife and transfix the card through the middle.

ALFRED I'm afraid it would require a special kind of knife with a very pointed and heavy blade. My penknife is small (*taking it out and opening it as if to throw. He takes cigarette from his mouth and drops it into a small vase and quenches it with the point of the knife blade.*)

> (ANNIE *drops the Ace of Clubs on the floor, and* ALFRED
> *throws twice at it unsuccessfully.*)
> (ALL *the smokers put their cigarette stumps in various vases.*
> ALFRED *closes the penknife and puts it away in his pocket.*)
> (*Card is left on floor.* JOHNNIE *drags over chair and sits on*
> MADAME BOSANQUET's *right.*)

MADAME BOSANQUET I find it very hard to visualize the various statuses of Society, which you say prosper in the South American Countries in which you have lived. I suppose life is hard and very real.

ALFRED Oh, yes—no quarter.

MADAME BOSANQUET Is there the duels? Are there killings through jealousy?

ALFRED Not as many as you'd think. I imagine there is a good deal at least of respect for the ordinarily understood values, and it is growing. Certainly, I have known of situations which it seemed to me could only end in bloodshed, and then, someone has come along and taken the hands of the enemies in his and clasped them together. Civilization always seems to arrive at a point, and stay there for a while, where blood-shedding isn't the cure for all troubles. Then, in a moment, we have passed that point and we are all at each other's throats again.

JOHNNIE   A man away from the place he knows best in the world for some years, is the man in the best position to judge of changes in civilization. He can see in the little world of his own what may be happening in the world at large. But the man would have to be shut off completely from ordinary news—shut away. A man in a darkened room for some trouble with his eyes would be in a just state to judge of what he saw when he came out into the daylight.

ANNIE   It must be terrible to see perfectly ordinary people who say 'that's a good day' and 'goodbye now,' killed in their ordinary clothes.

CLAIRE   Yes, the clothes make a difference. I think even a postman killed suddenly, with a bomb perhaps out of the sky, would look less terrifying than an ordinary labouring man.

ALFRED   Naval sailors, officers and men, even heaped dead would look less terrible to me than one Merchant seaman or a Merchant Sea Captain, lying dead on his bridge.

ANNIE   I know, I understand. I know it is harder to be brave in mufti.

CLAIRE (standing up)   It was hard for my husband to be brave at any time. He never told tales of bravery, and when he died, he died so brave that the two men that were saved when his ship was burnt, the only ones saved, walked the roads across Ireland to tell me how how brave he died. God took away from him at the last all physical suffering. I can tell by what the sailors told me. Some escaped gas of the fire took him, the men said. They saw him. He fainted into the very centre of the fire. They said there wasn't a crease in his face when he entered the very heart of the flame.

(ALL sit silent.)
(CLAIRE turns snow glass this way, and that, and then
puts it down again.)

(KATE appears at door at left, closes door, then disappears. Then comes again with cups of tea and little cakes. She goes round, all take cups. She is a rather small, bright, black-haired, healthy young woman. She is not an awkward maid. She is demure. She has a white apron (not too big), a black dress. As she gets to the door on left, on her way out, she looks back and then comes over to where the Ace of Clubs lies, between ANNIE and MADAME BOSANQUET, picks it up and puts it on the round table, between ANNIE and MADAME BOSANQUET. She then moves off through door on left.)

(ANNIE, *while this has been going on, has taken up a pencil from the table and on a sheet of notepaper started making a sketch, looking at* ALFRED, *who keeps his head in position.*)

ALFRED I didn't know you were an artist.

ANNIE I am not. But just sometimes I think I can get a likeness, and then I can't.

JOHNNIE She's very good sometimes.

MADAME BOSANQUET Annie is highly accomplished.

CLAIRE She's gifted.

ALFRED May I look at myself? (*Comes round table.*)

ANNIE Yes, it's as good as I can make it.

ALFRED It is very like me, I believe, but you haven't done justice to my snub nose.

(ALFRED *goes back to his seat.*)

ANNIE You were talking of people killing each other in duels.

JOHNNIE Duels will never come in again into fashion. People who want to kill other people wouldn't be content with one.

MADAME BOSANQUET Greedy, greedy, always greedy.

ALFRED Yes, I suppose laziness and greed are the two greatest requirements for man, without them he could not carry on.

CLAIRE Your opinion of humanity is not very high, sir, but you know best perhaps. Living in faraway places, where many of your friends are people living far away from their birth places. Now my nephew here, Johnnie, staying on where he was born, has to conceal his laziness and his horrid greed under a covering of artful mildness. When I look at Johnnie (*looks at him*) I find it hard to see him sticking a knife into anyone's side just for some sort of greed or any other reason. Can you see him so, Annie?

ANNIE No, Johnnie (*looking at him*) is the kindest person in Droleen.

CLAIRE So was his father. I mean his father still is.

JOHNNIE I hope his companions now find him kind.

CLAIRE I'm sure they do and anyway when he walks in at the door here, and I hope he will, he'll find people waiting who still believe him the kindest. Indeed he will.

ANNIE He will.

MADAME BOSANQUET It will be his right.

JOHNNIE He will never come here, though if he could he would. (*Takes, fumbling with it, telegram from his pocket.*) There was an accident this morning, he is dead.

CLAIRE Where?

JOHNNIE In the Jail Yard at work. Stone fell from a lorry, I suppose. Killed by a falling stone. And Alfred here now has the skeleton from our cupboard, my cupboard. I am sorry—I was taken off my guard, I spoke so quickly. I am deeply sorry, Aunt, indeed everyone.

(ANNIE *goes over to* JOHNNIE *and puts her hand on his and then returns to her seat.*)

ALFRED (*standing up*) Perhaps I am in the way at this time, at this time. May I withdraw?

MADAME BOSANQUET Sit down Alfred. Someone in the town would have told you anyway very soon. We are all sad for Johnnie and for ourselves. Johnnie loses a loved father, who, had he lived, would have been a sadness to himself, for though he could wipe the slate clean, for other people, for himself he would always have remembered that his friends, he would have thought, should be ashamed of him. He set fire to some goods—ah, you needn't look so interested Alfred, it was not what you would call political—he wanted to get the insurance money to settle his bankruptcy business.

JOHNNIE So that he could help me along to make a real gentleman of me, to educate me.

MADAME BOSANQUET There was no danger to anyone, it was an isolated store where the goods were. He bungled the whole thing, poor dear, and at the trial he confessed and the lawyer cried. He could have got him off, he said, and now he's dead and Johnnie has no father.

(JOHNNIE *takes out his handkerchief and gently wipes his eyes, and keeps the handkerchief in his hand for a little while.*)

JOHNNIE No father.

ALFRED I'm very, very sorry.

(CLAIRE *gets up and goes away by door on left. She is moved by the sadness of the moment.*)

MADAME BOSANQUET He was the kindest creature and all the town knows that.

ANNIE I am sure they do. You know that, don't you Johnnie?

JOHNNIE I do, I do.

ALFRED (*standing up*) I must say good-night. (*He shakes hands with* JOHNNIE.)

MADAME BOSANQUET Have a glass of wine before you go.

ALFRED Oh, no, thank you.

MADAME BOSANQUET Ah, do.

(ANNIE *goes out of door on right and returns with decanter of port and glass and a cake. Pours out wine for* ALFRED *and* JOHNNIE *who sip their glasses.* ALFRED *shakes hands with* MADAME BOSANQUET *and* ANNIE *who lets him*

out of door on right, and goes with him to see him off. JOHNNIE *standing,*
MADAME BOSANQUET *still sitting down, are silent and* ANNIE *returns.* JOHNNIE
sips his wine and eats a little cake.)

JOHNNIE   I'll just let him get on and then I must go.
MADAME BOSANQUET   Ah, don't hurry. Sit down.

(JOHNNIE *sits down.*)

JOHNNIE   Will you say good-night to Aunt Claire for me? I'll go now.
(*He stands up shakes hands with* MADAME BOSANQUET *and* ANNIE. ANNIE
goes towards the door on right with him, but he signals with his hands.)
JOHNNIE   No, no, you stay with Aunt Rose. I'll let myself out, good-night,
good-night.

(*Exit.*)

ANNIE   Have a little wine Madame Rose. (*She pours out a glass and brings
it to* MADAME BOSANQUET *and a little cake.* MADAME BOSANQUET *sips
the wine and eats the cake.*)

Curtain.

ACT THREE

Scene: *Grassy knoll overlooking small harbour and roofs of town. Side of Pilot's black wooden shelter on right; at left high board fence of hurley ground. Wooden seat to right of middle.*

PILOT—*middle-aged, tall, weather-beaten man, in worn sea-blue reefer coat, and trousers, peaked cap, all cloth, no white top, looking out of shelter, searching horizon with old binoculars showing the brass where the black is worn off.* PILOT *disappears into shelter.*

Enter, left, JOHNNIE *and* ALFRED.

ALFRED   After all I am sure you would have sooner I hadn't been unlucky enough to be present last night.

JOHNNIE   I don't care in the least and I don't care for your sympathy. My father was unlucky perhaps, and he was able to continue to live on, and he would have lived on and defied everyone in the length and breadth of the land; well, I'm being rather ridiculous, the length and breadth of the land wouldn't bother about him, and this little town wouldn't have bothered him. Perhaps he was lucky and perhaps I'm the unlucky one left.

*(*PILOT *appears again from shelter and looks out to sea with glasses.)*

ALFRED *(looking towards the* PILOT*)*   Isn't this place rather public?

JOHNNIE   Not at all, Joey's deaf as a post. *(He goes over to* PILOT *and shouts)* Any sign of the feller from the River Plate?

PILOT   Eh?

JOHNNIE   Is he in sight, that feller from the River Plate?

PILOT   River Plate. I had him a minute ago, I thought. But there's a bit of a haze down there. I think he's fumbling about there. Ah, I've got him now—he must be burning a horsehair mattress off a sofa. Here, look yourself.

JOHNNIE *(takes glasses, alters them, and after two or three attempts)*   Yes, I've got him. Well, he oughter have had a good passage—*(louder)* good passage.

PILOT   Good passage, plenty of wind, and a good passage for us all when the time comes, Mister Johnnie. *(He taps* JOHNNIE *on his breast.* JOHNNIE *gives him back the glasses and goes back to* ALFRED.*)*

JOHNNIE   We get a good view over the town here.

ALFRED   Your Aunts are very nice people.

JOHNNIE   Yes, yes, certainly they are.

ALFRED   They have been hospitable and kind to me. I very much appreciate it. I'm really a stranger from a far distant corner of the world.

JOHNNIE   Yes, too far distant in the world, too strange, too abnormal, too wonderful altogether, like yourself with your duels and your parrots, and first of all your harlequin's positions and all your old talk.

ALFRED   I had no idea I was bothering you. I was just trying to make myself agreeable.

JOHNNIE   Oh, and so you did indeed.

ALFRED   I can't help it if I've had adventures. God knows I don't bring them forward until I'm asked. I'm just as fond of making a figure of myself as the next one. But I don't think I go out of my way to do so.

JOHNNIE   Out of your way, out of your own way, no. But you ought to go out of my way. I'm tired of you. For two two's I'd take you down and dip you in the harbour, and leave you there.

ALFRED   Johnnie, you're not yourself. I quite understand, well I partially understand, I suppose, you're upset, in grief, and all that—your father and everything.

JOHNNIE   Perhaps.

ALFRED   But I am not able to let any man, whatever the circumstances, say he'll dip me in this, or any old harbour, and get away with it. I just can't have it.

JOHNNIE   No, I suppose not. Let's change the subject.

ALFRED   Well, I'm agreeable; what shall we talk about? Politics in France seem very odd just now, and in China the Yellow Peril seems to be an ingrowing peril, though I'm not so sure about that. We must be prepared for everything.

JOHNNIE   Yes, prepared to travel—travel light. Ready for anything. One shirt on, and one in the hand, a change of socks, a packet of razor blades, just enough to keep one clean chinned.

ALFRED   I know, clean chinned, clean limbed.

JOHNNIE   Yes, yes, just enough to keep the chin clean up to the edge of civilization, and then when we emerge on the other side of the bushes of Barbary, of barbarism I mean, enough edge on the blade left to clean up again; on the other side in civilization again.

ALFRED   You're in luck—in your imagination, if you believe that first comes a good spot, then a bad spot, and then a good spot again. I wish I could. Through the smoke into the stratosphere, and then into the smoke again, eh? On straight, on clear through the stratosphere into the—what?

JOHNNIE   (imitating a Christy Minstrel corner man)   Them sort ob questions 'ad spoil all da Teeology in da known world.

ALFRED   I'm sorry, I didn't wish to fly so high.

JOHNNIE   Well we've got to make the most of it and keep all our eggs in one basket.

ALFRED   Well that's profound of you. Whatever happens to the eggs, we are bound to have one good big basket anyway, more useful than a lot of little ones.

JOHNNIE   Sometimes, I dream of notable personages—it's inherited. My father used to dream of English political figures. Gladstone, Disraeli, and several others. The other morning I had a kind of nightmare. I was wandering in a very grey town, trying to catch a train and losing my way, and met Bernard Shaw, on a tall brown horse, and his beard and eyebrows were haloed round with the morning sun. Down where I was on the road it was all grey and misty and Bernard Shaw said to me 'Johnnie you oughtn't to be out so early in the morning without your breakfast, you ought to go home.' Do you think that has any meaning?

ALFRED   I'm sure it has, and this one big basket of yours, you could sew your waterproof over it and turn it into a canoe, and paddle away in it to a better pitch, and you couldn't do that if you only had a lot of dinky little baskets that wouldn't be capable of supporting you unless they combined. They'd let you down and you'd get soaked.

JOHNNIE   I believe you.

ALFRED   No one knows what to put their money in.

JOHNNIE   If they've got any.

ALFRED   Those that haven't any are the best off, they don't have to worry. But I have friends who have got money, a little, and they are always worrying about it, taking it out of one sock and putting it in another. They're the worst off friends—they are trying to conserve their strength, their capital, and every now and then it gets a bit less. I've got other friends, that are always tossing the stuff up and down, and 'pon my word they're as well off. They get the excitement anyway. I wish I knew how to make some money myself and I can't have enough.

JOHNNIE   I suppose you've come away with something.

ALFRED   Enough to keep me alive in a cheap country.

JOHNNIE   Well, this isn't a cheap country—in some ways.

ALFRED   I know that. If I lived here I'd have to take up something. I'm too old to enter one of the professions, and I expect they are crowded.

JOHNNIE   Yes, crowded.

ALFRED   And no one wants a clerk who can't keep an account of anything.

JOHNNIE   Do you know that Miss Jennings received an offer this morning for her to sell out her share of the Cinema? A big offer!

ALFRED   That's splendid. It shows someone thinks the property valuable.

JOHNNIE   Yes, and still she's inclined to accept it. The lawyer says it's a good offer. There's the lad with the cheque fluttering in his hand, standing on the site of the Cinema just waiting for Annie to take the cheque and hand over the papers she has.

ALFRED   I'm glad to hear this, if it gives Miss Jennings whatever she wants.

JOHNNIE   Yes, the money's enough and plenty. She could put it into something safe.

ALFRED   What?

JOHNNIE   Oh, just something safe, low, certain, steady interest I suppose.

ALFRED   It must be wonderful to have enough and plenty as you say, just coming in from something safe. Sit in a garden and watch the roses bloom, with, perhaps a gentle river tinkling at the foot of the garden, a little music coming from a distant native musician, with a harp under some umbrageous trees. All in a green shade.

JOHNNIE   Green gage?

ALFRED   Green gage Hell, I'm being poetic. Johnnie, I like you, you're alright. You stand you to your troubles well. You've got grit. You'll get on. You've only got to shake yourself a bit. Shake into harness and then nothing'll stop you. You'll go on from success to success. There's nothing to stop you. You've got education, and determination, that's what's wanted in the world now-a-days. It's better than a lot of mouldy capital. The thews, thews—that's a good word!—of your good right arm'll take you on, on, on to success. I see you a pillar of the Mercantile world in some great Eastern Country. What do you call 'em—a great a great Pro Consul, wielding power. That's it. Making yourself somebody. Making yourself felt. Cutting ice everywhere. Moving with the best, and having them kowtow to you. If I was younger I'd like to be at it myself. But I haven't got the stuff in me for it. A few years ago and I'd show 'em something. I'd have a palanquim and be carried around. No cheap motor cars for me. Men with battle axes running on each side of me, and I'd take a paper to any old Chief and I'd say—'Sign here,' and he'd sign and be glad to, and my Government, whoever was employing me, would not be able to do enough for me. And that's all before you Johnnie.

JOHNNIE   But how do I start, that's the trouble.

ALFRED   Oh, some fairy Godmother, or Godfather 'll come along, and give you a ticket to the fields of Glory. Where was the place in the Arabian Nights where the lad threw in the meat, and had eagles pick it out again stuck over with jewels, do you remember that? Good hunting!

JOHNNIE   I wonder to hear your reading such old child's story books as that.

ALFRED   I haven't read them for some time, but that's the idea. And those old stories are not so silly, if they are a bit romantic. Symbolical, that's what they are. Everything's symbolical if you look at it in the right way—I am.

JOHNNIE   Symbolic?

ALFRED   Yes, I am symbolic of something alright.

JOHNNIE   Yes.

ALFRED   I am symbolical of arrested civilization. I've been hampered. Climate and one thing or another, in my way. What I always wanted was an equable climate and no gunplay. Where I was it was always too torrid. I don't mind work. I've always revelled in it. I don't mind how much work I get so long as it's the right sort, where I can use my head as well as my hands. I was always intended for command also. Now, that's unusual, a man who can use his head, and his hands, and also is suitable to take command at any given moment. I've seen good things collapse just because the Chief in Charge didn't have just two of them ingredients, let alone the three. The three, hands, head and power to command, are practically a miracle and very rare.

JOHNNIE Some people in this town believe they're miracles then.

ALFRED Oh, yes, that's always so in little places. But have they ever proved it. Could they prove it here? Not they.

JOHNNIE Well, it's a dear old place if it is in a hole in the coast.

ALFRED Of course it's a delightful place—to come from. These little places can produce great men, if they can't use them. That accounts for your being thrown up, as it were. A star to shine in other firmaments.

JOHNNIE I'd certainly like to show the town what I could do if circumstances came my way. But this is a healthy place, lots of people come in for the day in the Summer time.

(*Enter* 2ND PILOT (MICHAEL) *on right.* 1ST PILOT *is looking out of shelter with glasses.* 2ND PILOT *touches him on the arm.* 2ND PILOT *takes glasses.*)

JOHNNIE If there were lodges by the sea, not too expensive, people would stay here for months and bring money into the place.

1ST PILOT All right, here, Michael. I think I'll take my watch below here. (*He goes over to seat and stretching himself along it composes himself for sleep.*)

JOHNNIE They'd have to put up a few shelters towards the North along the curve of the bay, for bathers. The Spring Board is a good place for swimmers, men bathers. You know where it is. Just a few yards to the north of the harbour. Not five minutes walk from any part of the town almost—deep clear water. Plunge in there before breakfast and you wouldn't get a better bathe in the world, I believe. It's the absolute ocean, and this time of the year, they say it's the seaweed's blossomings, it'll take your breath away with the ozone or whatever they call it.

ALFRED I meant to have a swim this morning, but I was late up. To-morrow morning I promise myself to sample it. It's a long time since I took a before breakfast dive. Mens sana in corpore dip. In the countries I've been it's been more in the line of the Dolce far Niente.

JOHNNIE They say the early morning is the best, but with good firm sands and a warm afternoon, the shore to the North that I'm talking about, would be very popular. Let alone people taking lodges here, ordinary lodgings would find they'd get lots of visitors, glad to pay well for reasonable simple comforts. And the two hotels we have, as well as the ordinary run of commercials, would find they could, by taking a little extra trouble, cater for visitors. A few children and buckets and spades, in a hotel hall never did anyone any harm. And they might have a soothing effect on some of those cross old commercials. Are you bothered with any at your place?

ALFRED   No I seem to be the only person staying. There are people in and out for meals.

JOHNNIE   Oh, yes, slack just now I daresay. The commercial business is generally a bit drained out after the fair. To-morrow morning the tide ought to be about right at the bathing stage. Michael (*calling to the* 2ND PILOT) What time's high water to-morrow morning?

2ND PILOT   It should be a grand morning for a bathe, very big tide, twenty past seven, high-water. It'll be a good day to-morrow (*looking at sky over the sea*). We're going to have a good spell, and time it was. Too many of those old gales. It's too early altogether to break up the year.

JOHNNIE   It's about time we had a little good weather.

2ND PILOT   We haven't had a real summer for years. Why, when I was a young boy it was so hot in the summer we were in and out of the water all the day long. And, even in school time, ye'd never see a feller with a dry head once June'd come in and maybe earlier some years. Then right on pretty well to Christmas, well, anyway, I often saw a score or more of us stripping off and plunging in on a Hallows Eve. But it's gone, all them things. Changed. The people haven't got the spirit for it now.

JOHNNIE   It's changed in my time.

2ND PILOT   It's changing every day. I wish I was dead sometimes. But that's a sin. There's nothing to do but just keep on doing what you're paid to do: looking out for an odd stinking old steam boat. Josey's got the right way there on the bench—Sleep. And look at the price of the medicine now. Why, some drinks varnish. They got no respect for their insides. Balsam's alright. I seen a man drink Balsam. But if you got it now it'd be adulterated. It's all a thing of the past.

JOHNNIE   I suppose they're content to go to see the films.

2ND PILOT   The young ones they go. There was one there one time. The orphans of the storm. Them God damn kids had a bitter deal, I tell you.

JOHNNIE   They don't have any dances in the Assembly Room late years.

2ND PILOT   No not a thing. They had a dance years back and a boy out of Boland's—

JOHNNIE   Boland's the drapers in Shop Street.

2ND PILOT   He fell on his head out of the window and broke his neck. You can see him behind the counter with his head on his shoulder. (*Sings*)

> Peek a boo
> Peek a boo
> I see you hiding there
> Peek a boo
> Peek a boo
> Come from behind the chair.

It's a sin to laugh at him, but it's a fact he don't mind. He's a bit of a curiosity for everyone. It was the drink did it, and it didn't stop him drinking either. It costs him nothing. All the travellers that come to the town like to take him out and buy the stuff for him, anything he fancies. They like to see him pour it as if he was going to pour it in his ear. He's a living curiosity. (*To* ALFRED) Don't you miss him while you're here, Sir.

ALFRED I won't. I'll go into Boland's. That's it, isn't it?

JOHNNIE Yes, Boland's.

(PILOT *searches horizon with glasses on purpose to see him.*)

ALFRED On purpose to see him. And if I get a chance I'll see him pour a libation.

JOHNNIE I'd forgotten the cause of his rye-neck. I'd got so used to seeing him about.

ALFRED Have you been here most of your life?

JOHNNIE All of it. I went to school here. Have a cigarette. (*Taking out case.*)

(ALFRED *and* JOHNNIE *smoke.*)

JOHNNIE I ought to have offered you a cigarette before. But I haven't been smoking much lately myself, and that's the way selfishness makes me forget. (*Offers cigarette to* 2ND PILOT *who smokes in a delicate manner.*)

(JOHNNIE *goes over to fence, left, and looks at hurling match advertisement.*)

JOHNNIE That was a great match. Any games we had here were so poor, I had given up going, but just by chance, I went to see that match. It was exciting and no mistake.

2ND PILOT It was a good match right enough. Like old times.

ALFRED I'd like to see a good hurley match.

JOHNNIE There won't be any more here this year.

ALFRED Of course, I've seen hockey, it's not like that.

JOHNNIE No, it's not like that.

ALFRED I understand.

2ND PILOT I seen some young ladies, and some young fellers out of the Bank playing hockey in the Infirmary Field one time. It was very nice to see.

JOHNNIE Hockey's a good game when it's properly played.

2ND PILOT I've seen them play croquet too. Of course on a specially prepared ground. That was in Plymouth one time. We went on a waggonette on a trip into the country, and we stopped in the village to give the horses some water. And I went for a walk by myself and I came on them playing croquet in front of the house, under the trees. I knew it was croquet the minute I saw it. I named it. I'd heard a man speak of it. It seemed to me a fair game. I liked to see them at it.

(*Enter* KATE *left with a coat over her apron which just shows below it, no hat.*)

KATE   Miss Annie saw you from the window up here, so she asked me to say would you look in on your way back, at your Aunt's, Mr Johnnie.

(ALFRED *smiles at* KATE.)

JOHNNIE   Say I'll be along in no time.

(*Exit* KATE *demurely without returning* ALFRED'S *smile.*)

ALFRED   It is really wonderful. What a view over the ocean there is from up here.

JOHNNIE   And we're not so very high up either. But we get an unimpeded view. On the top of Knockbrack you can see the wide ocean stript before you. You can take a car to the foot of the hill, but after that you must climb—rough going. It'll take you the best part of an hour but it's worth it.

ALFRED   We must arrange an outing to it.

JOHNNIE   Yes, one day when the weather takes up properly. It's no place to get caught on in a fog of mist. One false step near the highest bit, and good-bye to you. Though it's perfectly simple in clear weather. Just like mounting a staircase in your own house.

2ND PILOT   I never was there, it's too far. I was too long a seafaring man to be enamoured of walking.

ALFRED   That's so I believe. Sailors feel out of their element climbing rocks, while they have no fear of climbing up ropes into the sky with the sea waving about below them.

JOHNNIE   I think I had better be making my way down to the town.

ALFRED   And I should go to the hotel and see if there are any letters or messages for me. (*They move off left behind paling.*)

(PILOT *takes a chew of tobacco and looks out to sea with glasses.*)

Curtain.

ACT FOUR

Scene: *Small railway terminus of Portnadroleen. Side of Waiting Room and end of train on left. Entrance gate to station. Side of Goods Shed on right. Fence at back, over it Stationmaster's house with roses. Also, sea horizon, roofs of town, and masts of steamers. End of railway line with buffers, on right.*

(*Enter two elderly railway* PORTERS, *right, with mass of luggage piled on four wheeled truck. They bring the truck to rest.*)
(1ST PORTER *sits on the luggage, the* 2ND *leans against it.*)

2ND PORTER   This was a sudden plan they made to go travelling.

1ST PORTER   Yes, it's only yesterday Miss Jennings sold out her share of the Cinema, and I believe it'd astonish you the size of the cheque she got. It was then—I have it right—she was always intending to travel a bit. But it was at that instant she heard of an opportunity from some family dying, or backing out, and she got a whole row of cabins, for half nothing, from Liverpool, going a voyage into the wide world. Only start at once. With that girl it was always quick work, like her mother before her.

2ND PORTER   Oh, very sudden, quick, quick.

1ST PORTER   And her mother never had lashings of money like she has this blessed moment.

2ND PORTER   She taking all the friends too. They're no relation I believe.

1ST PORTER   No, no, not the very slightest. Just friends, just as much, and no more than you and me.

2ND PORTER   That's wonderful. She must have a great heart; aren't the old ladies very lively now to go trotting off on the wide ocean, visiting all the Islands, I suppose, and taking in America.

1ST PORTER   They're not so very old and the nephew is only a chicken. A bit of travelling wouldn't have done his poor old father any harm, if he'd been spared to this day.

2ND PORTER   It was the Lord's will.

1ST PORTER   The day began very mild. We'll have a good spell now. I'd like well to be an Old Age Pensioner. Wouldn't it be grand to be doing nothing all day, at this time of the year, but wandering on the green hills round the town watching the young lambs at their play.

2ND PORTER   This isn't the time of year for young lambs.

1ST PORTER   That just shows what an innocent mind I have that I wouldn't know but what it was their time.

275

2ND PORTER   I'm still active minded. Wouldn't it be a good scheme to be labelling this luggage.

1ST PORTER   Yes, busy, busy. (*He gets down from the luggage*—BOTH PORTERS *go off, left, and return presently with paste and a handful of labels*—LIVER-POOL. 1ST PORTER *dabs on the paste on the bags and trunks, and the* 2ND PORTER *puts on the labels.*)

1ST PORTER   That one's upside down.

2ND PORTER   Ah, what matter, ye'd never know what way them steam boats would be.

1ST PORTER   Did you hear who else is going with them?

2ND PORTER   No, who's that?

1ST PORTER   The servant, old James O'Brien's daughter. She'll be going as a lady's maid.

(*Enter* KATE *right, neatly and well dressed carrying a handbag to match her costume, and also a brown paper parcel which she puts on top of luggage.*)

1ST PORTER   Good morning to you. So you're off on your travels.

KATE   Off indeed, and we were packing all night, you never saw such a move in all your life.

(RAILWAY GUARD—*middle aged*—*peers round corner of shed to right. There is soap on his chin and a safety razor in his hand.*)

1ST PORTER   Here's another one that was up all night.

(GUARD *withdraws head.*)

1ST PORTER (*going over to side of shed and talking to the* GUARD *who is hidden*) Was it playing cards for the goat you were Sir? It's a grand thing the invention of the safety razor for a shaking hand. You ought to have taken a dip in the tide. It is the loveliest thing for a man that would be up all night Sir.

2ND PORTER   Kate, will you send us a couple of picture post cards?

KATE (*very slowly*)   If I send picture post cards to everyone that I met this morning walking up to the Station, I don't believe there'd be enough printed in the living world.

(*Enter* BOY *right*—*he is about* 10 *years of age, bare-foot and is carrying a small wooden case. He passes across the stage to left, puts down case inside of corner by end of train, returns and exits slowly, right. As he passes* KATE *and the* 2ND PORTER *he says*)

BOY   You promised me one, anyway.

KATE   And I'll keep my promise, Mickey.

BOY (*as he goes out*)   I have great faith in the women.

(*Enter stout, tall* APPLE WOMAN *with basket. She wears a green dress, an apron, and an old worn brown shawl.*)

APPLE WOMAN   Would there be any sort of a middling fair at Millish?

1ST PORTER (*turning from watching the* GUARD *shave*)   It'll begin when you get there.

2ND PORTER   There was a good few jobbers passing up the road early this morning.

APPLE WOMAN   If I get a ticket will the train go without me?

1ST PORTER   Not at all. If you want to go down the town again, it'll go with you and stand beside you like a little dog, till your business will be finished.

APPLE WOMAN   Is the Clerk in the Booking Office?

2ND PORTER   To be sure he is. That man is always there on the job. Train or no train, War or Peace, he'll accommodate you with a ticket.

(*Exit* APPLE WOMAN, *left.*)

KATE   Will the train start on time?

2ND PORTER   On the tick of it.

KATE (*throwing her chin to the shed where the* GUARD *is shaving*)   Is he alright?

2ND PORTER   In perfect shape. Anyway, you're not depending your life and property on him. It's the engine driver that is the whole works. (*Goes left, shouts*) Are you alright there Francis, throw some coals under her. (*Noise of coal being shovelled and a shovel striking iron.*) Don't be extravagant now. The motor car is much more silent.

(*Re-enter* APPLE WOMAN *left passing across stage and out to right.*)

KATE   There's a very heavy smell of the sea this morning.

2ND PORTER   Ah, that's a sign of good weather.

KATE   My ladies delayed talking to people coming up.

2ND PORTER   There's plenty of time.

1ST PORTER   Plenty of time. There always was since I've been paying any attention to it.

(*Enter* GUARD, *right, now shaved and spruced up.*)

GUARD   Yes, but the train starts to the moment (*takes out watch*) but that's not yet. I think it should be a good day. (*Looks up into the sky and out over the sea*) I wish I was coming back instead of going away. It looks very pleasant here by the ocean shore. When the Autumn is coming on and Summer is lingering with us yet, we are loth to let it go. Up there by the Junction it's a very lonely place. It's uncouth Miss (*to* KATE).

KATE   But it's very healthy.

GUARD   I wouldn't put so much by the health as by the entertainment. What have we to do there but watch the ducks washing themselves in the pond?

2ND PORTER   And wouldn't that be a very elevating sight, Sir. They quack when they're pleased.

GUARD   Oh, quack enough.

(*Re-enter* APPLE WOMAN. *She sits down on the ground right of platform with her basket beside her.*)
(*Enter* JOHNNIE. *He carries an overcoat on his arm and a second hat in his hand.*)

JOHNNIE   Did my Aunts not get here yet?

KATE   They stopped talking on the way, Sir, with some of the neighbours.

2ND PORTER   Now, Mister Johnnie, you'll be seeing the whole world and when you come back, God spare you that you may, and in good shape, you'll be able to tell us the whole history of the people of the world, friend and foe.

JOHNNIE   I'm sure I will.

1ST PORTER   Whatever you do don't go near America. It's a very enticing country. It's full of Irish.

2ND PORTER   And isn't that a good reason for him to go there?

1ST PORTER   But if he goes there, he'll not come back to his native air, unless he was to come back a millionaire and buy the town and make himself a Dictator.

2ND PORTER   And who would he dictate to?

1ST PORTER   Who but you and me.

2ND PORTER   Sure he can do that now—he can say 'put them items of luggage in the van' and we must obey.

(*The* TWO PORTERS *begin pushing the truck to the left until it is partly hidden. They begin removing the luggage.*)

(*Enter right,* MADAME BOSANQUET, CLAIRE GILLANE *and* ANNIE JENNINGS. ANNIE *has, as well as her handbag a bunch of travel advertisements—Railway Passes and Steamship Tickets.*)

(JOHNNIE *turns towards the three.*)

JOHNNIE   There's plenty of time, but still it won't be so long now until we are off. You have a great handful of documents there Annie.

(*He goes over to help* ANNIE *sort them out, putting tickets in her handbag. One of the travel papers which is large when unfolded shows a picture of a liner. It flutters to the ground. The* APPLE WOMAN *drags over to it, and picks it up and looks at it.*)

APPLE WOMAN   Ah, that's a lovely steamboat. It's grander nor any I ever seen. The one I went to seek my fortune in wasn't near as grand. I was only a young one maybe. But my idea of fortune was great, and now I'm telling lies.

(*Telephone bell heard off left.*)

JOHNNIE   It was a good boat brought you back anyway.

VOICE OFF LEFT   Come here, Driman, this instant.

1ST PORTER (*going off left*)   The Managing Director is calling me.

JOHNNIE   You must have had a terrible time all night packing.

MADAME BOSANQUET   I don't believe Annie got any sleep at all.

ANNIE   Oh, Yes I did.

MADAME BOSANQUET   She made us take a rest for an hour or two towards the dawn, and now I feel as fresh as paint. We had a little breakfast and we'll get something more soon when we get on beyond the junction.

JOHNNIE   I had a good breakfast a while ago, but I'm getting hungry again.

CLAIRE   You always had a healthy appetite. I hope you'll never lose it in the strange places we may be going to. I can't get over Annie stirring us all up like this on the spur of the moment. I didn't think we had it in us.

MADAME BOSANQUET   Well, if she didn't book the berths on the instant we wouldn't get anything so good.

ANNIE   I couldn't have done it by myself; it was Mullally telephoning and telegraphing, and working hard, over several hours, that made the whole thing possible. Johnnie would have done it too, but I wanted to get everything as much settled as possible before I'd tell him, but when he came on the scene he was great, buying trunks and getting them home on handcarts and everything.

MADAME BOSANQUET   And didn't little Kate work well?

ANNIE   She did, like a little Trojan.

GUARD   I must say you're very enterprising, and it's a great reflection on the intelligence of this town that the inhabitants could make up their minds so quickly, and get local assistance to help them carry out their important plans.

(*Exit left.*)
(1ST PORTER *enters left, followed by* GUARD.)

1ST PORTER   What do you think that fellow in the Booking Office says— he's had word by telephone from the lad at the Junction and he says—

'War is declared'.

JOHNNIE   What war?

1ST PORTER   He didn't say.

2ND PORTER   Hasn't that feller inside got the wireless to give him information, not to be upsetting us with tales from the Junction.

1ST PORTER   He has but he says that the feller at the Junction is quicker
always; at the same time he's a bit of a joker.

JOHNNIE   There's a law against spreading false news.

1ST PORTER   I'm sure of that, but this feller seems to be outside the working
of the law. He spreads anything he likes. He's got a notion about
things that might come to pass. Maybe he's a sort of a prophet. This
time he just said 'War's broke out,' and then he had to leave the
instrument to attend to some pig jobbers and I'm sure he wouldn't
be caught speaking before them. They live out of wars. However if we
have patience, we'll hear from him as soon as he's disposed of the pig
jobbers.

GUARD   If war was to be declared now, in any sort of a general way, it
wouldn't be much use in going to Liverpool looking for any sort of a
holiday trip on the wide oceans. They'd be closed to pleasure traffic
almost at once: and if they weren't it would be against my advice any
friend of mine would venture on the high seas, unless it was imperative
—death by drowning in the middle of the ocean is a poor entertainment.

JOHNNIE   I believe you.

GUARD   I would be inclined to tell anyone I knew to stay in their own
parish until the troubles blew over, unless a man had any particular
graw for any particular place; then I say, let him go there and prepare
himself for his latter end, and, if he's given an opportunity to fight to
defend it, then let him do so.

2ND PORTER   There might be no war come here at all.

JOHNNIE   When it starts it spreads.

(*Telephone bell rings*—1ST PORTER *goes out, left.*)

JOHNNIE   And there's some of those that were in the old wars who say they
liked them.

2ND PORTER   I don't believe a word of them. They'd like porter if they'd
get enough of it, but war satisfies soon.

JOHNNIE   It depends on the sort of war it is.

MADAME BOSANQUET   That's perfectly true, if you read history.

CLAIRE   I don't want even to hear of any more wars. I'm tired of them.
You're young, Annie, what do you say to them?

ANNIE   I don't know what I say. What do you think, Kate, of all this
talking of war?

(KATE *comes over to* ANNIE, *leans her head against her and cries a
while.* ANNIE *soothes her.*)

KATE I thought we were just going out into the wide world pleasing ourselves.

1ST PORTER He says he's still talking to the jobbers—they've lost something. The feller here couldn't make out whether it was a sack or a trunk, or maybe an umbrella. When he's busy the Junction philosopher is very thick in his speech. He says if it isn't war it means war, and it'll be money out of his pocket, anyway. It's hard for the Clerk here, even if he had human understanding, to make out what the lad's saying. He has to speak so guarded on account of the jobbers—them and their umbrella. Did anyone ever see a pig jobber with an umbrella? I never did. Perhaps they are not pig jobbers at all. Perhaps they are spies. That'd be a queer one. It would be easy for a spy to disguise himself so as to deceive a Railway Clerk.

2ND PORTER They have no penetration.

ANNIE What are we going to do about it, Johnnie.

JOHNNIE We might go on to the Junction and perhaps we'd hear something more definite there. But I doubt it, and then we'd have our luggage stuck there, if we didn't go any further. We'd have to wait there till evening unless we got a couple of cars to take us back. But, anyway, at the Junction if the Dublin train is on time there's not time enough to talk to anyone about the war, if it is a war.

1ST PORTER Oh, I believe it's a war somewhere alright. The clerk here says the junction lad doesn't sound a bit like joking. If those pig jobbers would only find their old sack, we'd know what to advise the ladies here and yourself, Mister Johnnie. Of course, if the war cancelled the sailing of the ship, that'd cancel the booking of the berths and you'd get your money returned. I don't say that the railway company'd give you back your fares, but the steamship company would have to. It's my opinion.

GUARD (looking at his watch) I'm afraid I must be moving out in a few moments now. What about the luggage in the van? Of course, you can come with me up to the Junction and I'd be delighted to have your company. I feel lonely and nervous. But I can see the luggage is a difficulty. If you get it to the Junction, how to get it back, a puzzle, till evening. And the porters at the Junction haven't got the manners our young friends here have in handling luggage. Indeed, God help us, they don't have time and before Francis has the train standing, those boys have the luggage hauled out of her up the platform and into the Dublin train.

(1ST PORTER signs to 2ND PORTER.)

1ST PORTER I think we'll take the luggage out of her.

(ALL the others standing dull and quiet, except the APPLE WOMAN who rises stiffly, and begins to make across the back of the stage towards the left. (The PORTERS return with the truck piled up with luggage.)

ANNIE   What are we to do now? I feel there is something we might do, and
yet I don't know what.

JOHNNIE   Perhaps in a few moments something more definite may come
through from the man at the Junction and there's just a chance perhaps
the sailing of the boat will just be delayed, perhaps twenty-four hours.

ANNIE   I'm afraid I can't believe that will be so.

GUARD (*left*)   I'm sorry ladies I must be leaving now. (*To* APPLE WOMAN)
Are you coming Ma'am.

APPLE WOMAN   I am. If there is a war a fair is the place to gather information
about it, and I have my return ticket taken and the Railway'll bring
me there, and back, to-night, or I'll have blood.

2ND PORTER   That's the way to talk to them.

(*Exit* APPLE WOMAN *left.*)

(GUARD *looks at watch, blows whistle and waves flag, exit
left. Train moves off.*)

(*Telephone bell rings, both* PORTERS *and* JOHNNIE *go off left.* ANNIE *takes
a suit case from the truck.* KATE *takes another and they give them to* MADAME
BOSANQUET *and* CLAIRE *to sit down on. They themselves lean against the
truck.*)

(*Re-enter* BOY.)

BOY   Did you miss the train?

ANNIE   We let it go without us—we changed our minds.

MADAME BOSANQUET   We thought we'd go later.

CLAIRE   The next train.

BOY   There isn't another train till to-morrow. (*He moves towards gate, right.*)

ANNIE   Wait a minute. I might want you to go a message for me.

BOY   Yes, Miss.

ANNIE   Isn't there a woman lives about half a mile away who has new laid
eggs sometimes?

BOY   There's a woman there does have fowls I know, just beyond the little
wood.

ANNIE   Well wait till I'd see what I'd want from her. She'd have a basket
would she?

BOY   Oh, she would miss. She'd have a grand basket.

ANNIE   I'll give you half-a-crown now and you'll tell her to give you as
many new-laid eggs as she can for that and you'll bring them back to
me here and I'll give you a sixpence for yourself. Will you do that now?

BOY   I will, Miss.

ANNIE   There's the half-a-crown, now you remember, as many as she can
give me for the half-a-crown, and they must be new-laid.

BOY   Oh, they must be new-laid.

(*Exit* BOY *along Railway line, to left.*)
(*Enter* JOHNNIE *and* PORTERS, *left.*)

JOHNNIE   The information, as far as we can make out—the man at the Junction has poor teeth and speaks very indistinctly—is that if the war is in the Middle East it is 'War Declared', but if it's nearer home it's 'War broken out'! But the friend that gave him the information has gone out to gather some news, but in the meantime I've been talking with Simon the Clerk here; there is no question of a joke. There is war somewhere, but whether it will effect shipping on this side of the world, or not, we don't know and I don't suppose it can make any difference to us whether or no. I am grieved after the trouble everyone has taken.

MADAME BOSANQUET   All Annie's trouble.

CLAIRE   That's what he means. That's what we all mean.

1ST PORTER   You wouldn't think of going to America. You could get to America if the Atlantic was to run dry itself, or perhaps better then, and it's the two of us would wheel the old barrow for you.

JOHNNIE   I'm afraid the Steamship people wouldn't change the tickets.

2ND PORTER   Oh, that's the difficulty. But they ought to be glad to have you.

1ST PORTER   Wouldn't it be a marvellous thing to be walking on the bed of an ocean in the company of that great Leviathan. It wouldn't be absolutely dry for a long time.

2ND PORTER   It'd be moist.

1ST PORTER   We might get short of food in the middle of the passage and all die of starvation. Our movements would be naturally slow, and we couldn't carry a great deal of grub with us on the old truck. I suppose they'd be great quantities of fish. Every day a Friday: and we'd have the place to ourselves. No one born outside of Portnadroleen would think of taking the journey. We'd make a great name of ourselves. We'd be like the heroes and great ladies of the ancient line of Heroes in Great Ireland of old.

2ND PORTER   We'd write our names on the Scroll of Fame, and if we had a little camera with us we'd get great photographs, and when we climbed up the beach in New York the crowd, and the Mayor of New York and the Fire Brigade, would be there to meet us with bands and the Hibernians and the Sons of Mayo. We'd have great writing home.

1ST PORTER   And how would you send the letter?

2ND PORTER   By aeroplane, how else? You must be in a queer old mediaeval state to forget the aeroplanes.

1ST PORTER   It would be more dangerous for them, for if the machine broke up they wouldn't have the soft water to be falling in. But the hard shingle or the cruel rocks. Even if they were meshy with seaweed, a fall on them from maybe two thousand feet would be a hard blow.

2ND PORTER   It'd make them more cheerful and anyway the sight of land all the way would give them great encouragement.

1ST PORTER   And anyone that would look down on us, pushing the old barrow up and down the hills and hollows of the main ocean, would get queer old encouragement.

JOHNNIE   The passengers would be allowed to take a turn at wheeling the truck I suppose.

2ND PORTER   Oh, there'd be no trouble about arranging that. If we were down a very deep valley we wouldn't be able to see where we were coursing to. We'd have to have a compass. At night we could steer by the stars in the blue heaven. Wouldn't it be wonderful for me to be lying on my back in the great flags of seaweed, with a couple of conger eels beside me, picking the shining stars and giving out advice?

1ST PORTER   It'd be a terrible heavy journey on the boots. They'd wear out very soon on us.

2ND PORTER   We'd walk in our bare feet.

1ST PORTER   But you wouldn't ask the ladies to do that.

2ND PORTER   I would not. They'd be sitting up on top of the trunks on the old barrow. When we are doing the thing we might as well do it properly.

1ST PORTER   I'm with you there.

(Enter BOY left, with heavy basket.)

ANNIE   You weren't long.

BOY   I met the woman and she coming along with a load of eggs herself, and she said to tell you to take the lot of them and give her another shilling or leave it with the clerk in here for her. Did I do right, Miss?

ANNIE   You did, you're a good boy. Put the basket down here by the truck. Here is your sixpence for you now.

(Taking out her purse from her handbag she gets the money, and also a shilling which she hands to JOHNNIE.)
(Exit BOY—by gate, right.)

ANNIE   Here Johnnie, do you mind giving this to the clerk inside. Don't ask him any more about the war; he'll tell you if he's heard anything. Anyway, I haven't heard the bell.

(Exit JOHNNIE, left.)

1ST PORTER   Will we take the eggs down to you with the luggage? We thought we'd take that down to you later in the dim of the evening.

ANNIE   Yes, that's the best.

(MADAME BOSANQUET, *and* CLAIRE *and* KATE *stand up.*)
(JOHNNIE *enters, left.*)

JOHNNIE   I said nothing to him only to tell him to give the woman a shilling for the eggs, and he said nothing to me.

ANNIE   I think we best go back now.

(ALL *move out by gate, right.*)

1ST PORTER   A war is a terrible thing if it is between people that speak the same language, but perhaps it is worse if they don't understand each other, and can only cry out like the wild things; though mostly they fight silently.

2ND PORTER   They say 'tis a glorious thing to be swinging a sword through the skulls of the people, but I don't believe it. If it is glory, it's not there. It's in the cold moon time creeping for your country, if it's for a country man must die.

1ST PORTER   Isn't it better for a man to die for something when he must, most times, die for nothing. They say that the spirit of a man dying in the might of his battle, takes the shape of a sword leaping from his body among the ghosts where all are equal.

2ND PORTER   I wouldn't hold with that old tale. There is great division among the warriors dead, all but some. There is a kind of a footpath of the clouds where only the greatest walk. All of a height and a kind of a humming noise about them like gold bees, that would be at the same time glistening and no man knows if he will be walking there. Ah'tis but for a time, maybe for a day in our way of thinking and then they go on where the dear God would have them. And anyone that would see that pass of great heroes walking he would lose his sight for a day, and when his sight would come again the memory of the march he saw would pass away out of his brain by the front of it, just as if you took your great hands and opened the forehead of him, and then closed up again—gone.

JOHNNIE   Well, I think war is a cruel, a beastly thing, however you look at it.

1ST PORTER   It brings out the bravest. It brings down the low ones into the mud, but it's not a necessity. It's a curse that is on the people.

2ND PORTER   Some people say they love it.

1ST PORTER   Ah, say, say, say, they'd say anything. A love-sick young man would die of love, and what is that to make of love a great thing. You'd think dying was the finish of a glory, a winning post, to listen to the talk off a platform, by a barrel head, before a market cross.

JOHNNIE   You are old men.

2ND PORTER   Not so old at all.

JOHNNIE   Well, I don't see anything that I would die for at this moment.

2ND PORTER   Because it's not put before you rightly. If I was to have the gift of speech this moment I believe I could find something you'd die for now, my boy, bright as you are.

1ST PORTER   Take no notice of that man. He isn't right. He's always got his head in the clouds and his feet in the old bog hole.

2ND PORTER   It's not that I have my head in the clouds but that you have your thought in your stomach waiting your breakfast. With me it's the emptiness of my stomach makes the brightness of my head. With you the hollow stomach makes the hollow head. 'Tis to our breakfasts the two of us should be going down this moment. This will be a long day, before it's finished.

(*Enter* ALFRED, *right. His hair is wet. He is not wearing a hat. He has a towel wrapped round his neck. He has a letter in his hand, pale blue paper, with an envelope to match.*)

ALFRED   I have only just come back from bathing. I found this note lying on the table in the hotel. It is from your Aunt, sent to the hotel last night but undelivered to me by the ridiculous people. They just left it lying on the table in the hall, supposing that perhaps it would catch my eye. I might have seen it this morning when I went out to have my bathe, but someone of last night's roysterers had left his hat on top of it.

JOHNNIE   I suppose she has told you of the sudden proposed journey.

ALFRED   Yes, and before I had time to properly read her note I hear that the journey is not taking place.

JOHNNIE   That is true.

ALFRED   The porters here are, I suppose, wondering what to do about the luggage.

JOHNNIE   These men know what they are going to do with it. They are going to take it back to-night in the darkness. If there is darkness in this town of burning light.

ALFRED   Some wild tales of Wars, or rumours of Wars, perhaps quite rightly has altered your people's plans?

(JOHNNIE *turns to porters.*)

JOHNNIE   I suppose we might say it's that, men?

1ST PORTER   Strong rumours.

2ND PORTER   Imminent.

ALFRED   War has its charm. It feeds something that all men and women long for—excitement. Indeed I have thought that if the range of guns could have been limited by the League of Nations, by making neutral lanes, sea lanes and land lanes, the tourist cruising companies could have continued to cater for their customers. 'Travel round the world and see the wars from a swivel chair.' Intervals, if any, filled with deck games fancy dress carnivals, and concerts for the benefit of the ship-wrecked seamen. You and your relatives, are, I suppose, the ship-wrecked passengers.

JOHNNIE   Yes.

ALFRED   Where the bullets whistling fly
Comes the sadder, fainter cry,
Help us brothers ere we die
Of—Ennui.

That's rather good, isn't it! It's a quotation, most of it. I think it's very apt. Anyway this war will most likely turn out to be a premature foreign correspondent stunt, and you will, after a little delay, be able to all start again on your trip. If the Steamship Company have really cancelled their sailing they'll have to refund—must do so.

JOHNNIE   Oh, certainly they must. Yes, they're sure to do that.

ALFRED   War can be very deadly, even a war fought at close quarters with small arms. People fighting in a forest have a tendency to get closer and closer until they're looking straight down into the muzzles of the other men's rifles, or hitting up the other one's revolver, and then letting him have the contents of yours, before he has time to bring his hand down again. Those who have learnt their business dodging round trees, make a poor fist of it among ditches, and on a roadway or a plain, they are completely demoralized. One man's as brave as another.

JOHNNIE   I wonder is that true.

ALFRED   Absolutely. It's the environment that is cowardly. But in a sense no man is brave naturally. He is the vessel into which bravery is poured.

2ND PORTER   The Vase (*pronounced vayse*) of Bravery.

1ST PORTER   The Vase (*pronounced vawse*) of Valour.

ALFRED   Quite so.

JOHNNIE   It would take time to work that out, to go back over history and to make sure.

ALFRED   But man has some attributes which are his own naturally.

JOHNNIE   Yes, I suppose so.

ALFRED   He is naturally good-natured, for instance.

1ST PORTER   Well, that's something to go on with.

JOHNNIE   I think I've got an idea of what you mean. But it would take a good deal of clearing up. The dividing line between what is natural, and what is un-natural is vague to me at present.

ALFRED   Not to me in this case.

JOHNNIE   Our conversation leads us nowhere.

1ST PORTER   I wouldn't say that. This man here is very instructing. He has a way with him, and that you would hardly expect from the look of him.

JOHNNIE   Oh, Mr Clonboise has travelled a lot in South America. He's a

relation of mine. If you'd go back far enough you'd find an ancestor of
his in Droleen.

1ST PORTER   I wouldn't doubt. I could see the family resemblance to some
parties in the town, if not to your own immediate family. He'll be here
for his health, I suppose?

JOHNNIE   Oh, yes, taking a rest.

ALFRED   I don't know yet what stay I'll make. I had a bathe this morning
and that was delightful. And of course it's getting on in the year. The
climate seems mild and equable. I believe at all seasons of the year this
should make a handsome place of residence, or at any rate a *pied à terre*.

2ND PORTER   It's healthy alright for anyone that has the constitution to
stand out the length of the winter and the spring. What has most of the
people slaughtered here is the price of drink, and that appears to be the
same everywhere in the present age of the world. We're all one level.

1ST PORTER (*beginning to pace up and down*)   Did any of us have our breakfast
yet?

ALFRED   I had not. I came away of course, when I found this letter, and
when I heard of the delay, of course, I simply ran up here.

JOHNNIE   Well, you'll be able to get a good breakfast now. An early
morning bathe always gave me a great appetite. The bacon and egg
always smelt better after you came out of the sea than at any other time.

ALFRED   I believe you this moment.

2ND PORTER   A breakfast late or early was always a good institution. I've
eaten a great many breakfasts in my life. I never missed one, even
when a child going to my school. I never was in such a hurry to go to
the Schoolhouse but I ate my breakfast first. My father, and his father,
missed many meals as well as their breakfast. That time will never
come again.

1ST PORTER   With God's help.

2ND PORTER   With God's help.

ALFRED   I had hoped that there would be less suffering in the world of the
future than in the old world. But even still there seems to be much
suffering in many lands. Evil distribution, or at any rate wrong
distribution of necessities and luxuries too. I predict, however, that this
country of Ireland will never see any great suffering again. Peace and
quiet ways beside the beautiful waters of the Broad Atlantic. Of course,
flying, aviation, will gradually bring other lands nearer. But visitors
from other climes will just pause here, birds of passage long enough to
open their purses and distribute some of their wealth and then fly on
again to Europe. The people of this country will then draw the curtains,
light the lamp, will switch on the Shannon Scheme and prepare to
spend the evening in happy quiet with a book or in searching for the
root of some strange gaelic word, heard during the daytime in the
Market place. The far-away worlds will clash and fight for empty
nothings—Money, Power, Variety. But here in Portnadroleen the wise

inhabitants like ole Brer Rabbit will just keep on 'saying nuffin'. They will have the better part. But I'm running on and keeping you all from your breakfast. Indeed, I'm devilish peckish myself this minute. (*Turns as if to go away right.*)

1ST PORTER (*who has been pacing slowly up and down*) You'll trip over your shoelace. It is undone.

(ALFRED *goes over to luggage truck. Puts up foot and bends over and begins tying shoe lace.*)
(2ND PORTER *steps over to him and takes revolver, a parabellum, from* ALFRED's *left hip pocket.*)

2ND PORTER (*levelling revolver*) Stand up now—hands up.

(ALFRED *obeys, with his back to the audience.*)

(1ST PORTER *goes to* ALFRED *and searches him for other arms. Takes his pocket book breast pocket, also* MADAME BOSANQUET's *letter which he hands to* JOHNNIE *who has been on* ALFRED's *right, not in the line of fire.* JOHNNIE *moves forward to take the letter.* JOHNNIE *stands holding the letter in his hand while* 1ST PORTER *goes through the pocket book. He takes out some paper money, looks at it and puts it back. He takes out passport and photograph; he looks at it and at* ALFRED. *Hands passport to* JOHNNIE, *who looks at it, and when* 1ST PORTER *holds his hand out for it, gives it back.* 1ST PORTER *also takes out a larger paper.*)

1ST PORTER Insurance, for travelling by rail, steamer and motor. Well, he's not travelling at the moment.

(*Puts pocket book into* ALFRED's *side coat pocket, neatly, pulling lapel down over it.*)

That ought to do him a lot of good. Turn round. (ALFRED *turns round, facing out*) Yo can drop your hands, but keep them in front of you. You're travelling. How far do you expect to go?

ALFRED I had originally meant to travel about on the Continent of Europe. And then I thought of staying here for the time. But I'm in your hands.

1ST PORTER Oh, no, you're not. Is he Tom?

2ND PORTER Oh, walk away if you like. (*He still keeps the revolver pointed at* ALFRED's *body.*)

1ST PORTER What's the revolver for?

ALFRED Where I was, up the country in South America, we were advised to carry a revolver always.

1ST PORTER Why?

ALFRED   I don't know—just protection.

1ST PORTER   Protection against what?

ALFRED   The natives might rise.

1ST PORTER   Oh, the natives might rise.

ALFRED   There was no sign of any trouble when I was there.

1ST PORTER   Were you ever fighting in war with this revolver?

ALFRED   Oh, no.

1ST PORTER   Or any revolver.

ALFRED   No Sir.

1ST PORTER   Have you killed many men? Fighting duels perhaps?

ALFRED   No, No, I never used it. I did fire it off, of course, practicing firing at a mark on the wall. The Mining Company wished us to. And at a bottle. I wasn't very good at it.

1ST PORTER   I suppose you did your best. Do you think you're dangerous now to this community?

ALFRED   Oh, I don't think so at all, I have no desire to meddle with anything. I read the papers, at least I have done so always, everywhere, in the past and wherever I am, I never understand anything. Perhaps I shouldn't read the papers at all.

1ST PORTER   Probably you'd be as well not to. The best thing for you to do is to eat and drink, and walk about, and smoke your cigarettes, you can smoke one now if you like.

ALFRED   Oh, thank you. (*Takes out cigarettes and lighter—offers case to* JOHNNIE.)

JOHNNIE   No thanks, I won't smoke now.

(ALFRED *holds the case out towards* 1ST PORTER *and* 2ND PORTER.)

2ND PORTER   No thank you, we chew tobacco at this time of the morning. It's too early for cigarettes. They're unhealthy things to the natives of this place early in the day.

ALFRED   I hadn't heard this.

2ND PORTER   You haven't been here long enough to hear everything yet.

1ST PORTER   You're free now, you can go. But mind yourself. (*He points off right.*)

(2ND PORTER *lowers revolver and drops it into the side pocket of his jacket.*)

ALFRED   I'm sorry if my having that revolver and coming here to the town has caused any unpleasantness, and I am really grieved about this trip for Mr Gillane and his friends falling through, and if I have annoyed anyone by anything I have said, I'm supremely sorry. I would sooner have cut my tongue out than hurt anyone's feelings. There are times really when I put my foot in it so foolishly that I wish I was dead.

2ND PORTER   Don't start wishing again.

ALFRED   Did I talk about wishing things before? I forget what I said.

JOHNNIE (*walking across to* 2ND PORTER)   What sort of a revolver is it?

2ND PORTER   Oh, up to date. (*Takes out revolver*) See Mister Johnnie, here's the safety catch. It's off (*touches it*). Now it's on (*touching it again*).

JOHNNIE   Show it to me here (*holding out his hand*).

2ND PORTER   Now it's off. (*Touches it again. Then opens it and takes out cartridges and drops them into his side pocket and hands the revolver to* JOHNNIE *who glances at it carelessly and hands it back to* 2ND PORTER. *Goes over to luggage and sits down.*)

JOHNNIE (*to* ALFRED)   I'll have a cigarette now, I think.

(ALFRED *takes out case and lighter*—JOHNNIE *smokes.*)

1ST PORTER   Now, Mr Clonboise, the best thing for you to do is to go along down the town with Johnnie Gillane and you can give Madame Bosanquet the latest news of the war, which is nothing at all. And you can apologize for being late at the station, if you feel like it. Now, Johnnie, rise up off the barrow. I think it would be best for us to push it into the goods office for the time being and off the platform.

JOHNNIE   That's the best thing to do with it. It's time everyone had their breakfast. It's time I had mine. If we all wait any longer it'll be lunch time.

2ND PORTER   And a while longer and it'll be tea time, and another little while and it'll be supper time. And it won't be long then till it's time to take a sleep. Because, in spite of what you might think, Mr Clonboise, the people of this town do get sleepy now and then.

ALFRED   I must give in to that if you say so.

JOHNNIE   Well let's be going.

ALFRED   Yes, let's be going. I ought to be the first to want to hurry away, for I think I'm the only one of us who had a bathe this morning to give me that extra touch of appetite.

(*Exit* JOHNNIE *and* ALFRED, *right.*)
(*After a moment* 1ST PORTER *goes to right and whistles through fingers.* ALFRED *re-appears right.*)

1ST PORTER   And you might call, on your way to your breakfast, at Miss Jennings and give her the war news. Goodbye now.

2ND PORTER   Let us heave along this load of clothes and boots, and general apparel, suitable to all the climates of the world. Let us heave it into the office.

(*The two* PORTERS *push the truck off left.*)
(*The two* PORTERS *re-enter left.*)

1ST PORTER   Now let us go down and get the breakfast. There is one thing
that would give me great encouragement if someone, some kind
Samaritan, would give me good winners for to-day.

(*Exit leisurely, right.*)

Curtain.

ACT FIVE

Scene: *Railway Station as before, but late in the evening. Red sunset sky right. Buildings dark. Light from left from Office.*

(*Enter two* PORTERS *gate right wheeling empty barrow. Whistle heard off left. Noise of train approaching.* ALFRED *in overcoat enters gate right and stands against side of shed, where he remains during the scene smoking several cigarettes.*
Enter bare-foot BOY *gate right. He passes across stage, exits left. Front of Engine appears left.* PORTERS *hurry off left.*
Enter left, APPLE WOMAN *with noggin bottle in hand, but empty, followed by* 1ST PORTER. *She gives him her railway ticket. She sits down on truck.*
Enter left BOY *with bundle of evening papers. Enter left* 2ND PORTER *and* GUARD. GUARD *takes one of the papers from under the* BOY'S *arm and opens it at the racing page.*)

GUARD   Did any Christian gentlemen here back Elkhome at twenty to one? And there is no answer.

(*Turning to the* APPLE WOMAN.)

Did you Madame? You did not I fear. But you sold your apples for your basket is empty, so I see is the noggin. (*Taking an empty bottle from the basket and holding it up to the light*) I wish I had seen it earlier in the day when it's heart was full. It was a good fair they tell me. Was it so Mary?
APPLE WOMAN   They were in grips at the commencement, but later on a great quantity of money was passing.
GUARD   Were there any good ballad singers there?
APPLE WOMAN   There were two, Sir, they had the town scoured twice of ha'pence.
GUARD   Isn't it an audacious thing that the ballad singer should go through the street singing full of porter, while our native poets do languish in the caves of the hills, perishing for recognition? They should be supported in affluence. They should be the guards on the railways, while I should be singing the praises of Erin, the brave and the free.

(*Exit* 2ND PORTER *left.*)

GUARD (*to* 1ST PORTER)   Has the day passed off here as usual?

1ST PORTER   Much the same.

GUARD (*turning up the newspaper's back page*)   There's a stop press piece of
news here that says that the rumour of war in the Middle East is denied
authoritatively. That gives the lie to what's in the front of the paper,
which describes the holocaust. Well, I'm glad it's over before it began.
I'm not ready for war yet. I haven't the heart for it. Not on a large
scale. A touch of private revenge would suit me well. There are a
couple of people in this town of yours, without offence (2ND PORTER
returns with lighted lamp) to anyone here present, that I could see bumped
off, if it was done quickly. There was a man I was playing cards with
last night. Well, he had great gifts but he was a nasty man to look at.
I wouldn't miss him if he was to be taken from me, not that I wish any
harm to the man. There was a man here one time that was Mayor.
There was nothing ever done to him. Some have charmed lives and
some are not so lucky. There was nothing else of interest in the paper
to the people of this town. (*Folds paper carefully and hands it back to* BOY.)
This town is very lucky. It's so self contained. The only trouble is that
there are too many ruffians at large in the streets. This place ought to
have had a jail.

1ST PORTER   It had once.

GUARD   That's a curious thing. The march of civilization. First a jail and
then no jail at all. And what do they do if by any chance they find
anybody, not a native, I'm not saying a native but a visitor, suitable
for incarceration?

1ST PORTER   They put him in a car and take him away I dunno where, and
they have to pay for the car. For a while this Railway used to pay its
dividends, taking away prisoners. In fact, I believe when the jail went,
the train came near to its death.

2ND PORTER   That shows you what a lot transport has to say to civilization.

GUARD (*sits down on truck*)   Now, you'd have to have your eye pierced very
tight on the facts of the case, to be certain whether the crime causes the
transport, or the transport causes crime. Look at war. You can't have
war without transport. If two nations are wishful to fight they cannot
fight until they are brought to some one place, at the same time, where
they can hammer it out. Napoleon said an Army walks on the stomach
of its weakest member. Now they either fly or go in a bus, except
when they go by water. The people in the town below us are sitting in
their chairs waiting for the news of the far corners of the earth, that this
young lad has folded against his young ribs. And instead of running
down to them with their nourishment, he stands here listening to the
words of Socrates sitting on a truck. Didn't he sit on a barrel? No, no,
that was another feller—an empty barrel.

1ST PORTER   What has been in it?

GUARD   History doesn't tell us, but I tell you, if I find any old artist out of a barrel sitting opposite me playing cards to-night and he's lucky, I'm telling you I'll be declaring war on him, I'm tired of leaving the unravelling of my heart strings in the Savings Banks of sweet Droleen.

2ND PORTER You find it very hard to get a man to stand up to you at all at the cards. It's what you begin with vengeance. You should take them slow, then creep up on them, and take the scalp off them.

GUARD There's something in what you say. I've been all my life too headstrong, and I get a name that goes before me. I believe that those I meet at the Card School here get their instruction from some head centre or other in some distant place, where they have the opportunity of studying that is denied to the benighted unfortunates of this town. If ever I become a millionaire I'll buy Droleen and sink it in the sea. It isn't good for me that there should be such a place. It causes me to sin. If it wasn't there I wouldn't have any bad thoughts about the place. (*Turning to* APPLE WOMAN) Let you, Ma'am, take no notice of anything you may hear at this hour in this place. There was a song once—'This Grand Conversation was under the Rose.' Did you ever hear tell of it?

APPLE WOMAN I did sir, it was a grand old song.

GUARD That was a song of great warriors. Greater than the one you see before you now. This boy here, that stands like Cupid with his share of arrows under his arm, is too innocent to have heard that song sung.

BOY Maybe I'll hear it yet.

GUARD You might if you mind yourself.

1ST PORTER I suppose there were towns in Ireland that you held your inquest on, long ago, before you set your foot in old Droleen.

(*It is getting darker. Light on left from Goods Office goes out.*)

GUARD I wouldn't name them. They're gone down the long hill of memory. Buried beneath the moss and the ivy. When I've finished with a town, there's not picking for a flea in it.

2ND PORTER If you want to say anything freely about this town don't let those present curb your animosity in any way. This woman here lives beyond the borough boundary. Myself and my co-directors are immigrants and this young lad here, he won't have grown to manhood's strength before you'll be under the nettles by the natural process of decay.

GUARD (*turning to* BOY) The way he speaks to me you'd think I hadn't a soul at all. My young hero, remember Robert Emmet died with a smile, let you try to live with one. But sometimes my feelings get too much for me. But when the sword, shining and bright, falls from my hands, it's you child that will grasp it and wave it, wave it. Where will he wave it boys?

2ND PORTER Where it is most wanted.

GUARD You're perfectly right, get strength in yourself little boy. Never stop to pass judgment on the old ones, they have their troubles and remember, if you wish them well, they are not able to help wishing you well. That's a long thing to say but a short thing to remember. (*Loudly*) Who's that feller standing in the dark corner in the shelter of the shed? Bring him out here.

(ALFRED *steps forward*.)

APPLE WOMAN   Holy God, you're not going to shoot him before my eyes.
GUARD   Do you not know that Agamemnon would not kill Apollo in the presence of Cleopatra? His hour will keep.
2ND PORTER   We shifted him this morning.
GUARD   Well, let him go to Hell out o' that.

(*Exit* ALFRED.)

GUARD (*getting up stiffly and slowly*)   Has the Goods Clerk gone?
2ND PORTER   Yes, his light's out.
GUARD   Then with youth in front (*with his left hand making a gesture for the* BOY *to start*) followed by Pomona of the empty creel, let us go down into this little town and see what diversion they have prepared for the Old Irish Chieftain and his gallow glasses. (*He walks after the* APPLE WOMAN *filing out right, followed by the* PORTERS, *the* 2ND PORTER *swinging his lantern*.)
GUARD   I'd put out that lantern. We're in mufti now.

(2ND PORTER *blows out lantern*.)

CURTAIN.

La La Noo

A Play in Two Acts

CHARACTERS

PUBLICAN *About 50. Handsome heavy face, slightly blue chin. Worn old hard felt hat. Old striped cotton shirt, no collar. Double-breasted brown tweed waistcoat. Stem of wooden pipe sticking out of pocket, short well-worn grey jacket, red-brown trousers, old dark green velvet slippers.*

STRANGER *About 55. Thin way-worn man. Red-grey moustache. Pretty good black felt soft hat. Dark blue tie. Old white shirt with soft turned down collar. Seedy respectable grey suit. Small neat old black shoes.*

1ST WOMAN *About 26. Well and neatly dressed. Small umbrella.*

2ND WOMAN *About 45. Well and neatly dressed in brown. Walking stick.*

3RD WOMAN *About 19. More brightly dressed.*

4TH WOMAN *About 20. Small, dark, but with white face, worn clothes, ragged shawl, broken boots.*

5TH WOMAN *About 23. Fair hair, fawny shawl, blue dress, neat shoes.*

6TH WOMAN *About 24. Brown hair, fawny shawl, dark red dress, neat shoes.*

7TH WOMAN *About 26. Sturdy. Dressed in workmanlike heather tweed, grey felt hat.*

ACT ONE

Scene: *Small public house, bar dingy blue with basin and two pint glasses. On left behind bar, dingy blue dresser with spirit bottles on top shelf, porter bottles below, and small glasses on shelf. Porter barrel behind bar to left. To left again, heavy door. Some hay under door. On floor in front of bar wooden arm chair. At back, window with dingy claret-coloured cotton half-curtain. Hanging lamp with shade in front of window. Green outside shutter standing against wall. Open doorway, green door to right of centre. Outside, scene of sandy road, bent grass, sea islands near, and high islands distant. Ocean horizon. Long stool in front of wall to right.*

(PUBLICAN *discovered standing behind bar with spectacles on reading a little paper like a bill. Enter by door* STRANGER.)

STRANGER God save all here.

PUBLICAN And you also, sir. (*He throws paper under bar and takes off spectacles.*)

STRANGER That's a fine day, or it was. It won't last I'm thinking, there's a lot of those heavy old clouds in the sky, and it's not to say that after the long fine hot spell we've had the weather is going to change in a moment of time. 'Long promised, long stand.' It's a good while, they say, since they had a hot summer here. I'll have a small whiskey.

(PUBLICAN *goes to bar dresser, takes a bottle, changes his mind, takes another, measures out a half one, and puts the glass before* STRANGER *on bar. Then, after a second or two, takes small jug of water from dresser and puts on the bar.* STRANGER *drinks whiskey at a gulp. Then slowly pours water into glass and drinks it.*)

PUBLICAN Nice scenery about here.

STRANGER I was at the Sports on the Strand beyond. I came away early and walked by the shore round the butt of cliff. I'll have a touch more of the pawnee, the water.

(PUBLICAN *takes up jug, sees it's empty, goes round bar, walks through doorway and to right, returns with jug full, spilling a little water as he comes. Stranger pours water into glass and drinks it slowly.*)

STRANGER This ought to be a healthy place. Nothing to worry you but the calling of the sea-birds to one another.

PUBLICAN   It's quiet enough indeed. I didn't go to the Sports. I'm sure there was good value there. There was a young lad, McGaw, from in the hills back here, did he win? They said he'd win the four mile race.

STRANGER   Oh, he did and easy. A fine handsome young feller and a good rangey way of running.

PUBLICAN   But what's the good of it to him?

STRANGER   Ah, well, it passes the time for him and keeps him out of harm's way. He has to mind himself and keep fit if he's going to have a chance to win anything. Health is everything. Health and a hard heart'll take you round the world.

PUBLICAN   You travelled the world I'm sure. And this is only a backward place for you. Myself and the Smith up the road is all the civilisation about here, and it's four miles before you strike the main road. A good road it is, hard as steel, well laid, well made, well stood.

STRANGER   I heard them speaking of it. People are always talking about roads. I tell you I saw more roads in my life than I ever want to remember. And the people I saw walking the roads, the bigger part of them weren't fit to be walking a road with honest men, it's what the half of them ought to be in a sack, with a stone in it, in an old bog hole.

PUBLICAN   Well, a good road's a good road. It goes from here to there, it keeps the order of civilization in a state of movement.

STRANGER   It does that indeed.

PUBLICAN   Before there were any roads in the country the people were very benighted.

STRANGER   Ah, but they had great innocence and kind hearts. It is the big cities of the world that spoil the humanity in the people and turn it into nothing but envy, obstruction and throat-cutting in the way of business. Hello, what's coming now? (*He is looking out of door to right*) A large body of women. I always heard it was unlucky to meet a large body of women in the morning early.

PUBLICAN   Well, it's not morning now. It's late in the evening.

STRANGER   I don't know but it might be unlucky any time of day to encounter them. They are marching down on us heavy, very strong and determined. There's a dark cloud over them, a bit of a shower maybe. They'll hurry away from it but it'll catch them in a half minute. (*Puts arm out of door*)

STRANGER   Here it comes. (*He moves from door down to front of counter. Sound of rain—slight.*)

(*Enter* WOMEN. 1ST *and* 2ND, 3RD *and* 4TH, 5TH *and* 6TH *side by side.* 7TH *alone, last to enter. They crowd themselves about doorway and in front of stool, shaking the few raindrops from themselves. Sound of sharp rain.* STRANGER *stands at attention.* PUBLICAN *takes off his hat and puts it on counter. Stranger takes his off to salute and puts it on again.*)

PUBLICAN   That was a severe drop.

2ND WOMAN   Yes, we didn't see it coming till it was almost on us. But indeed there was no shelter anywhere, except the Blacksmith's and this house, sir. We've been to the Athletic Sports and this young lady (*looking at* 4TH WOMAN) guided us along the road over the hill from the sea sand. Our intention is to walk on to the main road where we understand the 'bus passes, rather an extended walk, but you see we found that the only other way would be to go back by a private venture 'bus from the Sports and we all agreed that it would be terribly crowded, and we feared—I did, and some of the others agreed with me, that an accident might easily occur.

1ST WOMAN   It isn't a very bad road, I suppose, from here on. I hope it isn't too stoney.

3RD WOMAN   Is there any grass at its sides? I've got thin shoes on.

PUBLICAN   It's a grand road, but hard for walking. But it's not too bad and you can take your time.

(*He goes to bar dresser and finds paper on a hook there and consults it.*)

The 'bus won't pass by before two hours and a half I'd say. What time is it? (*He turns to* STRANGER. STRANGER *waves his hands outwards as if he said 'search me.'*)

1ST WOMAN (*takes watch out of handbag.*)   It's between ten minutes and a quarter past five.

PUBLICAN   There you are, she won't pass the crest of the hill where you meet the main road before eight, for she doesn't leave the harbour before seven forty-five.

STRANGER   You'll have a beautiful view of the ocean and the sun setting as you go up the road. You won't notice the time passing, or the hardness of the road. It has the Bay of Naples and Sydney Harbour and Rio looking like a bunch of faded flowers before you. You'll enjoy every moment, ladies. (*The sky outside is lighter.*)

7TH WOMAN   It's cleared off, we should be moving on I think.

2ND WOMAN   Thank you. Good afternoon.

1ST WOMAN   Goodbye.

3RD WOMAN   Good evening.

(*The other* WOMEN *just turn their faces towards the* PUBLICAN *and the* STRANGER—*all file out. The sky outside darkens.*)

STRANGER   The same again.

(PUBLICAN *measures out a half one.* STRANGER *pays for his drink, puts a little water in it, and sips but does not finish it. All the* WOMEN *return. There is a sound of rain.*)

3RD WOMAN   We went out too soon. There is another small shower chasing the larger one.

PUBLICAN   'Twas ever so, mam, here. You could never depend on it once the weather is in the way of breaking. The showers have no mercy on you.

1ST WOMAN   Still we had sunshine all day and the Sports were very delightful. In the first pony race when the jockey had his pony fall on the top of him at the fence, we thought he was killed. We were standing quite close to the jump—he lay so still. . .

7TH WOMAN   He was all right. It'd take more than that to kill that sort of a lad. When he got up after he came to himself and shook himself and found no bones broken, he went off laughing.

1ST WOMAN   Still it looked very much like a tragedy to me. While they were giving him first aid, I saw a tall man running towards us with a large bottle. I was sure it was whiskey and that he intended pouring it down the casualty's throat. 'Don't do that' I said, 'until a Doctor sees him.' They said there was a Doctor coming, and I did see a stoutish man riding across the land.

4TH WOMAN   Why did you stop the boy on the sand having the drink? What harm would it do him, but all the good in the wide world?

PUBLICAN   Where was the man coming from with the bottle?

1ST WOMAN   From one of the tents.

PUBLICAN   Which one?

1ST WOMAN   I think it was the second from the end, and the name on the banner over it was 'Dolan'.

PUBLICAN   Safe enough.

4TH WOMAN   Safe enough! Can you beat them publicans. Wouldn't you throw any spirit on a fire and it sinking, not to be forever scraping on the threshold 'Is it whose? Is it mine? Is it thine?' I hate all publicans.

7TH WOMAN   The Doctor soon had him in charge and standing up on his feet. Just winded, nothing more. The boy did right to lie still until the Doctor could get to him, if there is a Doctor. Of course, if a man is bleeding to death that's another thing.

STRANGER   Oh, yes, that's another thing.

7TH WOMAN   And the people are not so innocent, but they can stop a flow of blood.

5TH WOMAN   I do faint when I see blood.

6TH WOMAN   That's the truth, she does fall back.

2ND WOMAN   I think it's time enough to faint when you have done every-thing you can for the victim of the accident and by that time you've forgotten all about yourself and if you faint it is because you are thinking about yourself.

1ST WOMAN   I don't know altogether about that. I think it's physical with most people, unless there is some association with the falling of blood.

5TH WOMAN   It is for what it's shed that makes it worth its flow, I'm telling you.

1ST WOMAN   You're telling me.

6TH WOMAN   Aye, she's telling you.

4TH WOMAN   Blood is blood, wherever it flows or for who or whatever it flows.

7TH WOMAN   That's beyond me.

2ND WOMAN   Not as much beyond you as you think, or would like to think. I have seen blood shed for me, and I was neither proudful nor ashamed, but that's a while ago.

STRANGER   And it was right.

(*The* PUBLICAN *takes off his hat and scratches his head with a stroking gesture.*)

7TH WOMAN   Well, it's nothing to me and I don't want to see any man suffer.

6TH WOMAN   You do right. Why should they suffer wounds? Are there not enough wounds on the creation of the earth?

1ST WOMAN   Wounds enough!

STRANGER   Wounds enough on man and woman.

1ST WOMAN   I would hate to see any man die. I didn't see my father die. He was away from me when he died. I have no brother or sister and my mother died when I don't remember her. And I thought I was going to see the jockey boy die there on the Strand to-day. I was sick at it. I didn't want to see it. I am glad now, not only for him, but for myself. But surely I cannot expect to live all my life and see no man die. 'Tis too much to expect.

4TH WOMAN   I never seen them die. I seen them wither and when my back was turned they died on me. Wouldn't they put the life across you? They'd like to with their tricky ways. They're in hands with death the whole time, the dirty twisters.

5TH WOMAN   I don't care what you say, I'll see a man die and then I'll die myself and it won't be long either.

6TH WOMAN   She does always talk that way. I don't think it's right for her.

STRANGER   It isn't right. It's not healthy.

2ND WOMAN   She should be thinking of bright things at her age. Not gloomy thoughts. Youth is for flowers and gaiety.

PUBLICAN   There doesn't be much flowers about this part of the country, only the wild things. The Smith had a bit of a rose growing but it died on him.

2ND WOMAN   'Tis the wild things that have the real beauty.

STRANGER   You've said it, Madame.

1ST WOMAN   They put flowers on graves everywhere.

6TH WOMAN   It's nettles that do grow mostly on the graves about this part of the world. I saw graveyards in the Great Cities of America with figures of stone standing high, steps up to them and houses built under them, and pillars of marble and white caves with more statues standing within them, and some had flowers that never grow and so they never die. And maybe all the time, the young nettles smelling from their soft green leaves over the small little graveyard in a cleft of the hills, near my own home, were in the cave of my mind.

1ST WOMAN   I know that is so with me, also. A grave is ever a homely thing.

STRANGER   Every man should dig his own grave, if he's given time.

2ND WOMAN   Doesn't he?

STRANGER   That is so, Mam.

4TH WOMAN   I'll tell you what. I think you're all talking about death because you think 'tis so far away. Look at the people that are killed on the roads every day with the motor cars rushing at them. Isn't that a queer thing, and no one to care as if it is what they liked killing each other. I wouldn't mind if they killed the streels of the roads, like you might think I was. But they are in the habit of killing each other. People rich enough to have a motor car do kill others in the like shape and semblance of themselves. I knew a man once, a fine fair, high looking, handsome man, and he threw a sod of turf at a man in a boat, and the boat tipped over, and the man in it was drowned, and it was but a joke. But the man who threw the turf never lifted his head out of his breast as long as ever he lived. And now if every man who killed another man, or maybe a young child, with his motor, I'm saying if they all hung their heads it'd be a queer looking bunch of crooked necks you'd see walking the roads, and the lanes, and the streets of this country, and it's supposed to be only a backward place. I'm telling you, the countries of the world, I believe, are boasting every day of all their own they are in the habit of killing on their own roads, maybe every week in the year. It's what they ought to bury them in one place and not have the eyes of God weaving over the surface of the earth for little lonely graves. Maybe that's what they think'll make them grand, killing on the big style. I dunno. . . .

1ST WOMAN   I think this woman is right, we are getting into the way of thinking very little of a life. Holding it too cheap.

7TH WOMAN   It's the newspapers! I never read them. I hear the wireless, and that's enough for me. If I miss it and some important announcement is made, someone is sure to tell me. I suppose the newspapers cause more dyspepsia than anything else that has to do with us. That's why the papers are able to fill themselves full of advertisements of cures for dyspepsia. I can eat anything but I can't read a newspaper.

2ND WOMAN   I wouldn't like to miss my daily paper. I read at least one and a half every day. And I like the day best when I don't see the name of anyone I know, personally, in the paper. I like to feel that everything that happens in the news is nothing to do with me. Or at any rate, that

I myself, personally, do not come into it. Of course, it's impossible not to be affected in some way, even if it is only by the price of sugar.

PUBLICAN   It's the first thing I look for. I sell it.

STRANGER   It's a useful article. Beet sugar is fine and healthy. But the sugar cane is a better cane than the schoolmaster ever caned with.

PUBLICAN   I never saw a sugar cane with him.

STRANGER   Molasses hot with rum. It's a good drink for a strong healthy man.

2ND WOMAN   It is.

3RD WOMAN   I'd love to taste it. (*Turning towards* PUBLICAN) Have you any?

PUBLICAN (*taking down proper rum bottle, with sailor label, taking out cork and smelling the bottle*)   I have a little here but there's no molasses left with me.

3RD WOMAN   Oh, I couldn't bear to drink it by itself.

5TH WOMAN (*raising her head*)   Rum and milk together is a good drink for a delicate stomach in the morning.

7TH WOMAN   And not too much milk.

1ST WOMAN (*turning towards* PUBLICAN)   I hope the Sports are a great success. Are they for any object?

PUBLICAN   No object at all, only Sport. There's sure to have been a grand day for everyone. I never had a tent there myself. It's too wearisome getting ready and drawing all the stuff across over a twisty road, and I'd have to hire a horse. I have a little ass, but he wouldn't be able to take over all that hill on one journey though he's a strong lad.

1ST WOMAN   It *is* a bad road.

PUBLICAN   That's why there was no one on the road with you to-day except yourselves. There's none goes nor comes this way. Up on the ridge of the hills to the back of us there (*pointing to the left front*) is where the road from the Sports is, there'd be plenty of traffic along there. But you'd find no road from this place to it. It's what you would be all the time climbing stoney ditches. Pretty well a two mile steeple chase for you ladies (*looking round at the group of* WOMEN.)

2ND WOMAN   Our only way is to do as you advise, and catch the 'bus (*The light outside is always getting brighter*) and I'm sure it will be wise for us to start very soon now. We'll have to walk a little faster after our delay.

PUBLICAN   You'll have plenty of time. Just keep going steadily. I'm not much in the habit of walking myself. But I could start anytime now and be sitting on the bank a half hour before there'd be any need to be thinking of the 'bus coming up from the harbour.

2ND WOMAN (*turning towards* STRANGER)   And we're to look out for the sunset.

STRANGER   You won't be able to miss it, and it'll be a broad one to-night I'm thinking. Observe it well. If it's mad looking, with a tattered mantilla on its face, it'll be a bad day to-morrow. But if nice and sweet like this young lady, looking over her shawl (*he looks towards* 6TH WOMAN *who has shawl over lower part of her face. She drops her shawl and puts up her chin*) then the morrow will be as nice as you please. That's the way it goes. I often heard the old ones say so, and I often observed it for myself. It's an extraordinary thing the way the weather does back up the Almanac. I never saw an Almanac that was altogether wrong.

7TH WOMAN   It wouldn't be of much use if it was.

2ND WOMAN   Unless it went by contraries, like dreams.

5TH WOMAN   Dreams don't go by contraries. They speak the truth.

3RD WOMAN   I hope not.

4TH WOMAN   I don't care what way they go. 'Tis all a superstition.

1ST WOMAN   I don't know, I'd take a warning if it was in a dream or in a spoken word.

7TH WOMAN   Would you take it in tea leaves?

1ST WOMAN   Even in tea leaves I'd take it.

7TH WOMAN   When tea leaf prophecies are not common sense.

2ND WOMAN   What's that?

3RD WOMAN   Yes, what's common sense?

7TH WOMAN   Common sense, is anything practical that can be applied by ordinary practical people, that's common sense. (STRANGER *lifts his hat solemnly from his head and puts it on again.*)

STRANGER   I always take off my hat to common sense. There ought to have been a Saint called Saint Common Sense, some of these wise guys say.

6TH WOMAN   So you say, you say more than your prayers.

STRANGER   Oh, well, I . . . I watch out. I've got to watch out.

5TH WOMAN   God protect you.

4TH WOMAN   And us all.

1ST WOMAN   It isn't every gathering of women caught in a heavy shower has such a pleasant place to shelter in.

2ND WOMAN   Indeed not, and we're very much obliged to you, sir. (*Looking towards* PUBLICAN. PUBLICAN *bustles about and produces from under counter four bottles of lemonade.*)

PUBLICAN   Would you not now all take a drink of lemonade before you start your road. (*He turns to the dresser and gets a few glasses and a couple of mugs.*)

7TH WOMAN   Many thanks indeed, but I think we ought to be on our way. It's not so long since I, for one, had a cup of tea in a tent. I never saw a tea tent at a Races before. It's a new innovation.

2ND WOMAN (*shakes head*)   No, thank you all the same. (*Others shake their heads. All move towards the door but the* 2ND WOMAN *stops and shakes hands with* PUBLICAN *and then with* STRANGER. *Other women do the same in following order:* 3RD WOMAN, 4TH WOMAN, 1ST WOMAN, 7TH WOMAN, 5TH WOMAN, 6TH WOMAN. STRANGER *follows them to door and on to road.*)

STRANGER (*speaking on road and pointing left*)   Now up that hill you must go. It's a bit of a stiff climb at first, but after that it's easy, until, with a bit of up, and a bit of down, you get the level that'll carry you all the way. On the main road there's a comfortable bank under a tree, and you can see the road from the Westward and you'll be able to have a full view of the 'bus a couple of gunshots away, coming up from the harbour. Step into the road, hold up your hands, and the engineer'll stop. Now safe home to all of you. (*He takes off his hat and with it in his hand comes back into the shop and finishes his drink which is on the counter. The* PUBLICAN *turns from the window where he has been holding the short curtain one side and looking out. The* PUBLICAN *and the* STRANGER *turn their faces towards one another. The brightness is already going out of the sky.*)

Curtain.

ACT TWO

Scene: *As before—an hour later—heavy rain, sky very dark.*

> PUBLICAN *sitting on box outside bar.* STRANGER *in chair.* STRANGER *has drink before him and is eating a piece of bread and butter, and picking the shell from a hard-boiled egg, dipping it in a saucer of salt.*

STRANGER   I'm thinking those lassies will not be in very good shape this minute. If it'd held off half an hour later they might have been under the tree in the little wood by now. Though, even so they wouldn't be able to stay there all the time. They'd have to make up their minds to go forward at last. I don't think the grand sunset I was offering them'll be so grand after all.

PUBLICAN   It's a great thing to be able to take pleasure in a sunset. I think myself I saw too many of them. From the roadway there in front of this house, you could get a feed of them all the year round—all sorts.

STRANGER   I've seen as many sunsets as yourself and maybe more. I've seen dawns too, ones I wouldn't want to see again, queer ones that would put the terrors of death in your heart. Sometimes after rising from a cold bed, another time maybe rising from the hard ground.

PUBLICAN   Well, you're a strong looking man to-day. At the same time it's not a good thing for any man, after he's left his boyhood behind him, to get drenched to the bone and you'd not be far under that *(turning his face to look out of doors)* before you'd be as wet, if you don't mind me saying it, as an old cormorant. I can offer you the shelter of this roof for the night if this is any use to you. You can sit up in the chair there, or lie in the bed there beside myself. I'm a very quiet sleeper. Come on now, have another roziner on me. *(He fills out a good sized share of whiskey from the bottle into the* STRANGER'S *glass and helps himself to a smaller helping. The* STRANGER *goes to the door to look out at the weather. He holds left hand over glass to keep rain out of it.)*

STRANGER   You'd think that ought to be enough to douse hell.

PUBLICAN   Ah, there's not enough water to put out that fire, I'm thinking. But still—

STRANGER   I see so many devils going about that I think that place must be overflowed.

PUBLICAN   This is a backward place.

STRANGER   Isn't it better so. There's nothing to be ashamed of, to be in a quiet place. You ought to thank God for it, on your knees, you ought.

PUBLICAN   I do. I do.

STRANGER   I'm sure you do. What do you want with heavy death and destruction, doing no good to anyone only cataracts of harm to man made in the image of God.

PUBLICAN   I know that sir. It's just that a man that would be growing old thinks that if he'd once cut a lump of a stick out of a hedge, put on the brogues and rattled over the bogs and far away, he'd have something to be thinking about even if it gave him a sour stomach.

STRANGER   Anyone could understand that. (*He returns to bench and sits down, putting his glass on the counter.*) I believe now, if the weather doesn't brighten up completely in the next twenty minutes, I'll accept your hospitality. Perhaps the Smith'll be back before the night. We could knock a crack out of him. They're so fond of knocking sparks out of metal, they ought to have a spark or two in themselves. He might raise a song for us. I often heard a Smith sing well. They have great lungs, sparks and bellows, good enough.

PUBLICAN   I've heard him sing when he had a couple of pints.

STRANGER   Well, we'll give him a couple of pints whatever.

PUBLICAN   He'll have some in him when he gets home to-night. Though it'll be mostly died in him by then. He won't be home till the night's well on.

STRANGER   There's sure no law against him stopping here.

PUBLICAN   Well, not much, not too much law against him this night.

STRANGER   He'd be my guest, if you'll excuse me. Of course, this house is yours, and I'm your guest and many thanks. But with your permission I'd love to be entertaining the singing Smith. I'm not able to sing myself this long time. I think I got my throat scored in the middle of my life. However, I remember the words of some of the best of the old ones and if the Blacksmith falters I'll be able to put him on his way.

PUBLICAN   It's a great blessing to have a strong memory. I never was able to commit to my brain but very little of whatever schoolmaster thought I ought to have off. He often lost patience with me, and, I'll tell you the truth, I often lost patience with him. The only difference between us was that I didn't mention the fact. I'd like well this minute to be able to stand up and give out a good song to you, or perhaps some great speech from a classic man of the old times.

STRANGER   I'm sure you could if you gave yourself the courage. Stand up and it'll come to you. Stand up. (PUBLICAN *comes forward to front of the bar left, and raises right hand as though about to declaim. Opens mouth, then drops hand to side and shakes his head slowly.*)

PUBLICAN   No, it's not there. I haven't got it. (*He returns to back of bar.*)

STRANGER   It's your modesty tangles your tongue. 'Tangle tongue' that's that they used to call the hooch they used to make long ago. I'd say that it's a long time since your tongue was tangled with liquor. You have the fine healthy appearance to me of a temperate man.

PUBLICAN Oh, temperate enough. Though looking at the sea would often make a man dry. Still, I only take an odd spot because I seldom have company. The Blacksmith is from day to day a very moderate man. Perhaps because it's seldom he has anyone much for company but myself. We are company to one another, but not what you'd call jovial company. He tells me everything he picks up at the Fair, and I tell him anything I pick out of the Almanac. But you can't drink very hearty on them things. I make myself a cup of tea on the little fire I have here (*pointing left to where kettle stands*). There's a grand spring of water just to the south of me and it never fails.

STRANGER A lovely spring of water is a grand thing to contemplate and every man, even if he is drinking alcohol at the time, ought to thank God for all the good waters in the world for there's many a bad well and bad spring, where no man can drink and live, and to have to pull himself, and his horse, away from such a well, and such a spring, is a hard thing for any man.

PUBLICAN Yes, sir, a hard thing. The world away from us this day is full of terrible cruel things. There was vampires and dragons in the old days, long ago, if you could believe the old tales, and I could believe them, for there are raging vampires eating at the hearts of the people all over the world this evening, while you and me here in the quiet, are just talking a little encouragement to ourselves.

(STRANGER *stands up, puts left hand to mouth, then raises right hand, takes left hand from mouth. He is listening.*)

STRANGER God save them all, they're back.

(*He goes to the door.* PUBLICAN *goes to window.* WOMEN *all drenched with rain draggled and shining file in in the following order:* 4TH WOMAN, 3RD WOMAN, 5TH, 6TH, 1ST, 2ND, *and* 7TH WOMAN. *They stand in a half-moon, backs to the right wall and facing towards the bar, behind which the* PUBLICAN *now stands.* STRANGER *has backed into corner behind chair in front of bar.*)

2ND WOMAN We're drenched.
1ST WOMAN It came down in sheets.
3RD WOMAN In buckets.
4TH WOMAN I never seen buckets like them.
3RD WOMAN The devil's own buckets.
7TH WOMAN Perhaps he kicked them.
STRANGER If the devil kicks the bucket tell me.
6TH WOMAN Ah, tell you nothing.
5TH WOMAN We'll never get over this.
PUBLICAN And why not, Miss, people got soaked often in the country and were no worse for it.

STRANGER   He isn't intending to be funny with you ladies. He means there's no harm in the rain in this part of the Universe.

PUBLICAN   There's no venom in it.

STRANGER   It's only lately we were talking of rum and milk. Wouldn't this be the moment for it? (*Turning to* PUBLICAN) You have milk, haven't you?

PUBLICAN   Indeed, I have. I have a grand little cow that gives the best milk that ever met rum.

2ND WOMAN   I don't think we'd bother you with that.

PUBLICAN   Well, you'll have a cup of tea anyway. I haven't enough mugs for you all and I'm sorry. It's not right for you not to have something. I had the tea made for myself. (*To* STRANGER) Put in another handful of tea and the kettle is boiling.

(STRANGER *puts tea in teapot and crosses for kettle. He fills mugs and carefully drops a little tea in glasses and throws it out to warm them before filling them up. The* WOMEN *step up to bar, take their mugs and glasses and hold them in their hands as if to warm them. The* STRANGER *comes round with the sugar bowl, a black glass skillet with a spoon, white crystallized sugar. Each help themselves and drink slowly.*)

STRANGER (*raising his glass*)   Happy days.

(ALL *the* WOMEN *raise their mugs and glasses a little.*)

2ND WOMAN   We'll have to make another attempt to get away if there is still time, if it clears up at all.

1ST WOMAN   The tea is good. The weather not so bad now. I think we might make a dash for it again.

STRANGER (*to the* PUBLICAN)   Has the Mem Sahib any dry clothes to lend them?

PUBLICAN   Mem Sahib? Who's that?

STRANGER   The Missus—your wife. . . .

PUBLICAN   Ah, sure I'm an old bachelor.

STRANGER   I knew it. It was only a forlorn hope. Has the Smith e'er a wife?

PUBLICAN   He's an old widower.

STRANGER   Could you dry their clothes by the fire here?

PUBLICAN   I would and welcome but what good would a weeshie little fire like that be?

STRANGER   Would there be a fire left in the Smithy?

PUBLICAN   There would. He'd have banked it down before he went away.

STRANGER   And I could blow it up with the bellows. Have you any sort of rope or twine? I could make a line across above the Smith's fire and dry their grandeur for them. Have you any string. I never saw an old bachelor but he'd have a bundle of string.

PUBLICAN (*reaches under bar and produces large paper bag and throws out a tangle of string of various kinds which he begins untangling*) What will they be doing without their clothes? Won't they be perished?

STRANGER They could wait inside there till such times as their clothes be dry. (*Points to door.*)

7TH WOMAN That's a good idea, but what's it like in there? (*She goes over to door left and opens it a little*) It's full of hay, it seems dry. (*Other women follow her over and look through door.*)

1ST WOMAN It doesn't look very comfortable.

2ND WOMAN Well, it's good hay.

(STRANGER *comes over and helps* PUBLICAN, *knotting string.*)

7TH WOMAN It won't be too cold. The back of the little fire place should make it pretty comfortable.

PUBLICAN I wish I had something better to offer you. But you're welcome to the poor entertainment.

STRANGER Now, ladies, don't be shivering in the wet clothes. Just when you've got them off, drop them through the doorway there. You can tie them up in the two fawny shawls, if you'll be so kind, the way I can carry them up to the Smithy. I'll blaze up a great fire there and I'll dry them first class. I often longed to be blowing a smithy bellows.

(WOMEN *led by* 7TH WOMAN *walk off through door on left.* PUBLICAN *and* STRANGER *go on making a couple of long strings, walking across the floor to stretch each one out to see there is a good length.*)

STRANGER If I was wet as that I wouldn't be long peeling the stuff off me.

PUBLICAN I dunno. They do have a lot of buttons and pins.

STRANGER Did you ever hear of Liverpool buttons.

PUBLICAN What's them?

STRANGER Bits of string.

PUBLICAN Bits of string!

STRANGER The sailors in the old days they say used to sell their buttons to buy a last drink, so they tied their clothes together with bits of string.

(*A bare arm appears left and pushes bundle of clothes in fawn shawl. Two other bare arms help to push bundle out. Second bundle follows in the same way and door is pulled to. It is not raining outside but the sky is still overcast.* STRANGER *pushes string into his pocket and walks over left and in a polite and stately manner delicately picks up the two bundles and walks towards door at back.*)

PUBLICAN (*coming round from behind bar*) I'll give you a hand with one of them. (*He takes one of the bundles and follows* STRANGER *out of door and away to right.*)

Curtain.

Scene: *As before—half an hour later. Curtain rises on empty public house. The sky outside a little brighter.*

(PUBLICAN *comes to door along road from right, looks into shop and stands in doorway looking right. After a short interval along comes the* STRANGER. *They enter.* PUBLICAN *goes behind bar.* STRANGER *sits down in chair.*)

STRANGER   They're getting a great drying and they won't be too smokey at all. What about a smoke yourself? (*He takes out packet of cigarettes and offers it to* PUBLICAN. *But* PUBLICAN *takes pipe out of pocket, takes box of matches from dresser and hands it to* STRANGER, *who strikes match and puts box on bar, lights his cigarette and hands flaring match to* PUBLICAN *who lights his pipe. They smoke a short while.*)

PUBLICAN   They'll be glad to get their clothes again. The unfortunate creatures!

STRANGER   And why should they worry, good dry hay and there's a fashion for it now—the nude . . .

PUBLICAN   What's that?

STRANGER   The Nude, the Naked. The English pronounce it nude, the Yankees say Nood—it sounds fatter to me—the French say Le Nu.

PUBLICAN   La Noo.

STRANGER   Le Nu.

PUBLICAN   La Noo. La La Noo. French! That's French! If Schoolmaster was to hear me now talking French he'd rise out of the old mountainy graveyard where they left him. La La Noo. La La Noo.

STRANGER   You'd soon pick up any language. It's only a matter of taking fences and having no fear.

PUBLICAN   It must be a gorgeous thing to be able to speak maybe two or three languages. So that you could be entertaining two or three persons within yourself. 'The nude' says he 'the nood' is that right? 'The Nood' says he 'La La Noo' says I.

STRANGER   That's the way.

PUBLICAN   You must have had great travels.

STRANGER   Ah, not so much at all, but where the way turned I took, and the Oceans are very wide.

PUBLICAN   And wild. . . .

STRANGER   Wild. But still after crossing the great heaped seas you'd be glad to get ashore in some seaport where the houses might be made of paper.

PUBLICAN   Newspaper, is it.

STRANGER   Much the same.

PUBLICAN   It's a queer old house you'd make out of newspapers in this country.

STRANGER   Some people in the World think it very strange to live in a mud cottage.

PUBLICAN   I wouldn't say but I was born in one.

STRANGER   It's likely in the World that there's more houses made of clay than of stone, now, at this very moment.

PUBLICAN   I never heard that till you told me this minute.

STRANGER   Aren't there plenty of brick houses and isn't a brick dried clay?

PUBLICAN   That's right enough when you say it. But it's hard to beat a good house of stone. At the same time I'd like to see those paper houses. You could put an old stick through them, couldn't you? And maybe have some feller come out and chase you. I don't think paper houses would be any good in this part of the country. We're very quiet here but if we had paper houses it'd be different. You might live all your life here from your creepy stool to your coffin, and not a single thing to happen. But paper houses'd wake them up.

STRANGER   You take your life very peaceable. You didn't go to the races itself. But I suppose you couldn't leave the shop.

PUBLICAN   Oh, I might have locked it, I suppose. But there, I didn't feel any want on me to be on the Strand to-day, and if I had gone I would have missed yourself, hardy man!

STRANGER   You should take more pleasure in your life.

PUBLICAN   Well, I suppose I should. I have the broad ocean before me, and the clouds rushing over my head all day long and in the night, only it's so black I can't see them, unless there was a moon. Well, anyway, thank God for the moon, I suppose people in the distant places, if they knew I was here, would say 'That man has the wealth of the world in the air and the sea and his health.' Ah, to hell with their old talk. If I could get away and see some excitement, and some of the great scenery of the world, then, maybe, I would come here and be contented to draw down my own excitement out of the heavens or up out of the deep sea. But this was ever a quiet place, as far as men and women had anything to do with it. The great hosts of ancient heroes in their battles fought among themselves—God rest their great souls, in the crevasses of the mountains to back from us. They never took a sight nor a hearing of these paths, I believe. I have the feeling in the palm of my hand if I put it down on a path, and it was that the Great Ones that are gone over passed over that path, I would feel it trembling under my hand. Still, isn't that a queer thought for one man to have?

STRANGER (standing up) Go out strange man and put your hand on the road-way and tell me if any Great One passed there lately or long ago. Tell me!

PUBLICAN   Ah, no sir, I wouldn't like to have anything to do with them old things. It isn't right. The women's clothes ought to be pretty well dry by now. We ought to go and get them and bring them down to the unfortunate creatures.

STRANGER Whatever you say. I wouldn't say myself but they'd be perfectly dry. But I dare say they're dry enough. We left a great glow on the fire when we came away.

PUBLICAN If we had a melodeon we could have music. I'm sure you can play the melodeon. You look to me like a man that would knock great tingling out of a melodeon.

STRANGER You have too good an opinion of my accomplishments. Playing the melodeon is beyond me.

PUBLICAN If we had one now and played a dance on it, the ones inside could hear it through the door and be dancing for themselves.

STRANGER They'll have to do without any dancing, we'll get the clothes now. (*He goes to door.* PUBLICAN *comes round bar.*)

STRANGER Let's go.

(STRANGER *and* PUBLICAN *walk out of door and to the right. After a short interval they come back, each carrying a bundle of clothes. They go to the door left and the* STRANGER *knocks and calls out* 'Here's your clothes now ladies.' *He and the* PUBLICAN *leave down the bundles.* PUBLICAN *goes back behind bar, and* STRANGER *to his chair.* STRANGER *lights pipe. A bare arm comes out of door left and hauls in each bundle. Voices from behind door.*)

1ST WOMAN They dried them well.

3RD WOMAN They're not so crushed or crumpled as you'd think.

2ND WOMAN They're not very comfortable.

7TH WOMAN They're a damn sight better than they were when we came in with them.

6TH WOMAN That's mine.

5TH WOMAN That's right, it is yours.

1ST WOMAN My shoes are awful.

3RD WOMAN Who'd think of a laddered stocking now.

7TH WOMAN *My* shoes feel dreadful.

PUBLICAN (*leaning on bar*) They have a lot to say for themselves all of a sudden. They ought to be glad to have a couple of ladies' maids like you and me looking after their clothes.

STRANGER The Smith'll wonder what blew his fire away.

PUBLICAN We'll not tell him for a long while, we'll knock a bit of fun out of that. It's a pity we didn't leave one stocking itself up there, it'd be circumstantial evidence to puzzle him. He's a very hard-hearted man. We'd tell him a Queen came out of the sea to warm her toes at his fire while he was away.

STRANGER During his absence. You could tell him it was a mermaid, only mermaids don't wear stockings, that's certain.

PUBLICAN I never saw one.

STRANGER Well, you didn't miss much perhaps.

PUBLICAN Oh, I don't know about that.

7TH WOMAN (*behind door left*) That's mine.

4TH WOMAN Keep it, mam. I mistook it.

STRANGER An intelligent man would know his own clothes when he saw them, and would have them all on and be ready for the road long before this.

PUBLICAN That's it, ready for the road, but what road can they go? If they tried to climb over all the stone walls to back of us they'd get lost. And the other way they'd never get to the Harbour road in time to catch the 'bus now. How will we get rid of them?

STRANGER I'll think out a way.

PUBLICAN I believe you will.

(*Door on left is pushed slightly open. Voices from inside sound more clearly.*)

7TH WOMAN You musn't take that hat, it's not yours.

4TH WOMAN I'll have it because I want it.

2ND WOMAN Don't let her have it.

3RD WOMAN Oh, let her have it. It looks well on you, you wild one.

5TH WOMAN Isn't that an audacity.

6TH WOMAN Sure, she has it as a present.

7TH WOMAN Remove it.

4TH WOMAN Remove yourself.

(4TH WOMAN *comes through door, left, wearing bright hat, belonging to* 3RD WOMAN. *She walks across floor out of door and turns left past window and away.*)

PUBLICAN Isn't that a desperate and audacious character—well, they're better without her. Nothing'll stop her now. That one'd take stone walls flying. If the rest of these ones inside could follow her they'd get to the main road behind us. But they're too delicately nurtured.

STRANGER They haven't got the muscles for it. They haven't got the hearts for it. They're coming out now. . . .

(WOMEN *file out into the kitchen. Their clothes are wrinkled and pathetic looking.* 1ST *and* 2ND WOMAN *side by side.* 5TH *alone. The* 7TH *alone. Then* 3RD *and* 6TH *side by side. They stamp about in their dried shoes and pull down their shrunken sleeves.*)

STRANGER Ladies, you look grand. We haven't got a tall looking-glass for you to see yourselves, but I give you my word you'd pass anywhere for a garden party.

7TH WOMAN Good honest tweed will stand a lot of wetting and then come up smiling.

(*The* WOMEN *turn towards each other, inspect each other's clothes and smooth them down.* STRANGER *takes out packet of cigarettes and offers them to women—only* 6TH *and* 7TH WOMAN *accept.* STRANGER *strikes match, but* 7TH WOMAN *has lighter which she uses, and* STRANGER *lights* 6TH WOMAN'S *cigarette.*)

2ND WOMAN   Now, what are we to do? We can never get to the 'bus in time, as we have no conveyance.

STRANGER   It's a queer thing that there wouldn't be someone in this out-of-the-way part of the world that'd have a lorry that we could put these ladies on, and let them catch the old 'bus.

PUBLICAN   There's nobody here but our two selves and these ladies.

STRANGER   Why wouldn't the Smith have a lorry?

PUBLICAN   Well he has a lorry but he won't be back till the night.

STRANGER   Would he have petrol in it?

PUBLICAN   He would have it full up, for he was going to a Fair tomorrow morning.

STRANGER (*jumping up*)   Where is it?

PUBLICAN   Back of the Smithy, under a corrugated iron shed he has there. But, can you drive a lorry, for I can't?

STRANGER   I never drove one, but I have driven little cars.

PUBLICAN   I suppose they all run in the same way. But lorries are very headstrong, and you'll have a dangerous road for anyone that wasn't used to it.

STRANGER   I don't care. I'll put these ladies on the 'bus yet. I'll get the old lorry out. Show me where it is and I'll get her.

(PUBLICAN *goes to door with* STRANGER *and points right.*)

PUBLICAN   Up there behind the Smith's house. Do you get a sight of the iron roof. It's only an old hay shed. If she once starts with you I believe, brave man, she'll go all the way with you. If any man except the Smith himself could control her, you could like the Smith, and better, for there's plenty of times the Smith was afraid of her. I could see it in the face of him coming down the road there. He'd be afraid to loose her. But I'm saying once yourself gets her shaking along up and down these hills to catch the 'bus, she'll go as kind and as grand as a greyhound.

(STRANGER *goes off on road, right.* 1ST WOMAN *goes to door and looks out right over* PUBLICAN'S *shoulder.*)

1ST WOMAN   I hope he will be careful.

(PUBLICAN *goes in behind bar, takes from under bar green Old Moore's Almanac and sitting down with his back half turned to women, reads.*)

2ND WOMAN   Certainly, this is a great idea taking us in a lorry. I wonder ought we to offer to pay the Smith for using it. We could leave something here for him.

7TH WOMAN   We can talk about it with this kind person who is driving us.

6TH WOMAN   If I owned a lorry and six blacksmiths were stranded on a roadside I'd let them have the lorry and I would be insulted if they'd offer to pay me.

7TH WOMAN   There's the petrol.

6TH WOMAN   Is it ask for the price for the drop of petrol that would be taking them.

2ND WOMAN   We must only do what is right.

5TH WOMAN   What does it matter what we do the one way or the other?

1ST WOMAN   The weather is nearly cleared up completely, now we'll be able to see the setting sun that we've been promised. Will it be a wild one or a tame one, I wonder?

2ND WOMAN   I wonder!

7TH WOMAN   Whatever it is I'll be glad to see it. I was getting to think that we had no choice but to march through the night across half the country and in the hard dried up shoes we have it'd be no catch.

2ND WOMAN   But how would we have been if it weren't for the hospitality we received here from this kind man.

(PUBLICAN *puts down his book and turns towards the* WOMEN.)

PUBLICAN   I only wish I'd had better entertainment for you ladies. All knew was that it was good sound dry hay.

3RD WOMAN   I know it was dry for I've got some (*shifting her shoulders*) down my back still.

PUBLICAN   I'm sorry about that now. I knew it was dry, because it had to be dry, because the little cow I have wouldn't touch a mouthful if it'd have the slightest hint of a mouldiness on it.

2ND WOMAN   It was very good milk she gave us for tea.

PUBLICAN   Oh, the best always I'm glad to say. (*He puts book out on bar and begins reading again.*)

1ST WOMAN (*turning towards* 3RD WOMAN)   Your beautiful coat!

3RD WOMAN   It was a swagger coat, but it isn't swaggering any more.

2ND WOMAN   You could, I'm sure, bring it up again with a good ironing.

7TH WOMAN   Let a tailor do it. That's the best way.

6TH WOMAN   When it's properly pressed again you'll never know you were out in floods of the sky with it. But it's a good thing it was only rain. If we had been down by the lower road by the edge of the sea, and the waves beating on the rocks at the top of the tide, it would be destroyed by the salt water.

5TH WOMAN   Some say that the cloth to stand the salt water should be woven from the wool of the sheep that lives by the salt sea eating the salt grass.

7TH WOMAN   I never heard that. I never thought of it. But it's common sense
if you come to think of it.

2ND WOMAN   I wonder how far *(turning towards* 3RD WOMAN*)* your lovely
little hat has gone by now.

1ST WOMAN   I'm sure it's fluttering over the little fields and the boggy places
like a Will-o'-the-Wisp.

2ND WOMAN   What would be the feminine of Will-o'-the-Wisp?

3RD WOMAN   I can't think of anything. Sall-o'-the-Straw, that's not very
good.

2ND WOMAN   Ah, yes, Sall-o'-the-Straw.

3RD WOMAN   If it was Jack-o'-Lantern, the feminine of Jack-o'-Lantern
would be Jill-o'-Lantern. The people who made my hat never thought
it would be called a Jill-o'-Lantern.

5TH WOMAN   I think it is a very nice name for a hat.

6TH WOMAN   A cousin of my sister and me came on a vacation from
America one time, and out there all the girls were wearing big hats,
and my brother said that this girl never got married because a mason
on the top of a sky scraper fell in love with her when little hats were
the fashion, and when the big ones came in he never was able to pick
her out again.

2ND WOMAN   That's a sad story.

1ST WOMAN   I'm warned now. I'll never get a big hat or I'll be on the shelf
for ever.

7TH WOMAN   If a woman mason—there are women masons working in
some parts of the world—if a woman mason admired a man walkng
in the street below the sky scraper, she'd have great difficulty in picking
out one shining bald patch from another.

2ND WOMAN   Except by the shades—from Cerise to Ivory.

1ST WOMAN   Well, now, that's the old boys. Lots of the young ones have
beautiful glossy heads, regular thickets of curls.

2ND WOMAN   Yes, with rams horns—rams caught in the thicket.

3RD WOMAN   I think they put too much furniture polish, or whatever it is,
on their heads.

5TH WOMAN   It reflects the blue sky and the clouds, and the birds flying. I
saw a sea gull one time flying in the looking-glass of a young man's
head, and he not knowing it.

6TH WOMAN   It would only make them conceited to know a thing like that.

2ND WOMAN   If birds could be reflected on shining locks, so could a bee.
Bees in the bonnet.

1ST WOMAN   They are all liable to that.

7TH WOMAN   Yes, or bats in the belfries. Tipped, they're all tipped.

5TH WOMAN   They are not so tipped as they used to be I'm thinking.

6TH WOMAN   Some young boys are very wild. It isn't any harm in them.
But they haven't got enough to do with their energy and yet I wouldn't
like to see them made to go where they would not want to go, or

driven in any way. The good God will find a way for them in a good day.

5TH WOMAN   'Tis the truth. (*A slight pause.*)

2ND WOMAN   Our friend in need is, I hope, not having too much difficulty with the Smith's lorry. I wonder what the Smith would say if he knew what use it was being put to. (*Turns towards* PUBLICAN) Will the Black-smith be very wild when he hears that a gang of women have been making use of his lorry?

PUBLICAN   Not at all, mam, he'll be delighted that it was of any use to you. He's a well mannered and a well thinking man. Don't be standing up ladies, won't you sit down? That man up there is a long while starting her up. But it's likely he's oiling the engine and the wheels. I'd say he was a man who would take a lot of care of a machine before he got to starting it. Maybe I ought to go up and give him a hand.

2ND WOMAN   Not at all. He'll be along I'm sure as soon as he's got every-thing working properly.

PUBLICAN   He will have an easy job with her if she's in good trim but it'd never do if she stopped with him on the side of the hill between this and the 'bus.

1ST WOMAN   I hope it won't do that.

PUBLICAN   Not a fear of it. If she run off properly she'll go all the way and anywhere you'd wish. She's as wise as a—as a—as a machine could possibly be. It's a marvellous thing the inventions that have come into the mind of man from his earliest days for the purposes of propelling himself over the floor of the earth, or over the furious ocean, or along the devious rivers. The boat with an oar or with a sail, and then by steam revolving the paddle wheel or the screws, and then the electric engine, taking the great vessels full of tea and sugar, and all sorts of goods, and human beings all over the world, from one sea port town to another, and then will you observe man on the land on stilts in some places they say for the purpose of the viewing of the country. I walked on stilts when I was a young lad and I declare to you, mam, (*looking to* 2ND WOMAN) it didn't seem to me that I was getting any better view than if I was sitting at my ease on the top of an old bank. But it was a great change on the human being when they invented the bike. The machine that goes by the power of arithmetic. Schoolmaster used to tell me if you'd multiply the length of the old crank by the circumference of the wheel, I think, you'd get the proper speed you'd make. I'm sure it'd be in a ready reckoner. You never see a ready reckoner now, I suppose. I suppose, the education of the people now is so grand that they know all these things for themselves.

1ST WOMAN   I don't know them, I'm sure.

3RD WOMAN   And it wouldn't, I believe, do me a bit of good to know. I'd much sooner wait and let someone tell me.

PUBLICAN   But before the bicycle man had the horse to ride or it was the camel he had first, I forget. I never saw a man riding a camel. They ought to be powerful jumpers. Oh, no, that's the kangaroo. Those lads would think no more of jumping a daisy than of jumping this house. And after the horse and the bicycle, man had the motor car and that's the change of the whole world. Here to-day and gone to-morrow. Peace or War it's all the same to the motor bringing a doctor to a sick person, that might be dying but for his coming, or bringing cannons to be spitting death on men, women, and children. (*He goes to window, left-hand corner, pulls back short curtain and tries to look up road to the right.*) I never thought of the worst, or maybe it'll be the best in the end. The last invention of all—the aeroplane, to be flying through the air taking the people wherever they'd have a mind to go, or perhaps, taking them where they wouldn't want to go at all, and worst of all killing them with bombs dropped out of the sky. Isn't that a terrible thought that as soon as man finds a well he finds a poison to put in it.

(*There is a noise right of a motor engine working, and then silence and then again some hammering.*)

PUBLICAN   I wonder what will be the next invention for the transporting of the people. I forgot the under-water travelling in the submarines. Ah, but it was used for bloodshed from the first. Isn't that an ignorant and a savage thing, that what might have been a pleasure and an entertainment—to be down under the sea looking through the port holes at the fishes playing theirselves. . . .

(*Sound again of engine running. Then silence.*)

7TH WOMAN   He seems to be having a lot of trouble. We'll go up and see if we can give him any help.

PUBLICAN   Oh, he'll be here in no time. He's just getting her right. (*He motions to stool and chair, and brings round box.* WOMEN *sit about, not much room on stool, so* 5TH WOMAN *pulls* 3RD WOMAN *down on her knee.*)

1ST WOMAN   We'll be a long time sitting in the lorry.

PUBLICAN   Oh, not at all, you'll be no time. The machine goes by that hill flying, you'll hardly have time to observe the scenery. I think that it's a very strange thing with all the poets and writers telling us about the beautiful scenery of the world that we do be for ever inventing ways of flashing by it so that it's an impossibility for us to see it. Slow and steady might be better in the end. But that's not the way I ought to be talking to young women like yourselves with all your lives before you. It's all right for an old feller like me to be content with a bit of quiet old talk about the old days. But talking of old times is no pleasure to the young, they can't stay still to listen, and rightly. If it wasn't for youth dashing about and making new inventions we'd be walking backwards into the mists of the past.

3RD WOMAN   There were great heroes in the old ages, I know there were.

PUBLICAN   Yes, yes. But if it wasn't that you'd heard them and their deeds told out so well you mightn't think so much of them. They had poets and old shanachies to tell out their great deeds, and it was the poets that had the great thoughts.

2ND WOMAN   But great thoughts lead to great deeds.

PUBLICAN   I wouldn't doubt it. But all the same the men that told the tales were practised at the game; they had schools for teaching the telling of tales. They could sketch a small little thing, so that it'd look like a gold banner shining above a mountain, and the people would be lepping round with their old swords sweeping holes in the whin bushes, to be fighting the enemy whoever he was. That's the way the poets did it. Get them mad to fight and then let them fight. And afterwards whatever they did, be it little or much, make a great song and a giving out about it.

(*Engine heard off, running.* ALL *listen. The* WOMEN *stand up and move to the doorway.* 1ST, 2ND *and* 7TH WOMAN *on road outside the door, looking right at first and then turning their heads towards left following the movement of lorry.* 3RD, 6TH *and* 5TH WOMAN *in doorway itself.* PUBLICAN *has window curtain pulled on one side looking right.*)

PUBLICAN   He's going right. He's taking the lower road. He's going slowly at first letting the fall of the land tune her up a bit. He'll want to have a good look out for the old crooked tree on the lower side. He'll take her down to the junction of the roads and he'll stop her there until you all join him.

3RD WOMAN (*watching from doorway*)   Yes, he's looking out of the box of the lorry, he seems to be looking down on the roadway.

2ND WOMAN   Perhaps the track isn't too good.

7TH WOMAN   He's doing right. He doesn't want to get his tyres down in a boggy bit.

(*Faint noise of motor running then a low crash and silence.*)

3RD WOMAN   Oh, God! His head hit against the tree.

PUBLICAN (*coming round from behind bar*)   I can't see. I can't see. What happened to him?

3RD WOMAN   He was thrown out of the lorry on to the road. The lorry has run into the bank and stopped.

6TH WOMAN   He is lying in the road.

PUBLICAN   Did the wheel go over him?

7TH WOMAN (*coming into doorway*)   No, he was thrown out. His head must have struck the tree. He has not moved since he fell. Come, let us go down. (WOMEN *pass along, left.* PUBLICAN *follows them.*)

PUBLICAN   It was always the way.

Short Interval.

(2ND WOMAN *and* PUBLICAN *come in at door.*)

2ND WOMAN   He was only alive for a few moments after we got down beside him.

PUBLICAN   Yes, only a few moments.

2ND WOMAN   I don't think he felt any pain.

PUBLICAN   What's that?

2ND WOMAN   No pain, I think.

PUBLICAN   No pain. The shutter will be best. But I'll have something to throw over him.

(*He goes to window and pulls down the
curtains. He hands them to* 2ND WOMAN *in a bundle.*)

PUBLICAN   Do you take these, madam.

(*She folds them together in long folds, more neatly, and puts them over her left arm.* PUBLICAN *signs to her to go out of the door. He takes the shutter and drags it across barrel and box in front of the bar and goes out of door. The sky is cloudy with a tattered red sunset.* WOMEN *and* PUBLICAN, *he carrying dead body of* STRANGER, *appear left, pass window and in at door.* PUBLICAN *puts body on shutter. The body has one curtain under it and one over it. The head is towards the front. The* PUBLICAN *on left,* 2ND WOMAN *on right. Behind* PUBLICAN 6TH WOMAN *and* 1ST WOMAN. *Behind* 2ND WOMAN, 5TH WOMAN *and* 7TH WOMAN. 3RD WOMAN *follows carrying* STRANGER'S *hat, from which she is rubbing the dust with her handkerchief.* WOMEN *stand in a half circle behind feet of body. Falling back, naturally, into this order from left:* 6TH WOMAN, 1ST WOMAN, 7TH WOMAN, 5TH WOMAN, 2ND WOMAN *and* 3RD WOMAN, *who still holds the* STRANGER'S *hat in her hand.* PUBLICAN *stands to left in front of bar looking at body.*)

2ND WOMAN   I don't believe he felt anything.

1ST WOMAN   Ah, well, the lorry had gathered speed down the hill.

3RD WOMAN   But he was alive when we saw him.

7TH WOMAN   I am sure his neck was broken.

(3RD WOMAN *puts hat on dead man's breast.*)

2ND WOMAN   It is terrible, terrible, and there is nothing that we can do that I can think of.

1ST WOMAN   I think we should go away.

2ND WOMAN   Yes, let us start away.

7TH WOMAN   The lorry is quite alright. I could drive it. I can drive a lorry.

2ND WOMAN   Why didn't you say that before?

7TH WOMAN   I wasn't asked.

1ST WOMAN   You weren't asked—

2ND WOMAN   You can take us all away now. (*She turns her face towards* PUBLICAN.) Goodbye.

> (*She turns away and walks out of door followed by* 1ST, 7TH, 5TH, 6TH *and* 3RD WOMAN. *They turn left and pass window.*)

> *Short Interval.*

> (3RD *and* 6TH WOMAN *return.* PUBLICAN *is leaning against bar, left.*)

6TH WOMAN   It is a hard thing to leave you by yourself here with this poor Stranger dead. Is it what you would wish that if we meet any man on the road we would tell him what has happened, and to let him come himself or send someone, to be with you here in the night?

PUBLICAN   I thank you. You are good young women but I'll do well. The Smith will be coming along. He's not too far away this moment. He'll come in here and there'll be the two of us. The three of us—here for the night. God give you a good journey.

> (*Exit* 3RD *and* 6TH WOMAN, *passing window on left.* PUBLICAN *goes behind bar, gets matches and lights lamp. Behind bar is now dimly lit up, and front of bar in shadow and across to right of scene.* PUBLICAN *comes round bar and closes door, goes to wall and looks to Sports advertisement, takes it down, rolls it into a ball and wipes bar with it. Throws it under bar. Comes round to front of bar and sits down in chair. Distant noise of lorry starting and going away. The sky is darkening—the streaks of red sinking.*)

CURTAIN.

In Sand

A Play in Three Acts

CHARACTERS

ANTONY LARCSON.
JOHN OLDGROVE.
THE MAYOR.
EDITOR.
TOWN COUNCILLOR.
ALICE.
HER MOTHER.
HER FATHER.
MAURICE.
KITCHEN MAID.
CHAUFFEUR.
OLD SAILOR.
VISITOR.
GOVERNOR.
HOTEL BOY.
BROWN BOY.
BROWN GIRL.

PROLOGUE
The Green Wave

Left and Right as seen by audience.

FIRST ELDERLY MAN, SECOND ELDERLY MAN.

Scene: *Room with large window towards the right of centre overlooking roofs of a city, on an easel in the shadow towards the right is a framed painting of a wave, further to right small table with bottle of whiskey, glasses, jug of water and syphon of soda.*

(*Enter left two* ELDERLY MEN; *the* 1ST ELDERLY MAN *wearing an old dressing gown, the* 2ND ELDERLY MAN *is wearing overcoat, muffler and a hard felt hat.*)

2ND ELDERLY MAN   Well, here I am up in your sky parlour, what have you got to show me? You've got a view anyway—*walks towards window and looks out*—I see all the bounteous beauties of nature laid out before me. I see the Pillar and the Four Courts.

1ST ELDERLY MAN (*singing*) 'The British Fleet lying at Anchor and Admiral Benbow.' Are the Pillar and the Four Courts natural beauties?

2ND ELDERLY MAN They are natural features of the landscape or the roof-scape I should say. What about this picture now?

1ST ELDERLY MAN Take off your outdoor things.

2ND ELDERLY MAN Oh, I won't bother.

1ST ELDERLY MAN If you don't you won't feel the good of them when you go out. (*Helps* 2ND ELDERLY MAN *out of his top-coat puts it on chair to left, brings easel and picture forward out of the shadow and towards the window.*)

2ND ELDERLY MAN What is it?

1ST ELDERLY MAN It is a wave.

2ND ELDERLY MAN I know that, but what sort of a wave?

1ST ELDERLY MAN A green wave—well—a rather green wave.

2ND ELDERLY MAN What does it mean?

1ST ELDERLY MAN I think it means just to be a wave.

2ND ELDERLY MAN I like things to mean something, and I like to know what they mean, and I like to know it at once. After all, time is important, the most important thing we know of, and why waste it in trying to find out what something means, when if it stated its meaning clearly itself we would know at once.

1ST ELDERLY MAN If that wave could speak it might say, 'I'm an Irish wave and the Irish are generally supposed to answer questions by asking questions,' and the wave might ask you what was the meaning of yourself!

2ND ELDERLY MAN Agreed! Agreed! The wave could do that. If the wave could speak, but I wouldn't tell him—not that.

1ST ELDERLY MAN You're quite right you keep it to yourself.

(*Moves easel nearer to the window so that the sunlight falls full on it.*)

2ND ELDERLY MAN I see you like it fully illuminated.

1ST ELDERLY MAN Yes, I have a feeling that a wave seems less cruel when lit up.

2ND ELDERLY MAN You've been treating me in terms of wave. So I suppose you think I'd be less cruel if I was better lit up?

1ST ELDERLY MAN I wouldn't like to play any experiments with you.

2ND ELDERLY MAN No, I wouldn't like to have any experiments played with me! But I'm not such a Philistine as you might think. I admire a wave for its . . . its . . . art content, pattern, and these things. But the sea, the ocean itself, is just a great stretch of water to me. It's nothing but size. It's its moods that make it.

1ST ELDERLY MAN And yet you are impressed with bigness. I've heard you say that you felt smothered in a city of ordinary buildings. You longed for skyscrapers, twenty and thirty stories high, so that you could feel you were 'Expanding Upwards', you said.

2ND ELDERLY MAN That's a natural physical longing with the ordinary honest-minded man. We want to be rising above the sordid. I don't mean to say that Art is always sordid; but sometimes these modern examples of Art are sordid. Anyway I object to having any sort of Art shoved down my throat.

1ST ELDERLY MAN Yes, that's your only hope, keep on objecting. But don't you ever want to create a work of Art yourself?

2ND ELDERLY MAN Who, me!

1ST ELDERLY MAN You! Why not, unless you feel that man himself—the man in the street—is a work of Art in himself.

2ND ELDERLY MAN You've said it in a nut-shell. That's exactly how I feel. An honest man is a work of Art. An honest man who doesn't owe anybody anything and can go to his bank, and push in the door of the manager's office. No, nobody on earth could do that. They're not so brave or so reckless as all that. Everybody must, at least, turn a handle. Well, I say the man who's in no one's debt and can turn the handle and stump into his bank-manager and put a healthy sized lump right on top of his over-draught, just to keep it from blowing away, and no nasty questions asked about what he wants it for—I say that man is a work of Art.

1ST ELDERLY MAN And I believe—(looking at 2ND ELDERLY MAN)—he stands before me now. Yet I have known some men who might be called works of Art and who could not do what you can do.

2ND ELDERLY MAN Yes, that's just the sort of people you would know, and if they are works of Art, as you say they are, then they don't know it. They haven't got any confidence in themselves and that's what makes them paint pictures, and try and make works of Art just to look at. That's an idea! Talking to you, and looking at your wretched wave brought that out in me. I *never* had an idea about this sort of thing before. At least I never put it into words. Perhaps it was lying dormant until you annoyed me with your green wave.

1ST ELDERLY MAN If my Green Wave annoys you we can easily turn our backs on it—but here better still—(goes to easel and turns face of picture inwards)—we'll turn its back on us.

(2ND ELDERLY MAN joins 1ST ELDERLY MAN by window;
1ST ELDERLY MAN opens window and both look down.)

2ND ELDERLY MAN I see men as flies walking, and horses drawing carts and old-fashioned side-cars, jaunting cars! I don't believe I ever saw a jaunting car from as high up as this—do look how extraordinary the jarvey looks with his whip held out horizontal as if he was fishing, and the horse looks very odd and long shaped, and the passenger too looks very funny, most undignified and sprawled. It's funny to think you would look like that, if you were in the car down there, seen from up here.

1ST ELDERLY MAN   And so would you look funny too, and lots of people, even more consequential than yourself, would look mighty funny when seen by a bird, if a bird would bother his little eyes about such things.

2ND ELDERLY MAN   I don't suppose he would and anyway if you were down there, on that car, and I was up here, or I was down there and you up here, neither of us would be able to draw the other's attention to the ridiculous appearance of the other.

1ST ELDERLY MAN   Look! there's a man I know, I'm sure I do. There's something about the way he cranes his head forward that's familiar to me, and look he's buying a newspaper from a boy, and he's waiting for the change. I bet it's a shilling, yes, yes, I'm sure, that's elevenpence the newsboy had to fish out for him.

2ND ELDERLY MAN   (*turning away from window*)   What about having one more look at that picture of yours?

1ST ELDERLY MAN   Better leave it as it is.

2ND ELDERLY MAN   Who painted it anyway?

1ST ELDERLY MAN   I don't know. It's not signed and no one I have shown it to has any idea.

2ND ELDERLY MAN   Where did you pick it up anyway? In some old junk shop up the Quays, I expect.

1ST ELDERLY MAN   I didn't pick it up in any old junk shop on any old Quays—I bought it from a man who sold nothing but pictures—had a shop full of them, all sorts. Well, he did sell something else, he sold home-made toffee. He couldn't tell me who painted the picture, but he said it looked at me as if it liked me, so I bought it. But I see it's beginning to worry you again, so next time, before you come, I'll get some artistic friend of mine to paint some buttercups and daisies on the side of my green wave and turn it into a green hill-side, and then it won't worry you any more. But come—(*walks towards table*)— what about shoving down our throats some of the native wine—(*hands bottle to* 2ND ELDERLY MAN *who helps himself to whiskey*) what will you have, plain or fizzy?

Curtain.

ACT ONE

SCENE I: TIME: *An Autumn evening many years ago.*

TONY LARCSON, *an elderly man, pale, clean-shaven, dark grey hair, is lying in bed (left of centre), slightly raised on pillows—white nightshirt.*
JOHN OLDGROVE, *a man about forty, with brown short whiskers and moustache, clean shaven below the line of mouth, hair left above but clipped close. He is dressed in a brown jacket and waistcoat, blue trousers, black boots, half-Wellingtons, but trousers not stuffed into boot tops.*

There is a shaded lamp on the table, throwing very little light on LARCSON, *but illuminating* OLDGROVE. *The bed is a four-poster with dark green damask curtains and lining to back of bedhead. There is a glass-fronted book-case over drawers to the left—door to the right. Long, hanging bell-pull between door and bed foot.*

> *Right and left as they appear to the audience.*

LARCSON (*in a low, clear voice*) Well, my boy, now is the accepted time. I accept it anyway, and you must accept it too.

> (*He puts his right hand on the right hand of* OLDGROVE,
> *which is resting on the quilt.*)

I haven't got to be giving you hints, or beating about the bush with you. I haven't got to begin twisting the quilt edge or crying 'hark' every time there's a ticking noise in the wainscoting. I suppose Catherine told you something of what the Doctor said a day ago. He did me the honour to make no bones about it. Indeed, I could have wished just at first that he wouldn't have honoured me as so brave. However, it's me that will have to make bones of myself. Oh, forgive me, John, the vanity of the joker. Joking to the last. All that need is dead for me, as between our two selves. Five or six days, Jack, if I keep on drawing lucky breaths, or maybe it might be only hours and one of five days has gone.

OLDGROVE But isn't there something in the strength of your constitution— a temperate life . . . .

LARCSON I asked about those things—first he used long words that I couldn't understand. When he was Hick Heck Hocking my mind was following my eyes out of the window. One time I would have *looked* as if I understood to save my face. But I thought a man with such a short tether needn't worry any more about whether he appeared to have any Latin or not, so I asked him for simpler words—and I'm satisfied.

OLDGROVE Mister Larcson, you have great courage. It gives me courage to see you so.

LARCSON No courage, just quietness. I'll tell you one good thing, the best of the news, no pain, no fussing, perhaps in my sleep. I often thought, when I thought of such things, that 'in my sleep' would suit me best, and I don't suppose, all the same, that I was unique in that, and I wasn't unique I suppose either when I used, in the full of my health, to bury myself in style. I fancied going up to Glasnevin with two or three bands, but if only one, I wanted the Girl Pipers playing: 'I know my love by his way of walking'. When I planned my funeral I always floated above the procession myself, and I am telling you now, it was particularly grand to me to see that Pipe Major swinging up her baton in the air.

OLDGROVE You aren't tiring yourself talking to me, Larcson, my dear friend, is it good for you to give your mind to such things so much?

LARCSON It is good for what I am pleased to call my mind. I had another ending, dying on a quay wall after saving a beautiful little girl child from the dark waters, some of the people carrying the child to hospital and some of the people standing round me watching me gasping out a hero's death—no pain, no fuss, except a certain amount of friendly fuss—but I never could satisfy myself with my last words. There I go, Jack, teasing you again. I must give up teasing for evermore. It's right I should. I don't have to do any heroic actions now even if there was time, so I should stop all teasing. With God's help as long as this life lasts with me I'll tease no more.

OLDGROVE Would you like me to read anything to you?

LARCSON That is an idea. It reminds me of a plan I have had in my head the last few hours, turning it over gently now and then. It's a plan for a memorial to myself that'll hurt nobody.

OLDGROVE You never wanted to hurt anyone.

LARCSON More often than you thought, but I was lazy. In the book-shelf on the middle shelf there is an old green book of the Poems of Tom Hood. I read old poems in it soon after the Doctor and I had our talk. I could have waited until you came and asked you to read to me from it. But I remember what I want to remember—when I was a boy I was very fond of the poems of old Tom Hood and there was one 'Forget me not'. All sorts of forget-me-nots ending up with:

> 'Six tons of sculptural marble
> As a small forget-me-not'.

Well, now, that's not what I have in my mind, but I have written out here, just roughly put it down in pencil, a plan I have that'll hurt nobody.

(Takes folded paper from table, and with his left hand makes effort to pass it to OLDGROVE. OLDGROVE *stands up and takes paper.)*

OLDGROVE   Am I to read it now?

LARCSON   No, not now. It's just a few notes. I'll tell you now what it is, and I want you to go to James and get him to write it out fair and legal and so that there can be no mistake about anything and then bring it round to me any time to-morrow in the afternoon before I get sleepy, and bring along James' old clerk, and the young one to witness it when I sign it, and also to be able to say I'm clear and able to know what I'm up to. It mightn't be necessary to have all this paraphernalia, as it's only a wish, a thing I would like to have carried out when I am gone, but it might as well be done well and strong, and it'll amuse the old clerk and the young one, to have a glimpse behind the scenes of an old oddity's last days. I won't have you witnessing my hand, because that mightn't be correct if this plan is considered part of the real will, because under that you get, you know John, your share of what there is.

OLDGROVE   You are very good to me.

LARCSON   And you. It isn't much. If the locust ate a many years, perhaps I ate the locust in the end, and there's precious little left now. So it's well that:

> I will not long delay
> for the corn,
> Or for the oil,
> Or the wine that maketh glad
> The heart of man.

OLDGROVE   Wouldn't you like to rest a little now, and I'll leave this paper under your pillow and then I can come back in an hour's time, say, and you can tell me your plan.

LARCSON   Oh, I'll have plenty of time to rest. Give me a sup of that stuff in the glass and I'll heave ahead.

*(*OLDGROVE *takes glass from table and puts it into* LARCSON'S *hand.* LARCSON *drinks a little, slowly, waits, drinks a little more, hands glass back to* OLDGROVE.*)*

LARCSON   He says it's twenty years old. He thinks that a great age, and so did I once but, just now it doesn't seem to me so extra old, though whiskey and men aren't the same thing, though they have many things in common, and though, I suppose, they punish each other. Still I don't have to worry about it now. When the bell rings for the last lap the egotist doesn't feel his egotism making either lead or feathers to his heels—and here is my plan—

—THE MEMORY OF ANTHONY LARCSON—

I want you, or James, or both of you, between one month and three months after I'm dead, sooner than that would be a botheration, and longer might be too long, and someone in the town might say: 'And who was Antony Larcson?', and that would be painful to the faithful and the few. I want you to choose between you a nice little girl of about ten years of age, born in the town, of parents born in this town. You'll think my mind with Pipers' Bands and everything is running on nice little girls, but in this case a little girl is the only choice. A boy would think the whole affair woman's work, beneath him, and my memory would get a bad start. When you have found your suitable little girl she is to go, with her people, and James, or yourself, just after the last of the low water spring tide, to the far strand and there just above the water's edge she is to write with a stick in the sand:

TONY, WE HAVE THE GOOD THOUGHT FOR YOU STILL.

She's to wait there, and all of you are to wait, until the water has flowed in over the writing, and then you are to give the little girl a very large bag of very nice sweets, and you are to, as soon as you get back to town, pay into a Savings Bank ninety pounds to stay there in the Bank for her till she is twenty-one years of age, accumulating compound interest. I don't know what the money should amount to by then, I never was any good at arithmetic, anyway it'll be time enough. Do you understand, is it clear enough?

OLDGROVE   Clear enough. We'll have trouble, I'm thinking, over our choice. The parents of the little girls who aren't chosen, and me and James living on here catching the black looks. It won't do James any good in his business.

LARCSON   And I'm sure there must be lots of nice little girls born of lovely parents themselves belonging to this town. Maybe you'll have to draw lots among the little girls.

OLDGROVE   It'll worry James. It'd be an awful come down for a lawyer to have to draw lots. By nature they must believe that everything can be done by argument. They could make water run uphill by argument, they believe.

LARCSON   They are great men of faith.

OLDGROVE   I wouldn't like to be a lawyer, perhaps having to act against your best friend. You could refuse, but if you were hard up you'd start thinking of your wife and family and how it's an unlucky thing to refuse good money.

LARCSON Well, Jack, you haven't got any wife or family to be bothering about. You'll be one not-so-old bachelor carrying out the wishes of a genuine old bachelor. This used to be a great town for bachelors long ago, it was full of them, but of late years they've been captured in numbers. I think the young women are advised by their aunts —that is if the aunts are settled and out of the running themselves— how to catch a husband. I believe they band themselves together as soon as a new eligible bachelor appears in from over the hills and far away. They band themselves together to all have a try for him, but they're under a bargain, as soon as he shows signs of wavering towards one of them, for all the others to stand clear until she either gaffs him or fails; in that case they all come back to their prey again.

OLDGROVE They're awful. I think, Tony, you mustn't be tiring yourself, now. You should try and rest a little. I'm thinking just now that when James and I have to choose the little girl for your money—but let us hope there is a mistake made by the doctor, they do make mistakes sometime; they'll tell you, some of them, that mistakes can be made, let us hope so, and you may be here with us for a while longer yet. . . . I'm thinking whenever we have to choose the young girl there'll be some scalded hearts among the fully-grown young women of this place. There'll be snorting in Gath and a publishing of it in Askelon. Can't you picture them, Tony, but you must be resting yourself now and not bothering yourself with such thoughts. James and I will be well able to take care of ourselves. You always, in the past, had grand ideas. Indeed, you often told me ideas and plans that would have shaken up all the old Bank Managers of this place, retired, and in active service. But you never put any of your plans into operation—you had too kind a heart to want to upset anyone. But I wouldn't have cared. If I had the ways and means I would have shaken this exquisite old town upside down, including their worships the Mayor and Councillors. I'd just love to take them on a marvellous grand picnic to the Island, and then to have the boatmen slip away with the boats and leave the city fathers to entertain themselves. They'd light a fire as a signal of distress and all round the shores I'd have the people lighting answering fires—as signals of joy. I wouldn't appear in it myself. I'd have an alibi. I'd manage to be seen somewhere else altogether at the time of the goings on. But I don't suppose any alibi would satisfy them unless I was in my grave at the time. Oh, it'd all be a lot of fun, of course, and nobody a bit the worse. As soon as they saw the joke, the Mayor and the Councillors would be laughing all the time thinking of each other keeping vigil on the Island. And I would not leave them in misery too long. I'd send out the boats to them pretty soon, and the makings of a bowl of punch in every boat just to warm them up. But I talk a lot and you must be resting, Tony. If I hadn't talked so much you would have been asleep by now.

LARCSON   No, Jack, I like to hear you talking.

OLDGROVE   I'll go now (*standing up*) and I'll come in to-morrow, with the paper all made out.

LARCSON   Come to-morrow, yes, but don't bother about having the paper made out at all. You understand, I know, what I want done. It doesn't have to be tied up in any legal form for I know you will carry out— that's how they say it, 'carry out'—my wishes. Good-bye, Jack, for the present.

OLDGROVE   Until to-morrow. Have a little rest, now.

(LARCSON'S *eyes are already closed, as* OLDGROVE *lets himself out of the door, closing it gently.*)

LARCSON   No pain, no fuss, 'perhaps in my sleep,' he said.

Slow Curtain.

SCENE 2: *Sand by sea, low rocky point with sea mark, on right. Sky overcast, it is raining. Distant hills.* THE EDITOR *of the town's weekly newspaper, with spectacles, wearing pepper and salt suit, and small cloth cap.* THE MAYOR—*tall hat, frock coat, white waistcoat, grey trousers, ends roughly turned up, light dust overcoat.* OLDGROVE *as before, with low-crowned derby hat, carrying bouquet of Michaelmas daisies and roses, also pointed stick with bunch of many coloured ribbons on it, and a large bright blue, plush-covered box of sweets.* OLDGROVE *has an umbrella which he holds over the* MAYOR. *Three* TOWN COUNCILLORS, *wearing overcoats. One has a walking stick, and one has an umbrella, with which he tries to shelter the other Councillors, in turn.*

EDITOR *on extreme left behind* MAYOR. OLDGROVE *on* MAYOR'S *left, the* COUNCILLORS *grouped on his left.*

THE MAYOR   The young lady is already claiming woman's privilege by keeping us waiting. Ah (*looking off, away right*) I see three figures now emerging from the village. One of them is quite small, Miss Alice, no doubt. The others will be the parents. They'll be drenched before they get here if they have not come properly prepared. These al fresco affairs should take place in the summer months. Not that our summers have been very magnificent lately. I think, with your permission, Mr Oldgrove, and my Councillors, owing to the inclemency prevailing, it would be an act of unkindness to ask this child and her papa and mama to allow themselves to be detained here a moment longer than

necessary for the carrying out of the wishes of our departed brother—
I think I may call him brother. So with your permission, I say, I will
read some few words I have jotted down here, which will, I trust, put
us *au fait* with the matter now in hand. (*Puts on pince-nez, takes papers
from breast pocket and reads*) We, my friends, citizens and indeed I may
say citizenesses, are gathered here to-day on the shores of the wide
ocean, so gentle in summer, when the zephyrs epitomize the character
of the all too fleeting moments, so rude, rough and boisterous in
winter though (*looking up from the paper and turning towards* OLDGROVE
and the COUNCILLORS) I'm not sure that the equinoctial gales aren't the
worst time of the year, and if this isn't the first of them threatening now
I'll be agreeably surprised. First comes the rain, I've noticed, and then
the wind clears away the rain and the sun comes out and you think it's
going to veer to a good hard quarter, and then it backs and the wind
and rain come howling down on you and the slates and the chimney
pots go flying through the sky (*continues reading*) and boisterous in
winter . . . gathered here to carry out the last wishes of a distinguished
member of our community—Mr Antony Larcson—who was taken
from us but a bare six weeks ago. He has gone to his eternal rewards,
where we must all go in God's good time. For some of us that day
cannot be very far off. For some of us the long vista of the years which
stretch before us gives me the thought and the hope that they may be
years full of sunshine and the singing of the little birds who bring only
messages of gladness.

1ST COUNCILLOR   Hear, hear!

(THE MAYOR *turns his face towards the* EDITOR *who
makes a mark in his notebook.*)

THE MAYOR   While for some of us The Autumn of the sere and yellow leaves
is approaching with no uncertain tread, for others, for one other at
least, the primrose bud is unfolding itself in the ambient airs of hope
and promise. A certain politician, I have been informed, has pre-
empted the primrose for himself and his admirers. I do not mention the
flower in any political connection, pro or con. The primrose flourished
before the politician was drawing his first breath of life, not to say
cutting his first tooth.

2ND COUNCILLOR   Very true.

(THE MAYOR *turns his face towards the* EDITOR
who makes a mark in his notebook.)

MAYOR   Dear friends, and fellow citizens, Antony Larcson was ever a lover
of the old town. Its interests were ever in his thoughts. When he burnt
the midnight oil of study, in nine times out of ten the study was ear-

marked to, in some subtle way perhaps hardly observable to less brilliant intellects than his, earmarked to the advantage of all humanity and therefore, as the most human spot he knew, to the advantage of the old town. He, when he heard the first notes of the Last Post, the first rattling of the curtain rings which presage the final drawing of that dark curtain which hides from all human eyes, if not from all memory, a frail and tottering human being leaving the stony pastures for, we hope, a bright and gladsome land beyond the veil.

When he heard that bugle call, our noble friend set himself like a classic hero of old with his back to the tall pillar, and did bend all his senses to the supreme effort of the survey of all the tombs and memorials of all the ages, from the pyramids of the far desert to the lonely, small cross of boards driven into the earth above a narrow space, shouldered in among a crowded concourse of the dead on some mountain eyrie of those who, in spite of all the savants, cling still to the Immortality of the Soul.

Our friend, I have no doubt, considered all forms of remembrance, everlasting flowers, feasts of honour—men remember much in gratitude when in their cups, the ancient heroes tell us. He gave a passing thought, no doubt to the ringing of bells once a year for ever and always. But belfrys rot and tumble down in decay. Or men's ears grow heavy and sluggish to the sound of oft repeated bells—'Who was that for?' 'I don't know who, some old fellow that died in the old days long ago.' 'It's a pity they wouldn't put the price I suppose he left for the ringing to some better purpose.' That's the sort of talk the ringing of bells gives cause to after the passing of many years. Our friends, no doubt, could have had a posthumous portrait painted of himself from a photograph. I have in my possession myself an excellent Carte de Visite which, though executed some years ago, is unfaded and gives a very fine impression of this friend of ours. Should a portrait in oils have been his wish, it would have been hung within the Mayor's Parlour, where it would have been an incentive to the young men of our ancient land when on the threshold of their careers. But 'simplicity' and not 'excelsior' was the word emblazoned on the banner, which our late citizen carried in his strong right hand. There is a something in simplicity that appeals to us all, perhaps. (*Lifts his head from reading paper, which he holds in his hand, but does not read again.*) Perhaps it is that there is so much of the child even in the hardest of us all, and we know that it is only the hard who have survived the last generation in our town. Whatever may have gone on in other places, you know, as I know, here it has been tooth and nail. Get a good hold and never shift it till you get a better. It has been down, or be downed. I never killed a man, even in thought, though maybe I let a sinking man go down the third time. No, I have many things I'll suffer for in my last hours—but no—I might have seen them go twice, but before the third time I held out a hand—that is all

I can say for myself, and I hope it will be accepted when I'm moaning on the hinges of the door. Maybe it would have been better if this man, whose wishes we are following out today, had never decided to leave these wishes which are in a sense a criticism of our bad old ways, and a criticism I say on even the best of our ways.

What he left for this purpose would hardly pay for a new pump up on the Mail Coach road, but a pump would have shown he appreciated the goodness and the virtue of cleanliness. The ways of men, and especially men on their death-beds, are strange ways, and not be understood by those who stand in their full health, not thinking of their last hours, but of the hours which keep coming towards them like waves of the sea, some with crests of glistening foam on them and some dark as blood, no two waves alike. I speak out of my heart, and I don't care who hears me, and if it wasn't for the hope that I may keep my chin up above the on-coming waves, with the help of God who made me, if it wasn't for that I tell you, I would raise my hands above my head and let my cursed old body sink into the depths (*The sky is getting lighter.*) But here comes the sunlight in time to welcome this little maid. She and her fond and proud—proud they should be—parents, are almost upon us.

(*The* EDITOR *comes forward and takes the manuscript of
the* MAYOR'S *speech from his listless hand.*)

But there is another group of people coming into the green land now at this moment, as I am a living man, 'tis the woman pipers' band. (*He turns his face towards* OLDGROVE.) I see the hand of young Oldgrove in this, and I know what they are playing.

(*Pipers' Band heard, far off, playing: 'I know my love by his way of walking.' All the time coming slowly nearer. The sunlight is gathering strength, and shines on* ALICE *and her mother and father, as they enter right.* ALICE, *a girl of almost nine years of age, nicely dressed, small slip of paper in her hand.* MOTHER, *woman in the thirties, well and pleasantly dressed.* FATHER, *not very tall, wearing waterproof and carrying umbrella and* ALICE'S *waterproof. Band playing all the time, coming always nearer.* MAYOR, COUNCILLORS, OLD-GROVE *and* EDITOR, *take off hats.* ALICE *and* MOTHER *bow,* FATHER *takes off hat.* OLDGROVE *moves forward and hands* ALICE *ribboned stick.*)

MAYOR   You are welcome, Miss Alice, to the far strand by the Ocean Shore and the sun shining in the sky welcomes you. Come now, down to the tide's edge and let you write those kind words you have, I believe, in your little hand this moment.

(*Drum Major and one or more of band now appear on right, as they finish tune.* MAYOR, EDITOR *and* COUNCILLORS *make way for* ALICE *as she walks to edge of sea.* ALICE *saying each word clearly and separately, reading from paper as she writes.*)

ALICE   TONY - WE - HAVE - THE - GOOD - THOUGHT - FOR - YOU - STILL.

(OLDGROVE *hands her the box of sweets—and to her Mother the bouquet.*
Box has picture on it of a cottage covered with roses.)

MAYOR   Do I get a kiss?

(ALICE *puts stick and box of sweets on sand, goes to Mayor, who stoops. She puts her arms round his neck and gives him a kiss, takes the* MAYOR'S *chain in her hand and looks at it.*)
(*The* EDITOR *takes out his handkerchief and unobtrusively wipes his eyes.*)

MAYOR   Now we must wait until the tide flows over your calligraphy, Miss Alice.

(*All turn faces towards the sea, silently, then, after a time, all file off right. The band waits a few moments, then playing 'The girl I left behind me', follows. Sound receding. Empty stage for a space of time, then*)

Curtain.

ACT TWO

TIME: *Twelve years later.*

Scene 1: *By a bay, on left summer-house of an Hotel, gaily painted. A flower bed, a white balustrade, suggestion of arbutus tree on right.* ALICE *and* MAURICE *enter left along shore.*

MAURICE   Alice, you are very kind to let me call you Alice, so very kind to a man twenty years older than you.

ALICE   Why not, Maurice?

MAURICE   Why not, indeed, 'why not' you say 'this old man might be my father,' and surely you think a few weeks acquaintance in a tourist hotel should warrant a short name for such a one. But, Alice, I put my cards on the table, win or lose, and should there be no one else, no young man near your home, in which case I am too proud to fight against a young man for your love. But if there is no other, then, as my heart was my own till I met you . . . then I ask you to marry me.

        (ALICE *says nothing, but walking along the beach
           begins writing on the sand.*)

MAURICE   Oh, why do you keep me waiting for my answer? But I must have patience, and what is that you write upon the sand?

ALICE   I write TONY – WE – HAVE – THE – GOOD – THOUGHT – FOR – YOU – STILL.

MAURICE   Then there's another, and Tony is his name.

ALICE   Tony is dead long ago.

MAURICE   But still you remember him. But you are too young to spend a life mourning. I ask not that I should supplant Tony in your heart, I will only ask a hearing for my love.

ALICE   Tony died when I was a child, Maurice.

MAURICE   Then take good time to consider, I won't rush you. I could say that I could give you a life of comfort, and perhaps I might even say of luxury, though perhaps not so luxurious as you have with your own people. I will get a motorcar, though it may be so well turned out, nor the chauffeur so well trained as your own. My own coachman is strong and intelligent and, if I ask him, he will learn to drive a motor car for you. I have no secrets. I am a fairly wealthy man. My grandfather and my father were carriage builders and I, an only son, inherited the business. It is an honourable and ancient trade, but if it is too ancient for

343

a youthful age and, if the motor car drives the horses from the roads,
then we must fit engines into our carriages. I am not an old fogey but
still I will always love the sound of horses' hooves on a road. My dear
creature, I have nothing to hide.

ALICE   I have something to hide, or something that perhaps I should hide. I
should perhaps say only 'good-bye' and then after I leave tomorrow,
we would never meet again.

MAURICE   Wait! Oh, wait! Think, think, don't say anything yet.

ALICE   I have something to hide. I am a fraudulent visitor of a few short
sunny days. That motor and that chauffeur are not mine. I pay for these
by the week. And now my holiday is over I pack my clothes, look how
new they are (*she holds her arm up towards him*) and I will never wear
them again in an hotel like this one. I will go back to my work. I work
in an office and I keep some of the accounts and type-write the important letters. But (*looking down on the sand*) TONY - WE - HAVE - THE -
GOOD - THOUGHT - FOR - YOU - STILL.

MAURICE   What fraud is there in all that? If, to test me, you had told me you
were a forger you would have found me stand the test. Try me how
you will I am a determined man. Test me as you will.

ALICE   It is Tony's own fault. When I was a child, an old gentleman called
Antony Larcson died, and I don't think I had ever seen him, but, if I did,
I never knew him. I often saw old gentlemen walking along the pave-
ments in the old town, but I knew the names of few of them, and this
Mr Larcson, I don't believe he ever knew I was in the land of the living.
No, I was chosen by two other people. You see, he left a sum of money
to be paid to a nice little girl born in the town, of town-born parents,
who, after he was dead, had to write on the Strand:
    'TONY - WE - HAVE - THE - GOOD - THOUGHT - FOR - YOU - STILL'.
And the nice little girl had to be chosen by Mr Oldgrove—a friend of
Mr Larcson and his solicitor—and they chose me. Perhaps they put my
name in a hat with a lot of other nice little girls. And anyway I was
chosen, and with my mother and father, and the Mayor and some
Councillors, and a band of girl pipers, and Mr Oldgrove, I went down
to the far strand and wrote:
    'TONY - WE - HAVE - THE - GOOD - THOUGHT - FOR - YOU - STILL'.
and I was given a lovely box of sweets, the biggest I had ever seen. We
waited till the sea came in again and covered my writing. And whenever
I find myself on a sea strand for all the years that have gone by I write
to encourage Tony. I looked on him as a good friend—didn't he give
me that great box of sweets, and the money—I didn't think such a lot
about that at the time for I didn't see it. Mr Oldgrove used to call on my
people and me from time to time, and say it was growing. And he used
to always laugh, and stop to talk to me, whenever he saw me trotting to
school or back again. Then he died. Then my parents died. And I was
alone, and a solicitor—not the one who was at the choosing of me, he

had died years before—and this solicitor handed me a cheque, my
fortune—by then it had grown to a hundred and twenty pounds.
My office salary could keep me easily enough. I had no one in the world
to think of except number one. So I set out to give number one the
time of her life. I didn't think it was owing to me for anything I had
done except to be lucky. So I made up my mind to blow the lot on a
grand holiday. I bought a lot of clothes and I hired the motor car and
the chauffeur and I didn't hire it until I'd gone a long way from my
native home. See what a designing minx I was. And as soon as I saw
you, see what a designing minx I am still, I said to myself, 'If that man
asks you to marry him—don't hesitate, say yes.' But my conscience,
you see there is such a thing as a minx conscience, said: 'But only after
I have told him what a cheat I am.' Now you know, sir.

MAURICE   Now I know I have my first kiss. (*She holds up her face, he kisses
her, takes her face in hands and kisses her again.*)

MAURICE   Do you think Tony would object to an old boy if I wrote also
on the sand (*he writes*)

'TONY WE HAVE THE GOOD THOUGHT FOR YOU STILL'

(*Taking* ALICE's *right arm through his left hand and lifting her hand to
his lips with his right hand. Exit both, right.*)
(*After a pause, enter on left,* KITCHEN MAID *leading by the hand*
CHAUFFEUR.)

KITCHEN MAID   Oh, the air here by the sea tastes lovely after that stuffy old
kitchen. Oh look! Look what somebody has written on the sand.

CHAUFFEUR   I expect I know what it is, and who wrote it. It's something
about a chap called Tony and my lady wrote it. Whenever we come to
a bit of sea shore she always writes that (*looks down at sands*). Yes, that's
her writing, but somebody else has copied it.

KITCHEN MAID   How lovely, get me a stick and I'll write it myself (CHAUF-
FEUR *goes to left, breaks off small branch and brings it to the* KITCHEN MAID
KITCHEN MAID *with head on one side—considering writing—reads:*)

'TONY WE HAVE THE GOOD THOUGHT FOR YOU STILL',
your lady must be cracked.

CHAUFFEUR   Not at all. She's a wise woman.

KITCHEN MAID   What does it mean? What she's written.

CHAUFFEUR   Ask me another.

KITCHEN MAID   Well, she's rich and happy and grand, so here goes for luck
(*writes on sand*). I'll tell all the girls in the hotel and we'll all have the
good thought for Tony, whoever he is, and if he's dead let him rest his
soul in peace and happiness. But perhaps you would sooner I didn't tell
the rest—just to keep it to myself—to ourselves.

CHAUFFEUR   I don't seem to care what you do about it.

KITCHEN MAID   All right sniffy, here write it yourself, it can't do you any harm and might do you a bit of good, unless you're quite satisfied as you are.

CHAUFFEUR   No, I would consider it too much of a presumption to write what my lady wrote—in a sense a kind of forgery.

KITCHEN MAID   If that's all the forgery you ever do you'll do well. I'd write anything on any old strand in the wide world if I thought there was luck and virtue in it.

CHAUFFEUR   Luck and virtue don't always go together.

KITCHEN MAID   Now, Mr Petroleum, keep your wide eye on the wide ocean.

CHAUFFEUR   All right, all right, I'll send you some post cards from some of the places I may be visiting with the car. I see a lot of places one way and another, and very interesting architecture—scenes in markets and what not, lakes and mountains, and I'm expecting to be on the Continent:

> On the Continong
> Tray bong, tray bong,

as the song says. Next season should be very instructive. Monte Carlo, a shocking place for the gambling, and Ostend, similar I understand, but different. Rome, Venice, all canals, going around in boats, I believe. Germany—lager beer in large china mugs, very nice too. I like lager in the summer but for all the year round old fashioned gold old four-ale takes a lot of beating. I like it. But when I'm driving I touch nothing, lemonade and a dash, no more. They can't bear the smell of liquor on you. And, after lunch as soon as they climb in, I get a whiff of every sort taken backwards. As it comes over to me, Chartreuse Whiskey, Burgundy, Chablis, Sherry. But I speed up pretty soon and when she gets going, the breeze she makes carries the old scents, the perfumes of the wash-'em-downs, away along the road behind us. I daresay the hardworking country folk standing in their little old fields enjoy the smell of other people's good drinks what they'll never taste themselves. But I daresay it may be a good thing for them, in the end, give 'em a hope for better things, make 'em ambitious, if that's a good thing. And as to smoking—no chauffeur that values his place, smokes in his hours of duty. I think my people have always thought almost worse of the smell of tobacco than of liquor, and that's why, as we're not going out again to-day, I'm going to light the pipe.

(*Takes out pipe and tobacco pouch, fills pipe and lights with match. He sits on end of balustrade. He smokes, looking out to sea.*)

There's something very imposing about the sea. I should like to own a lot of sea, and I'd like to have a yacht to go about on it. I've seen the very yacht that would suit, painted all white with rosy coloured curtains on the cabin windows. Fine large, long yacht with a bright brass funnel, that'd take a lot of polishing I should think, but I would have to do it . . .

(KITCHEN MAID *is slowly walking along sea to right.*)

I hate polishing brass work after a dirty run. Of course in fine weather on dry roads it's nothing, it's child's play, just a touch of the paste, let it settle itself and then rub it off—and there you are—they can see their faces in it. Make you laugh, some of them, you'd think they would sooner look at something better than their old phizzes. There's no accounting (KITCHEN MAID *moves off right*) for tastes . . . I'd sooner be looking at your nice little face, Miss Molly . . . hello, she's gone!

Curtain.

Scene 2: *Ten years later by a tropical ocean.*

(*Left and right palms; in front of them shrubs with large flowers. A distant point of land with trees.* MAURICE *and* ALICE *on a seat left.*)

ALICE   We will soon have been completely round the world, won't we? We will be able to say we've been round the world. That used to be a wonderful boast with people one time. But there isn't anyone who could have had such a splendid and beautiful time as I have had, most happy of women, making a long circle with my Maurice.

MAURICE   I'm too old for you, my dear. I'm not able to climb the highest mountains.

ALICE   I have seen a plenty of men who could climb the highest mountains without loss of a breath, but I have with me one with whom I'd sooner climb a two-foot-high hillock, than own a mountain of gold, climbable or unclimbable; my man Maurice owns my heart. (MAURICE, *leaning towards her right hand which is on his shoulder, kisses it and recites*)

(*Pause.*)

    I've got a white hand on my shoulder
    Such a beautiful white hand on my shoulder.
An old, broken-down sailor drifted into the bar of the hotel just now and gave us a song, he called it 'White Hand.'

ALICE   Had he made it up himself?

MAURICE   Oh, it was nothing, sentimental. He hadn't made it up, I heard it before—a week ago in one of those islands to the East'ard. He sang it all right but melancholy—I heard it before that again.

ALICE   Don't bother about it.

MAURICE   Well, it was a sad enough song.

ALICE   Tell it to me and get it out of your mind or share it with me.

MAURICE (*who is now standing up*):

> Away Oh,
> Away Oh,
>
> We got a ship—a happy ship and a happy crew
>
> Away Oh—
> Away Oh,
>
> And a fine old man—and we got music too
>   A happy ship—and a happy crew
>
> And Away Oh,
> Away Oh,
>
> We're sailing away
> To where there's parrots
> Among the palms and girls
> In the shadow
> Shadow lands
>
> And Away Oh,
> Away Oh,
>
> But I've got a white hand on my shoulder
> Such a beautiful white hand on my shoulder
> Such a thin white hand on my shoulder
> Captain Death's got his hand on my shoulder
>
> Away Oh,
> Away Oh,
> Away Oh.

(*Pause.*)

It's a miserable sort of song to sing out here. I think.

ALICE   It is gloomy, but nothing could be gloomy here for long.

MAURICE   No, not gloomy long, but long days can be too long.

ALICE   This is a nice place to stay. I think we should stay here for some time.

MAURICE   Yes, for some time.

ALICE   Presently we'll get our things unpacked properly. I haven't remembered Tony yet, give me your stick.

(*She takes* MAURICE'S *stick and goes to water edge and writes on the sand.*)

MAURICE   Tony must be remembered round the world now all the time. A great many people, far more than we ever knew anything about, must have written his epitaph. If we go round again we'll be tying a double true lovers' knot in his memory.

ALICE   I'll go round the world with you as many times as ever you want to.

MAURICE   We're fancy free, nothing to stop us except misfortune—other people's misfortune—or our own. We can keep moving like the finger on the wall but we don't write anything on the wall—only on the sand of the sea-shore.

(ALICE *comes towards* MAURICE *who looks right.*)

MAURICE   I see a figure a long way off coming this way and I know who it is—it's my old lugubrious singing sailor—come we'll stand in the shadow of the trees and watch unseen while this old man of the sea comes to Tony's memorial.

(MAURICE *and* ALICE *stand to left.*)

MAURICE   I don't suppose he has very good sight, or is much of a reader anyway. But I hope he won't pass by unseeing.

ALICE   Oh, I hope not, I hope he will be interested. I hope he will follow my lead in honour of dear Tony. If he does it will be the first time I have actually seen anyone except yourself write my memory after me. You haven't seen anyone either, have you?

MAURICE   Oh no, though I have several times seen the writing was fresh and new. Here he comes, he walks very stiffly, he's stiffer than I am and I am sure he's ten years younger than me. God give him good luck, I don't think he ever had much.

(*Enter* OLD SAILOR *right. He sees words on sand, looks down at them, takes from pocket glasses, puts them on, reads. He goes down on his knees, takes dash knife from his pocket, and with its point writes on the sand. Rises from knees and moves off behind trees left.*)

MAURICE   (*looking left*)   Here's someone else coming, it's a boy from the hotel, he's carrying a note or something for me on a tray.

(Enter left brown native boy, carrying tray with cablegram on it—he wears a short white jacket and flowered cotton kilt.)

MAURICE *(taking up cablegram)*   I don't want this, I don't care about it. I wasn't to have any business messages at all, we neither of us were to be bothered. We left everything arranged for, didn't we? Yourself as to the home, and myself as to the office. Well, here goes.

(He reads cablegram, he is moved, he looks towards ALICE.*)*

Let us sit down just for a few minutes. My wife *(he pauses, then speaking slowly)*, I have a sad story to tell. I am worth the money in my pocket—the clothes I stand up in. The new works have been burnt out. They were only half completed but nothing now remains. Every penny the firm had was in it. They were uninsured.

ALICE   Come, my dear, let us go to the hotel, the room is shady. There is a fan working, don't talk about anything for a little while, we are together now, we have each other.

MAURICE *(rising)*   Each other.

(They move off left.)

Curtain.

ACT THREE

Scene: *Same as Act Two, Scene 2.*

Many years later.

(*New seat left, bright chromium-plated, flowering bushes trimmed down, but tall palms remaining. Enter* OLD SAILOR, *more decrepit-looking, with* VISITOR (*a man about 35 in grey linen suit, large brimmed grass hat, guide book under arm*).

VISITOR   I suppose you know this Island well?

OLD SAILOR   I know it, I suppose, as much as ever I will, I have never moved from it since I was cast up on the coast away there to the East (*points left*). I was a young man then. The people on the Island thought a lot of me. For three years I never did a stroke of work. The people brought me anything I wanted, they thought I could work miracles. The usual thing, you've read about it in books, I have no doubt. They thought I could heal their animals when they were sick, and themselves. I did what I could. One thing I stopped them of, some of their most awful cures, dreadful! shocking! I could tell you all about them, freeze your blood, though that wouldn't be any harm in this climate. Anyway, to hear me would only bore you. When they were tired of feeding me for nothing, they gave me a little canoe and I went fishing, and by and by I got me a little patch, and I found I was able to grow a few sweet potatoes and, one thing and another I made out.

(*All this time the* OLD SAILOR *and* VISITOR *have been approaching the seat.*)

VISITOR   Let's sit down, it's as cheap to sit as to stand.

(*They sit down,* VISITOR *on left*—VISITOR *offers tobacco pouch and cigarette papers.* OLD SAILOR *rolls cigarette as does* VISITOR, *who brings out match box and lights the* OLD SAILOR'S *cigarette—they smoke silently.*)

VISITOR   You've had an adventurous life.

OLD SAILOR   Humdrum enough—twelve years at sea, in sail all the time. I never stubbed a nail, never had anything worse to put up with but gales of wind until the old Phoebus Apollo, well, she wasn't an old ship, she was a lot younger than I was, about one quarter of my age and Phoebus Apollo wasn't her name, it was just what I like to call her. We were at anchor here in the bay, off-shore wind, what there was of of it, when about the darkest hour of the night, the wind went slap round and blew straight into the bay and broke her up. On those rocks to the East, you could have seen them there at low tide. Me and the Old Man were all that got ashore alive and he died before morning. I think he got broke up inside pounding on the rocks, anyway he didn't seem to me to have any want to live. It was so dark, not a sign of a moon or a star, we couldn't see each other's faces. But he knew my voice. I couldn't know it was him by his voice, it was too far gone away, only by the feel of his sleeve with the braid on it. He heard no other voice but mine and he, I think, was pretty sure I was the only one left except himself. So just before dawn, he set out on his last voyage. Sir, I laid my ear flat on his breast and I never got a whimper out of it. Yes, I believe he was a fine man. He was going ashore for good after that voyage. They always say that. I'd never set eyes on him until I saw him standing in the office at the port we sailed from.

For years I was living nice and easy with my little garden patch and my fishing, and then another Alexander Selkirk come along and he traded with the inhabitants. He traded with me. Well, he was a man who was as little fond of hard work as I was, but he hated work and he fretted for hating it. I didn't fret. I think I fretted that night I was washed up as much as ever I wanted to. So it didn't fret me to catch fish and trade them with Alexander the Second. He'd opened a store by that time, and I took rum in payment for my trouble. Good genuine Sailor Man Rum it was too. First and last I must have consumed a row of barrels of it as'd reach from here to the beginning. After the passage of years Alexander got word of some sickness among the people. They weren't showing much interest in trade. So he got a doctor to come over to the Island and stay a while and make them so as they could trade again. Just before the doctor left, having cured the people so as they weren't listless any more—he gave me a sharp look and he told me to knock off the Demon Rum. He said if I didn't I was for the happy hunting grounds. I said, 'What of it? Maybe I'll be the same there as here.' 'Maybe,' he said, 'but you won't have such an easy passage, you'll get complications. Shall I tell you some of them?' he said. 'No,' I said, 'and if I want to, I can imagine better than you could tell me.' I've got a vivid imagination, you require it on this Island if you're to hold your own against the extraordinary flowers and birds and insects and the colours of the illuminated seas that do abound, 'Well,' he said, 'I've told you.' 'Yes,' I said, 'Doctor, in your capacity as a doctor you've told me.' I took a last pannikin to him as his big canoe went over the tilt of the horizon. Last pannikin, I never took another.

VISITOR   Did you not have any adventures with cannibals and such like?

OLD SAILOR   When Alexander died, and he'd been making money, had it stacked up in a bank far away, his nephew came along with a couple of improved hard cases, and he handed over the store to them. They stayed with us a little while. They drank up all the rum that was left and then they just disappeared, melted out of the sight of men—some thought they took hands and floated out beyond the reef and sunk each other. The inhabitants said I was the natural heir to the store. I couldn't say anything about that, but I distributed everything on the shelf fair and even among them. Then we all sat down to wait. After a period of time a crowd of people came from far away, well dressed, very clean. They came in a big schooner with an auxiliary engine, first I ever saw, very smart, and these people, they began measuring up the flat land here by the beach, and they gave me a little book and a pencil to make a note of the measurements and they were making their own notes also. I considered they were anxious to form an opinion of how much my intelligence amounted to and how much experience I had of the sins and sorrows of the great world from which, they thought, they came. They went away and presently they sailed into the bay again. They'd brought carpenters and joiners with them and a lot of little white tents for them to live in and they fell to and built a large sized hotel. They sailed away then finally, they didn't come back, no visitors came. There were no fixings in the hotel. Just a beautiful shell. There was just one toy they'd left behind them, one of these patent bottle openers clamped to the counter. I'd never seen one till I saw this one. They weren't invented when I was in the world. But when the hotel builders went away it made an amusement for us on the Island. We found three bottles and a good double handful of corks, and any time anyone felt like amusing himself he corked an empty bottle, put the neck in the machine, jerked over the lever and drew the cork. After a time the corks got completely shredded out so we had to get some soft wood and make our own corks. But they didn't come out of the bottles so well. However we had our memories of the first corks to fall back on. Memory is always a good garden to fall back on. If you weren't so restless in your mind, sir, I could tell you out some of my memories. I mean the one I manufactured for myself out of the ghostie air. These boys and girls, old and young of this Island, have their own special manufactured memories. Well they've all got two sorts. The ones they talk of and the ones they keep to themselves. So have I. You'll find yourself the same way if you make a little stay here. But perhaps you're moving on. Though I daresay they could make you comfortable enough here. But on the other hand if you take the next steamboat away to some other place you'll feel you've made a move and done something. The hotel up above us now is, I believe, very convenient and grand in every particular. I've never been through it, some time I might ask for the job of delivering some great personage's boots to him on a silver salver. But you mark my words, this hotel will never be to the old inhabitants of this place, the old ones that remember, but a poor misted shadow of the first one, which was rambled through up stairs and down stairs, and when the roof had fallen away and side planking moulded into dust, I tell you we that skipped through it were like moths in a skeleton. And when the people came and built this last hotel it would be hard for them to find the shape of the old foundations.

(VISITOR *is reading guide book.*)

I was always standing around while the building was going on and they got used to me. I was used to them, from the beginning. The architect, the directors of the company, plenty of them, all mighty flush of money I should say, and then the chef when he came; and the electrical engineer, who fixed up the lighting and all. I was used to them. The engineer thought he knew more than anyone, and he used to give the inhabitants little electric shocks, make 'em squeal. But there was one strong lad who thought he was so brave, he wouldn't give a twitter, and the engineer kept raising the strength and before he knew that he was up against an obstinate brave one, he pretty near shrivelled up that man of courage. He only just turned it off before it was too late.

VISITOR (*looking up*)   No, it's not late, I don't think it's ever late in this place.

OLD SAILOR   You're learning.

(VISITOR *reads guide book.*)

OLD SAILOR   I used to talk a different way to each of these people just so as to suit the measure of their understanding, but it would be a mistake to make any attempt to alter oneself to talk to you, sir, for you are so simply, honestly, and straightforwardly true that falsehood would ring flat on you like a smasher's coin on a hardwood floor. Later on, when the hotel got going, the visitors began coming and staying on, some of them, for a long time. The management found that the visitors got melancholy if they didn't have something they could understand to look at, and to be amused with. So they encouraged me to hang around the place and entertain the people—any old way. Tell them my life, my lives, shipwrecks by land and sea. The management thought I ought to give them some ancient legends of the old chieftains of the Islands. But when I tried to get the chief who was living then up in the hills to the back to talk, he wouldn't tell me anything unless I promised not to tell it off again to anyone. The management then told me to take a day off and make up some legends myself. But it was too great a strain,

I wasn't able to make up anything. I wasn't scared that I'd lose my job because I knew the visitors wouldn't put up with anyone but me. They were used to me. For a while, quite a while, two or three seasons I kept them interested in some paintings I got the knack of making. They were two in number, a distant Island green with palms like mop heads sticking up out of a blue sea. As well as blue and green I had some light red and a yellow, lemon yellow, and I gave them a picture of a canoe on the water with a sail, and a setting sun. They used to give me five dollars apiece for those paintings. I got the planking I painted on from the management. But after a lapse of time the visitors got to paying me ten dollars a head to give them the knack of it, and the most of them, those that had any power of concentration, got so as they could paint those two pictures themselves. So the painter-artist occupation died on me. However, like most of the people here, I could swim about a bit in the waves, and I used to go out with the bunch of swimming visitors. There were lots of the original inhabitants who could make rings round me as a swimmer, but the visitors felt safer if I was with them, than if they had half a hundred of the brown boys and girls dolphinating themselves among the tall green seas. They believed that the shark always goes for the pale legs first. Fed up, they believed, long ago, with the brown and so the visitors thought if I kept farthest out Old Man Shark would swallow me, and while he was getting me down, they'd have time to go ashore. I swam around for years till I got a bit stiff for it. 'Brave,' you'll say. No, I wasn't particularly brave. You see, walking around the beaches for years under this sun with only a little kilt on me, my legs were only theoretically white.

The management of the hotel changed, from time to time, but I was always around getting the run of my teeth, and now and then, a stiver or so for pocket money. Not much dinner and very little dinarlee. You see, I had let them see how little contented me. I could do with very little of everything, and I hadn't got anyone who would particularly expect to have the shaking out of my long stocking. The management wouldn't have liked me to look too prosperous. I wouldn't have cut so much ice with the visitors if I'd appeared too grand. One time a visitor going away in the steam boat, as he was going up the side, let his swell white topi, with a green lining, flop into the water. I was there in my canoe, and I hooked it out of the sea for him, but he said 'keep it'. So for a few weeks I wore it around. But the management said, 'No, I don't think so. The visitors aren't so keen about you in that. Makes you look like Government House. They like Government House all right sometimes. But they come here to get away from it.' That was a long time ago. Things have all changed since them days.

(VISITOR *is unfolding map in guide book and studying it.*)

But so far I've been able to hold my own and I've been lucky, when one thing failed another came along. One customer sunk, another rising out of the sea. When I got tired of swimming around in the high breaking rollers I came inshore into the shallows, as you might say, where no shark with his wisdom teeth cut would think of coming. I discovered by a mere accident, that I had a husky old sailorman singing voice, and a few of the old inhabitants gave me praise for it, and I'll tell you, they are very particularly critical about singing. The young ones as well as the old ones don't mind criticizing anything they don't think absolutely up to the mark, and in a way it's a compliment, because, if they didn't think something of you they'd just make a sort of purring noise and change the subject. They were made glad with my singing. I only had one old song; you've heard it I daresay, you've heard it often.

VISITOR Oh, yes, I heard it.

(*He folds up map and continues reading guide book.*)

Switzerland must be a very interesting country.

OLD SAILOR There's few who travelled these seas who haven't heard 'White Hand' but most always they'd heard it sung by a tenor with a little round mouth always making too much of himself and not enough of the song. But when they heard my rum gum and old salt tack moan out that song with good respect, they were got right where they lived, and they stayed on, because they didn't use old 'White Hand' up. After the first night they heard me they never would let me sing it more than once of a night. Like men in the shadows, with one candle, but plenty matches, they'd light and blow out light, light and blow out, making old 'White Hand' and me last. You'll understand there was no question of passing round the hat after the song, nothing ever of that kind, always the artist. But the management appreciated the fact that I was keeping the visitors hanging on just to hear me sing 'White Hand'. You think you've heard it sung but not you, for you tell me you've never been here before, and unless you heard me and 'White Hand' you never heard her. I am not conceited about it. No, I'm proud to be the lucky one caught with the right throat at the right period of my life to give out that song. And when I stopped singing it I stopped in full swing. You'll perhaps wonder why—it was a long time ago now when I stopped.

(VISITOR *turning to back of guide book, looking up something in the index.*)

OLD SAILOR Everything is changed. I'm changed a little myself. But before my joints got altogether stiff I got a new amusement for the visitors.

The management thought a lot of it; they told me, actually told me, I was holding their slippery visitors from slipping away. I went up top-side among the hills and I had one of the old inhabitants teach me a few steps of one of the old-time dances. It had to do with a harvest, much like you might have had away back home one time when they have thanksgivings and put corn in the churches, and pumpkins, and flowers of the corn, little blue ones and poppies; that's the flower they make the drug of, long sleep. I'll be thinking of my own long sleep sometime or other, I suppose. But the tourists; they thought it was a cannibal dance. The thanksgiving in the twirls of my legs they thought, were to signify the strength and elasticity I had taken to myself with the gobbling up of my enemy. Of course the tourists of those old days were an innocent type. I wouldn't say they were harmless. But they weren't very complicated in their minds, and they were generally satisfied with their own first view of anything—hit or miss. 'Cannibal Dance,' they said, and cannibal dance it was. What time is it?

(VISITOR *is reading, makes no answer.*)

Well, you're right, don't look at your watch; here, time isn't of any consequence. Everything is changed but there being no time they couldn't change time, not even the complexion of time. Another lucky touch I had for the visitors, and it was good for me personally, I got good hard money out of it, and I salted it away in the safe in the office and I drew on it. But unfortunately there was nothing much I could buy with it on account of me giving up the rum so long ago. So my capital lasted too long—like Dives in the Good Book it weighed me down. The way I made the money was cutting little toy canoes out of a couple of bits of bamboo and a leaf for a sail. And when the wind blew off shore, and out through the smooth water where the barrier was open, my little canoes would sail away and away oh. The visitors would buy these canoes for half-a-dollar each just to see them sail away. Strange, when I painted pictures of canoes I got a crown apiece. But when I made one, I couldn't get more than half-a-dollar. I tried to raise the price but they said they could make them themselves. They couldn't, not so's they'd sail away.

That trade lasted me a while but they tired of them in the end and I was glad; it got to be monotonous (*he looks off right*). Here's a woman, as fine a woman as ever lived, coming from the West.

VISITOR   They seem very fine women to me.

OLD SAILOR   Stand up Sir!

(*Enter right* ALICE, *now old and stooped; she is dressed in a thin grey linen—rather full skirt and jacket, wears a large brimmed grass hat. She carries a tray with cords over her shoulders—a few large shells are on the tray.*
VISITOR *and* OLD SAILOR *stand up—*SAILOR *takes off his hat.* VISITOR *takes*

off his hat. ALICE *bows, passes slowly across the stage by the water's edge and exits left.*)

OLD SAILOR   Yes, I have reason to say as fine a woman as ever lived. When we got our first Governor here—he said as soon as he looked at me he felt discouraged and he wanted to retire me, and without pension— peremptorily like that. But this lady, she talked up for me, and I was retained, as before, without pay. The Governor said, 'I'll call him the old souvenir,' and he laughed and so the lady laughed and I laughed. She was always good and kind to me. Broke to the wide herself, she gave me the helping hand, let me work her garden a bit for her, raise the few vegetables for her and saw that the management gave me a little share of pocket money and my grub every day. And she had had her own troubles. She stood up to them like a good'un. When she first came here, with her husband, a fine man, as fine a man as ever I saw, though I saw him once only and for a short time. When she came here everything must have looked grand to her, fine Island, flowers the brightest in the world, fine hotel, and she and her husband with plenty of money to spend, to throw about them. And then in a moment— there comes a cable (came on the same steamer as themselves) packed aboard from the nearest cable station and that was far away. Hard luck, but anyway they had their last run in peace and quietness. And this cable her husband he opened it up and in a moment he took a seizure and died in an hour. He was broke. Everything at home gone up in flames. There wasn't the price of a drink left for the widow when the funeral was paid for. The management they acted fine and square I'll say. They never asked her to pay them anything ever. Presently they gave her a little grass-roofed house they had in the grounds with a little garden patch and all. When she had time to pull herself together she got into this trade of selling these shells. Visitors like yourself like to hold them to their ears—say they can hear the billows roar. It took her all her time to keep her courage. You see, every human being about seemed rich, the management and the visitors with money to spill, and the original inhabitants wealthy in their good nature. All rich except her and me. That's why she had a sort of pity for me. And another thing, I took her orders from the first. One night under the moon I was singing 'White Hand' to the boys and girls. And after I was finished she came away from her cottage door and she said to me: 'Don't ever sing that song again', and I quit it right then and there. I suppose it was a bit ridiculous me singing a song like that when my voice was beginning to get pretty well croaked.

All these years she's made out not so bad, enough to keep her alive and always in good heart. I never seen the cable that'd knock her out.

She's seen all the changes here same as I have. Governors—we've had them. She was here a long while before the first of them was wished on us, and he wasn't so bad. He was willing to learn. And we here, we Islanders, saw that he learnt a lot. We had him pretty well drilled. He sailed to his Boss away off, they had given him orders to show up somewhere else, but he died before he got there. I reckon he died of a broken heart. After that we had them in a string, one after the other, short term men, short term so's they couldn't get the cockles of their hearts tangled up too tight. As soon as they said 'Earthly Paradise' some little visiting bird, and not a bird of paradise, carried word away to the Boss, whoever he was. And the Governor packed his traps and lit out in a canoe, for the steamboat that had brought him his walking-away papers. The Captain's order was 'Give him time to break the seal and read his letter, then blow your whistle high, and keep the steam squirting through it, till you see his canoe coming away from the beach.' I know that's the facts, the Captain told me his own self. He is a noble Captain, he isn't of this world nor yet of the next. He's a kind of go-between, standing there on his bridge, with his hand on the engine-room telegraph, always whiffling in the soft airs between sky and seas. He has a heart in his breast he has, and he'd take the ring and pit himself against anything, his mate told me. He said, 'You see him once butting into a hurricane, and you'll say what man like that does, man can do—with the help of God.' I never knew but three steamboat captains and all since I washed in here. All good men first class. But this one, he's got a bit of a list, but he's going yet, is the King Pippin of them all.

Some of these Governors had hardly time to see their shadow in one full moon before the whistle blew for them. Then they bred a new kind of Governor, full of biz, doing things, making roads, cutting straight up into the country, all laid out with powdered coral, very fine to look at. By and by a burst of rain came and washed out the roadway, here and there, and everywhere. And there were the Governors who were all for suppressions. These stumps of trees here, that's the work of one of them and he's gone long ago, someone else had a better idea I suppose. Yes, those trees were of the flowering sort, large and full of scent, and the girls had the fashion of putting them in their hair so the Governor said, 'It makes them too attractive,' so he cut 'em down in their prime. Oh, yes, some of them had brains no doubt, misused brains, great on improving us. I'm improved, I'm sure, if you'd known me when I first came here you'd find it hard to recognize me now. I went to night school here, one or two rainy seasons, and you'd be surprised if you knew all I learnt. It's no burden to me and I'm thankful for that. The only thing I'm sure of is that I will die and I knew that from the first. Even you, sir, will die, I suppose you know that, unless you live until the world comes to an end under you, crumples up and sinks into the empty. Even then I don't suppose you'll consider it satisfactory living floating on the edge of empty.

But these suppression governors, they didn't last much longer than the earthly paradise ones because they weren't able to show results. There was nothing left to suppress, not so they should notice. We got sly. This is the slyest Island on all the seas. I wouldn't tell you only I know you're not listening, you bloody little numbskull. These suppression Governors never did much good for themselves after they left here, I believe, because when the steamboat came for them they couldn't face defeat calm and quiet, and they used to fill themselves up with the home. And they mostly picked them out of the canoes in a bosun's chair, making Authority look like nothing at all. We've got no full Governor just at the moment. The last of the make-'em-goods suppressed himself out of this life by putting his foot through the bottom of a canoe. He said to the man who owned the canoe, 'You shouldn't attempt to take passengers in that canoe, look, it's rotten,' and he gave the bottom boards a bang with his foot, and he was right, the boards were rotten and he went through down to the bottom of the lagoon. They got him up and worked artificial restoration on him for a time but he never came back. A new Governor will be on the way out to us soon now (*looking left and standing up*). Here comes this lady with the shells (*he catches* VISITOR *by the shoulders with a tight clawlike grip*). You get up and buy two of her shells, one for each ear, give her two quid for the pair, no haggling, you've got it, haven't you?

VISITOR   I've got it. (*Taking roll from pocket and standing up.*)

(VISITOR *and* OLD SAILOR *walk towards* ALICE: VISITOR *takes two
shells and pays* ALICE: ALICE *hesitates, shakes her head.*)

ALICE   It's too much.

(*But* SAILOR *insists on her taking the money, he closes her hand over it.*
ALICE *moves along edge of sea and exits right.* SAILOR *makes* VISITOR *hold
a shell to each ear.*)

Curtain.

Scene: *Same as Scene 1. A year later.*

(*Enter* VISITOR *right—*NEW GOVERNOR *left, he is wearing white topi,
tussaud silk short jacket with three silver stars on left breast, pale blue shirt,
turned down collar with black bow tie. Yellow cord riding breeches and high
tropical laced boots. He has a revolver in holster and is leaning on a dark
brown silver-mounted walking stick.*)

NEW GOVERNOR (*as they meet close to seat*) I give you good morning, sir, I am the Governor of this Island and I like to make myself known to all visitors. It is my invariable custom and I find it is appreciated. I have never yet received a serious rebuff; you, I understand, have made a previous visit here, I believe at a time when there was no Governor in residence and things were a tiny bit higgledy-piggledy. We have, I am glad to say, been able to put everything into order. Almost everything, of course there is always something in this part of the world among the outposts of civilization where there is a little more to be done, a little more polish to be applied. You have hardly had time yet, no doubt, to compare the present with the past. Your previous visit was a year ago, I understand.

VISITOR I notice a very great improvement. There's an air of respect to be observed by the merest tyro in observation, everywhere.

GOVERNOR I am gratified that you were able to observe a change for the better. Though, of course, what you have observed must as yet be but a skimming of the surface. (*Impressively*) There is a deeper culture, a planned culture. This you will observe, I hope, later. Do you plan— intend to make a stay of some duration?

VISITOR I hope to be able to make a considerable stay if I find myself comfortable. During the few hours I have been here I have experienced a strange, but very pleasant sensation, that of being in a chosen and appointed place. As though the Supreme Being and myself had collaborated in placing me here—my spiritual home.

GOVERNOR You want to watch out all the same. That feeling may come from the sense of order that is, and is to come. But we must recognize that man cannot live by order and order alone. There are other component parts such as hope—that is, the hope for more order.

VISITOR I feel that. By the way, there was a familiar figure to be seen when I was here before, an old man of the sea in worn clothes and a very poor hat.

GOVERNOR He died a few months ago. He sat down on the seat, he didn't move, and when I sent one of my native attendants down to see why he sat so long—I can see this seat with my binoculars from my study in Government House—he found that the old man was dead. He was quite a feature here, someone had given him the title of the Old Souvenir.

VISITOR Poor soul, he seemed to me very worried about something, I'm glad he's at peace. There was also a person here I noticed, a lady, no longer young, a peripatetic seller of sea . . . of shells. How is she?

GOVERNOR Dead, dead also. Only a fortnight ago. She had been ailing some time, but was cheerful, I understand.

VISITOR I'm glad of that.

GOVERNOR One evening she came down here just before the fall of night. She was observed to write something on the sand with a stick, no one was able, it appears, to discover what she wrote. I trust it was nothing scurrilous. There is a certain trouble here from time to time about slogans. But we will be able to get the matter well in hand I have no doubt. After the lady had left the strand I sent one of my attendants down to see for himself what was written. But the tide had risen over it, whatever it was. The lady couldn't be questioned because she was exceedingly ill; in fact, as soon as she regained her residence, a doctor had to be procured and, in spite of his every effort, she passed away before morning. Quite a large funeral—seeing the cavalcade was of such considerable dimensions I thought it advisable myself to attend. I have had reason to believe that my action was appreciated.

VISITOR   Her life had been a life of some severity, I was informed when I was here.

GOVERNOR   I got no particulars. The people, including the hotel people, were vague.

VISITOR   I don't like vagueness.

GOVERNOR   Nor I.

VISITOR   I used to be rather vague myself, always studying to improve my mind, listening to others, not listening to myself, letting myself be ridden over rough-shod. I wasn't a worm—but I was worm-like. Now I feel quite different, I feel at this moment a commanding something that envelops me and is part of myself. I have a desire to help others.

GOVERNOR   That is most commendable of you and I am sure you will find many that you will be able to help. Even if they themselves do not realize it.

VISITOR   In this matter of slogans I would suggest that certain slogans only be permitted.

GOVERNOR   I am seeing to that, thanks for the suggestion all the same. I'm having a list of slogans prepared, any of which can be used.

VISITOR   Right, and anything outside that list, any free-lance slogan, to be barred absolutely. That's the talk! I haven't as yet seen any writing on the walls.

GOVERNOR   There aren't many walls. First take your wall, then write on him. That drives the people to the sandy beaches; we have plenty of them. In the old careless days they used to scrawl all over the Island shores personal remarks about the reigning Governor and his immediate friends in the community. It got so embarrassing that some of my predecessors used to employ a man and a horse to obliterate the writings with a brush drawn forward and backward by the horse. Evil persons who were not in true sympathy with authority used to detain the man, and the horse, by various dubious tricks. One was to tell the man that there was something most shocking written on a far beach. Something that should be removed before the people could see it. Then when he had hurried away out of sight, with his horse and harrow, they'd bring a large concourse of their friends down to our beach here to make merry over the work of the scandalous would-be wits. They drew caricatures on the sands, also of leading well-disposed citizens and of the Governor himself.

VISITOR That was too much.

GOVERNOR If you have any suggestion to make as to suitable slogans, it will give me the greatest pleasure to incorporate them. I have no apprehension in inviting *you* to make suggestions. But I was sadly disillusioned when I invited one or two of our visitors a week ago and found their only ideas were some purely ephemeral cry from the heart. I say cry from the heart, because their suggested slogans were only for the purpose of advertising some commodity in the manufacturing of which they had a personal interest.

VISITOR That is not right. You said just now, Governor, that walls were somewhat of a rarity here.

GOVERNOR Yes, very rare. The materials for building walls is rather a problem to come by. We have coral rocks but transporting them from the coast is very troublesome and labour here is diffident. But I like these problems, and no doubt I will find a way of procuring the right materials at the right moment.

VISITOR You, no doubt, have some sort of a jail, probably surrounded with a wooden palisade. Poor stuff, doesn't make an impression like a wall. But you don't want a wall all round a jail. One good high wall standing up by itself, on a plain, is all that is required. If you build a wall to encircle your prisoners, after a few attempts to climb it, your prisoners, owing to low initiative caused by prison diet, give the thing up like an uncrackable conundrum and lie down in its shadow. But my idea is a single piece of wall, it can be a long or short piece, just as you think necessary. My single piece of wall, if it is properly constructed, high and difficult, attracts all the inhabitants who either attempt to climb it, or give advice and encouragement to others. The most alert and able, therefore the most criminal of your people, will be most active in the climbing. So there, at any time you want them, will be your criminals merely for the taking. I have these ideas. I give them away as soon as they come to me. See here, Governor, should you ever find yourself in a corner of any kind, no matter how important, or how trivial, just give me the word and I'll bend my mind on to something. In this matter of permitted slogans——

GOVERNOR Would you like to see the list I have been preparing? Would you like to run your eye over it? (*Takes typewritten paper from pocket and hands to* VISITOR) They're alphabetical.

VISITOR (*looking down list*) Yes, yes, seems to meet every want. You might add, 'Art for Art's sake'. I say, what's your revolver for? Are you afraid of the natives?

GOVERNOR Not particularly.

VISITOR Is it loaded?

GOVERNOR   Yes, there's one cartridge in it only.

VISITOR   Isn't that a risk? You might miss with the first shot.

GOVERNOR   No, I will not miss with the first shot.

VISITOR   Well, you know your own business best. Now, Governor, tell me something, here, sit down where the Old Souvenir sat (*points to corner of seat.* VISITOR *walks up and down, hands clasped behind his back*). Now, Governor, tell me, where's your nearest inhabited land?

GOVERNOR   About five hundred miles away.

VISITOR   You've got no cable connection nearer than that?

GOVERNOR   No, and not there.

VISITOR   What's your link with the outside world?

GOVERNOR   The steamer. The same as left you here just now.

VISITOR   When do you expect it will call again. Not for a month or so, I suppose.

GOVERNOR   Since you ask, she'll be back here again tonight.

VISITOR   The devil she will! That alters things. Oh, well. Quick action is the best in the end sometimes. Why is she coming back so soon and where's she been to?

GOVERNOR   You are interested in her. Well, sir, the Captain has sailed to the west, to an island, a deserted pineapple island, and he aims to get a few bunches just as a private venture.

VISITOR   What time will he be back here?

GOVERNOR   At the fall of night. He'll lay off until the moon gets up; we've a full moon here tonight. He can't run in through the break in the reef at night except under a full moon. But as soon as the moon's up he'll steam right in and drop his anchor, right here in front of us. He aims to have a couple of days rest for himself and the crew.

VISITOR   He does, does he?

GOVERNOR   He deserves it. They all do. Getting a lot of pineapples in the heat of the day is tiring work. He will be able to relax here.

VISITOR   I sincerely hope he will be able to do so. You said just now, Governor, that I was a man of ideas, I am—Item A, Item B. You are a man trained in obedience and in training others to obedience. Well, I have no experience as a teacher or a trainer. Just now I got a genuine first-class idea. I'm going to remake this place, or rather start it right away from scratch. I'm going to make this place an independent State. You will retain your Governorship, with a slight difference. You will be called 'Chief' just as the First Engineer on a steamboat is called 'Chief', I will be the Evident—you know, Self-Evident.

GOVERNOR   Dictator?

VISITOR   No, no, 'Dictator' suggests a time lag—a Dictator says do so and so and so, and then it gets done or sometimes it doesn't. I am the man who when he says a thing goes, it goes, I don't mean 'goes away' so much as goes like a clock goes. Do you follow me? Do you take my point?

GOVERNOR Perfectly, it's self-evident.

VISITOR Well, the first thing we've got to set out is a Constitution. I'll rattle one out of my head right away. In the meantime there are some things for you to do. We've got to have something in the nature of an Armed Force, and something in the nature of a Flag. For the flag bring me here a collection of any materials suitable for a flag-making, from Government House, and the Hotel. And as to the Armed Force. How many men have you employed directly, or indirectly, about Government House?

GOVERNOR Eight houseboys, two carpenters, two painters, a couple of builders' labourers, a butler and five gardeners.

VISITOR How many is that?

GOVERNOR (*after counting*) Twenty, I make it.

VISITOR Good, are there enough arms for them?

GOVERNOR We've got a signal gun and two presentation swords, and we've got no ammunition for the gun.

VISITOR All the better, we don't want them to hurt anyone and we certainly don't want them by an accident hurting each other. Untrained men should never have firearms. They can carry spears with blunt ends. Got any spears?

GOVERNOR Not at the moment. But the carpenters can soon make some wooden ones. One-piece ones.

VISITOR And you might put a bouquet of flowers in the muzzle of each of the signal guns. Another thing we must have is a new Motor Road.

GOVERNOR There isn't a motor in the place, because up to this there hasn't been a single road suitable for motoring. There's a very ramshackle road, climbing into the interior, starting from the hinterland of the hotel.

VISITOR I hate the word 'hinterland'; it was very popular once; it always suggests, just what no doubt it is here, the ash heaps behind an hotel. You must have a Motor Road, we *must* have a Military Force, and we *must* have a Flag. You'll think 'must' is to be the key word. But you'll find it's nothing of the sort. 'Must' in plans should have a final letter added to it. The penultimate letter of the Alphabet. And so you get musty—that's rather funny, eh? I don't think being funny generally is such a bad thing in an Evident. But still sometimes it gives a wrong impression to people who don't understand fun. It's a queer thing but mostly everybody is impressed by solemnity. Even if they are solemn themselves. I shouldn't think all the same that our people were very solemn. I have, when I was here before, heard them laughing in the woods at night. About the Motor Road (*thinks with chin in hand*)— what time's low tide?

GOVERNOR Quarter past three.

VISITOR Very good, get your carpenters to prepare a quantity of rough stakes, then send any four unskilled men you have along the strand to the left here, and let them, on the smoothest part, stake out a double track motor road, for just as far as they can go. How far do you think that'll be, Chief?

GOVERNOR   About seven miles, I should say. I've never been all the way myself. It's a long way to walk, and I don't like walking in this climate. You know, Evident, your Evidence, that the tide will have turned and begun coming in a good way before the four men have finished marking out the road.

VISITOR   What a mathematical brain you have (*claps his hands*). Put as many men as you can spare on the job and I say, this is good, let half start at each end, and then they'll meet in the middle, and if the tide begins coming in on them too fast, they must curve the road inwards in front of the tide. I should have liked to be able to say we had a dead straight Motor Road. But curved like Cupid's bow will be delightful. We have to constantly be adjusting ourselves in the face of the enemy. In this case 'the Enemy' is the oldest one of all. By the way, how goes 'the Enemy', (*he takes out watch which is in a fob pocket*) not so bad, we've only used up about half an hour so far. Ah, but there's still a lot to do. We've got to have a Swimming Pool. That's really one of the first things. Catches the idea of the youth. I don't know why it's necessary to catch Youth's Idea. I haven't time to go into it now. Where can we have our swimming pool?

GOVERNOR   The people here have the entire Pacific to swim in, they wouldn't know what to do with a swimming pool.

VISITOR   I'm sure you are right. But it doesn't make any difference. Get one of your painters to take a pot of aluminium, no I'm tired of aluminium, a pot of moonlight blue paint, and walk along the shore till he comes to a naturally formed pool among the rocks and then let him paint up the words 'Swimming Pool'.

GOVERNOR   I don't think he'd know what moonlight blue was. Shall I send him down here to you with his paints and let you mix the shade you want?

VISITOR   Oh, dear, no, thank you very much. I can't do everything. Let the painter choose any nice blue he likes. The great thing is to have him happy in his work. The foundations of our Society are to be built, as you will see, on happy craftsmen. Another thing we should have is a Picture Gallery. Have we got any pictures?

GOVERNOR   I have a couple of the Old Souvenir's paintings, and a mountain scene; it's after an oil painting. I picked it up myself, in a curiosity shop, just before I went aboard the ship to come here. I very nearly gave it to the Captain, as he took a fancy to it. But now I'm glad I didn't. It'll be a nucleus, and the hotel has a number of engravings and a tinted portrait of one of the first directors. And there was a lady visitor who spent a season here many years ago, and painted a number of exotic water colours of the Island and presented them to the hotel, in exchange for her bill receipted. I say 'exotic' but don't misunderstand me, sir. This Island is exotic but these paintings were exotic in another way altogether. I wish the Old Souvenir was still with us, he'd organize a painting squad among the original inhabitants, some of them are very deft with their fingers and very competent draughtsmen, as we know by their caricatures on the strand. However, we're going to stop that part of their activity under the Limited Slogan Order.

VISITOR   Oh yes, that must not be forgotten above everything else. The Limited Slogan Order. To return to our Picture Gallery. I suppose the hotel people would let us have their pictures on loan and give us the use of, perhaps, the large drawing-room. And how many pictures do you think you'll be able to get together?

GOVERNOR   I couldn't say exactly, a few dozen anyway. The Hotel Management I am sure will give us every possible assistance they can—this not being the regular season, you yourself being the only visitor, they have time to be agreeable. When the rush is on they'll have no time to give to the music of the spheres which, as Pythagoras taught me, is a perfect harmony, and that is what we take it you aim at for our New State.

VISITOR   You've said it.

GOVERNOR   The Hotel Management in their days of rush recognize no chiming bells except the bells of the cash register.

VISITOR   Wait a while, we'll tax that. In the meantime, what's the next thing we've got to have before our ship comes home, with the Captain in it? Everything must be working like clockwork. Everything, I say, before he arrives. We've got to do the best we can right away with the materials we have to hand. Later on we'll be able to work on the fine ancient system of trial and error. By the way, that's an idea. I'll incorporate it in our Constitution. The national motto shall be 'By Trial and Error' and there's more in it than meets the ear. Try your criminal before he makes his first slip, his first Error, and becomes a criminal, and draw lots, pick your victim, put him in the dock, try him before a judge and jury, convict him, or find him not guilty. Explain to him from the first, of course, that it's only an imaginary trial. I say 'him' advisedly, because if we happened to draw a young woman she'd argue—and that would bring our courts into a farcical light, and the women would join all together and laugh us out of court, out of our own court. I may not be as brave as a lion but I know the courage of a hen.

GOVERNOR   I suppose I ought to be getting the various works started.

VISITOR   Yes, yes. And, I say, we will have to have a Race Course.

GOVERNOR   But there are no horses on the Island.

VISITOR   Doesn't matter. First get your Race Course, then somebody will bring the horses along. Horses won't race without a race course and they won't race without bookmakers either. That's an idea—we might make ourselves into a bookmaking firm. I'd cry the odds and you'd be my clerk.

GOVERNOR   Wouldn't that be derogatory to our position?

VISITOR   No, not under the Incognito Rule—I'll have to put that into the Constitution. The Evident and the Chief will have the power of becoming invisible in law, at will. And while we have decreed ourselves as invisible it will be a criminal offence for any citizen to say, 'I see you, Evident.' or 'I see you, Chief.'

I feel a little tired now. Before tackling the Constitution, I think I'll have tiffin. Will you join me, Chief?

GOVERNOR   I'd love to. I've never had tiffin with an Evident before. But I'd like to get some of these matters, which have to be put in order, started at any rate. I'll just get a snack at Government House.

VISITOR   Oh yes, and we must have a Library. Firstly, a Reference Library (we won't have *Who's Who*, I'm not in it), a ready-reckoner and the poets, and we will want an Atlas. Then in the Library proper, some fiction, crime tales. This, I know, is a practically crimeless Island, but the citizens won't realize that unless they've got some idea of the goings-on in other places. 'You can't enjoy anything without contrast,' as the Great Mogul said when he took iced rice with his curry. That's settled. You'll meet me here after I've had tiffin.

(*Exit.*)

VISITOR (*returning*)   I say, you don't think my title, 'The Evident', will make people think of 'the usual', like bacon and eggs for breakfast?

GOVERNOR   It wouldn't have occurred to me for a moment.

VISITOR   You're a good fellow, all right. 'Evident' it is.

(*Exit.*)

(GOVERNOR *fans himself with Topi.*)
(*Exit.*)

Curtain.

SCENE 3: VISITOR *discovered striding up and down in deep thought, hands clasped behind back. Enter left* GOVERNOR *followed by brown boy from Hotel who is carrying a great quantity of coloured curtains, chair covers and cushion covers.*

VISITOR   What have we here?
GOVERNOR   The Flag.
VISITOR   Oh, I forgot the Flag. I've been so busy on the Constitution; well, first things first. Let's at it.

(GOVERNOR *signs to boy who drops the cloths in a heap partly over the seat and partly on the ground. He then stands by, turning his face in wonder from the* VISITOR *to the* GOVERNOR *and back again. The* VISITOR *and the* GOVERNOR *rummage among the heap. What the* VISITOR *doesn't approve of after holding up, he lets fall. What the* GOVERNOR *holds up, the* VISITOR *shakes his head at, and the* GOVERNOR *lets it fall, until the* GOVERNOR *finds two cushion covers, claret coloured and silver diamond. He hands them to the* VISITOR, *who is delighted with them, holds one up and admires it.*)

VISITOR   It is our flag.

(*Arranges one of the covers over* GOVERNOR's *left shoulder,
keeps other in left hand.*)

Presently you'll have it run up to the top of the flag pole. And now for the Constitution (*he strides up and down*).
GOVERNOR (*to* BOY)   Take these away (*pointing to a heap of cloths*) and return each to the place from which they came.

(*Exit* BOY.)

VISITOR   Be seated (GOVERNOR *sits down*).
VISITOR   Complication is the thief of time. Therefore, by allowing a perfectly simple breeze of the brain to advise me, I have simplified the Constitution so that it will fit on half a sheet of notepaper. And then, I am speaking metaphorically, for our Constitution will not be a written one. It will be simply photographed on the tablets of our two memories. A kind of book-keeping by double entry. The Constitution is retrospective. Firstly, every citizen of this country has, always, been free. Secondly, the Government has consisted, always, of an Evident and his Chief, assisted by a Parliament, consisting of the Lefts and the Rights who are always equal and up to the present only the first part

of the Constitution has functioned. The second part is now about to begin functioning.

GOVERNOR   Excuse me, how are you going to keep the Lefts and the Rights equal?

VISITOR   Beautiful simplicity again (*pointing to right over water*). See yonder in the lagoon, the Old Ceremonial Double War Canoe lying at anchor. That is our Parliament House. You and I will sit in the middle and the representatives of the two parties each in their own canoe, and you know how cranky these old war canoes are. If the number in one canoe exceeds the number of the other the whole concern will begin to tip over and I will then of course have my vote for what I think best, and should by any chance, owing to the different weight of individuals, there be any difficulty about trimming the two canoes, I will use you as a trimmer. So Parliament will float on an even keel.

GOVERNOR   I see a difficulty in your scheme. The people here are splendid swimmers and wouldn't in the least object to upsetting Parliament.

VISITOR   I've thought of that. None of the members will be allowed to attend Parliament except while wearing their best modern suits of clothes. This will make them careful. You and I will of course, wear our swim suits, in your case 'with decorations'. I see you have them. How have you been getting on with our plans?

GOVERNOR   The carpenters are busy making stakes. We can't get along with the motor road, of course, until the tide has receded. The painter is painting his Swimming Pool Notice Board. In the meantime willing hands are marking out the Race Course. Others are assembling the pictures for the Picture Gallery. This is necessarily a rather slow piece of work, because my people having seen so few examples of Representational Art, are naturally very interested, and are constantly taking pictures out into the sunlight to view them better, and at their ease. If the attendant is alone in this viewing, he seems to be able to concentrate on the matter in hand, and to understand the picture, no doubt in his own way. But if two or three, with their pictures held out before them, happen to meet out of doors, immediately a discussion arises as to the merits or demerits of the various pictures. In some cases these arguments have engendered so much heat that it has been necessary to send out pickets to bring the picture bearers in. However, the exhibits are going up on the walls now, fairly smoothly. Though a certain amount of trouble is caused by partisans of certain pictures wanting them hung in the best places. The assembly of the Library is not giving so much bother, because unless the books have illustrations, my people are absolutely impartial about them. Later on someone will have to see that all the books are the right way up, and arranged in some sort of order. The great thing is to get the shelves furnished. It is a strange comment on man in his more primitive form, that he should be most anxious to understand what he sees. While he is often entirely unambitious as to the understanding of what he hears. Combining the eye of eagle with the, comparatively, carefree ear of the parrot, who thinks human speech was invented so that he could learn it off by heart. This is an interesting thought. Do you not think so?

VISITOR   I do, I do, indeed. How's the Armed Force getting on? Have they had any drill yet?

GOVERNOR   Oh yes, there is a lot of drilling going forward, they are very enthusiastic about it. They take turns putting each other through their lessons. They, of course, have to select one of their number for the part of drill sergeant in the more complicated items such as form fours. They don't like drilling in their bare feet, they consider that they are unable so to produce a martial tread. Luckily I was able to find a cupboard full of old boots in Government House. At this very moment they are shaking the earth.

VISITOR   The Parliamentary Canoe will have to be carefully overhauled. But that needn't be done today. That's the advantage of a retrospective Constitution. Parliament has already functioned, in imagination's Echoing Canoes. If I hadn't hit on this sort of Constitution we would have been put to the pins of our collars to have the whole concern in working order before the Captain comes in tonight. As it is I know we won't be able to rest on our oars until the day is far advanced. But before the moon rises everything will be accomplished. I don't suppose in the whole world so much will have been done in so little time. Have you got your Slogan Notices made out yet?

GOVERNOR   They are now being made out by the receptionist at the hotel. She very kindly offered to help. She's very intelligent. I daresay she's nearly finished them now. I'll go up there and see how she's getting on.

VISITOR   Yes, that would be well done. I'll be considering any further embellishments, which might tend to add to the importance and dignity of Our State. It's very hot down here, you might send a boy down from the hotel with one of those large garden umbrellas.

(*Exit* GOVERNOR.)
(VISITOR *sits on seat.*)
(*Enter boy with umbrella which he fixes over seat.*)

Curtain.

Scene 4: *The same; later evening. The stage is dimly lit.*

(Enter left GOVERNOR *dressed as before and* VISITOR *in full evening dress with flag round waist. Slogan Notice pasted on tree-trunk, right.)*

GOVERNOR   See, I have got my Anti-unpermitted Slogan Notice up.

VISITOR   I'm glad to see that. It is most important. Do you know as the hour grows nearer for the arrival of the steamer I have been getting just a little bit jiggity, and, as soon as I knew that it was actually lying out there waiting for the moon to come in to us, I was so worried about the Captain that I went and had a little talk with the lady receptionist at the hotel. She completely reassured me.

GOVERNOR   She is a most intelligent young lady, I have always found her so—and most helpful.

VISITOR   Yes, indeed, I talked lightly about things in general for a few minutes, to put her at her ease, and then I asked her, plump, how would the Captain react to the New State and she told me that we need not give ourselves any trouble whatever on his account. She said, she knew for a fact, he had told her himself, that he was 'absolutely fed up' (those were his words) with 'rampaging the wide oceans', and he'd welcome 'with a heart and a half' the moment when he could retire from the sea and settle down somewhere on shore, and there was no place in the whole world he'd like better than this Island. Then without committing ourselves, I broached the subject of the crew and the ship. She said that I had no doubt heard that sailors were supposed to have wives in every port, and in the case of this special crew it might be said that they had wives in every port—but this one. That would be a reason for them being wishful, perhaps, to settle down here. Then I touched lightly on the subject of the ship, treating it rather as a joke. I asked if we could use it as the nucleus of a Navy, or perhaps as a Floating Summer Palace for you and me. She reassured me about that at once. She said they practically had the brokers in for months travelling with them, apparently to and fro all the time. She said the claim against the ship (she has a genuine business head that girl), could be satisfied by giving the brokers' men a quantity of the unwanted fittings, a canoe, water, provisions, and full directions for getting home. She's taken a lot of worry off my spirits. *(Pause)* It's been a long day, a long day for both of us. I could have done nothing without you, Chief. What are ideas and plans without someone who will carry them out. *(Pause)* I wonder what the people up in the hills think about the new State?

GOVERNOR   Oh, they've probably heard nothing about it yet, and even when they do, it will be next door to impossible to know what they are thinking about, or anything else. I don't think that they think as we understand the word. Their thought processes are of quite a different order to ours I do believe. But like the climate here, they are benign. Benignity is one of the most difficult things to deal with in a subject people. That is if you have to fill up any large space in your report for home. You see, they don't realize that they are a subject people at all.

VISITOR   Well, they are not a subject people any more, and you don't have to send any more reports 'home', as you call it. (*Slaps him on the shoulder.*)

GOVERNOR   Of course not, I forgot that for a moment. I would throw up my hat in the air, but in this warm, and gentle climate, such exuberance would jar the sensibilities—all right in harsher, more northern latitudes, but not here.

VISITOR   We've got everything through at such a pace today, that we'll be glad to take a few days off. With ruck-sacks, we might go for a short walking tour into the interior, of course, only walking in the cool of the mornings and in the evenings, resting during the day. We might make ourselves up as natives of some distant Island, or at any rate we could wear false moustaches, like the Pasha and his Vizier, in the old story. We'd listen to everything we heard. You, I suppose, know the language?

GOVERNOR   Only a word or two, I'm sorry to say.

VISITOR   All right, then, we'll have to bring along an interpreter. He can carry our impedimenta. During our walk we will be able to make ourselves *au fait* with whoever are the most important people. The leaders of what we may call the Mountain Society. And then later, when we have our Floating Summer Palace in the lagoon we'll be able to give a reception. Of course the invitations will have to be sent out very carefully—the more I think of this walking tour the more important it becomes. You see we will have to understand perfectly the different stratums and cliques among the higher classes of the people. We don't want to step off the wrong foot. We'll have ice cream. There's sure to be a refrigerator on the steamer. That will be in our favour at once. Every guest, as they come on board, will be handed a cornet and the major domo will instruct the people how to lick them in the approved manner. After our rest among the hills we will come back to civilization with such energy that the proroguing of Parliament will be child's play to us. I see the scene before me. The Great Double War Canoe now turned to the uses of peace, a sword beaten into a plough-share. Myself sitting up under the canopy in the forward part, and yourself, ever on the watch moving here and there. Seeing all the members into their places Left and Right. When the canoes have ceased rocking about, and are quite still, I will stand up. I think I will be wearing ceremonial robes of some kind. Something in the nature of regalia is always appreciated, and you must have a costume

also. I may think these details out myself. But I rather think I will seek
the advice of the young woman receptionist. I think she has taste, and
at any rate a woman's nature lends itself better than man's to the
blending of shade. Man is ever rombustious and crude in these matters,
delighting in sharp contrasts, like the Great Mogul. But I remember
I used him before as a simile. That shows I'm really tired. Whenever
I'm tired I begin repeating myself, and everything isn't finished yet.
The meeting with the Captain is bound to be exciting. I first thought
we'd meet him on the beach and welcome him to our New State.
Then I thought that would be rather abrupt, knock him off his pins,
his sea legs, as it were, so I got Miss Receptionist to agree to tell him
about the change and then have him led towards the Picture Gallery,
where we will be standing ready to receive him formally. I see you
haven't changed, and I think you are right. My full dress appearance
will symbolize authority at its blandest. First I thought of a black tie
and a dinner jacket. But I discarded the idea at once. 'Tails,' I said to
myself, 'it must be.' Uncomfortable, very, in the tropics but tumbling
about in ducks, or a lounge suit, while symbolizing Democracy at its
highest, coupled with the Parliamentary Man and shining in the face
of the eleven stars, is surely more than an anachronism, and far less
than the Eternal Verities. 'Captain,' I shall say, 'speaking for myself and
for my intrepid, tireless and cultured fellow-worker on the Path of
Freedom, I welcome you, wayworn from the deep and dangerous
furrows of Neptune Realm, to our State which at one and the same
time is the newest and oldest establishment of this planet, afloat and
now ashore. The calm and urbane rigidity, no—placidity—of a firm
land being substituted for a heaving deck. You behold us, no doubt,
through rosy spectacles. After a while you will notice this island
earth beneath you is trembling. Do not be alarmed. The trembling will
be caused by the marching feet of myself and collaborator marching
forward to greater expansion, remember that, as the poet says—

> Love itself
> Must rest

And where we rest we bivouac—on the Paths of Freedom.'

(*Enter boy from Hotel, Left,*
carrying a note on a tray.)

VISITOR   A note for me (*holds it in his hand, turning it about*).
GOVERNOR   Read it, sir.

(VISITOR *opens note, reads hurriedly, he is distressed.*
Reads again, slowly.)

VISITOR   It is from the Receptionist.

GOVERNOR   Yes, the Receptionist. What is it about? What does she say?
Unless it's personal.

VISITOR   No, it's impersonal. She says (*reading*) 'You'll have to call your
revolution off' ('Revolution'—I thank you Miss for that word) 'until
the end of the year. The pilot who brought the steamer in has just come
up here in a hurry. He thought the management ought to know—
the ship's full up of tourists. It's the earliest commencement of the
season I've ever known.'

GOVERNOR   Anything else?

VISITOR   'I have to jump to it now, yours in haste.'

GOVERNOR   Anything else?

VISITOR   Only 'Keep your chins up.'

VISITOR   (*after a pause*)   I think I'll go in and change.

(*Exit* VISITOR.)

(GOVERNOR *sits down wearily in seat, takes off Topi and wipes head—sits
dejected, after a time rises, walks over and looks at slogan notice on the right,
walks slowly across in shadow of tree left, when Enter right two Brown-
Skinned Lovers. The moonlight is growing strong.*)

BROWN BOY   (*handing girl his spear*)   Write something good on the strand—
something to bring us luck.

BROWN GIRL   I can't see to write anything yet, wait a moment (*looks right*)
until the moon comes up over the tress (*a pause*). What shall I write?

BROWN BOY   Anything that will bring us good luck. I think the old things
are best.

BROWN GIRL   So do I. I'll write what we have always written (*she writes with
spear point, saying the words*)
TONY – WE – HAVE – GOOD – THOUGHT – FOR – YOU – STILL.

GOVERNOR   (*stalking across the stage*)   What have you written?

BROWN GIRL   Is that you, Governor? I've just written what we always write.

(GOVERNOR *goes over and looks down.*)

GOVERNOR   Is this taken from the list of Permitted Writings put up on the
tree there?

BROWN GIRL   No, Governor.

GOVERNOR   Did you read the notice?

BROWN GIRL   Yes, Governor.

GOVERNOR   Well, why do you think I put it up?

BROWN GIRL   Oh, I thought you just put it up for putting up. Anyway it's
on harm what I've written. We say it brings good luck. You try
yourself. (*She puts spear in* GOVERNOR'S *hand.*)

GOVERNOR   Who was this Tony—some shepherd of the hills, eh?
BROWN GIRL   I don't know sir—he just brings us luck.

(GOVERNOR *drops his stick and takes up spear
and writes, saying:*)

TONY – WE – HAVE – THE – GOOD – THOUGHT – FOR – YOU – STILL.

(*Enter left* VISITOR. *He has changed his tail coat and white tie
for his grey short coat and a black tie.*)

GOVERNOR (*looks at* VISITOR, *then down on sand at writing. The moonlight is
shining on his decorations Three Stars.*)   What have I done, I who was
given these Three Stars (*he touches them with his fingers*) each for seven
years obedience and for causing others to obey, I have disobeyed my
own ukase.
     But I have obeyed alone.
     I have disobeyed alone.
     I will die alone.

(*He pulls revolver from holster and
raises muzzle to his chin.*)

VISITOR   Don't let him—don't let him.
BROWN GIRL   Oh no, Governor.

(BROWN GIRL *throws arms around* GOVERNOR. BROWN BOY *siezes his right
hand—and wrests revolver from him.* GOVERNOR'S *topi has fallen off—Girl
and Boy release* GOVERNOR. *He stands with his face covered with his hands.*)

BROWN GIRL (*looking down on sand.*)   Don't be fretting yourself, Governor,
look. (*She pulls his fingers away from his eyes.*) Look at the sea's edge!
The tide is coming in now fast, look, look, the waters are covering up
and washing away everything that we have written.

(*As she speaks she and all the others, gazing down at the tide's edge,
move slowly backwards towards the front of the stage.*)

CURTAIN.

Appendixes

APPENDIX A

First Productions of the Plays of Jack B. Yeats

HARLEQUIN'S POSITIONS

First performed at the Abbey Experimental Theatre on 5 June 1939. The Settings were designed and painted by Miss Anne Yeats and constructed by Gearoid O h-Iceadha. The cast was as follows:

MADAME ROSE BOSANQUET	Evelyn McNeice
CLAIRE GILLANE (Her Sister)	Sheila Maguire
JOHNNIE GILLANE (Their Nephew)	Robert Mooney
ANNIE JENNINGS	Anne Potter
ALFRED CLONBOISE	Wilfrid Brambell
KATE	Moira McSwiggan
GUARD	Gearoid O h-Iceadha
FIRST PORTER	Michael Kinsella
SECOND PORTER	Dermot Kelly
APPLE WOMAN	Sarah O'Kelly
BOY	Finbarr Howard
FIRST PILOT	Victor Boyd
SECOND PILOT	John McDarby

The Play was produced by Ria Mooney and Cecil Ford.

LA LA NOO

First performed at the Abbey Theatre on 3 May 1942. The Settings and Costumes were created by Michael Clarke. The cast was as follows:

PUBLICAN	Brian O'Higgins
STRANGER	W. O'Gorman
FIRST WOMAN	Cathleen Fawsitt

SECOND WOMAN	Florence Lynch
THIRD WOMAN	Nellie Manning
FOURTH WOMAN	Brid Ni Loinsigh
FIFTH WOMAN	Mary O'Neill
SIXTH WOMAN	Maureen O'Sullivan
SEVENTH WOMAN	Eve Watkinson

The Play was produced by Ria Mooney.

THE GREEN WAVE

First performed at the Lantern Theatre, Dublin, on 29 September 1964. The Setting was designed and painted by Liam Miller and Noel Keating. The cast was as follows:

FIRST ELDERLY MAN	Paul Clarke
SECOND ELDERLY MAN	Denis Merritt

The Play was produced by Patrick Funge.

IN SAND

First performed at the Abbey Experimental Theatre on 19 April 1949. The Settings were created by Gene Martin assisted by Leslie Scott, and the Costumes were designed by Gene Martin and executed by Eileen Tobin. The incidental music was specially composed by Gunther Stumpf. The cast was as follows:

ANTHONY LARCSON	Pilib O Floinn
JOHN OLDGROVE	Noel Guy
THE MAYOR	Traolach O hAonghusaigh
EDITOR	Denis O'Donovan
TOWN COUNCILLOR	Bill McCormick
ALICE	Grania O'Shannon
HER MOTHER	Mollie Griffen
HER FATHER	Bill Shawn
MAURICE	Liam O Foghlu
KITCHEN MAID	Rite Ni Fhuairain
CHAUFFEUR	Sean Mac Shamhrain
OLD SAILOR	Brian O'Higgins
VISITOR	Raghnall Breathnach
GOVERNOR	Eamon Guailli
HOTEL BOY	Brendan Clegg
BROWN BOY	Micheal O hAonghusa
BROWN GIRL	Angela Newman

The Play was produced by Sean Mac Shamhrain.
The Prologue *The Green Wave* was not played.

APPENDIX B

Sources of the Texts

My Miniature Theatre; Holograph manuscript in the possession of Miss Anne Yeats.

Timothy Coombewest or Esmeralda Grande: Holograph manuscript in the possession of Miss Anne Yeats.

James Flaunty or the Terror of the Western Seas: Published version issued by Elkin Mathews in 1901.

Onct More's Great Circus: Drawings and manuscript in the possession of Miss Anne Yeats.

The Treasure of the Garden: Published version issued by Elkin Mathews in 1903.

The Scourge of the Gulph: Published version issued by Elkin Mathews in 1903.

The Wonderful Travellers or The Gamesome Princess and the Pursuing Policeman: Holograph manuscript in the possession of Miss Anne Yeats.

The Deathly Terrace: Holograph manuscript and typescript in the possession of Miss Anne Yeats.

Apparitions, The Old Sea Road, Rattle: Published versions issued together in one volume as *Apparitions* by Jonathan Cape in 1933.

The Silencer or Farewell Speech: Manuscript and typescript in the possession of Miss Anne Yeats.

Harlequin's Positions: Typed acting version and manuscript in the possession of Miss Anne Yeats.

La La Noo: Published version issued by the Cuala Press in 1943.

The Green Wave and *In Sand:* Published version edited by Jack MacGowran and issued by the Dolmen Press in 1964; also manuscript in the possession of Miss Anne Yeats.

In addition to the above materials I have also consulted the author's own copies and proofs of his published works and early drafts of the various plays.

APPENDIX C

How Jack B. Yeats Produced his Plays for the Miniature Theatre

by the Master himself.

I produced my first card board plays on a stage about eighteen inches wide. But I found that only a very small audience could look on at one time, so I had a stage made with a proscenium opening three feet eight inches wide and one foot ten inches high. The stage was made like a box, with the front (in two pieces) top and side in the form of doors. When opened, the front and top made the sides and top of the proscenium. This larger opening allowed an audience sitting five or six abreast to get a very good view without being able to see through the wings to the hands of those who manipulated the figures. The whole stage end of the room was curtained off, and from once the audience took their seats they had nothing before them but my card board actors and card board scenes. The figures were about nine inches high fastened firmly to laths of the same tone as the stage and by these laths the figures slid along. They could not move their limbs so the plays were written to suit the stiffness of the actors.

The old 'Penny Plain and Tuppence coloured' plays were adapted from full grown plays like 'Three-fingered Jack, the Terror of Jamaica,' or 'Paul Clifford' or 'Mazeppa', plays which were full of sword fights and pistollings, swoonings of ladies and poisonings of cups. Things impossible to do with card board figures. So the old makers of the miniature plays did the only thing they could, they had a different figure for every action and stage directions such as this:

'*Jack*. No words; obey or perish. (Jack binds Rosa's hands with a cord. Draw off Jack and R.H. Pl. 7. she leans against wing L.H. put on Jack at table Pl. 5).'

or this:

'*Quash*. No hurry, Jack, take it easy. 'Cause him going to send you down below to see your ole friend.
(Desperate combat. Jack disarms Quashee when a struggle takes place. Draw off figures combating and put on Jack and Quashee bottom of Pl. 6. Jack is about to strangle Quashee when Tuckey with pistol R.H. Pl. 6 appears at top

380

of rock between the two scenes. He fires and wounds Jack who leaves go his
hold. Quashee then springs up and stabs Jack in the breast. Draw off the
figures and put on Quashee stabbing Jack R.H. Pl. 6. Enter Sam L.H. Pl. 6.
from behind set piece, and Tuckey R.H. Pl. 4.')

In colouring my scenes I used coloured papers very largely which
saved time and paint. Lightning was suggested by a zig-zag cut in the
back cloth covered with blue paper down behind which, at the right
moment, a light was dashed. For foot lights I used night lights with
reflectors. For coloured fires I used red and green matches, used them
good and plenty!
   The titles of my plays were:

> 'Esmeralda Grande,'
> 'The Treasure of the Garden,'
> 'James Flaunty,'
> 'The Scourge of the Gulph,' and
> 'James Dance, or the Fortunate Ship Boy.'

There was also a pantomime called 'The Mysterious Travellers, or
the Gamesome Princes and the pursuing Policeman', and I had two
circuses. The pantomime was good fun to make because of the
mechanical 'business'.
   The clown smoked real smoke out of a little clay pipe. He also
fished from the quay with a practical fishing rod. There was also a
pillar letter box with a door which opened and showed the clown
hiding inside, then snapped to again, and
             There was a town crier who rang a bell.
The making of the circuses was good fun too. The 'Procession of All
Nations'. Japan with those delightful little paper lanterns with toy
candles inside. And the four horses abreast in the Ride of all Nations.

> The Riders of old Rome who in prehistoric days guided their antideluvian
> horses mid the catacombs and pyramids of that noble City without saddle
> or bridle.
> The Cowboys.
> The Egyptians stated without error to be the most marvellous horsemen in
> the entire universe from the Indian Ocean to the Carribean Sea.
> The Bull-fighters of Spain, and the ring master spoke of the 'sanguinary
> sawdust of Seville'.

The words of the plays were of course spoken behind the scenes and
it was at times hard to make the voices of the characters sufficiently
different, and after talking for some time in the husky voice of
Captain Teach one found that for a scene of two all the characters
were speaking their lines in the same deep notes. From the time one
had acquired the throat of piracy, one had to be very careful, for it

was not right that Jessie Henderson should speak with the same voice as Willie McGowan or Bosun Hardbite. The two voices used in the Adventurers Oath in Esmeralda Grande were easier to produce. A deep roar for the Captain, and for the crew as they repeat each line a fear-struck wail which gradually grows feebler as the thing goes on.

And now, looking back, I think my audiences liked the oath best of all, better than the red fire of the flare on the sinking *Linnet* and better even than the green shine of Esmeralda Grande.

(from *The Mask*, Florence, July 1912.)